To Olive Rich

Our good friend

James H Stewart
November 6, 1991

Rubles and Dollars

Rubles and Dollars

Strategies For Doing Business In The Soviet Union

James L. Hecht

HarperBusiness
A Division of HarperCollinsPublishers

Library of Congress Cataloging-in-Publication Data

Rubles and dollars : strategies for doing business in the Soviet Union /
   [edited by] James L. Hecht.
      p. cm.
   Includes bibliographical references and index.
   ISBN 0–88730–487–7
      1. Soviet Union—Economic conditions—1986–   2. Soviet Union—
   Commerce.   3. Soviet Union—Description and travel—1981–
   I. Hecht, James L.
   . HC336.26.R79   1991   91–27845
   3326'732247—dc20   CIP

Printed in the United States of America

91 92 93 94 CC/RRD 7 6 5 4 3 2 1

Contents

Acknowledgments   *vii*

Introduction   *ix*

1/ Why Do Business in the Soviet Union?   *1*
      James L. Hecht

2/ Understanding the Culture   *13*
      Mario R. Dederichs

3/ Daily Economic Life in the U.S.S.R.   *29*
      James R. Millar

4/ The Soviet Work Force: Problems and Opportunities   *47*
      Walter D. Connor

5/ Managerial Decision Making   *63*
      Paul R. Lawrence
      and Charalombos Vlachoutsicos

6/ Corporate Experience in the Soviet Union   *81*
      James L. Hecht

7/ Joint Ventures: A Practitioner's View   *93*
      Roman Pipko

8/ Operating in Moscow   *113*
      Tom Laurita

9/ Doing Business Outside of Moscow   *125*
      Elisa B. Miller

10/ The Pioneers 139
Gail Friedman

11/ A Soviet View 151
Yevgeniy Y. Pompa

12/ Financing Joint Ventures 169
Lawrence J. Brainard

13/ Legal Aspects of Doing Business 185
Richard N. Dean (Part I)
James A. Forstner (Part II)

14/ The Future of the Soviet Economy 205
Herbert S. Levine

15/ The Future of the Soviet Union 225
Lawrence E. Modisett

16/ Action to Take 247
James L. Hecht

Notes 257

Recommended Books 269

Index 279

About the Authors 287

Acknowledgments

To paraphrase Winston Churchill, seldom has one person owed so much to so many.

My indebtedness to the 15 contributors goes beyond the fine chapters they produced. Many already were stars, but all were willing to work as a team. I am grateful for their punctuality, civility, cooperation, and talent.

Two people whose names do not appear in the Contents contributed directly to the book. Lori L. Schipper did a great deal of the research that was required for the list of over 100 recommended books. Patricia Walton's skill as a translator allowed Yevgeniy Pompa to write his chapter in his native Russian, yet have it published in excellent English.

I am deeply indebted to Virginia A. Smith, the executive editor at Harper Business Books. Her vision was an essential part of the book's genesis; her intellect resulted in many significant improvements between the initial drafts and the final manuscript. The book also benefited from the skillful editing of Jonathan Ewing and Nola Lynch.

Many people provided information and suggestions. One who was particularly generous with his time was Paul Surovell, whose information base as editor of *Interflo,* a journal which covers Soviet trade, was of enormous help. Those who reviewed more than one chapter and gave useful suggestions were John M. Carpenter, Antony W. E. Pell, and Eric Stubbs.

A great many others contributed to individual chapters. For example, I am indebted to over 100 people for information included in Chapter 6.

Special recognition should be given to James K. Oliver, my

mentor at the University of Delaware during my transition from scientist/businessman to scholar. Moreover, had it not been for his effectiveness in championing me for an academic appointment without traditional qualifications, I do not think this book would have been written.

Looking back, this book would probably not have been written were it not for two other people who had the vision to support nontraditional projects with which I was associated in the past. For this support, I am grateful to Elwood P. Blanchard, Jr., and Robert E. Naylor, Jr. Dr. Naylor also contributed some useful insights to a chapter I wrote.

The cost of producing this book was paid in part by my project at the University of Delaware. I am grateful to the University, and also to the Amoco Oil Company, Asea Brown Boveri Incorporated, and E. I. du Pont de Nemours & Company for providing financial support to the university for this effort. Earlier financial support for activities that led to this book was provided by grants from the United States Institute of Peace and the Greve Foundation.

Finally, an indispensable role was played by my wife, Amy Blatchford Hecht. Despite her own responsibilities as a university dean, she always found time to discuss my queries on content and wording—and to nurture in me the desire to strive for excellence.

Introduction

To be an important player in the global marketplace of the future, a company must have a strategy for the Soviet Union. The purpose of this book is to improve that strategy and to assist in its implementation.

This purpose has posed several problems. The first was the breadth and complexity of the subjects that had to be included. Consequently, rather than write a book alone, I decided to share authorship. Even if I had spent years doing research, I would not have had the knowledge and experience of the contributors to this book. The breadth of their knowledge is apparent not only from the titles of the chapters but from the diversity of their backgrounds. Five have doctoral degrees in economics and three in law; others have advanced degrees in business, history, political science, sociology, international relations, chemistry, and chemical engineering. Two of the contributors are professional journalists.

Books consisting of chapters written by different authors often are not well integrated. I have attempted to prevent this from happening by being an active editor. For example, an anecdote popular with those who specialize in the Soviet Union was used by four different contributors in their first drafts. In the published book it appears only once. If the reader does not find this book as well integrated as if it were written by a single author, I as editor take responsibility; all the contributors have acceded to my requests to delete material covered in another chapter.

The worst problem that was faced was the rapid pace of change in the Soviet Union. For a company working in the U.S.S.R., neither this book, nor any other, can replace the need to use Soviet specialists who are up-to-date.

Consequently, this book focuses on presenting information and experiences which will be of value for many years. During the months that the book was being edited and produced, we did not make revisions when something of consequence occurred in the Soviet Union. Thus, the ruble wages reported in the book will be much lower than those that are in effect when this book appears. Also, there is no mention of the transfer of many of the nation's coal mines to the control of the Russian Republic. However, the value of the book is demonstrated by the fact that the book predicts that such changes are likely to happen. In addition, more basic information—such as the future costs of Soviet labor in hard currency—will remain fairly accurate for many years to come.

A problem that did not exist was to find ways to make the book interesting. Doing business in the Soviet Union is as challenging an assignment as exists in today's business world. Westerners who work in the Soviet Union must be diligent, persistent, resourceful, and patient. Their lives are always interesting.

CHAPTER 1

Why Do Business in the Soviet Union?

James L. Hecht

The reason for doing business in the Soviet Union is the same as the reason for doing business elsewhere: to make a profit. Moreover, the magnitude of the opportunity is unmatched in the world. The Soviet economy is about the size of that of Japan, yet there is virtually no effective domestic competition and foreign firms are welcome. The dismal economic reports currently coming from the U.S.S.R. indicate that there are difficulties associated with operating there. But the downbeat reports usually ignore two factors that make possible relatively rapid economic improvement: the Soviet Union's enormous wealth in natural resources and its relatively well-educated labor force.

Most good business opportunities in the Soviet Union will be long term, but profits can be made in the near term also. Success requires an understanding of the country and its people and the recognition that it is necessary to operate a business differently in the U.S.S.R. from elsewhere.

For multinational industrial companies the Soviet market must be viewed as more than a profit center. Because the U.S.S.R. produces about 12 percent of the world's GNP (gross national product),[1] success in the Soviet market is not merely a potential source of profit, but an opportunity to increase global market share, the elixir of the multinational corporation.

When a company increases its share of the market, the cost per unit of product is decreased since research and marketing costs are spread over a larger volume of business. In addition, an increase in market share results in a decrease in relative production costs as a result of economies of scale. Thus a company that increases its share of the market has the option of further strengthening its competitive position—without decreasing profitability—either by lowering prices or by expanding research and marketing

1

to accelerate the development of new products and more efficient production processes. Market share is particularly important to competitiveness in product areas for which research and marketing costs are high.

The experiences of Caterpillar, the world's leading producer of earth-moving machinery, and Komatsu, its principal competitor, demonstrate how the Soviet Union can make a difference in the competitiveness of a company throughout the world. Just as the location of its corporate headquarters, Peoria, has often been used to symbolize the American heartland, "Cat" symbolizes the success of U.S. industry. In 1980 Caterpillar's sales were $8.6 billion a year, exactly three times as high as the Japanese company Komatsu's. Not surprisingly, Caterpillar's share of the Soviet market was 85 percent, while Komatsu's was 15 percent.

But then Caterpillar suddenly was unable to compete in the Soviet market: the U.S. government restricted exports for political reasons. By the end of 1982 Caterpillar's share of the Soviet market had deteriorated to 15 percent and Komatsu had captured 85 percent.

Caterpillar was so large and dominant that this shift of over $100 million a year of business might not have made a large difference were it not for the fact that in 1982 there was a sharp decrease worldwide in the demand for earth-moving equipment. In 1983 Cat's sales were only $5.4 billion, and even by 1985 sales had recovered only to $6.8 billion, less than 80 percent of the 1980 figure. However, helped by the large increase in Soviet business, the sales of the smaller Komatsu declined less than 10 percent during this period.

Thus Komatsu was able to avoid making the severe cuts in research, development, and marketing that Caterpillar had to take; as a result Komatsu was in a better position to compete against its dominant U.S. rival. Not surprisingly, in 1988, after the market had recovered and Caterpillar's sales had grown to a record $10.4 billion, Cat's sales were only twice Komatsu's. While there were other factors, there is no doubt that the increased market share provided by the Soviet market significantly aided Komatsu in improving its global competitive position.

For a multinational corporation to use the U.S.S.R. to increase market share, its management must understand how to compete successfully in the Soviet Union. Most Soviet business must be structured in ways other than compensation trade (i.e., sale of product for cash payments in a currency that can be converted to other currencies). In addition, there are vast differences in business culture between the U.S.S.R. and the Western industrial nations.

Greater cultural differences are encountered in the Soviet Union than in most other countries because—along with a unique historical experience—the Soviets have had 70 years of an entirely different economic system. In an economy in which bonuses have been given for exceeding production goals, with no attention to costs, it is not surprising that labor and energy have been used poorly. In a society in which all factory output has been bought by the state, it is not surprising that market research and quality control tend to be ignored.

The uniqueness of Soviet business was apparent to me in a meeting that I participated in. An American business executive clearly had the attention and interest of the three Soviet executives to whom he was describing a medical device he could set them up to manufacture. The Soviets asked many excellent questions, but they showed no interest in the packaging, even though they had been told that the packaging was a key part of the product. The Soviets were very intelligent and, in areas of science and technology, well informed. But in their society attractive packaging has not been necessary to sell products and, in the absence of a packaging industry, the functional benefits of packaging have not been well understood and are seldom utilized.

The problem that foreign firms most frequently mention as limiting business with the U.S.S.R. is the Soviets' shortage of hard currency (i.e., a convertible currency, such as the dollar). In recent years the Soviet Union has had only $25 to $30 billion a year to spend on imports from the industrial nations of the West. Most of this hard currency has come from the sale of petroleum, natural gas, and products derived from these resources. However, billions of dollars' worth of other natural resources, such as gold, diamonds, platinum, palladium, chromite, and rhodium, are also exported each year. In 1991 the Soviets may be able to increase their hard-currency earnings by taking advantage of their position as the world's largest producer of petroleum. In the past Soviet oil exports have been on the order of a billion barrels a year, but much of this was exported to Soviet client states at bargain prices, and usually in soft currencies. In 1991 the Soviets will no longer offer such politically motivated bargains and will sell petroleum only for hard currency and at market prices.

Unfortunately, the Soviets have been forced to spend a significant part of their limited hard currency on food and grain. Agricultural chemicals (mostly pesticides)—for obvious reasons—have also had a high position on the hard-currency shopping list, as have machinery (particularly machinery used in oil fields), technological know-how, high-technology products needed by Soviet industry but not produced in the U.S.S.R., and some pharmaceuticals.

Because of the magnitude of these needs, relatively little hard currency has been allocated elsewhere. However, like low income parents who lack money to meet pressing needs, but who somehow give their children presents at Christmas, the Soviets have spent small amounts of hard currency for consumer products. Because of rising expectations, hard-currency spending on consumer items is almost certain to grow in the future. This trend is likely to be accelerated by the fact that Soviet enterprises that generate hard-currency sales now have the capability to use some of their profits to purchase Western goods.

While most Soviet policies are being flayed at home, hard-currency allocations—like the Moscow subway—have been relatively free of criticism and are not likely to undergo major changes in the near future. Consequently, the best way to enter the Soviet market, particularly for companies that are not selling high priority items, is to structure the transaction so that it does not require the Soviets to pay in hard currency, using such forms of business as countertrade, coproduction, and joint ventures. This also is the best way for companies that are already selling to the Soviets to expand their market. A Soviet view of why such arrangements are mutually desirable is given in detail in Chapter 11.

Countertrade has existed since the beginning of recorded history in the form of barter. One well-known example of countertrade involving the Soviet Union is the sale of Pepsi-Cola to the U.S.S.R. in return for Stolichnaya vodka. Since Soviet demand for the Pepsi has exceeded U.S. demand for the vodka, Pepsico is now also taking ships built in the U.S.S.R. in exchange for product. Pepsico will either sell or lease the ships as part of a complex business arrangement involving Fram Shipping of Bermuda, which basically is a Norwegian company.

Most foreign companies are not going to be able to do as well as Pepsico in the near term. Pepsico established its ties with the Soviet Union many years ago; the chief executive officer of the company, Donald M. Kendall, built solid relationships with Soviet political and business leaders. As a result, Pepsico was able to negotiate deals for two of the limited number of Soviet-made products that can be marketed in the West successfully. An important lesson from Pepsico's success in countertrade is to get in early.

Good trades can still be made if a company's management is imaginative and enterprising. For example, the number of potential Soviet products will be greatly increased if the deal is not limited to a simple exchange of products. The Soviets might supply a product for a developing country (where state-of-the-art quality is not as important); the developing country, in turn, would supply a product to the Western nation involved. Although the transaction becomes more complicated, an advantage is that the opportunity for profit is increased since the Western corporation participates in two transactions.

A type of countertrade that has hardly been used, but that has potential, allows the Soviets to supply a service, such as contract research. For example, the Monsanto Chemical Company is financing biological research at the Shemyakin Institute in Moscow with some of the money it receives from sales in the Soviet Union.[2] The Soviets are world class in many areas of basic research, and the cost of supporting a scientist in the Soviet Union is at present only about one-fifth of what it would be in the West.

In the area of applied research, many Western companies should be able to develop mutually beneficial relationships with organizations that are part of the Soviet military-industrial complex. As a result of large cutbacks in military spending and military research, these organizations are anxious to expand into civilian uses to maintain jobs for their employees, and they are not reluctant to involve Western companies in the conversion process. In the U.S.S.R. military contractors pay more and provide better benefits than other employers, so many of the best scientists and engineers work for them; that is one of the reasons the Soviets have frequently matched, and occasionally bettered, the accomplishments of their American counterparts in the development of military equipment and the exploration of space. This type of cooperation is a good opportunity for Western high-technology companies.

Coproduction is a cooperative arrangement in which part of the product is produced by the foreign partner and part is produced by the Soviet Union. For example, suppose the product is made by assembling components *A, B, C,* and *D.* In a coproduction arrangement, the foreign partner might manufacture *A* and *B* and ship these to the Soviet Union; the Soviets would make *C* and *D* and then assemble the product. For its role, which could include supplying technology, the foreign partner might be compensated by receiving a certain amount of the final product for every 100 units of *A* and *B* furnished, but many other arrangements are possible. In all of the many ways it can be applied, coproduction involves a high degree of cooperation; but the foreign partner does not make an investment in the U.S.S.R., and both the foreign participant and the Soviets have separate organizations.

An example of coproduction is the manufacture of an elastomer similar to DuPont's Hypalon, a major ingredient in certain types of synthetic rubber. The Soviets first manufacture high-density polyethylene, the raw material for Hypalon. The Soviet-produced polyethylene is then shipped to a DuPont plant in Northern Ireland, where it is converted into an elastomer using the Hypalon process. All of this product is then shipped to the Soviet Union for domestic use. By participating in the manufacturing process the Soviets obtain the elastomer for a much lower price than they would by purchasing Hypalon. Another example of coproduction is the manufacture of ambulances by the Riga Automobile Plant in conjunction with Mariani of Italy and two Finnish firms, Tamro and Ajokki.

Joint ventures are the best-known form of Western–Soviet cooperation. Much more has been written about joint ventures than about other forms of cooperation for several reasons. As explained in Chapter 7 and other parts of this book, the peculiarities of Soviet law have often led to business arrangements structured as joint ventures when other forms of cooperation would be satisfactory. From the Soviet viewpoint, joint ventures are a very desirable form of cooperation because they furnish badly needed capital, technology, and business know-how.

A joint venture has many potential advantages for a foreign partner. A joint venture maximizes the opportunity to become established in the U.S.S.R. For a mature product, a joint venture in the U.S.S.R. can be a way of increasing global market share; for a new product, the Soviet market also offers a unique opportunity to move down the experience curve, as I will explain later in this chapter (p. 9). A joint venture can also lead to significant sales in the U.S.S.R. by the foreign partner while the Soviet market is being developed in advance of manufacturing by the joint venture in the U.S.S.R. However, since any joint venture, even between U.S. companies, has problems, undertaking a joint venture in the Soviet Union must be viewed as following a high-risk strategy: taking a greater risk in order to reap a greater gain.

Joint ventures in the U.S.S.R. have two major problems. The first, which is widely recognized outside of the Soviet Union—although not always by potential Soviet partners—is the matter of "repatriating" profits—a problem which will exist as long as the ruble is not a convertible currency. The other major problem is the inadequacy of much of the supply infrastructure.

With respect to the repatriation of profit, one possibility is to gamble that at some time in the future the ruble will be convertible. That is not a bad risk, because convertibility is a goal to which the Soviets are committed and that is in their interests to achieve. In fact, starting in 1991 ruble profits can be converted to hard currency in an auction process, although not on very favorable terms. However, relying completely on the eventual convertibility of the ruble is unlikely to result in a good joint venture. Convertibility may take a long time. In the meantime, additional hard currency for equipment that cannot be obtained in the U.S.S.R. may be required if profits in rubles are to be used to expand the venture. In addition, it may be necessary to use hard currency for purchases necessary to operate the enterprise—such as raw materials or replacement parts not available in the Soviet Union. Thus, unless the foreign partner is willing to make continuing hard-currency investments without being able to repatriate profits, it is necessary to generate some hard currency—even when the partner is willing to invest in the Soviet Union for the long haul and to defer profit taking. The fact that foreign investments in the Soviet Union often involve not only one or more companies but also one or more banks makes hard-currency generation even more of a necessity. (Details on financing are given in Chapter 12.)

There are three basic ways that a joint venture can be structured to repatriate hard currency. One is to sell part of the joint venture's products for rubles and to export the remainder for hard currency. Another is to sell all of the products produced by the joint venture in the Soviet Union, but to have an agreement that allows the joint venture to purchase, for rubles, exportable products such as petroleum, cotton, or chemicals. A third variation, which can be used only for certain types of joint ventures, is to generate sufficient hard-currency sales in the Soviet Union.

The unique business opportunity offered by the Soviet market is demonstrated by a hypothetical example of a joint venture that would both serve the Soviet market and be a source of low cost exports. Consider the case of a product dominated by three producers with worldwide sales of 400 million pounds of product a year at $1 a pound. One producer has 50 percent of the market; the other two have 25 percent each. At the present time the Soviet Union imports 4 million pounds of this product in direct proportion to each company's global market share.

The joint venture would include as its foreign partner one of the two firms that currently sells only 100 million pounds a year. The joint venture, with a $60 million contribution from its foreign partner in cash, technology, and know-how, would build and operate a plant to produce 60 million pounds a year of this product. Of this amount, 40 million pounds (9 percent of global use) would be sold for a good price in the Soviet Union; the remaining 20 million pounds would be sold in export markets at 80 cents a pound, displacing competitive products. This could be done because, with competition in the Soviet market nonexistent and domestic demand high, the Soviet market will easily absorb 40 million pounds, even priced at a slight premium.

Thus, by entering the Soviet market through a joint venture, a weak producer would increase sales from 100 million pounds to 160 million, almost as much as the strongest producer, whose sales would now be about 185 million pounds. The third producer would continue in a weak position with sales of only 92 million pounds. The joint venture partner would have strengthened its global competitiveness by a strategic move which can be carried out only in the Soviet Union. For example, there are many advantages to investing in Pacific Rim countries to provide low cost export capacity, but even in a country as large as South Korea the domestic market for this product would be only about 8 million pounds; therefore a noncompetitive domestic market does not do much to lower the cost of exports without decreasing profitability.

Thus a joint venture in the Soviet Union offers much of the same advantage to a multinational company that Japan has offered to Japanese companies—a very large market in which goods manufactured abroad are at a large disadvantage, thereby allowing a domestic manufacturing operation to sell domestically at a premium price and export at a price that competition cannot match. In his book *Trading Places,* Clyde Prestowitz documents how practices of this type have allowed Japanese companies to dominate a number of key industries.[3]

There is, of course, a negative side to the approach in this example: namely, the foreign joint venture partner may already have more than enough capacity to serve hard-currency markets throughout the world and does not want to compete with the products being produced in the U.S.S.R. In that case, the other basic method of repatriating profits, by having the joint venture agreement include a contract to buy for rubles exportable products, is the way to do business. This method is often viewed with disfavor by the Soviets, who are reluctant to export goods needed in the U.S.S.R., particularly raw materials.

However, it is much more advantageous for the Soviets to use their petroleum exports and other exportable materials to provide hard-currency profits for joint ventures than to purchase products from the West. For example, if an enterprise controls $10 million in exportable goods a year, that enterprise can use the resulting hard currency to purchase $10 million a year of products needed by the enterprise or desired by the employees of the enterprise. But if the exportable goods instead are offered to several joint venture partners as profit for investing $50 million in new Soviet plants to make the products that otherwise would be imported, the Soviets would end up with about $50 million a year in products not available in the U.S.S.R. That certainly is better than having only $10 million worth.

Regardless of how profits will be repatriated, joint ventures involving the manufacture of products should always be structured so that the products can be sold in world markets at competitive prices. Even if the plan is to generate sufficient hard currency by other means, changing conditions may make the export of product produced in the Soviet Union desirable at some time in the future. For example, some years after the joint venture is begun additional capacity may be needed in the West; if conditions have changed for the Western joint venture partner, this capacity may best be added by increasing Soviet capacity and using the excess for export.

To produce products that can compete in world markets the supply infrastructure is crucial. Manufacturing follows the fundamental law of computers: Garbage in, garbage out. Without high quality raw materials it is impossible to get a high quality product. But raw materials of sufficient quality are often not available in the Soviet Union. When McDonald's opened its restaurant in Moscow, the press described how the overall project had included not only a food processing plant but even the production of potatoes and other supplies. Fortunately for McDonald's, the raw materials required for hamburgers and french fries are relatively simple.

At the opposite end of the spectrum is automobile manufacturing, which requires a very large number of components, many of which the Soviets currently are unable to produce. Thus it is not surprising that Ford decided not to go forward with a proposed joint venture to make automobiles. What is a little surprising is that Ford invested so much time in an idea that was many years ahead of its time. However, the supply infrastructure problem would not prevent an automobile company from establishing a joint venture to make certain automotive components. There are components for which the supply infrastructure in the Soviet Union is sufficient for manufacture and export.

If the foreign partner is willing to use a joint venture as a producer for sales elsewhere, the Soviets have an important comparative advantage: a low cost, skilled work force. Wages will probably vary a great deal in the near term as a result of price reform measures (i.e., removal of large government subsidies on many products and services); after price reform is complete, the cost of Soviet labor should be less than 30 to 40 percent of U.S. labor costs since per capita Soviet GNP is about one-third of that in the United States. Moreover, until price reform is complete, companies that hire Soviet employees will enjoy a bonanza. In 1990, 400 rubles—$67—was a high monthly wage.

There is a price to pay for the low cost work force. It will be truly low cost only if used in tandem with skillful management which succeeds in selling workers on high productivity and quality. As previously mentioned—and as discussed much more in other chapters—these qualities have not been part of the culture of the work place.

Thus joint ventures involving on-site facilities in the U.S.S.R. can provide short-term benefits in addition to enormous long-range opportunities. The story of some of the pioneers who have established such joint ventures is given in Chapter 10. Not only is a joint venture an excellent way to "show the flag," but it gives the foreign partner a base for further operations. Relationships are very important to Soviets, and companies that establish a presence in the U.S.S.R. will have an advantage over competitors who are newcomers. Donald Kendall of Pepsico recently was quoted as saying, "I think anybody who has a product that can be marketed in the Soviet Union is a damn fool if they don't go over there now and get started. If they wait until all the conditions are right, someone else will have the business."

Finally, a joint venture in the Soviet Union may serve as a desirable way for the foreign partner to develop new consumer products. By providing a very large unfilled market, the U.S.S.R. virtually guarantees a good product a long ride down the experience curve. The worst case scenario would be that a product developed in the U.S.S.R. fails in the West, but with far less loss than if introduced in the West. Moreover, by marketing it in the Soviet Union, a product which would have failed in the West could be converted into a global winner.

The experience curve is a law of economics—as solid in theory and human experience as the law of gravity, but recognized only relatively recently. It has been found that the cost of a product (adjusted to eliminate the effects of inflation) decreases as a function of the amount of product that has been manufactured. The rate of this decrease in cost varies, but typically it is about 20 to 25 percent for each doubling of the volume manufactured. This relationship describes quite well the economic experience for all products—whether chicken breasts, integrated circuits, disposable diapers, or motorcycles. The decrease in cost arises from three sources: learning, technological improvements, and economies of scale.[4]

Consider a specific example of how a joint venture in the Soviet Union could help an American company develop new products for global marketing. For years food companies have considered commercializing the so-called plastic can, and several companies, such as Hormel and Campbell Soups, have recently introduced products using this type of packaging. These products do not look like ordinary cans and are packaged in flat plastic containers. Food packaged in plastic cans will usually taste better than canned food because the containers geometry permits less heating to sterilize the food. Depending on the plastic used, food can be stored at room temperature for up to five years. Because of these differences, the packaging often is described as shelf-stable.

This product concept has advantages and disadvantages. The quality of the food can be higher than that of canned food, but is not as good as that of frozen food. However, the new product is more convenient to store and use than canned and frozen food. And although the initial cost falls between canned and frozen, as energy costs increase, food in shelf-stable packaging will become cheaper to produce than food in metal cans. Whether such a package will become an important commercial product worldwide in the twenty-first century is a question, but there is no question that if hundreds of millions of such packaged units were produced and sold, the experience gained would make the plastic shelf-stable package less expensive and of higher quality. However, to gain experience by producing and marketing in the United States will be costly. In order to get the new product into supermarkets already crowded with an overabundance of other products, the new product needs to be priced low at a time when small volume makes its cost high. Even then, sales—and therefore experience—will likely be slow. Unless the new product is quickly accepted by consumers, losses mount and the pressure is on to withdraw the product.

What a difference the Soviet Union would make. There would be plenty of room in the stores for new shelf-stable food products and, provided that the quality was satisfactory, people would pay a premium price for it. After production reached a moderate level, costs would be down and initial problems would be resolved. This would be the time to ship modest amounts of product to the United States or Western Europe, where sales would bring in hard currency for profit or for materials not available in the U.S.S.R. If the product from the Soviet Union were not a success on the first try, modifications could be made for another attempt at Western markets. Thus the market in the West could be tested and developed from facilities in the Soviet Union which would operate at near capacity because of the strength of the Soviet market.

The desirability of doing business in the U.S.S.R. must be judged by more than whether operations in the Soviet Union will be profitable. For example, a U.S. company needs to ask at least two additional questions. The first is whether doing business will be good or bad for the United States. The second is whether Soviet trade will have a favorable or unfavorable effect on business elsewhere, particularly in the U.S. market.

The use of trade as an instrument of peace has long been recognized. Two centuries ago Alexander Hamilton wrote, "The spirit of commerce has a tendency to soften the manners of men, and to extinguish those inflammable humors which so often have kindled into wars." Theories of social psychology, such as those of Morton Deutsch, support Hamilton's eloquent words;[5] experimental studies have shown that relationships improve when competing groups work together on a common goal.[6] A good example of how economic cooperation can contribute to peace and prosperity is the European Coal and Steel Community—and all that has evolved in Western Europe as a result. Studies show that between 1954 and 1965 there was a marked change from hostility to amity by the French for the West Germans and by the West Germans for the French—reversing feelings derived from centuries of bloody conflicts.[7]

Doing business with a foreign country can affect a corporation's business in the United States, at least negatively. Trade with South Africa is an example. However, even when tensions between the United States and the U.S.S.R. have been high, a clear majority of the American people have favored more trade. A study in May 1984 by the Public Agenda Foundation asked whether it would be acceptable to expand trade with the Soviets and make other cooperative gestures—even if that made the Soviets stronger and more secure. Of a representative sample of Americans, 55 percent said that increased trade was acceptable; only 40 percent said it was not. Among college graduates, 63 percent said it was acceptable and 33 percent said it was not.

In times of less tension the support for increased trade has been much greater. In a summary of American attitudes toward the Soviet Union and communism, Tom Smith of the National Opinion Research Center gives the results of five studies by Louis Harris and Associates during the period 1970 to 1974.[8] During this time 70 to 75 percent of Americans favored expanding trade with the Soviet Union; only 12 to 21 percent opposed more trade.

Until recently U.S. business leaders whose companies had significant sales in the Soviet Union were in a difficult position. Not only did they not wish to alienate customers and shareholders with strong feelings about helping "an evil empire," but during most of the 1980s business firms did not wish to appear pro-Soviet in Washington. The good will of the administration and Congress would be needed in areas more vital to the needs of the corporation than the Soviet market. Although there were exceptions, these conflicting forces usually were resolved by pursuing business in the Soviet Union as well as possible while keeping a low profile.

Such caution is no longer necessary. The great changes that have taken place in the U.S.S.R. have been matched by changes in corporate thinking as well as in public opinion. A study of corporate attitudes toward U.S.–Soviet trade, completed early in 1989, found that only 7 percent of the 46 companies that replied felt that such trade would negatively affect their domestic image; 28 percent thought it would have a positive effect, and 65 percent believed it would have no impact.[9] Events that have occurred since then would shift the response even more toward the positive side.

In fact, it has been shown that doing business in the Soviet Union can help a company's business throughout the world. Because of the extensive media coverage generated, hundreds of millions of people associate McDonald's with a restaurant in Moscow where an enormous number of people wait in line, often for more than an hour, to spend (on average) one-half a day's pay for a meal. Thus, by skillful public relations, McDonald's has used its operation in the Soviet Union to improve the perception of its restaurants elsewhere to an extent that might not have been accomplished had the company spent on additional advertising the entire $50 million it has invested in the U.S.S.R.

Doing business in the Soviet Union must be based on making a profit. But profits calculated only from sales and costs will usually be lower than the true benefits.

CHAPTER 2

Understanding the Culture

Mario R. Dederichs

Russians like to think of their country as "eternal Russia," an ancient land with a very special people and a spirit that has matured over centuries of self-imposed isolation. Seventy years of communism have strained but never completely broken this concept. Despite all their claims of internationalism, the rulers of the Soviet Union kept foreign influences in their society at bay. And while proclaiming the lofty goal of creating a new *homo sovieticus* (Soviet man), they rekindled Russian national feelings when it seemed necessary—as Stalin did in rallying the country against the German invaders in what he called the Great Patriotic War.

These days of *glasnost* (openness) and *perestroika* (restructuring), lifting many restrictions of oppressive rule, are marked by a return to ancient roots, to the "eternal" spirit of the Russian nation. The revival of Mother Russia provides anybody who has to deal with this country a compelling reason for trying to understand its rich cultural heritage.

But be warned: It is not going to be easy—and Russians are not going to make it easier. Although they will appreciate the effort, deep down they are convinced that no foreigner can ever grasp what it means to be Russian. Winston Churchill's admission of futility in calling Russia "a riddle wrapped in a mystery inside an enigma" pleased the Russians by confirming their distinct character.

When I had just arrived as a correspondent in Moscow, I met an old and knowledgeable Russian poet at a Moscow reception. Well aware of the German obsession with what we refer to as *russische Seele,* he asked me, in perfect German, "So did you also come to find the Russian soul?" I politely replied that, at least, I would attempt to. He shrugged and smiled broadly behind his huge gray beard. "Take my advice and give up," he said. "We don't even know ourselves what it is."

I heard the same skepticism from Russians over and over again during my four years in the Soviet Union. My secretary used to grade foreigners by their level of understanding. Once she said of a colleague who had spent most of his life studying the Russian language and culture and traveling the country, a man so engulfed in his love for Russia and so attuned to its customs that many people, at first glance, took him for a Russian: "He has grasped a little."

The attitude is ageless. In intellectual circles, I was confronted with a poem by Fëdor Tyutchev, a nineteenth-century man of letters and diplomat who spent many years in Western Europe, that echoed my bearded poet's reluctance to share Russia's secrets. Tyutchev berated his countrymen in 1830:

> Be silent, hide and keep
> Your feelings, dreams a secret,
> In the depth of your soul
> Let them rise and set
> Like the stars at night,
> Enjoy them—and be silent.
> How can your heart reveal?
> How can somebody understand you?
> Does he conceive how you live?
> A thought spelled out is a lie,
> Stirring sources darkens them;
> Enjoy them—and be silent!

Secretiveness is a hallmark of the Russian character born out of a mistrust of foreigners and a distinct feeling of inferiority. Outsiders arriving in the wide plains between the Urals and the Carpathian mountains included some of the most ferocious forces in history: the marauding horsemen of Asia, Huns and Mongols; the messianic Teutonic knights and the overwhelming armies of Poland and Lithuania; the stubborn Swedes of Charles X and the terrible Turks of the sultans; Napoleon's Grande Armée and Hitler's Wehrmacht. Eventually, the Russians overcame all of them, but only at the price of enormous devastation and suffering, the latest cruel example being the more than 20 million Soviet victims of World War II. The lasting impact, enforced by every invasion, has been suspicion of foreigners and a feeling that telling them anything increases vulnerability. Over the centuries, Russians were humbled by superior forces from outside, more modern, more efficient, more inventive. They had to suffer for their backwardness and tried to gain some protection by being mysterious. If they could not be stronger, at least they could hide their weaknesses. Or, to quote Tyutchev one more time:

> The stranger's proud glance
> Won't grasp and notice
> What shows and shines clandestinely
> In your humble nakedness.

Czars and commissars alike enforced this attitude. Foreign travelers were discouraged from seeing too much, from meeting too many people. Sigismund von Herberstein, an imperial envoy who visited Moscow in 1517 and 1526, described how his delegation was met at the border by Russian escorts sent by Grand Prince Basil IV, who not only guided them to their capital but also kept a watchful eye over them along the way. One escort, Herberstein reported, "Stays behind, not to honor the ambassador, but to make sure that nobody is following or turning back." The early traders who came to Russia—Germans, Dutch, and English—were settled apart from the native population. Moscow's "international district" was called *nemetskaya sloboda* (the German suburb), and it was only here, in a different world, that Peter the Great acquired his taste for Western ideas and skills which turned him into one of Russia's great reformers. But periods of openness—the term *glasnost* was used as early as the eighteenth century—were followed by decades of backlash and xenophobia.

The czars were constantly alert to "evil" Western thoughts poisoning the Russian mind and possibly undermining their absolute authority. Nicholas I, who ruled from 1825 to 1855, was a case in point. Foreigners were admitted to his empire for diplomatic, commercial, and scientific purposes. Beyond that, they could only be spies. The French travel author Astolphe Marquis de Custine told a customs officer in Kronstadt, the port of Saint Petersburg, upon his arrival in 1839 that he had come only "to see the country." He immediately came under suspicion. "This is no reason for a journey," the officer said. The Marquis entered the country nevertheless and wrote one of the most enlightened books ever about Russia and the Russians. Many of his pointed observations are still valid to this day: "The country is organized in a way that, without the assistance of the agents of power, no stranger can travel there conveniently or even safely."

Even though the Soviet Union is now opening up to foreign involvement as never before, foreigners still have to cope with the "agents of power," starting with the militia who guard apartment buildings occupied by foreigners. Their role was to provide 24-hour surveillance. Only recently, as violent crime surged in Moscow, has their role as protectors been appreciated. Traveling without the assistance of ministries, trade organizations, or the state tourism agency (Intourist) is still very difficult. As it entered the 1990s, many parts of the huge country were still off limits for foreigners, starting right in the outskirts of Moscow. In 1987, I missed a prescribed route on a car trip to Vladimir and was promptly stopped at the next militia post. (These installations dot the highways all over the countryside.) I had to fill out a protocol form. The next day, a Foreign Ministry official reprimanded me, stressing that no deviations from an "open road"—open to foreigners, that is—were permissible, "not even by one meter."

I suspect another reason that so much of the countryside is closed to outsiders is because Soviets are simply ashamed of the appalling poverty and backwardness of a great many villages. Russia is a land of many contrasts, but none is sharper than the gap between this image of misery and the "official picture" exhibited on slick color photographs in the showcases of the Novosti news agency on Moscow's Zubovsky Boulevard. They show polished government palaces and marbled metro stations, towering universities and huge hydroelectric plants, imposing nuclear missiles and spectacular spacecraft, graceful ballerinas and resourceful athletes. But faced with the marvels of Western society, from high tech to Big Mac, many Russians regard their own achievements of today as painfully inadequate. As the country proceeds in facing reality, the shroud of secrecy gradually lifts.

More often than not, Russians express their pride by pointing to their cultural heritage, which has contributed, as they say, to "the best in world culture," from the golden-domed spires of Orthodox churches to the ageless masterworks of Fëdor Dostoevski and Leo Tolstoi and the enthralling music of Peter Tchaikovsky and Igor Stravinsky. In the absence of light-hearted popular culture, Russians read and reread their classics. In crowded subways, many passengers dig not into the pages of *Pravda* but into a worn-out edition of Anton Chekhov's drama *The Three Sisters.* Anyone with a sense of culture will be delighted to entertain a dinner party by reciting extensively from Alexander Pushkin's poems—and American guests should be prepared to reciprocate with a few lines from William Shakespeare or Walt Whitman. Increasingly, the Russian Orthodox Church and other religious groups, long restricted or even banned, are making a comeback, and it is surprising how strong their influence on public life still is after 70 years of "godless communism."

Nothing could be more insulting for a Russian than being called *nekulturny* (uncultivated). Once I asked a peasant woman selling apples at a roadside in the country if I could take her picture. She asked me to wait for a moment, then rearranged her head scarf, explaining: "Otherwise people abroad will think we are *nekulturny.*" Another matron in a museum in the medieval monastry city of Suzdal, which featured old icons and prayer books as well as Meissen porcelain and French jewelry, inquired: "Did you examine everything closely? All this has been made by our Russian people."

Foreigners are forever regarded as guests entitled to see only the best. Foreigners, said Grand Duke Monomakh (1053–1125), have to leave the country completely satisfied. "Nobody likes a visitor to his home who checks for dirt under the carpet," a current official once explained to me. It even hurts many of my acquaintances that an increasingly critical and inquisitive Soviet press these days exposes so much dirty laundry to public scrutiny. Pride remains a major element of the Russian character—one that no foreigner may violate with impunity. But isn't that true of all nations?

Many travel restrictions never made sense to me, as they involved no areas of military significance. Take the "diplomats' beach" on the Moskva River northeast of the capital. Foreigners were assigned to one side of the river; Russians crowded the opposite bank, within eyesight but out of reach. The only plausible reason was to prevent contacts. This attitude is easing under *glasnost,* but many Russians who have no formal business with foreigners are still ingrained with past prohibitions. During the time of Stalin, one Moscow resident told me, he would not even dare to pass an Intourist hotel on the same side of the street for fear of being seen close to a Westerner. In the xenophobic perception of the 1930s, every foreigner was a spy. The sinister legacy of Stalinism, the fear of persecution, lingers on, especially among older people. "They were taught never to trust anybody outside of their immediate relations," a Soviet manager who was trained in the West sighed. "Mistrust—that's why our society cannot be normal for a long time to come."

So, for anyone who wants to explore the "Russian soul," there remain unchartered waters even as this society is opening up. It goes without saying that the better you speak Russian the better equipped you will be for the task. Many non-Russians balk at the Cyrillic alphabet, but this is definitely the easiest part of the language. Two or three days of study will enable you at least to decipher street and subway signs. Although retaining this writing system may involve an inkling of isolationism (the Czechs, after all, with a similar language, manage quite well with Latin letters), linguists agree that it serves best in expressing in one character sounds that we need several for, such as "yu," "zh," or "shch" (read Ю, Ж, and Щ). Most characters appear familiar anyway, even if pronounced differently, because they originate from Greek. The language, however, with its complex grammar, is difficult to master. If you only listen to it, it sounds unexpectedly soft, even melodious. Not only lovers of Glinka operas will confirm this.

One aspect of the alphabet in particular reveals a lot about how Russians view themselves. The alphabet ends with Я (ya), which also means "I," and the personal pronoun is never spelled with a capital letter. Individualism comes last in a society where a single person never counted for much. In relation to the powers that be and that were, the individual was weak, unprotected, vulnerable, dispensable. Only now is the concept of individual rights and liberties making real headway in the Soviet Union. In the past, an individual had an impact only as part of a group—the clan, the village community, the military unit, the work collective, the party cell. Russians love the protection and the anonymity of the group even at the price of conformity. The importance of the community in Russian culture is rooted in past struggles for survival. In czarist Russia where serfdom ended only in 1861, the village community *(mir)* was held collectively responsible for acts of individual members.

Communism was able to build its collectivism on the well-prepared ground of self-denial. This principle reached right to the top. Collective leadership was the rule in the Communist party. Although leaders like Stalin, Khrushchev, and Brezhnev placed themselves into paramount positions, they always took care to preserve at least the pretense of collective decision making. All Politburo decisions had to be unanimous. Uniformity of opinion and the ban on "factionalism" kept the party monolithic until *perestroika* initiated major upheavals. Unfortunately, this attitude has prevented any real democracy, any sense of individual civic responsibility, and any tradition comparable to the Roman understanding of *civitas,* the enlightened French idea of *citoyens,* or the more duty oriented German concept of *Bürgersinn,* not to mention civil courage of the sort described by John F. Kennedy. Comrades always had to serve the interest of the party and, by extension, the interests of the party-dominated state with all its institutions. Dissent was suppressed, and dissidents were outcasts. The late Nobel peace prize laureate Andrei Sakharov, whose exceptional advocacy of democracy was redeemed shortly before his death, certainly deserves a chapter in any new *Profiles in Courage.*

On the economic side, the tradition of uniformity of ideas and behavior to this very day—and probably for a long time to come—stymie individual activity, even though it is becoming recognized that personal effort and initiative are essential in a new market-oriented economy. Group activity remains the rule, from factory brigades to private cooperatives. "Who do you belong to?" will be answered by indicating a group, an organization, a party cell; it used to be a question that helped to identify people with certain positions and views according to their group. This starts in kindergarten and ends in the retirement home. Uniforms, not only in the military, dominate Soviet life. In many state factories and state farms, Russians not only share the work place with their group but the cultural club, the sports grounds, the vacation resort, the sanatorium, and the hospital as well. When traveling inside the Soviet Union, frequently I had to skip breakfast in hotel restaurants because service depended on the correct answer to the question, "Which group do you belong to?" Replying "I'm on my own" was no good. Wrong answer. No service.

Getting rid of these attitudes is the biggest future challenge for reformers. Many fear that change may revert them into the other extreme—overemphasizing individuality, greedy egotism, and unsocial behavior. *Anarchy* is a key word that, for the older generation, raises the specter of vengeful peasant revolts and atrocious civil wars.

Beyond the group, of course, there is the identification with the country, the nation, and the people. Even under more favorable conditions, this never comes easily in a multinational society like the Soviet Union, which has more than 100 different ethnic groups. This is why, for the time being, we are dealing with "Russian" rather than "Soviet" culture and behavior. Understanding them is the key to the world's largest country.

It is fascinating to note that the perceptions non-Russian Soviet citizens have of Russians differ considerably from the way Russians portray themselves. Public opinion polls have made inroads in the Soviet Union. In one of the first "national character" profiles, published by the weekly newspaper *Moscow News* in 1990, the question was how Russians characterize themselves and how this matches the views of their compatriots on their most important characteristics (Table 2-1).

I do not agree with all the results but, in general, they come close to reality. For me, it is surprising to find the highest rate of approval for "open-minded" and "simple." Russians certainly make good friends once they open up—but that usually takes time. If they do, they share everything with you: their bread and vodka (lots of vodka!), their joys and sorrows. The emotional nature of friendships with Russians tends to stun foreigners, for often it is much more than they are willing to invest. I still cringe when one of my best Russian friends ends his letters with "I love you."

Not all these relationships, especially between business partners, are sheer generosity and selflessness. A Western businessman told me how he tried to escape from what his Russian acquaintance described as a traditional ritual for sealing a friendship: to exchange watches. The Russian had a Soviet-made $10 model, the Westerner a gold Rolex.

As for "simple," the term refers to the Russian background of rural heritage. Most urban Russians are only second- or third-generation city dwellers, still tied to the simple life and habits of generations of peasants. There is perhaps no word that is more likely to start tears rolling than *rodina*. This translates as "motherland" because *Rossiya* is feminine, Mother Russia. *Rodina* has the touch of crumbs of black earth, the smell of birch forests in springtime, the softness of waves on the Volga River, the

Table 2-1 Russian versus Non-Russian Views on Characteristics of Russians

Characteristic	Russians Saying Yes	Non-Russians Saying Yes
Are Russians:		
Open-minded, simple, easy?	66%	48%
Patient, consistent?	59	39
Hospitable, kind?	59	40
Peace-loving?	55	35
Ready to help, good neighbor?	55	36
Industrious, like to work?	53	24
Reliable, loyal?	28	17
Lazy?	25	29
Freedom-loving?	22	15
Full of energy, motivated?	8	8

SOURCE: *Moscow News* (English Edition), 27 May 1990, p. 8.

warmth of a summer evening with family and friends on a wooden bench at the dacha, the exhilaration of children frolicking on a snowy hill, and the tranquillity of a moonlit winter night in the taiga forests.

Whenever they have a chance, Russians leave their cities to spend some time enjoying country life, even if their dacha is nothing but a shack without electricity and water, and their vegetable plot is hardly worth the effort; even if they have to walk for miles to the next bus stop or the next grocery. This is where their roots are. "It's the only place where you can enjoy life," Grisha, a young Moscow painter, told me while pouring more hot water from a coal-fired samovar to dilute the tea extract in his cup for a perfect mixture. "In the city, you can only work." His little cottage in a forest 50 miles from the capital was surrounded by a fence 10 feet high—just like his neighbors'. Being a "good neighbor" is apparently not the most important aspect of country life.

I should more eagerly agree with the self-description of Russians as "patient." Patience remains an all-encompassing virtue and at the same time a form of suffering that drives outsiders crazy. Patience and endurance—*terpeniye* is *the* Russian word to remember—penetrate all walks of life. It is the way a peasant sows and waits, knowing that it is useless to do anything unless Mother Nature plays along. No need to get upset about a dry spell. Eventually rain will come or it won't. Getting upset makes no difference at all. When translated to urban life and modern industrial society, this habit makes no sense anymore. Most obstacles today are of human origin—under human control. But that is Western thinking, not Russian.

My wife one day got stuck between floors in an elevator. When nothing happened within 10 minutes, she got tense. "We've got to do something," she told a Russian trapped with her. But he stayed absolutely calm: "If it takes too long, I'll just roll up my sweater and sleep in the corner. They will come and get us out of here, no matter when."

If there is a line in a shop, Russians approach the end and briskly ask: "Are you the last one?" Then they take up their place and wait as the line moves forward at a snail's pace. Sometimes it may take hours before a customer arrives at the counter to buy meat, oranges, vodka, or theater tickets. But "time is money" is a Western concept, too. In Soviet stores, lines zigzag like sidewinder snakes, but everything proceeds quietly. No hassle, no protest—unless somebody tries to cheat by jumping the queue. Even when sales clerks turn their backs to the clientele and engage in seemingly endless chatter, hardly anybody criticizes them. "Shouting achieves nothing," said Soviet writer Maxim Gorky a long time ago. The rule still applies. Anger only hurts feelings and, in any case, you want to be on good terms with the clerk so that maybe she will sell you some rare "deficit" goods from under the counter. But the general lack of politeness is being handed down: nobody opens a door for an old lady, nobody offers a seat in the subway to a tired shopper.

Terpeniye means "endurance," and Russians, in some strange ways, almost enjoy it. They profess a certain pride in their ability to suffer: Did they not overcome all those wars and famines, shortages and inconveniences, dictators and *apparatchiks* in the end? An impatient farmer is a bad farmer.

"What can you do?" my Russian friends would reply when I drew their attention to the nonsense of waiting, the waste of time and energy in the shops, where you may have to stand in three lines—first for choosing goods, then for paying, and finally for picking up purchases. "It's the same for everybody and it has always been like that," they insist. It is a collective burden, shared by millions, and thus easier to bear.

But it makes too many Russians indifferent, apathetic, and fatalistic— qualities that are not helpful in transforming the country to an efficient and productive modern society. Even President Mikhail Gorbachev frequently admits to this braking mechanism: "It sits deep down in everyone of us, including myself." He has also said, "We are overburdened by old habits." On the other hand, an absence of patience and endurance might have destroyed social peace and civility long ago.

For anybody who does business with Russians, these old habits create major difficulties. Unfortunately, the effect is increased by a lack of material incentives for working harder. Sneering at ridiculously low salaries, Russian workers like to say: "The state pretends to pay us, so we pretend to work." Economist Nikolai Shmelev, like so many reformers, complains about "massive apathy and laziness" on all levels of economy, big and small. The messenger of a Western bank in Moscow gave me a telling example of his idea of swift delivery. In front of a crowded elevator, he rejected attempts to make room for him. "Oh no, you go," he said. "I've got time. I'm on duty."

The economic system has suffocated individual efforts. Every item of production was planned, and fulfilling the annual or the five-year target was completely sufficient. Even where "overproduction" was possible, most factories or farms hesitated to exploit this opportunity. It would only mean higher targets next year. Generously, the state planning commission (Gosplan) often reduced production goals when they were not met. In many instances, this system was so rigged by constant changes, even outright cheating, that many economic statistics turned out to be distorted and unreliable. Some Soviet economists claim that no five-year plan was ever fulfilled.

A *kolkhoz* (collective farm) in the Volga region, for instance, had to register a bad potato harvest one year. But the regional party newspaper reported that this very farm overfulfilled its plan by 10 percent. So the farm managers stopped worrying and just adopted the newspaper's figures in their official production summary. Nobody cared to check. This may help to explain the poll percentages under "industrious," "reliable," "lazy," and "full of energy."

Our Western approach to this problem would be that there is nothing that cannot be solved by a decent pay hike. But additional money is useless without additional consumer goods. Many of my friends in Moscow and Leningrad had an easy way with rubles. "Toy money," they called it. More important to them was *blat,* which means "pull" or "connections": You know somebody who can deliver the goods, mostly from the expanding black market, not necessarily for money but for a favor in goods or services you could provide or arrange. *Blat* works on reciprocity, one hand washes the other. My Moscow driver, who was very handy, never had problems in acquiring rare goods like a car windshield or childrens' shoes or coffee. In return, he repaired Volga engines and electrical appliances. This unofficial and unsanctioned network cushions many hardships and shortcomings of everyday life in the Soviet Union.

Blat is an extended version of family ties for mutual assistance that tend to be more common in poor countries suffering from such shortcomings in all areas. They fade away as consumer and social services become more readily available. In the Soviet Union, family relations are still very tight; Russians, children and adults alike, would never address their parents as Father and Mother but always in a loving diminuitive like *Papa* or *Mamuchka.* One negative effect that both the *blat* networks and close family ties have is that they reduce the mobility of the labor force, an increasing necessity of modern industrial society.

More seriously, all attempts to innovate meet with a distinct lack of a business culture. Before the October Revolution, what little industry there was remained in the hands of a small group of indigenous entrepreneurs and foreign investors. Under communism, every trace of capitalism was uprooted. Success resulting in modest wealth for merchants and farmers turned them into "parasites." The fate of the kulaks, peasants who managed their private land more efficiently and more successfully than others and thus happened to be somewhat better off than their neighbors, spread terror all over the countryside in the 1930s: Most of them were deported, killed, or starved. They were, as Stalin proudly proclaimed, "eliminated as a class." *Profit* was a dirty word for decades, synonymous with *robbery.* It is one of the painful ironies of Soviet society that the very qualities that are in demand today for a market economy and profitable business used to land people in jail as "economic criminals." Since Russians have long memories, the fear lingers on that changes might be reverted, new freedoms canceled and old restrictions reestablished. It happened after Lenin's free-market experiment, "new economic policy," (NEP), in the 1920s and, more recently, after the "Kosygin reforms" in the late 1960s. Over and over again, Gorbachev has assured his countrymen that this time, "reform is irreversible." However, there is a joke that Ivan, who has obtained a new hearing device, now wants some new glasses, too, because "I would love to see what I hear."

The first semiprivate entrepreneurs under *perestroika,* engaging in limited "individual labor activity," mainly in the form of cooperatives with 5 to 50 people in the service sector and in agriculture, had to bear the brunt of the antibusiness mood. These businessmen—for lack of their own term, Russians call them *"bizinesmen"*—were derided as speculators as soon as they made some modest profit with their restaurants, repair shops, and dairy farms. Disregarding the fact that their performance was much better than in any branch under state control, public anger focused on the "excessive" amount of profit they made. If a lunch in a state restaurant costs an average 3 to 4 rubles and a cooperative takes 20 to 25, isn't this "speculation" and "reckless exploitation"? Some bureaucrats joined the fold, upset by salaries for a cooperative waitress that were five or six times higher than their own. Many of the pioneers of private business in the late 1980s found themselves cut off from the state-run supply network and harassed by narrow-minded regulations and inspections.

Here, we meet with another braking mechanism, which poet Yevgeny Yevtushenko once described as "our worst handicap"—envy. In a society where, in theory at least, everybody was equal, a person who stands out in terms of income or property raises suspicion and jealousy. Once the privileges of the state and party hierarchy, the "more than equal" class of the *nomenklatura,* were no longer a taboo topic, there was popular support for stripping them of their perks—chauffeured limousines, special shops and hospitals, better apartments and schools, foreign travel and vacation hideaways. A cruel Russian anecdote perhaps gives the best insight into the extent of that mean-spirited mood: A fisherman catches a fish who tells him that he is actually a jinxed prince. If he were returned to the river, he could grant three wishes to the fisherman. So the old fellow starts: "You see, my neighbor has a nice farm, a pretty wife, and a very good milk cow . . ." The fish replies: "I understand, you would like to have the same." The fisherman angrily responds: "You don't understand a thing. I want him to lose all that."

Another obstacle that has to be removed in the Soviet Union is "administrative methods," which stands for mindless bureaucracy and endless red tape. Foreign residents and visitors, just like Russians themselves, have to deal with almost impenetrable "administrations," state committees and institutions to which efficiency is an alien and undesired concept. In establishing a foothold in Moscow or Leningrad, foreign companies and individuals have to endure a lengthy test of patience. Every little step is arduous and time-consuming—getting an apartment or a driver's license or a customs clearance or an international telephone line. Difficulties are not limited to the beginning, but the experience gained in the process is certainly helpful the next time around.

Like every bureaucracy, the Soviet variant devours huge amounts of paperwork. *"Bez pisma nikuda,"* Russians say, meaning, "You get nowhere without a letter." Businessmen accustomed to quick deals over the telephone are in for culture shock. Letters, documentations, negotiations seem to be all pervasive. The need starts at the lowest level because every Russian holder of authority exercises power to the hilt. A European commercial representative once forgot his *propusk,* the identity card that gave him access to his office building. The doorman, who had seen him every day for a year, refused to admit him. Without a *propusk* you are a nobody. There is hope that economic reform, boosted by Western management training and an erosion of central authority, may tackle this obstacle.

Even then, there remains a major irritant: an inconsistency of character and behavior that baffles foreigners. You meet an official one day and he is all smiles and politeness. You meet him a week later and he does not even recognize you. You establish what you think is a friendly working relationship with a Russian employee and you are stunned at how mute and rude he is occasionally. Perhaps these sudden shifts of mood result from the hardships of Russian life and the whims of nature, the chilling winter days and the clouded gloom of the "mud season" in fall and spring. Perhaps they are in line with a generally pessimistic attitude toward life, an obsession with the darker side of existence and a legacy of dashed hopes that has kept the somber works of Dostoevski and Maxim Gorky on the best-seller lists. "An optimist," a Russian saying goes, "is just a badly informed pessimist."

Women seem less affected by this phenomenon than men. They are usually more balanced, more motivated, more reliable. Since more than half of the Russian work force consists of women, this may be a consolation. Women now get better grades than men at universities and are making inroads in a male-dominated society. Women also do less drinking, the scourge of Russian society, a problem that affects productivity as well as social life. I cannot imagine what Russia would be without its women. They bear the brunt of hardships, usually performing what they call the "double shift": their work in a factory or office plus the chores of household and child care and looking after their husband's needs. Russian men tend to be pampered "pashas," relaxing on the sofa in front of the TV while their wives shop and cook and clean and wash. "It hurts me to see you working so hard, darling," a Russian husband in a cartoon tells his wife, who is busy in the kitchen. "Please, close the door."

The motivation of upward mobility is most apparent in women, many of whom direct textile factories, social and welfare agencies, and educational establishments. The majority of physicians and teachers in the U.S.S.R. are female. In business, they follow careers not so much for their personal ambitions but in a constant quest to improve the lot of their families. While increasing numbers of women in the West make decisions between career or family, married women in the Soviet Union just cannot afford not to work. In the West, emancipation usually means to find self-fulfillment in a full professional career, while the goal of most Soviet working mothers is to be able to stay home and devote their time to children and household, just as their mothers and grandmothers used to do. Children are showered with affection and catered to, even if that often produces selfish brats. Where else but in Russia would an old woman in the subway give up her seat for a perfectly healthy child?

The Soviet Union is a multiethnic and multicultural country. Traditions and attitudes differ considerably between different nationalities. Even Ukrainians, who are closely related to Russians, have a reputation for being more industrious, more ambitious, and more eager. In terms of business aptitude, many inhabitants of the republics in the Caucasus', such as Georgians and Armenians, have a wider tradition and experience in trade and commerce—and it shows. A disproportionate number of new cooperatives is run by dark-haired "southerners" as is, admittedly, a large part of the black-market trade. Kazakh, Kirgizian, and Turkmenian sellers at open farm markets in Russian cities like to engage in jolly good bargaining in the old tradition of Oriental bazaars. People of the Baltic nations— Estonians, Latvians, and Lithuanians—come closest to Western perceptions of work and business, being orderly, hard-working, and efficient. Their countries formed part of the market and trade networks of the German Hanseatic League and Scandinavia long before Russia opened up to foreign commerce. In the Russian Republic, it is striking how many of the most active trade representatives, diplomats, factory directors, scientists, and artists are of Jewish origin. Many Jews had established contacts with foreigners at a time when authorities discouraged this.

This short excursion into the charcteristics of other Soviet nationalities cannot do more than sensitize the reader to this additional complexity in doing business with the Soviet Union. However, Russians will constitute a majority of business contacts in the U.S.S.R. for some time to come, and Russian culture has influenced the behavior of other Soviet peoples considerably. Consequently, the following guidelines may prove useful, even if some should become superfluous in the rapid sequence of current changes.

1. Be patient.   Don't get overwhelmed by all the nasty little intricacies of Soviet life, business, and bureaucracy. Be firm in your positions and never show your anger. Be prepared for lengthy delays in applications, orders, appointments, anything. Don't become restless when your partners don't start talking business immediately. They just may want to take your measure or they may not have their act together. Don't get upset when things do not run smoothly or go wrong. You will only get ulcers. Try and try again. Calm persistence pays off. If you flunk the test of patience, you and your business could be in trouble.

2. Learn Russian, at least some.   Although you can assume that many people doing business with you will speak some English, you will encounter partners even at the top who do not. In any case, conduct all your negotiations with a trustworthy interpreter even if you have some command of the language. A personal introduction in Russian will always be appreciated and nobody objects if you continue through your interpreter. Russians do not expect you to speak their language and you will score points by trying. In everyday life or in contact with Russian workers and employees, some understanding of the language is always helpful. Only a very small percentage of the population speaks any foreign language properly. Outside the cities, you would be lost without the ability to ask for directions, order a meal, or identify yourself to an officer of the GAI traffic police.

3. Establish personal contacts.   This advice, of course, applies to business in any country but it carries special significance in the Soviet Union. Knowing the right people, sometimes just the right assistant, will help you to cut through red tape and avoid long talks with underlings who cannot decide anything anyway. In times of change, when many ministeries, state committees, and trade organizations are experiencing massive reorganization, an established contact may seem like an anchorage in a stormy sea. Go for the top, if you can, and use high-ranking officials for cross-connections into other organizations you have to deal with.

4. Get it in writing, and follow through.   "You can take my word for it" can be a nice expression of rapport. But don't rely on it. Politely insist on putting things down in writing, not only the final version of your contracts but also fix agreed positions during negotiations in letters of intent. Don't shy away from the paperwork. Your copies will come in handy whenever there is disagreement over previous deals or commitments. Business in the Soviet Union runs along more formalistic lines than in the West. But if you don't play by their rules, you may be in for some unpleasant surprises. In dealing with employees on all levels, do not assume that an order once given and a job once delegated will be executed as you expect. Follow up as often as you can. For a long time, control and the threat of sanction has been the only efficient stimulation in Soviet economy. Take a cue from a phrase that President Ronald Reagan used to irk Mikhail Gorbachev: *"Doveryat no proveryat"* (Trust but verify).

5. Don't hurt feelings.   Russians are very proud, and losing face is very painful to them. The concept of showing the right face is Oriental in origin, a heritage of hundreds of years of Mongol rule over Russia. So in the Soviet Union it is even more advisable than in the United States or Western Europe not to engage in shouting matches. Don't expose mistakes in front of superiors, don't question qualifications, and avoid insulting people or the things they cherish. If you disagree on anything, politics included, state your position clearly but mince your words. If you talk about home, try not to be boastful. Stay clear of resentment caused by comparisons, even though Russians have a special penchant for Americans and love *"nashi-*

vashi" (ours-yours) discussions. Russians have memories like elephants, enhanced by constant note taking in negotiations, and they recollect things when you may have long forgotten. Of course, they remember a good thing as well as a bad one.

6. Stay straight.   In all your activities, official and private, don't do anything that makes you vulnerable. The Soviet Union still has a powerful security apparatus. Nothing may hurt your business activities more than getting compromised by breaking laws or regulations, even minor ones like illegal money exchange, black market caviar purchases, icon smuggling, or traffic violations. Avoid even the appearance of corruption but be prepared to exchange little gifts or souvenirs. A box of Swiss candy can work wonders in getting preferential treatment at a theater ticket counter, an Aeroflot booking office, or in a hotel. On some occasions, you will be coaxed into drinking vodka at official dinners or private meetings, another test of character. Join in but know when to stop. Female executives are exempted from these "manly" games, but they have to overcome a lot of male bias. Being resolute and competent may reward them with even higher respect than for their male counterparts.

These recommendations do not guarantee success, and you should be flexible enough to adapt and amend them according to your experience. But let me add a last word of warning: Almost nobody who is in the Soviet Union for a long time escapes the "Moscow blues" (which is not confined to Moscow). Some scientists blame this depressive mood on the lack of sunshine during those long, cold, dark winters. The main symptom is a decreasing tolerance for all shortcomings. So when you get fed up with sloppy service, common intransigence, and tasteless *bifshteks* (beef steaks), you know it is time for a weekend trip to Helsinki, Stockholm, Berlin, or London, where you can relax in a nice hotel and enjoy all the things you missed in the Soviet Union. During my time in Moscow, we used to call these remedial excursions "coming up for air."

CHAPTER 3

Daily Economic Life in the U.S.S.R.

James R. Millar

In the face of turbulent change since 1917, the Soviet family has remained the fundamental unit of Soviet society and the household has always behaved very much like its economic counterpart in the "capitalist" countries.* Families have worked to earn income, decided on their own spending priorities, and made purchases in stores and other markets. The reforms since Gorbachev came to power have only increased the need for Soviet households to be economically self-reliant.

Almost 70 percent of the Soviet population now lives in regions classified as urban. This is a recent development, and a large proportion of the urban population of the U.S.S.R. is first-generation. Approximately 20 percent of the Soviet Union's labor force is still directly engaged in agricultural pursuits, as opposed to less than 2 percent in the United States. The exodus from the rural community has been exceedingly rapid during the last decade or so, averaging about 2 million persons per year. This rapid outflow from the rural sector reflects in part the much poorer standard of living in rural areas of the U.S.S.R., and the outmigration is further impoverishing the rural community, because the young, the energetic, the educated, and the ambitious are the ones who are leaving.

In comparison to the United States or Western Europe, the U.S.S.R. is still heavily rural. The gap between living conditions and professional prospects in rural and urban areas is much greater than in the West because of the sheer size of the country and its inadequate transport network. The

---

*This chapter draws upon Chapter 4 of my book *The ABCs of Soviet Socialism* (Urbana: University of Illinois Press, 1981). It has been recast, revised, and updated for this volume.

relative isolation of rural communities is far greater than in the West; the scarcity of private automobiles and trucks in rural areas is a contributing factor to this isolation. There is no equivalent in the U.S.S.R. to the American farms' pickup trucks, which are available to take members of the family into town on evenings and weekends. Some regions are so remote, in fact, that there is virtually no exit during much of the winter. Television does reach most of these otherwise isolated areas, but its message is the superiority of urban life, especially in choice cities such as Moscow, Leningrad, and Kiev.

One may not simply decide to live in a city. In order to obtain an apartment or room in a Soviet city legally, a person must ordinarily be employed in the city, but it is hard to find employment unless one already lives there. A person who wishes to live in Moscow could sign up with the labor exchange and take a chance on being assigned to Moscow, but no one would expect so farfetched a hope to come true. Moscow is the most difficult city of all to move to permanently. Restrictions on movement to desirable cities such as Moscow can be circumvented, but essentially only by exceptional professional success, subterfuge, or *blat. Blat,* probably the most important of these, is a term that refers to the use of influence to advance one's own or one's family's interests.

There is a hierarchy of living conditions in the Soviet Union, with Moscow and other republic capitals at the pinnacle and the remote villages of Siberia and Central Asia at the bottom. Moscow, of course, stands at the apex. The upward slope measures more than access to cultural events, such as the Bolshoi Ballet or the Mayakovsky Theater, or to paved streets. Moscovites live at the center of political power, which acts as a magnet for all of the good things in Soviet life. Food supplies are more reliable in Moscow than elsewhere. Industrial commodities designed for consumers gravitate to Moscow. Housing is superior; the provision of child care centers is more adequate; and so it goes. The same is true for the capital cities of all the republics, relative to their hinterlands.

Since Moscow is the political hub of a highly centralized bureaucracy, it is the best place to get things done. Moscow is the city of *blat* (connections), a city that reflects the best and the worst in the U.S.S.R. People who live elsewhere in the U.S.S.R. must make periodic trips to this political and economic Mecca of the Soviet system to have petitions heard, to meet with superiors, to buy commodities available nowhere else, and to have lavish vacations. Peasants come to Moscow from the outlying regions with their bags packed with fruit, vegetables, honey, and anything else that can be sold on the *rynok* (private market). After selling everything, they proceed to spend whatever they have earned, buying things for themselves and their friends; and they return home with their bags packed with clothing, toys, rugs, china, meat, and phonograph records. Although the details differ, the other major urban centers of the U.S.S.R. serve similar roles for those who live outside their gates.

The legal status of private property is being expanded today. It has always existed in the Soviet Union, but it has been greatly circumscribed by comprehensive state (public) ownership of the "means of production," which are defined to include all land, mineral wealth, and most of the fixed and working capital. Private individuals have always been allowed to own, and have been free to sell either privately or through state stores that take a commission, a wide range of items of personal property. These include not only articles of clothing, television sets, refrigerators, and other personal effects, but also certain types of capital equipment, such as hand tools, typewriters, gardening supplies, and the like, plus such large items of nonproductive capital as automobiles, apartments, houses, and dachas. Moreover, some forms of state property have been treated as if they were private property and have been used by private citizens for personal gain. Families may trade state-owned apartments with each other for mutual benefit; a newly formed family, in which the wife and husband each hold a one-room apartment, may trade these for a two or three-room apartment that houses two families. Similarly, a state-owned apartment located in a desirable city such as Moscow may be traded for an apartment in a less desirable city, plus a "consideration."

Buying, selling, and trading of personal property is a perfectly legal and open activity either through state consignment outlets or directly. Certain locations in each city have become trading centers where advertisements are posted and meetings are arranged for purposes of direct trading. The owner of the property, or the property right, is free to charge what the market will bear, without government interference. Legal marketing, of course, shades imperceptibly into illegal trading. Certain types of transactions are proscribed, such as the exchange of rubles for foreign currency, but even this has become common in major cities despite the threat of severe sanctions. It is also illegal to serve as a middleman in private transactions. That is, one may not legally purchase goods for the purpose of reselling them for personal gain. The deciding factor is intent, because a large number of such private transactions do in fact take place at a profit to the seller. It is also illegal to purchase an apartment or an automobile for the purpose of leasing it out or otherwise using it as a source of income. Reforms that are currently under consideration are likely to reduce restrictions on middleman activities, but popular sentiment is highly adverse to these kinds of transactions because they are viewed as speculation and exploitation of special advantages at the expense of the consumer.

Although no private individual may own land in the Soviet Union, every citizen who is in good legal standing is provided with access to land for private use. For satisfactory work, collective farm workers receive a plot of land on which to build a home and to maintain a kitchen garden. The legal situation for state farm workers is different, but actual arrangements are essentially the same as for collective farm workers. The great bulk of privately produced and privately marketed food products derives from these two types of private-plot agriculture. Rural workers not engaged directly in agricultural employment, such as schoolteachers or clerks, are also provided access to plots of land on which to build homes, keep animals, and tend gardens. Urban dwellers are also provided access to small plots of land on the outskirts of town, where they may build a *dacha* and keep a garden. Because the location is not ordinarily convenient, city dwellers rarely build substantial dwellings on the plots. They normally build summer and/or winter retreats, and most of them are primitive, with few modern conveniences. Ownership of freestanding homes is, therefore, primarily a rural phenomenon. The ways in which urban dwellers gain access to plots of land are complex and varied, and the size of the plots to which individuals are entitled varies by type of access. A worker may obtain a plot of land through the enterprise for which he or she works. A military officer ordinarily receives a plot through the military bureaucracy. Individuals not otherwise covered may obtain plots of land through the city administration, or through a cooperative arrangement, and so forth. Over one-half of the privately held plots of land in the Soviet Union today are held by members of the nonagricultural population.

It has become increasingly popular for individuals to build, or purchase, apartments under cooperative arrangements. Many cooperatives have been organized by employers, such as a factory, the Academy of Sciences, Moscow State University, or Gosplan. The usual arrangements call for 20 percent down payment and the remainder in installments, frequently without interest. Apartments purchased in this way are expensive relative to the subsidized rents of state-owned dwellings, but offer the roomiest and most comfortable living quarters available in the major cities. A group of private individuals may also arrange to contract for construction of a condominium and borrow a portion of the cost from the state bank. Interest is charged normally at 2 percent per annum. Apartment ownership affords the individual in the Soviet Union the largest and probably the most lucrative investment available for private ownership and potential gain. (Individuals who purchase an apartment do not pay anything for the land on which the building sits, which is a considerable benefit in any major city.) Owners of homes and apartments report themselves as much more satisfied with their housing than do those who rent from the state. Current plans to sell state-owned apartments to their tenants makes good sense, therefore, both fiscally and politically.

In addition to apartments, automobiles, and other consumer durables, individuals may purchase jewelry, paintings, rare books, and similar items. Individuals may also own financial assets, which include currency, savings accounts with the state bank, and state 3 percent lottery bonds (i.e., returns are distributed by lottery periodically). A type of checking account is now available to certain Soviet citizens, but it is of little domestic use in an economy in which almost all payments are made in cash. Apart from interest receipts on savings accounts and winnings on state lottery bonds, income from property is illegal in the Soviet Union. One may lend money to a friend, but charging interest would violate the law. Under certain circumstances one may receive something in consideration for subletting one's apartment or for renting a room (a "corner") to a student, but it is not legal to go into the business of taking in boarders or renting out apartments. Recent reforms may lead to the creation of joint-stock ownership of certain enterprises and thus legal dividend income. In general, however, property income still represents an insignificant source of legal income to households because of these ideological restrictions on unearned income.

All private personal wealth may be legally inherited in the Soviet Union. Survivors ordinarily have first claim even on the family's state apartment or dacha, and in this respect certain aspects of private ownership attach to them.

All other property, with the sole exception of collective farms, whose members are supposed to have indivisible (that is, inalienable) rights in the farm's capital stock, is publicly owned in the Soviet Union. Therefore the profits of state enterprises and rental payments of the population residing in state housing are paid into the various governmental budgets and used to finance investment in state enterprises, construction of new housing, and other state outlays.

Current reforms have been designed to expand private ownership of productive plant and equipment, but they have met with considerable resistance. Opposition to private ownership of land is particularly strong.

Private enterprise is not prohibited, but it has been severely restricted by limitations on hiring others for personal profit, on private middleman activities, and on private ownership of the land and productive plant and equipment. What domestic private enterprise does exist is therefore necessarily small scale. The line between legal and illegal private enterprise is not easy to draw. Individuals may sell newly produced items that they or their families have produced, for example, on private plots; and they may sell secondhand items, too. A writer may hire a typist to type manuscripts; families may hire housekeepers and babysitters; and anyone may hire work to be done or repairs to be made around the house, even though such hiring may contribute to the employers' personal incomes by making them more efficient or by freeing them to earn more money elsewhere. Although private enterprise has been restricted in the past to the sale of products of private agricultural plots and to one-person enterprises for home repairs or such sideline activities as seeing patients or clients after work, it has been ubiquitous and significant in almost everyone's life.

Cooperatives skirt a number of the limitations placed on private enterprise, but they remain for the most part small scale and focused on services such as restaurants or on contracting out to state enterprises. The cooperative sector has grown rapidly since 1985, but the public seems to disapprove of both cooperatives and private enterprise as a matter of principle.

The difference between profiteering and making a fair profit is not generally distinguished by the population. Making a bundle on a good idea or on the clever anticipation of consumer wants is considered speculation, not just good business sense. Thus far tax and other restrictions on the cooperative sector have kept it quite small scale, restricted in scope, and precariously profitable.

Most Soviet citizens work for the state in one way or another, and most elderly people these days receive state pensions. Although at one time an attempt was made to maximize the share of earnings that the worker received in direct nonmonetary benefits, this is no longer the case. Education is free, including higher education, in which success in entrance examinations assures all successful applicants free access plus a stipend. Medical care is free, too. Prescription drugs are highly subsidized, as are public transport and even the apartments that most urban dwellers rent from the state. Meals are served very cheaply, both in schools and at places of work, and child-care facilities (when available) are provided essentially free. Even so, the bulk of the typical Soviet household's income is received in money, which necessarily implies the existence of retail outlets in which households may choose the ways that their incomes are distributed among the various goods, services, and financial assets that are available—hence the importance of urban retail markets in the U.S.S.R.

All urban areas are served by official state retail outlets. The bulk of urban household income is expended in these shops. Soviet marketing follows the general European pattern, and most state retail outlets specialize in exclusive categories of products, such as fish, meat, and dairy products; bread and confectionery items; clothing; drugs; paper supplies; and so forth.

Prices are fixed for state retail outlets and are not subject to bargaining. Apart from cooperative restaurants, which are designed mainly to attract foreigners, restaurants and hotels are all state retail enterprises. Uniform pricing frequently causes anomalies. For example, most meat markets do not grade the meat that they sell by the cut. Butchers divide the meat into portions that are equally composed of good and poor portions. The flat, low price per kilo is "justified" in this way. If one knows the butcher, the effective price for "good" cuts may be very low. In the same vein, prices are exactly the same in good restaurants as in bad ones. Consequently, a meal in a good restaurant is a great bargain, and will cost no more than an indigestible meal in a poor restaurant. A meal in a "closed" dining room—that is, one that has an exclusive clientele—is also a bargain because the status of the organization ensures access to quality supplies, while prices are the same as in other state restaurants.

Two kinds of subsidies apply to state retail outlets. First, many food products are substantially underpriced and are directly subsidized by the state budget. Most meat products, especially beef, are examples. Underpricing tends to cause queuing for the products affected, because at state-quoted prices, which retail outlets cannot legally vary, these goods are a great bargain. Second, uniform pricing and the restricted mobility of the typical Soviet customer cause customers of poorly run shops and restaurants to subsidize the well run. Because the better managed shops cannot expand and compete with the poorly run, these differences tend to be self-perpetuating.

An experienced and energetic Soviet shopper learns when and where to shop for particular items in order to take advantage of peculiarities caused by uniform prices, uneven distribution of commodities, and variations in quality. The system rewards specialized knowledge, friendship, and reciprocity. Goods do not get distributed evenly, and the farther one lives from a major city the less likely that any desirable commodities will ever appear. Meat, including beef, is usually relatively plentiful in Moscow; but 200 kilometers away none is to be found most of the time. Moreover, goods are not distributed evenly within the confines of a city such as Moscow. For complex and little understood reasons, certain shops tend to get better and more reliable supplies than others. A certain buffet in a student dormitory, for example, may almost always have beer in stock, while regular retail outlets run dry for days at a time. State retail outlets also operate "casual" stands and kiosks for "surplus" items at irregular intervals. An alert shopper learns that certain corners frequently have temporary outlets where particularly desirable goods (such as oranges and apples in winter) are sold when available. By keeping an eye on these locations, by remembering which stores nearly always have milk or beer or better meat, and by staying alert to the formation of a queue anywhere, a smart shopper can maximize procurement of what Soviets call deficit commodities. The term is used to refer to goods or services that are in short supply all or most of the time. Although there are exceptions, deficit commodities are underpriced items in the state retail network, which causes excess demand to exist for these items. Even foreign firms operating in Moscow have not been able to break the mold. The wait for a Big Mac in Moscow's McDonalds often is one hour or more.

It pays to make friends with sellers in the U.S.S.R., for nearly all the desirable goods that are sold in Soviet state retail outlets are in deficit supply and require the exercise of purchasemanship, the technical equivalent of salesmanship in an economy like that of the United States. A judicious gift may get deficit commodities set aside for you. Tickets to the Bolshoi Ballet, for example, ordinarily are impossible to obtain from a ticket window in Moscow. Either they are specially ordered for tourists, high officials, and special purposes or they are distributed under the counter. Soviet shoppers worth their salt develop networks of contacts among those who sell or distribute state retail products and services which allow them to jump the queue for deficit commodities, that is, to buy at the "back door." The recipient of such a favor may not always be required to pay extra for it, but he or she incurs a reciprocal obligation for the future.

Most deficit commodities and services are provided through state retail outlets, and the individuals who market them can collect what economists call the monopoly rents on these scarce and underpriced items. That is, the employee is in a position to capture a part, or all, of the difference between the actual price established by the state committee on retail prices and the (higher) price that would be required to clear the market (that is, exactly match the number of buyers with the number of items available). For all purposes this is a property right individuals acquire by default from the state and are able to exchange for the other deficit commodities they desire.

The second type of retail outlet is the *rynok,* or "collective farm market." About one-third of the value of all retail food sales in the U.S.S.R. flows through the *rynok,* which is an unfettered market where farmers and others who have grown or produced their own products may rent a stall (and refrigeration if necessary) to sell them. Collective farms may ship their surplus produce to the *rynok,* too. Every city has one or more such markets. Typical products available are carrots, potatoes, pickled cucumbers, tomatoes, peppers, apples, pickled cabbage, honey, cheese, fermented dairy products, dried mushrooms, flowers, spices, seed, and fresh meat in winter time; the list includes more fruits and vegetables in summer. Prices are generally much higher at the *rynok* than in state retail stores, but one is free to haggle. Many Soviet shoppers visit the *rynok* at least once a week. Quality tends to be higher, and some items sold there are unavailable in other retail outlets. Anyone planning a dinner party would be certain to visit the *rynok* to buy a delicacy or two. The role of the *rynok* is probably less significant in Moscow than it is elsewhere as a source of staples such as potatoes, milk products, and meat, because these items are more readily available in state outlets in Moscow. As a general proposition, it is fair to say that the *rynok* plays a pervasive role in the supply of food products to the Soviet household, and all would be poorer without it. Thus, most Soviet households have dealt regularly with a legal free market for day-to-day needs.

The third type of retail market available to urban dwellers is a private, informal, legal market in homemade and secondhand commodities, in apartments, and for certain personal services. Much of this private trade is barter, and some of the items that are traded, such as state-owned apartments, are not in fact the property of those trading them. In addition, certain individuals sell their labor services informally. Any person with a skill, such as in repairing electrical equipment or hairdressing, may work on the side on his or her own time. Whether the activity is legal depends upon the nature of the service, the source of spare parts or equipment used, and the social implications. Unskilled women frequently do laundry for busy single men, and they may help in shopping, child care, and cooking on a strictly private basis.

This third category of legal informal marketing is difficult to identify uniquely, for it shades off into illegal economic activities on the one side and into legal state-organized secondhand markets (which operate on a commission basis) on the other. This open exchange of personal property is also important as a means for redistributing durable property from those who no longer require it to those who need it. As with garage sales in the United States, in the process everyone is made better off without anyone's being harmed.

Illegal market transactions comprise the fourth and final type of retail market in the Soviet Union. This market is very complex and includes a range from relatively innocent to quite sinister economic dealings. Because these transactions are illegal, the outside observer can obtain only a very sketchy impression of them, but the evidence suggests that illegal trading is widespread. A large proportion of the Soviet urban population is implicated—at least on a petty level. Illegal transactions are described variously by Soviet citizens. Soviets talk of obtaining goods *nalevo* (on the left), *po znakomstvu* (through a contact), *na chernom rynke* (on the black market), and *po blatu* (through pull). Each describes an important aspect of this market. Buying *po znakomstvu* is perhaps the most common and least criminal of all. In many circumstances it is more improper than illegal. Normally in this type of purchase no direct pecuniary gain is involved for the friend, who instead merely earns a reciprocal claim upon the purchaser. Purchases on the black market are ordinarily from private entrepreneurs who operate for a profit. *Blat,* on the other hand, can be accrued either by bribing someone or by being someone important with whom others seek to curry favor. The most colorful phrase, buying *nalevo,* is the most general: its meaning encompasses the entire range of illegal and semilegal activities that take place in the Soviet system.

The most desirable consumer goods and services are in deficit supply most of the time, yet prices on these deficit commodities are kept constant. Since Stalin's death, every attempt to make consumer prices flexible has failed mainly because prices would rise if deregulated. Thus the Soviet economy is a permanent sellers' market. Queues always develop when these commodities become available, and those who deal in them for the state cannot but be tempted to take advantage of their strategic monopolistic positions to increase their own incomes, to curry favor with superiors, or to benefit their friends. Oddly enough, then, the traditional institutional structure of the Soviet economy actually fostered a large volume of petty trading, petty middleman activities, and petty private enterprise. Today the Soviet Union is an acquisitive society, a nation of marketeers. An enormous amount of time is absorbed in shopping, selling, trading, scouting, and queuing for deficit commodities. The privatization movement under Gorbachev is gradually broadening and deepening the acquisitive instincts of the population, but it has not yet succeeded in converting the Soviet economy into one in which the burden of marketing is shifted from the buyer to the seller—hence the great dissatisfaction of the Soviet consumer.

By the most careful Western estimates, consumption per capita has more than doubled since Stalin's death in 1953. The fact that deficit commodities remain numerous reflects both the incredibly low standard of living at the end of postwar reconstruction and the continuation of official price policies that tend to perpetuate such deficits. In planning the volume of consumer goods and services to be made available, Gosplan must consider two dimensions. First it is obvious that the total value of consumer goods and services provided by the state must have some relationship to the quantity of labor the state intends to employ and the average earnings of these workers. Second, the more developed the society is, the proportions in which the different consumer goods are produced (that is, how many automobiles, refrigerators, and sewing machines, and how much meat, milk, and wool cloth to produce) must bear a definite relationship to the way in which consumers wish to distribute their incomes among them. The output of consumer goods has increased very sharply in the U.S.S.R. over the last 25 years, but changes in the composition of output have not kept pace, helping to perpetuate the existence of deficit commodities. Output growth also slowed in the late Brezhnev years, and there have been declines in certain output totals of consumer goods during Gorbachev's reforms, seriously aggravating an already critical problem.

Prices in state retail outlets are set by a state committee of the Council of Ministers, and they reflect many factors other than supply and demand. Prices on many items of food, such as bread, meat, and milk, have been set below cost, whereas prices on certain scarce luxury goods are set relatively high, approximating supply–demand conditions. Therefore, willingness to stand in line becomes a factor in the distribution of many goods, and the final result is a distribution of goods and services that is probably more equal than the distribution of money income. To some extent, this is deliberate policy, but it also reflects a policy of stability in retail prices that Soviet leaders have promised the population ever since Stalin died. Accordingly, apart from surreptitious price changes, mainly on nonessentials, official retail prices have increased only marginally in more than three decades. The Soviet population clearly appreciates this policy, for it prevents the erosion of their savings by inflation; and this is particularly important in an economy in which installment payments and other forms of credit buying are not available to consumers. Unofficial prices are rising sharply today as reforms are being introduced, causing great distress, especially for the poor and the nearly poor.

The policy of price stability has of course had adverse effects. For many food products, notably products of animal husbandry, retail price stability has led to massive subsidies by the state, for the real cost of producing agricultural products has been rising rapidly since 1953. Relative prices for industrial commodities and for agricultural products are completely unrealistic, therefore, and an adjustment between industrial and agricultural prices and within each sector, is long overdue. Thus far, however, the political leaders have apparently felt that trading *nalevo* (that is, under the counter) and all that it implies in the way of petty economic crime and large-scale black-market operations is more acceptable than the adverse political reaction increased prices are expected to bring.

In addition to a policy that fosters the persistence of deficit commodities, the system of state retail sales outlets is inadequate for supplying the Soviet consumer. Space for retail sales is inadequate. Poor service and inventories that cannot be sold have no effect upon the incomes or incentives of retail service workers. Retail outlets cannot respond to their customers' preferences in any case, but must retail what they receive. The only room for maneuver they have is on an individual basis, which means *nalevo*.

The scarcity of the more desirable consumer goods and services has become institutionalized officially as well as privately. Whereas the private response has been to expand *nalevo,* the official response has been to create special shops which permit selected people to avoid queuing for deficit commodities. These special groups include foreigners which is understandable in a country anxious to earn foreign exchange—but they also include certain Soviet elites as well. The temptation posed by the existence of deficit commodities yields special stores, restaurants, hotels, and recreation centers, with curtained windows to screen out unwelcome eyes, for high-placed party and government officials and for other successful people. The right to purchase deficit commodities in special stores or by special order is clearly a powerful incentive in the Soviet economy. Yet the persistence of deficit commodities is having a negative effect upon the fabric of Soviet life. Because of its location as the center of the government and of the tourist trade, and because of the relative wealth of the city's population, Moscovites are better dressed, better housed, better fed, better entertained, and more sophisticated than Soviets in other cities. Moscovites are also more alienated than any comparable population in the U.S.S.R. Certainly the city is a hotbed of criticism of the government and party. Nonetheless, what is true of Moscow is true in one degree or another for other parts of the U.S.S.R. The Soviet retail distribution system is sluggish and works only in fits and starts. The farther one gets from Moscow, the less effective it is; the smaller the community to be served, the poorer is the supply.

Moscow and other large Soviet cities are black holes in the Soviet system of retail distribution, which is why smaller communities rarely see deficit commodities in their stores or on their streets. That such commodities appear first in the major cities encourages villagers to visit periodically to exploit their availability, and city folks always buy extra for their relations in less favored retailing regions. In this sense Moscow is the supermarket of the U.S.S.R., for the Soviet retail distribution system relies heavily upon private cash-and-carry distribution of deficit commodities beyond the confines of Moscow. An examination of the personal cargoes of individuals returning to Novosibirsk, Omsk, Tomsk, or Irkutsk will provide confirmation of the actual volume of private distribution of deficit commodities. All major cities serve similar roles.

Rural areas are officially served by what is known as consumer cooperatives, but this network had a truly separate existence only years ago. Today these outlets are indistinguishable from state retail stores (except, perhaps, in being more poorly stocked), and the network's employees are now state employees. The consumer cooperative network is, if anything, less efficient and effective than the state network, primarily for the reasons given above. Consequently those people who live in the thousands of villages that compose the state and collective farms of the U.S.S.R. must rely much more heavily than urban dwellers upon their own productive efforts and upon the rural *rynok,* which is a more informal market than its urban counterpart. Rural dwellers in warm agricultural regions fare quite well when it comes to vegetables and fruits, which are deficit items in northern cities even in season. Opportunities to trade these products in urban markets can offer substantial profits. Even so, a drawback for all who live in places distant from major cities is the need both to transport their own products to market and to carry back industrial products at their own expense. Having a relative or two in a major city is an essential condition for living well in most rural regions. Thanks to the recent rapid urbanization of the U.S.S.R., most people do have urban relatives.

As indicated above, the Soviet overall standard of living has more than doubled since Stalin's death in 1953. While this may seem difficult to believe when one examines Soviet life today, the evidence indicates that the standard of living in 1953 was not materially different from what it had been in 1928, and 1928 was probably not much better than 1913. For 40 years, then, Soviet living standards remained approximately at the prerevolutionary level.

The most striking advances in living conditions for anyone who has watched these improvements over the years are in clothing, including shoes; the supply of food, particularly in animal husbandry products, fruits, and vegetables; housing; and in ownership of consumer durables and automobiles. Twenty years ago, any foreigner in Moscow stood out like a sore thumb because of the quality and cut of his or her clothing, and shoes were a dead giveaway. Vegetables and fruits were simply never available in the wintertime; and the amount of meat regularly available today is striking by comparison, despite constant carping. Housing construction has continued at a high rate for several decades now, and renovation of older dwellings has also been carried out on a large scale. The number of square feet per urban dweller has increased modestly despite a rapid increase in the size of the urban population, and the quality of new apartments has improved, if only because the new ones are self-contained, not communal. Actual construction quality has probably declined, however. Some consumer durables that are commonplace today were rarities only 20 years ago. Even peasants have refrigerators today, although many complain that they stay empty most of the time. Sewing machines are widely owned, as are, of course, radios, television sets, and stereo systems. Finally, anyone who visited the Soviet Union in the early 1960s and returned for the first time today would be amazed by the number of private automobiles on the streets of Moscow. In the 1960s even Moscow looked like a huge construction site or a giant factory, for the streets carried mainly trucks and buses. The few automobiles were official cars or taxis.

Unquestionably, there has been a large increase in the Soviet standard of living over the last 25 to 30 years, but this increase has not been evenly distributed geographically (or ethnically). A visit even to a large city in Siberia, for example, takes one back to the way Moscow looked 10 or 15 years ago. Until recently, queues had diminished everywhere, and they existed in the major cities mainly only for "luxuries"—for the best meat, for premium butter, for cucumbers or lemons in March, and so forth. The complications of *perestroika* have led to a resurgence of shortages for many products. Once they start, shortages tend to be self-perpetuating for particular commodities, for there are runs on them whenever they do appear, and everyone seeks to maintain a long-term inventory to hedge against empty stores.

The population has money, and it has the habit of queuing, and it will be a long time before queuing is eliminated from Soviet shopping habits. Scarcity-mindedness causes individuals to buy large quantities of scarce items when they appear. They buy for the future, for their relatives, and for their friends. Thus, as a hedge against doing without, individuals provide the storage space for many items that are not actually scarce. This is, of course, the logic of a sellers' market. The buyer must bear the costs of locating, transporting, and inventorying products. Psychologically, Soviet shoppers have also been traumatized by shortages, and they have organized their lives in such a way that queuing, taking advantage of unexpected appearances of deficit commodities, and sharing with friends and relatives are integral aspects of everyday life. The long years of sacrifice will take an even longer time to be compensated for and forgotten. Meanwhile, everyone shops with determination, a pocketful of rubles, and detailed knowledge of the needs and preferences of a dozen or more friends and relatives.

All able-bodied citizens are under considerable social pressure to contribute gainfully to the economy, and the labor participation rates for men and women are exceptionally high by world standards. Legal measures are also possible and have in the past been invoked against those persons who are designated "social parasites." Recently, able-bodied individuals, including those who are alienated from Soviet society, have been allowed to remain outside of regular gainful employment as long as some family member is prepared to guarantee support. If the person in question is a woman with young children, she may withdraw from employment voluntarily to care for them and her husband with little notice. The need to supplement family income and the desire for careers greatly inhibit this outcome, however. The wives and children of well-to-do, successful members of Soviet society are not troubled by antiparasite laws either. There are many other Soviets, most of whom are beyond the age for retirement (60 for men and 55 for women), who have the choice of supplementing their incomes by working as coatroom attendants, doormen, watchmen, and so forth. A large proportion of the existing Soviet labor force is, thus, completely free to work or to withdraw from employment as it sees fit. As a result, the Soviet labor force must be regarded as a function of individual evaluation of real wages, as it is in labor markets in capitalist countries. Thus we describe the labor market as open but heavily regulated. As *perestroika* progresses, the Soviet labor market will eventually be virtually a free market, comparable to Western labor markets.

The labor market comprises a complex collection of markets—some public, others private; and it is a huge market because it touches the life of every Soviet household and every enterprise and organization. Because it is an open market in which individuals exercise freedom of vocation within broad limits, it is more accurate to conceive of labor as having been centrally managed rather than planned, for planning under such circumstances can mean little more than the extrapolation of current trends. Except in wartime, direct central allocation applied only to the military service, to the penal system, and to available educational slots. The remainder of the labor force is self-allocated by incentives provided in public and private employments, and the intensity with which individuals work in any given employment is also self-determined.

In general, any person may also legally use skills in order to earn, or to supplement, income; he or she may also join with relatives or friends in a cooperative. A person who knows how to repair electrical equipment may freely and legally repair TV sets for a charge or with the clear intention of collecting a reciprocal favor at a future time from the set's owner. It is legal today for the repairer or the repairer's cooperative to receive cash payments for services rendered. The situation, however, is rarely so neatly defined. It would be illegal, for example, for the repairer to use spare parts taken from his or her official place of work, to use stolen tools, or to do the repairs during working time in the state shop without billing the customer officially. All of these things do occur because private work space is limited, tools and spare parts are not available except in the public sector, and working time is routinely "stolen" in this way.

Plumbers, carpenters, repairmen of all sorts, individuals who own private cars or even those who chauffeur for the state, can periodically earn a personal profit on the basis of their skills or their access to state property. Although it is technically illegal to do so, chauffeurs for state officials frequently use time that they know will be spent waiting to taxi individuals for private gain, and the state pays for the gasoline. Some individuals specialize in approaching foreign tourists in hopes of buying or begging some prize item for subsequent (illegal) resale, or in the expectation of obtaining foreign currency in exchange for rubles. Many individuals manufacture *samogon* (illegal drinking alcohol) in their kitchens, and those who make it well can exchange or sell it as a sideline. Drivers of state-owned taxis frequently take advantage of late-night fares to earn something over and above the standard fare, to sell liquor after hours, and to refer clients to prostitutes. Petty private enterprise was common in the Soviet Union before *perestroika* and it is rampant today, but the economic system has not responded structurally to these changes and much petty private enterprise in the U.S.S.R. is therefore obliged to commit petty crimes to function.

For deficit commodities or services, rubles are frequently useless unless mixed with *blat,* friendship, or a contact in the black market. *Blat* can get one out of a difficult spot, it can help one jump a queue, and it can be used for personal advancement. Where legality ends and illegality begins in these instances is hard to determine, and anyone who is involved in these kinds of transactions takes a certain risk in doing so. Interestingly, this implicates almost every household in the major cities of the U.S.S.R. and no small number of rural folk, for whom producing *samogon* is the most frequently cited crime. The exceptions are likely to be officials so highly placed that *blat* works silently for them. There was a time when it was said that *"blat* is higher than Stalin." Today it is accurate to say that *blat* is the only hard Soviet currency.

The volume of illegal and quasi-legal economic transactions in the U.S.S.R. today should not be exaggerated. No figures and no official estimates are available about them, but no one doubts that private trading, both legal and illegal, is extremely pervasive. The sharp increase in the role of *nalevo* markets in recent years may serve as a measure of the breakdown of the creaky, inefficient centralized retail distribution system. Private and cooperative enterprise have become essential to the functioning of the Soviet economy, but they are still regarded with suspicion by many in the leadership and by a large share of the public as well. A return to strict labor controls, a resumption of forced labor, and much more extensive policing of economic activities would be required to extirpate petty economic illegal activity. No current leader has indicated the willingness or the capacity to pursue so drastic a course, although one does occasionally hear nostalgic references to the public "order" that Stalin maintained.

A major source of inefficiency in the Soviet economy is the ineffectiveness of the material incentive system in state enterprises. Much emphasis has always been placed in Soviet industry upon moral incentives—the gratification workers and managers may obtain from doing good work. They include the awarding of medals, winning competitions, having one's name or factory written up in the newspaper, and the like. Moral incentives were important sources of productivity gains in the 1930s, during World War II, and afterward; but they have apparently lost much of their effectiveness today. Unfortunately the system of material incentives has never been thoroughly overhauled to reflect its increased significance as the prime mover in inducing efficiency and conscientiousness. Moreover, persistent shortages in retail outlets also undermine the effectiveness of material incentives, particularly where people cannot be fired for laziness or have their salary docked for lacking ambition. Obviously a society in which acquisition of the most desirable commodities requires either queuing or *nalevo* involvement in the economy is one in which a clever worker may find advancement to a more responsible or otherwise demanding position no advantage whatever. The move up may reduce the time that he or she has available for queuing, or it may remove the individual from the strategic position he or she occupies with respect to deficit commodities or *blat.*

One problem that wholesale nationalization did "solve" is periodic layoffs resulting from business fluctuations. The fact that Soviet enterprises do not lay off workers when sales or profits lag is, of course, the obverse side of the job security problem that managers face in trying to use the labor force efficiently. Soviet citizens value job security highly, and they can be expected to resist its loss. Hence the population's ambiguous and inconsistent stance vis-à-vis economic reforms. Everyone wants the benefits of a more efficient economy without losing job security or other welfare entitlements, such as free medical care, subsidized food products, and cheap housing.

From the family's standpoint it does not matter whether transactions involve the private or the public sector, but when things go wrong in the public sector the state is blamed. Most households in the U.S.S.R. have more than one primary wage earner, and most also receive some direct payment from a state agency. A grandparent may live with the family and draw a pension. He or she may also work at a part-time job; in any event, the grandparent would be fully occupied helping in queuing for deficit commodities, walking the baby, sitting with the children, gardening, and helping with the housework. The family may have a child in the university or in a technical school, in which case he or she would receive a stipend that would be contributed to the family's weekly income. Spending the family income is also a collective affair, involving state retail markets, the *rynok,* private trading, and *nalevo* markets, without anyone paying much attention to the breakdown among them.

Family members old enough to be responsible normally carry a substantial sum of cash with them at all times against finding unexpected deficit commodities. Everyone in the family knows what these are and what a reasonable price would be for them. What the family does not spend is set aside for purchasing large durable goods, such as an automobile, refrigerator, stereo set, and furniture. Consumer credit or layaway plans are unheard of. Some Western observers claim that Soviet families are unable to spend as much as they like in Soviet markets and that they are therefore accumulating savings unwillingly. This is a most unlikely conclusion for the simple reason that households do not have to earn more income than they wish. The amount of income that a family earns is determined not by the state but by the collective decision of the members of the household. Because queuing is so important a function in the acquisition of deficit commodities in the Soviet Union, it will always pay for one member of the family to increase his or her free time for queuing rather than to work at a job from which the income would be of little use. Moreover, as savings pile up, the temptation to steal time from the place of work to shop is irresistible, especially since it is difficult to get fired. The problem today is not an excess of rubles per se but a fear of devaluation, which is making private saving in the form of rubles risky.

As long as individuals are free to make their own purchases in the market and as long as individual households may elect the total number of hours that they wish to be employed, planners are not able to determine unilaterally either the total volume of labor forthcoming in the economy or the total amount and composition of consumer goods and services that it will make available. This constraint is enhanced by the presence of private employment and private retail markets. It is further enhanced by the opportunities that individuals have to convert public property into private means for personal gain.

If the state wishes households to contribute more to economic activity, it must provide something in exchange, and that has increasingly come to mean commodities and services rather than promises of a better future, cradle-to-grave minimal subsistence and security, or assurance against a foreign threat. In this respect the member of a Soviet household does not experience a different economic world than does his or her counterpart in the West. A Soviet who is suddenly transposed into a capitalist economic environment is not disoriented by the difference, although the plethora of goods and of choices available is normally overwhelming at first. Neither is a Western shopper disoriented in Soviet markets. The difficulties involved are irritating, but not completely strange, for there are queues in the West for certain kinds of sporting and cultural events, and there were queues for gasoline in the 1970s. As late as the 1960s the Soviet leadership sought to increase the share of consumer goods and services that were distributed in kind or free of charge. This followed from an ideological aim in the long run to distribute goods and services to the population according to the criterion of need rather than according to economic contribution. This aim has been completely abandoned today, but the economy remains heavily burdened by welfare entitlements.

Thus the Soviet household is not innocent of the way markets operate. It deals and has dealt in markets every day. Moreover, the extent of marketeering has increased steadily since Stalin's death. These markets, however, have historically been heavily regulated, and they have been greatly distorted as a result. A permanent sellers' market is one that places an enormous burden on the buyer. Thus it is that Soviet households have had mixed feelings about *perestroika*. As sellers of labor power, they are fearful of losing their job security. As buyers of consumer goods and services, households want a greater supply at no increase in price. This is perfectly rational behavior for individual households, of course, but, collectively speaking, the result is a disastrous contradiction that no one individual can solve. If everyone would work a full day as efficiently as possible, more and better quality products would be available. If only a few improve their work they will merely subsidize others without benefiting themselves. Hence the need for economic reform, which, as discussed in Chapter 14, will be very difficult to accomplish.

The Soviet leadership has finally decided to abandon traditional central planning of the Soviet economy, but it has yet to establish the kinds of institutions that are required to make central management of a modern mixed economy work. As the traditional Soviet administered economy sags into terminal collapse, the situation of the Soviet household is becoming much more difficult. More and more commodities are in deficit, and empty stores are multiplying. Increasingly, production is sacrificed in an effort to increase time spent searching out and making special deals for deficit commodities, or in seeking to earn or buy foreign exchange.

In order to change the current economic outlook, which is one of looming catastrophe, the leadership must convert the economy from a sellers' into a buyers' market. Until that task is accomplished, no reform will succeed. To date, for example, even foreign firms have found it difficult to maintain normal customer relations in the face of insatiable demand. If and when reforms succeed, Soviet households will have no difficulty learning how to behave in a market-oriented economy. It will seem strange to see goods actually in stores and no queues at the doors. The adjustment to reduced job security and to higher prices and fewer welfare entitlements will be difficult, of course, but the traditional system of central planning has broken down irrevocably and is no longer an option. One can only hope that the transition from central planning to market institutions is peaceful and mercifully short.

CHAPTER 4

The Soviet Work Force: Problems and Opportunities

Walter D. Connor

The success of business organizations depends in large measure on how well employees perform. U.S. business managers constantly exhort employees with the importance of quality work performance—and support their position by spending tens of billions of dollars every year on employee training programs. Companies considering operations in the U.S.S.R. that will require Soviet personnel need to understand the Soviet work force and how it can best be used.

Work in the U.S.S.R. means for most a five-day, 40-hour week. Workers are not well paid; the average wage is 260 rubles a month—an amount that a tourist can get for less than $45 at the official rate. Low wages have necessitated two wage earners per household, and it has been observed that the wage structure "is designed to oblige both a husband and wife to work full-time."[1] Long before it became common in Western Europe and the United States, women in the Soviet Union were employed outside the home, even during children's infancy.

Soviet workers can retire at age 55 for women and 60 for men—in some occupations, even earlier. The relatively early retirement places a potential burden on the state's pension system,[2] and is one reason that pensions have been low. Today's average pension for nonfarm workers is about 75 rubles, a figure that leaves most retirees below the official poverty line. Consequently, many Soviets work full time past the retirement age. Because pensions have not been indexed to increasing living costs, the percentage of those working past retirement age increased from about 15 percent in the mid 1960s to 32 percent in the early 1980s.[3]

In practice, blue-collar workers often work less than 40 hours a week. When needed inputs from another factory have not been delivered, workers are idled—a frequent occurrence. At such times, excused absences to shop or to rest can be obtained readily—an aspect of informal human relations in Soviet industry. The down side is that when the inputs finally are delivered there may be "black Saturdays" (and Sundays) in order to achieve a production quota. Thus Soviets have reason to fear products produced at the end of the month when quality—never in serious competition with quantity in Soviet factories—goes out the window to meet the monthly production quota.

Soviet workers have lived in a world where they and their managers have been judged almost entirely by physical output. The base wage of many workers is increased 50 to 70 percent as a result of bonuses for equaling or exceeding production quotas. Product quality and product cost have seldom been the concern of workers or managers, since marketability was never an issue in the command economy.

As in the West, many managers and professionals work far more than 40 hours a week. However, given the shortage of office space, many academics and other professionals work a good deal at home, and are entitled to extra apartment space for this purpose. Most specialties that require a college education—particularly fields traditionally staffed by women, such as medicine, education, and social services—are not as well paid as skilled work in heavy industry, but the opportunities for moonlighting for the educated are much better. High school teachers and college instructors can charge stiff hourly rates to tutor for college entrance examinations; doctors and dentists get high fees for quasi-legal work outside the socialized medicine sector. Thus real incomes in the U.S.S.R. are very different than the official statistics would indicate.

The quality of the work force depends heavily on the quality of education. At first glance, the figures are rather impressive. The USSR has gone from an undereducated, backward country before World War II to one in which a majority of the working population, independent of age, has attained at least eight years of schooling. Table 4-1 details this increase. Progress has been most notable in the manual worker category. Vast numbers of uneducated peasants, drafted into burgeoning heavy industry in the 1930s, have given place to educated urbanites.

Soviet students today in first through eighth grade attend comprehensive schools with a nationwide, standardized curriculum that places

Table 4-1   Percent of Work Force with at Least Eight Years of Schooling

	1939	1959	1970	1979	1987
Manual workers	4.5	32.5	54.3	73.2	84.5
White-collar workers	51.5	89.6	95.3	98.1	98.9

SOURCE: *Trud v SSSR* (Labor in the U.S.S.R.) (Moscow: Finansy i statistika, 1988), 10.

heavier emphasis on mathematics and science than American students of the comparable age range (7 to 15) are likely to encounter in most public schools. After eighth grade, students sort themselves into three tracks, giving some indication of their aspirations:

- An extension (ninth and tenth grades) of purely academic schooling, the curriculum and extension of academic work of the earlier years, aimed essentially at preparation for higher education.

- A "specialized secondary" institution or *tekhnikum,* providing, over a two-to-three-year period, combined academic and paraprofessional training.

- A three-year "secondary vocational-technical school," which gives, purportedly, the equivalent of ninth- and tenth-grade academic training along with vocational education below the paraprofessional level, to produce skilled blue-collar workers. The real level of the academic training is generally poor.

All three tracks give a high school diploma, and thus contribute to nationwide statistics showing relatively high educational levels, especially among the younger population. In 1987, 61 percent of workers under 30 had diplomas from the purely academic school, and another 20 percent from the *tekhnikums.*[4]

Educational *quality* varies rather widely within these generally encouraging figures, however. While the vast majority of youth today complete 10 years of schooling, the variation in the quality of teaching and facilities is great, both in academic and vocational education. Much of the recent growth in 10-year educational attainment has been due to the secondary vocational-technical school, which added academic courses to old-style, low level vocational schools. The result *is* a diploma, but not really the educational level of the 10-year academic school.[5]

Though an academic high school graduate will have more math and science in 10 years than an American gets in 12 years, and be better grounded in these subjects, the results are often uneven. In many areas, physical facilities in schools, from the building itself to basic lab equipment (to say nothing of nonexistent computers) lag well behind even the schools of America's most troubled urban areas; in *no* area are they likely to exceed the U.S. average. If not the most critical problem, this still limits various kinds of hands-on experience American students now acquire naturally both in schools and with home computers.

Actual demands on students have likely declined over the years, as more 14- to 17-year-olds have continued on in the eighth through tenth grades, which were formerly populated in the main by the children of professionals and managers. "Grade inflation," driven partly by teachers' and school administrators' concerns that they be seen as successful in their missions, and partly by sympathy, is generally acknowledged to be a major problem. The gap between the proclaimed and actual levels of education has taken on, in the words of a recent Soviet commentator, "frightening dimensions."[6] In a 1988 survey of 27,000 first-year students in colleges and specialized secondary institutions, a third of the first and half of the secondary category were unable to pass examinations testing the 10-year-level knowledge that was their ticket of admission in the first place. Many students cannot, by the fall, pass the same exams they crammed for in the spring. Since high schools vastly overproduce graduates in relation to the number of spaces available in full-time higher educational institutions, admission usually is highly "competitive." Yet many seemingly well prepared tenth graders do very poorly on the college entrance examinations they have opted to take. In the Georgian Republic in 1987, two-thirds of college entrance applicants received an "unsatisfactory" grade on the examination, and only 40 percent of those who had received medals for some aspect of their high school academic performance passed.

The lesson is fairly clear: "What Ivan knows and Johnny doesn't" represents nowhere near as large a gap as statistics on hours of instruction and emphasis on difficult subjects in the curriculum prompt us to assume. One cannot thus assume a very high degree of expertise in science and mathematics among teenage Soviets simply because they possess a diploma. Urban, middle-class teenagers, especially in the larger cities of the European areas of the country and in the Siberian part of the Russian Republic, will have a good deal of the basics. From these students, reading skills commensurate with their education, mathematics through some calculus, and a firm base in chemistry and physics (less in biology) can be expected. Rural school graduates and working-class youths who are often products of the combined academic-trade school, will show more flaws in these areas. In the Central Asian republics, the paper figures on school completion yield statistics showing this essentially third world area to exceed the very European Baltic republics. They also inflate massively the percentage of the indigenous population fluent in Russian, when perhaps 20 to 30 percent are really at this level, a fiction revealed in the difficulty of using Russian as the language of command in the Soviet armed forces.[7]

Western business needs for large numbers of well-educated workers are most likely to be met in the European urban areas. In these areas, the major caveat is the danger of assuming a degree of learning more than the average student acquires in 10 years. But it is unlikely that problems of *basic* literacy and numeracy would be so pronounced as in some younger elements of the U.S. labor force. Culture and the work ethic may well be more important, given certain minimal educational levels, than formal schooling in determining employee desirability.

Higher education is divided between *universities,* with multiple departments and disciplines much as in the West, and *institutes,* offering degrees in a single discipline or a few closely related ones. In either case, with few exceptions, the time from matriculation to the bachelor's-level degree *(diplom)*, is five years, assuming a full-time program. Many people, after a longer period, receive undergraduate degrees after a program of night school or correspondence study.

Graduate degrees are the *kandidat* and the *doktor*. The first, usually requiring three additional years of work encompassing a dissertation, falls, in American terms, somewhere between the master's level and the Ph.D. The degree of *doktor* is usually acquired in the early middle stages of a (successful) academic or research career, after a good deal of prior professional work. A fair share of graduate degrees are conferred not by universities or normal institutes, but by research institutes under the Academy of Science or various ministries.

Kandidat and *doktor* degrees are less common than are American M.A.'s and Ph.D.'s. Undergraduate level higher education output is high by international, if not U.S., standards. The United States in a typical year produces about 3 million high school graduates, takes 60 percent of these into two- and four-year colleges, and graduates about half the entrants four years later. The U.S.S.R. graduates a somewhat larger number from secondary school, but admits only about a quarter to all higher education, including part-time evening and correspondence programs, and five years later graduates about 80 percent of the entrants.[8]

The numbers for both countries are larger, proportionally, than is typical in the traditionally more exclusive systems of higher education in the United Kingdom and much of Western Europe. But what should be appreciated about the higher educational enterprise in the U.S.S.R. (as in the United States) is the qualitative diversity of institutions and programs, and of their human products.

Universities, with their various departments, are generally regarded as superior to all but a few single-discipline institutes: harder to get into and conferring a better education. That education, however, is narrowly specialized by American standards. In a university or institute, students specialize over their five years. Within universities, the mathematics and science departments, especially physics and chemistry, are typically the most demanding, and draw the best students. The education is good, but theoretical, in that shortages of high-tech instruments and other equipment tend to limit experimental training and experience. Institutes tend to be quite specialized, as are their products. Engineers, of whom the U.S.S.R. produces many, can be construction materials engineers, shoe manufacture engineers, and so on. Training is narrow, more like the training of technicians than of bachelor's-level engineers in American institutions.

The pecking order among universities is rather clear: Moscow State University sits at the pinnacle; Leningrad and Kiev follow; and the level of training in the universities in the Baltic republics (Estonia, Latvia, Lithuania) is also high. In the Baltics, command of Russian among the educated, despite local nationalism, is high as well. Indeed, some years ago when the Brezhnev regime moved to impose the "education exit tax" on would-be émigrés as a way to deter the outflow, the charges were largest by far for products of Moscow State University, less for Leningrad and Kiev, and lowest for a whole category of specialized provincial institutes. While the tax was lifted, it was a clear signal of the value the Soviet system placed on various components of its educational product line.

On the whole, then, graduates of the major universities are likely to be initially more intellectually talented, have worked harder and passed more hurdles in getting *into* them, and learned more from better faculties, especially in the sciences. They have passed through a narrower bottleneck than do American undergraduates to emerge with their degrees.

Institute graduates are a mixed lot. Provincial institutes in areas like agronomy, for example, draw many whose main interest is in getting a *diplom* per se and who have no desire to pursue work in the field of the degree. Such institutes are less selective and have more space for the marginal 10-year graduates. Certification by such is no strong guarantee of professional expertise or interest in the field of the *diplom*. There are some exceptions, like the Baumann Technical Institute in Moscow, but in general, the farther from the developed European areas, the more an institute *diplom* requires independent checking of an employee's knowledge.

Thus, while highly trained manpower—holders of *diplom,* or better, *kandidat* or *doktor* degrees—in the sciences can be *very* good indeed, and is certainly "underpriced," Westerners need to be selective. In Georgia, many Soviet employers were rejecting the graduates of that republic's own universities and institutes as unqualified for hiring.[9] With respect to business and entrepreneurial skills, it goes without saying that Soviet higher education has not been given to instilling these.

In the area of vocational education, reviews of Soviet performance are mixed. While the paraprofessional *tekhnikums* are taken seriously as venues for acquiring specialized knowledge, the vocational training in the secondary vocational-technical schools (SPTUs) comes in for criticism, as does their academic component. Part of the problem is pedigree. The SPTU is based on grafting an academic program to a vocational school (PTU) which gave basic work training to eighth-grade graduates but no academic training or diploma. PTUs and the SPTUs suffer from a bad image—as places where underachievers are sent and where problems ranging from drinking to delinquency are rife.

Another part is performance. Most SPTUs are limited to a narrow range of specialties, since many operate under the sponsorship of a particular plant. Poor instruction and lack of facilities and tools for adequate training are major complaints.

Allowing for a certain amount of hand wringing in any assessment of vocational education, it does seem that, on the whole, the Soviet program yields marginal results. These include poor matches between skills acquired and actual job requirements, and a fairly high rate of attrition from the jobs that were the target of the training. One study in a metallurgy plant showed that in the vocational school it sponsored 46 percent of the students did not like the specialty they were learning; an evaluation of trainees concluded that 44 percent were not adequately trained. Fifty-five percent of the young workers were unsatisfied with their jobs, and six years later only 20 percent of the graduates remained in the plant.[10]

In effect, this means that the U.S.S.R.'s planned, production-oriented economy—surely one that should have had some advantages in the vocational training area—offered more promise than performance. By and large, Soviet workers have learned the job on the job: on the factory floor, on the assembly line, at the construction site. The readiness to acquire skills, then—a certain basic literacy and numeracy, and willingness to learn—are likely to be cardinal factors in the workers an employer wants. The vocational schools have not produced them.

If work performance falls short of the goals Soviet academic and vocational education have set as reasonable, how does it compare with performance in the West? Products of 10 years of academic education in the European urban areas are, on the whole, likely to be able to cope with job manuals, operating instructions, and training in which basic literacy and numeracy are required better than many average urban high school graduates in the United States. Functional illiteracy is less likely among this Soviet population than in U.S. cities. As one moves out of these areas, toward rural, backward areas like Central Asia, one can assume less by way of basic educational background, less ability to read work and training manuals, especially if they are written in Russian. Involvement of Westerners in the Soviet economy has not been deep enough, nor thus far of such duration, as to develop the base for industry-specific assessments of how Soviet workers measure up to their counterparts in the West in trainability. What is more clear is that work performance has long suffered, in comparison with the West, from the way the economy is organized.

The Soviet labor force also suffers from problems related to the work ethic and the organization of work. Organizational aspects of the economy have worked to erode the rationale for high quality work. Factories have been allocated labor and materials and have not had to market their output since it is assigned to a destination by central planners. There has been little incentive, therefore, for managers to economize. Workers have been safe from unemployment, as their enterprises were safe from bankruptcy. Workers thus *have* come to behave in a way that is rational in these circumstances. A market economy will, if it takes root, discipline the work force to increase efficiencies and quality, as it is doing today in Poland and what was East Germany.

There are regional and cultural variations in the work habits foreigners will confront. These are likely to persist, even within the better developed

European regions of the U.S.S.R. The Baltic states of Estonia and Latvia—nations of a "Nordic-Western" tradition and a Protestant religious heritage—are ahead of other areas in productivity and general work performance. Both the lesser duration of their time under the Soviet political and economic system, and a heritage of rather highly developed skills and methodical approaches to work, play a role here. Striking as their relative prosperity may be within the U.S.S.R., more striking is their poverty, shabbiness, and inefficiency compared with Sweden or Finland. In the rest of the U.S.S.R., the problems are greater.

Thus the Soviet labor force as a whole has been poorly utilized. Full employment at rather low wages has been unproductive. Workers have been deployed to produce goods and services that are inadequate to give their modest pay purchasing power. This hardly motivates effort, much less excellence. From it derives the standard saying, "We pretend to work, and they pretend to pay us." In many industries, underinvestment in all but basic production machinery has meant that for each production worker the number of auxiliaries engaged in material moving, storage, and maintenance is very large. The typical Soviet factory uses large numbers of workers for the lifting and hauling that forklift trucks accomplish better, faster, and cheaper on Western factory floors. The failure to motivate quality work by positive or negative sanctions has meant that quality has not been built into the production process and quality control has depended on inspectors at the end of the line whose own jobs, wages, and bonuses have depended on their not being too demanding, since too many rejects would cut "plan fulfillment," and hence the bonus funds from which they, as well as those they inspect, draw much of their pay.[11]

Overall, given the state's commitment to honoring its full-employment promises, plus the reluctance to invest in auxiliary technology, the numbers employed in even sophisticated imported plants have been striking. For example, a chemical complex imported wholesale from a Dutch/Italian maker employed 178 workers in its original form; in the Soviet Union employment was 806.[12] Problems of work quality and productivity have interacted to produce a downward spiral that current reform plans aim to reverse.

Much of the labor force has come to the conclusion that it *has* been poorly utilized. Yet it is hardly likely that things can improve soon, given previous experience of partial reforms and their negligible results. Pre-1980 Soviet studies showed fairly low degrees of satisfaction with work—averaging around 55 percent,[13] less than in similar U.S. and Western European studies, where expressed satisfaction ranges around 80 percent. An early 1980s study showed a decline to only 35 percent "fully satisfied."[14] Beyond *job* dissatisfaction, however, lies a growing discontent with labor organization itself. The whole world of work is not "working" as it once did for a simpler, less educated population, more modest in its aspirations. If there is a kind of political and intellectual exhaustion of nonmarket organizational patterns in the U.S.S.R. today, there is also popular exhaustion with the prevailing pattern. More of the public now than ever before believe that the factory or office working within the organizational blueprint of centralized control *cannot* work well.

Over the past 25 years, various experiments, falling woefully short of systemic economic reform, have attempted to liberate some factories from centralized bureaucratic controls, to give managers more hiring-and-firing discretion and workers more autonomy in work organization and opportunity for increased earnings. Without exception, they have fallen afoul of a tendency for the system to reject them as anomalies, as the body's immune system fights an invading bacillus. "Guaranteed" delivery of needed inputs falls short because supplier factories may not be part of the experiment; contrary to promises earlier made, the output target of a factory is raised by central authority, cutting into the bonuses the lean work force was promised for above-plan production.[15]

Thus, economic policy has undermined motivation. Excess effort and good work results did not guarantee extra earnings. Social policy considerations and the labor hunger of an extensive-growth economy have meant that "bad" work, absenteeism, and low effort did not result in lower earnings. All this contributed to the "dependency" of much of the Soviet work force, the readiness to opt for "guaranteed pay with low effort" rather than "high pay for high effort." But while citizens are still reluctant to part with the old dependency, and do not have an alternative concept with which to replace it, they know that the underpinnings of the old system have eroded beyond hope of restoration.

Clearly, a lot of bad habits have been learned that need to be unlearned—by the work force as well as its bosses. In addition, jobs generally no longer meet the aspirations of a better educated labor force. They are tilted heavily toward goods production rather than services, and to semi-skilled, unskilled, and auxiliary jobs within that production sector. Thus a foreign investor will find it easy to attract ambitious, skilled, hard workers if they will pay a just premium. Hiring the best in the U.S.S.R. will be the exact opposite situation of foreigners seeking to hire in Japan, where the best are hard to attract.

Average pay for Soviet workers in 1990 was in the area of 260 to 270 rubles per month. This represents an increase of nearly one-third since 1987, much greater than growth in GNP or the supply of goods in demand. Workers in heavy industry, such as mining, typically earn a good deal more than the average; those in trade, services, education, and consumer-oriented industries earn significantly less. By any standard, this is low pay since 270 rubles equals $445.50 at the old official rate of $1.65 to the ruble, $44.55 at the new, more realistic rate for certain tourist and business transactions.

The best Western estimates put Soviet "real income" and living standard at about one-third of the U.S. level—and some have felt this to be too high,[16] as have Soviet analysts to whom *glasnost* has given louder voices. Soviet workers are—as has become clear to them—poor, by any European standard, and getting poorer. This has been, in the past, a poverty cushioned by several factors, which have influenced both expectations and behavior. Medical and educational services have been free, while heat and electricity charges have been nominal. Rents in state-owned apartments, stable since 1928, have been a minuscule portion of the average household's monthly income, though waiting time to acquire an apartment has been long. Basic foods—bread, milk, meat—have been priced at well below procurement cost, with state budget subsidies taking up the slack.

Soviet citizens, thus, paid little for many necessities, but were forced to astronomic outlays, compared with their Western counterparts, for major appliances, clothing, automobiles, and the like. Table 4-2 gives some examples from 1986 surveys by the research division of Radio Liberty and expresses the cost of items in time worked. For comparative purposes, data are given for Moscow, Washington, and Munich prices.

At the food counter, the basic Soviet rye loaf has been cheap because it is sold at less than half the procurement cost of the grain that goes into it. Potatoes are also a good deal in Moscow, as in Washington. But beef and chicken show the disadvantage of the Soviet earner, and hint at the very high percentage of the typical household budget that must go to food. These are state store prices—where beef, at "111 minutes per kilo," is also priced at less than half its procurement cost. They are, then, the prices posted on often empty shelves. In the collective-farm "free markets," where supply and demand set the price, beef will sell for four or more times the state price—but it is available for those who can pay for it.

Table 4-2 **Work Time for Consumer Needs**

	Moscow	**Washington**	**Munich**
Bread (minutes/kilogram)	11	18	19
Beef (minutes/kilogram)	111	46	140
Chicken (minutes/kilogram)	189	18	17
Potatoes (minutes/kilogram)	11	9	5
Color TV (hours)	669	30	54
Small car (months)	45	5	7
Large refrigerator (hours)	274	72	75
Rent for small (50 square meter) apartment (hours)	11	55	24
Man's suit (hours)	118	18	33
Bus fare (3 kilometer ride) (minutes)	3	7	7

SOURCE: Keith Bush, "Retail Prices in Moscow and in Four Western Cities in October 1986," *Radio Liberty Research Supplement,* January 21, 1987.

Household durables, "white goods," a small car (in the Soviet case essentially a 1970s Fiat), all cost the Soviet worker relatively dearly. Putting an ill-fitting suit on a man's back takes a month's work; the American spends half a week's pay for an ordinary suit. A bus ride is cheap for all, but cheapest for the Muscovite.

The striking difference—what leaves the Soviet something to spend or save for that suit, or TV—comes through in housing cost. Effectively, by the Tuesday noon of the first work week of a month, the Muscovite has paid his monthly rent; the Washingtonian (not in expensive Georgetown or Chevy Chase, but in Landover or Dale City) hits that point only a week later.

In today's Soviet economy, old practices are dying and old expectations are being violated, but new market mechanisms have yet to take hold. For Western business, the ability to pay better than a traditional Soviet enterprise will be important in keeping workers pleased. The ability to make a go of an enterprise, while government bites the bullet and closes money-losing plants, will also be a plus. The new possibility of losing a job should make for more committed workers as well, but will also generate major tensions. While the Soviet government admits to a growing number of unemployed, workers on the whole are not psychologically ready for this contingency. As the economy moves more toward the market, more workers will be forced to face it, and to realize that the old system of state-subsidized, money-losing enterprises offering a secure job is fading. Such workers should, after a necessary adjustment period, understand better the logic of a labor market that allows for layoffs and dismissals.

At least as important for some time will be a factor alien to American managerial calculations in rewarding a work force: the uncertainty of workers' abilities to turn the coin in which they are paid into the food, goods, and services they want and need. Enterprises that pay high wages by Soviet standards, but that are located in areas of poor supply and can offer few goods or amenities, have run into deepening troubles. The wave of strikes in the coal fields in July 1989, effectively crippling much of the energy sector, was a textbook case of the revolt of the highly paid but poorly served.

Enterprises that can operate internal company stores are thus possessed of a strong hand. Western businesses that secure these arrangements for their work force will provide strong positive incentives for performance and effort. Ultimately, it should not be necessary to operate this way, but as long as retail trade is in disarray, the company store will be an important incentive.[17]

Considering the work force broadly, as we have done, ignores the important fact that 51 percent of the workers are women.[18] Predictably, they dominate office work—pink-collar in the U.S.S.R. as elsewhere—and constitute by far the majority in education at primary and secondary levels, in retail trade, and in social services. Most physicians are women; however, men dominate as hospital heads, professors of medicine, and directors of research institutes. Light industries—food-processing, textiles, clothing, and footwear—are both heavily feminized and relatively low paid. Despite the large numbers of female operatives these fields employ, however, there are enough women left over to be heavily evident in construction work as well, usually in unskilled jobs. Westerners are still surprised by the numerous women in evidence at construction sites, hauling and stacking bricks, shoveling gravel, and doing other heavy work.

Although most women work because one household *needs* two earners, many value their work and enjoy the company of their fellow workers. They would find daily life in a small apartment less desirable. Still, if housing was more comfortable, and if single-earner families could survive economically, a number of women on which we can only speculate *would* quit.[19]

Women workers bear two interrelated burdens. They are generally underpaid, and they are laden with household responsibilities. Jobs usually held by women inevitably pay less. It is as if planners assumed that the full-time woman worker is the secondary earner to a man in the household and that her pay is thus supplementary. To the degree that this assumption has been followed—even in the face of a high divorce and abandonment rate, and hence a large number of households headed by women—it has been self-fulfilling. Because of their socialization to certain stereotypes, and because they have less choice, women take low-paying jobs doing "women's work."

Why do they have less choice? Because of the second burden—that of child care, housework, and shopping. Women shoulder the brunt of all of these, given the unheroic performance of most Soviet men. Men report "helping"—but not much—with housework and shopping. Hence, women often seek not a job per se but a location, a set of working hours that best allow shopping (after work or during), and closeness to nurseries and kindergartens where children are taken during working hours. This burden means that women report having much *less* leisure time than men, and also goes some way toward explaining an apparent paradox. Women, poorer paid and often in boring, repetitive jobs, typically report higher work satisfaction than men because of lesser demands, the lesser centrality of work, and the lower expectations women have for their jobs.

Generalizing broadly, women workers' needs are ones that Western business might respond to in very positive and creative ways. In one study, women in seven plants were asked which quality—technical competence or human relations skills—their predominantly male foremen needed to cultivate. Managers were asked the same. The results were exactly the opposite. Women voted 65 percent in favor of human relations skills; managers 65 percent for technical competence.[20] The work-plus-family burden accounts for the preference by women. Ideally, "flex-time" and part-time work alternatives not typically available in Soviet factories and offices would help. In their absence, women have coped within their work group in a more informal manner, depending both on fellow workers and on understanding managers.

Consider an office with seven women employees. On a given day, news at the outset is that a local store has stylish shoes—items, given the Soviet economy, in short supply. Varya is deployed with a list of sizes to queue for herself and four others in the office. Six cover for one missing. Varya is still lined up in the early afternoon, when local milk stores receive their daily allotment, so Masha goes out to buy a bottle for each of six others, plus cheese if available. About the time that Klavdiya must leave to pick up her Yuri from kindergarten early for a doctor's appointment, Varya returns, with shoes for three. Two sizes were unobtainable. She helps cover for the missing Masha and for Klavdiya, who is gone for the rest of the day. Masha then returns, with milk for all. Of seven workers, three have been absent enough of the day for the count to be somewhere in the order of five rather than seven person-days, an average one for productivity and a good day for shopping. Tomorrow will be similar.

Women workers rely on these arrangements. Women émigrés often cite what they miss most about life in the U.S.S.R. as the mutual support, the help in carrying out their roles as mothers and shoppers as well as workers. They miss the work group, the *kollektiv*.

Dividing the burden is very logical. Hours of most service and retail establishments, for a long time, senselessly duplicated office and factory work hours, in a society of near-total employment. A memorable cartoon in the Soviet humor magazine *Krokodil* shows a woman factory worker, just having exited the factory gate at 5 P.M., at a dry-cleaning shop outside its gate with an armful of clothes, being refused as the shop closes, with the words, "We, too, work from whistle to whistle" (i.e., nine to five). During the day, had she managed to visit the cleaners, the woman would have found it less than fully staffed, because the Varyas, Mashas, and Klavdiyas who work there were *also* out doing their shopping.

What women workers need, then, is flexibility built into the job and a retail sector that works reasonable hours. There have been progressive trends toward the latter in recent years. One element of flexibility would be the opportunity to buy consumer goods, or order them, within the plant. Another would be improved day care for preschool children under plant auspices. Well-designed, well-managed facilities of this sort are short in the U.S.S.R. The state has never committed resources sufficient for the nation-wide network of day care centers required by the virtually 100 percent female labor force participation.

All in all, there is much that Western business could do to attract skilled, educated women workers that is not being done by Soviet domestic enterprise. These areas are only some, but they have the virtue of being possible to deal with in the near term, without confronting the deeper and longer-standing issues of occupational segregation, equal pay for equal work, and so on.[21] Recent evidence indicates that, more and more, women, especially the better educated, are coming to evaluate their jobs in terms of intrinsic interest, challenge, and variety. Businesses that offer such work and fair rewards to younger Soviet women workers should be able to engage some of the best. These firms will then confront another challenge, the reluctance of Soviet men to take women in positions of authority and responsibility seriously. That problem will require some deep changes in culture and habits for its eventual resolution.

Before concluding, mention should be made of two other problem areas of the Soviet labor force: alcohol abuse and strikes. The former is persistent, the latter is a result of recent changes.

Alcohol abuse ranks high among chronic Soviet labor problems—especially among the "core" Slav nationalities (Russian, Ukrainian, Belorussian) who make up nearly three-quarters of the population and work force. The problem is historic, as well as contemporary. According to one story, when the tenth-century Prince Vladimir determined to take then-pagan Russia into some type of monotheism, his emissaries shopped around in Western Catholicism, Eastern Orthodoxy, Judaism, and Islamism—rejecting the latter out of hand because its alcohol ban was inconceivable to a Russia whose "joy was drink."

Drinking on and off the job is mainly a male indulgence, through women's rates of alcoholism are rising. Alcoholism derives in part from Russian culture, which equates being able to hold a great deal of alcohol with being a "real man," in part from a lack of other leisure opportunities. Alcohol abuse causes major health problems, many industrial accidents, much down time, and high rates of absenteeism. One careful estimate placed total losses due to alcohol abuse at about 8 to 9 percent of Soviet national income in 1980.[22]

Losses also include an extraordinary number of people who die from acute alcohol poisoning. An estimate based on calculations for the late 1970s is that about 20 of each 100,000 Soviet citizens died annually in this manner. Rates across a range of other countries averaged about 0.3, leaving the U.S.S.R. more than 60 times ahead in this kind of mortality.[23]

Alcohol abuse as a labor and health problem has been hard to crack. Abuse ranges from overconsumption of vodka, wine, and beer to the ingestion of colognes, antifreeze, brake fluid, and other substances which whether taken by mistake or in the context of a classic binge, explain why a death rate by "acute alcohol poisoning" can rise as high as the U.S.S.R.'s.

Gorbachev's early crackdown on the alcohol problem backfired. Cutting the number of sale points, restricting the output of vodka and other "strong" spirits, and raising prices markedly led not to a moderation of the abuses, but to major losses of state tax revenues and a tremendous increase in illegal distilling (moonshine production), which, besides further imperiling health and performance, caused a massive sugar shortage. There was no evidence that, outside of some executive-suite alterations in "three-vodka" lunches, the crackdown had any real or lasting moderating effect on productivity and safety in the work place. Today the campaign is over and the problem persists. The "scope of alcohol abuse and the severity of its impact on Soviet society are unique in terms of international experience."[24]

Soviet therapy techniques for alcoholism are, generally, primitive. Aversion therapy, using a medication that makes the drinker sick when he or she returns to the bottle, is one method. Court-imposed compulsory "medical and labor" treatment—in institutions resembling prisons more than hospitals—and massive antialcohol propaganda have been tried but yielded little. Only now are self-help modes, such as Alcoholics Anonymous, with a good record in other countries, making some inroads. Firing was never a major means of disciplining the drunken worker.

The problem of strikes and labor stoppages, for the present, is not a critical one though this may change. Western managers should have, as the previous pages indicate, resources to provide positive incentives to workers and employees, which are the best guarantee against strikes. Until recently, in any case, many factors, especially political repression, conditioned workers against any use of the strike weapon. But today the Soviet economy faces more strikes than at any time since the 1920s. Moscow's *diktat* no longer runs reliably enough to prevent strikes via fear of retribution. Economic performance and the supply of food, goods, and services have declined, creating grounds for protest. Long-suppressed ethnic tensions seek, and find, modes of expression in militant action, including work stoppages. All these contribute to the growing strikeproneness of the work force.

The strikes that paralyzed the Kuzbass, Donbass, and Arctic coal-mining regions in July 1989 were economic in both motivation and effect. Here, workers highly paid by Soviet standards rebelled against a legacy of poor supply, underinvestment in housing and infrastructure in their areas, and the coal ministry's extraction of much of the funds mines earned. Politically critical as the effects were, and however ominous the threat to the economy of another such coal strike, or similar actions being threatened by Soviet oil and gas workers, these economically motivated stoppages are still less significant than other economic problems.

A more serious problem in the future may be secondary effects of long-term labor disruptions whose roots lie in virtually insoluble ethnic, rather than economic, grievances. These accounted for the majority of man-days lost to strikes in 1989–90. In the first quarter of 1990, for example, the whole U.S.S.R. saw strikes claiming 9.4 million workdays of which 8.8 million were lost in Azerbaijan, whose dispute with Armenia over the Nagorno-Karabakh region, and anger at Moscow over its failure to resolve the issue, resulted in the refusal to work being used as a major weapon.[25] Given the tendency of Soviet producers, as well as their suppliers, to be monopolists, factories idle in one area of the country will have major effects in other areas. No alternative supplier, in most cases, is ready to step in and fill the gap. Thus the Azerbaijani militancy, which crippled much of that republic's economy, has radically cut the U.S.S.R.'s output of oil-drilling equipment, a virtual monopoly of the industrial area around the republic's capital, Baku. The resulting effects in the oil fields of Siberia have been severe. Azerbaijani unrest also had direct and indirect effects (via Armenia) on tobacco and filter production, creating in a nation of unreconstructed and unapologetic smokers the cigarette shortages of summer 1990,[26] which provoked strikes and mass protests in several industrial cities.[27] In what is left of the Soviet planned economy, labor disruptions may well increase, particularly should economic conditions continue to worsen or economic strikes result from nonethnic political grievances.

Thus the problems and opportunities provided by the Soviet work force are both large and clear. The opportunities stem from the availability to foreign companies of the best people from a large, well-educated work force. The problems derive from the necessity of changing the work culture and developing management techniques that will promote productivity and quality.

CHAPTER 5

Managerial Decision Making

Paul R. Lawrence
and Charalombos Vlachoutsicos

To be successful, joint ventures require more than agreements which make strategic sense; they require more than good answers to the hard problems of currency exchange and material shortages: they must be able to jointly manage operating issues. Even joint ventures between U.S. partners are likely to experience operational difficulties. U.S.-Soviet joint ventures will be more difficult since the partners have no shared cultural heritage and a scanty base of shared management knowledge.

Given the history of adversarial relations between the two countries and the lack of exchange, few American and Soviet managers have experience with each other's management systems and, as a result, are likely to hold distorted views of each other. Managers from both countries appear to assume greater differences and fewer commonalities than actually exist. More knowledge of each other's customary management systems and practices is greatly needed to provide a baseline of mutual understanding from which joint ventures can be launched.

This chapter provides information on decision making in U.S. and Soviet organizations. It is based on a comparative study that was jointly conducted by researchers from the Harvard Business School and the Institute of External Economic Affairs (IEEA), the research arm of the U.S.S.R. Foreign Economic Commission.[1] To the best of our knowledge, our study represents the first time such a binational team of scholars and practitioners have been able to conduct in-depth, on-the-spot, top-to-bottom research in Soviet as well as U.S. factories on management issues. In the spirit of *glasnost,* the Soviets were completely open in granting information.

The study found that Soviet managers have many misconceptions about American companies. They were surprised, for example, to find American companies to be as employee-oriented as they are. They expected more ruthlessness, and were surprised at the amount of consideration given to workers and the amount of care and due process provided when, for example, someone had to be discharged. They were also surprised to see that new product work is continuous and ongoing. Soviet decision makers are more likely to say, "We put in a new model years ago; maybe it is time to think about a new one."

The study also found that American managers had misconceptions about Soviet managerial behavior which, at best, were half-truths. These include:

1. The two management systems are mutually exclusive.

2. The Soviets know little about management. Their system has failed and failed widely. They are basically trying with very limited success to apply Western management methods.

3. Western management methods and techniques have proven vastly superior to those of the Soviets.

At the heart of the difficulty for non-Russians in understanding the Soviet system lie two features that our study has revealed for the first time. The first is the structural task unit (STU), which is crucial to the way Soviets operate their hierarchies. The second is the surprising degree of grass-roots democracy.

In the United States the hierarchy functions by a chain-of-command system; managers are expected to communicate up and down the command ladder one step at a time. The classic organization chart (shown as Figure 5-1) reflects the Western attitude toward the kind of authority superiors have over subordinates. Although they must perform assigned tasks and they must continuously inform and occasionally seek decisions from their direct superior, subordinates in our system are recognized to be separate links in the chain of command. Their position and its assigned authority is their own turf. Moreover, no one, neither superiors nor subordinates, can short-circuit the chain of command except in unusual circumstances. U.S. managers take this method for granted and are decidedly unhappy when their superiors or their subordinates bypass them. The main problem of the chain-of-command system is that superiors often find themselves isolated from the reality of their area of responsibility by the wall that their immediate subordinates form to obstruct their direct contact with lower echelons.

The authority system in Soviet organizations differs conceptually from that of the hierarchical system of Western companies. The core of the traditional hierarchical structure of the Soviet enterprise is the *podrazdelenye,* which we call structural task unit.[2] There are production STUs

Figure 5-1   Classical Functional Authority Structure in U.S. Enterprises

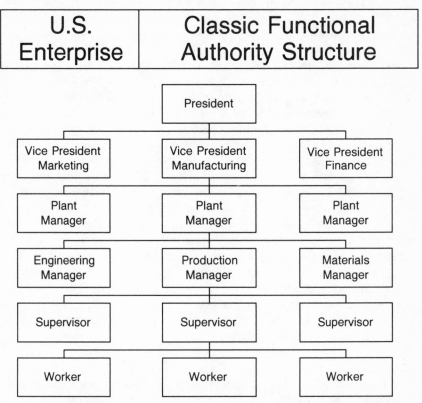

(*proizvodstvnye podrazdelenye*) and administrative STUs (*administrativnye podrazdelenye*). The STU is a group charged with performing a specified task. Members of STUs refer to themselves as "we," and they show an astounding cohesion, solidarity, camaraderie, and loyalty to one another and to their leaders.

Not all Soviet managers are STU leaders. For example; deputies and staff people are not STU leaders. A reliable indicator of which managers are line STU leaders is whether or not they were elected by their subordinates. Elected managers are line STU leaders and provide the backbone of authority in the enterprise. According to *perestroika*'s Law on the Soviet State Enterprise of June 30, 1987, the STU manager was to be legitimated by being elected by his or her subordinates and subsequently confirmed by superior authority. This election process has been modified by decree of the Supreme Soviet of June 4, 1990. The new rules strengthen the hand of the owner but still provide for significant grass-roots input.[3]

Soviet enterprises are themselves STUs, and each contains as many STUs as are necessary to perform its assigned tasks. In order to present the STU concept we have developed the chart shown schematically in Figure 5-2. As can be seen, each STU is a microcosm of all larger ones and a model for all smaller ones.

The largest STU of the enterprise is the enterprise itself. If an enterprise comprises more than one plant, it usually contains five hierarchical levels of line STU leaders: the director general of the enterprise, the general manager of each plant, the workshop managers in each plant, the foremen in each workshop, and the brigade leaders under each foreman. If fulfillment of a task entails crossing STU boundaries, managers are always expected to go up the hierarchy to their common boss for every decision.

The top STU leader of the enterprise is its general director, whose influence is felt everywhere, from the executive suite to the production floor. The general director is a walk-around, face-to-face manager. The "ideal" Soviet manager is an administrative perfectionist who demands discipline and implementation of assigned tasks and creates a sense of purpose and pride in his or her subordinates. To be perceived by subordinates as a good leader, a manager must inspire confidence in his or her effectiveness, as well as show personal concern for the well-being of all subordinates. The most crucial quality of the ideal STU leader is a willingness to take responsibility and a readiness to exercise authority by making final decisions and assigning clear tasks to subordinates.

The power of STU leaders in an enterprise can be compared with a nested set of the traditional Russian *matrioshka* dolls. The largest *matrioshka* doll contains all the smaller dolls, just as the power of the general manager contains the power of all the smaller STU leaders. And just as each progressively smaller doll contains all the smaller ones, each progressively lower STU leader has authority over all the subordinated STUs. Even the lowest functionary, the worker (the tiny solid doll inside the stack), can be viewed as an STU leader: though without subordinates, his or her authority rests in a clearly specified realm of responsibility *(kompetencija)*.

STUs operate on the basis of written and unwritten rules. The following are some of the rules by which we have found STUs to operate.

1. All members are to be strictly accountable for their actions. The authority and area of responsibility assigned to each and every manager are taken very seriously by peers, subordinates, superiors, and outsiders. They constitute an assigned duty—an obligation to society, to the enterprise, and, above all, to the immediate STU. For every employee the area of responsibility is his of her legitimate turf and is never meddled with by peers.

2. Subordinates are to be unconditionally obedient to superiors. Discipline is an essential ingredient of the system and is explicitly stipulated in

Figure 5-2   STU System of Authority in Soviet Enterprises

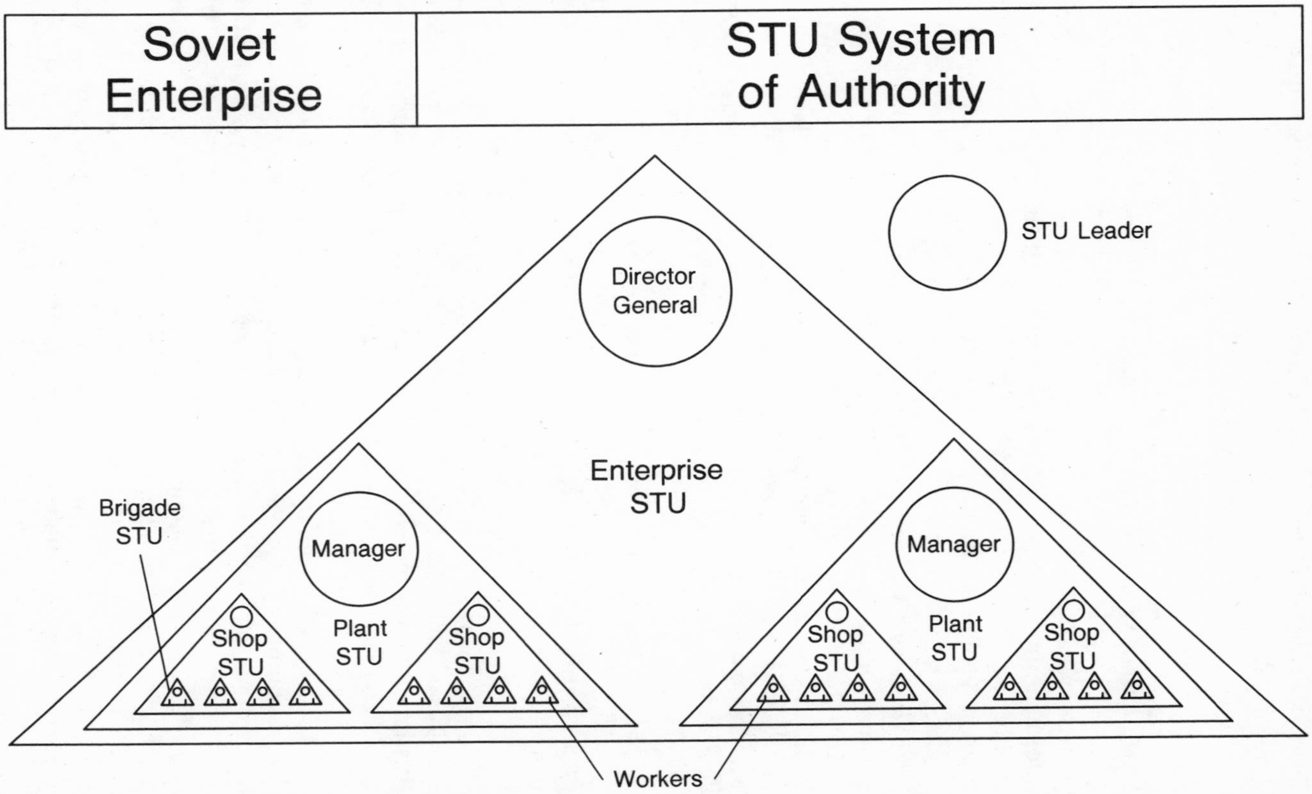

Soviet Enterprise	STU System of Authority

STU Leader

Director General

Manager

Manager

Enterprise STU

Plant STU

Plant STU

Shop STU

Shop STU

Shop STU

Shop STU

Workers

Brigade STU

Articles 2 and 14 of the Law on the Soviet State Enterprise. Otherwise, as always in Russian history, it is feared that confusion and anarchy will ensue.

3. STU leaders bear the complete responsibility and are bestowed with broad authority and complete administrative power for managing their STUs as a whole. As shown in Figure 5-2, the responsibility of each STU encircles all areas of authority and responsibility within their domain. An informal, implicit deal is made between STU members and their leader: members must obey the leader's instructions, and the leader must protect them and stand up for them in every way to everyone outside the STU.

4. Whenever STU leaders consider it necessary, the system allows them to bypass immediate subordinates and communicate directly with, and give instructions to, any member of their STU at any level. Subordinates from all levels also have the right of direct access to leaders. We have found that managers are expected to post office hours when they are available to meet with any employee (or even members of employees' families) who wish to consult them directly on any matter whatsoever.

5. STU members are bound to one another by confidentiality as to the inner workings of the group. In fact, divulging information to outsiders, even on trivial matters, needs the leaders' explicit approval. STUs function as collective entities that are practically impossible for outsiders to penetrate.

Closely knit groups have always been a part of getting things done in Russia. Examples include the peasant communes, peasant and army cartels, the village *mir,* and rural and plant brigades. In essence, all these groups are STUs.

The STU system offers considerable advantages in terms of the vertical integration of Soviet enterprises. These direct contacts can create strong bonds of personal loyalty up and down the hierarchy, and greatly enhance the leader's perception of what actually goes on in the organization. However, this unique combination of tradition and formal system consistently overloads vertical communication channels and reinforces the doctrinal desire to maintain centralized control. STUs can be one of the great strengths of the Soviet enterprise, but these cohesive groups often lead to excessive compartmentalization of the affairs of organizations and are very hard to integrate horizontally. Even simple acts of direct coordination between separate STUs do not happen—everything is expected to go up and over the channel through the shared STU superior. Thus STUs make it very difficult to carry out direct lateral integration in the enterprise.

The other dominant feature of the Soviet management system, one that is difficult for many non-Russians to comprehend, is the apparent contradiction between centralization and grass-roots democracy in decision making. The essence of the Soviet decision-making system STUs rests on deep-rooted Russian traditional management principles: one-person leadership *(edinohachalie),* collective leadership *(kollegialnost),* and collectivism *(kollektivnost).* These principles are closely interwoven. They can be traced far back in Russian history and have evolved from inveterate values and priorities.

Collective leadership has its origins in the collegial decision making of the medieval Russian peasant commune; it is defined by Soviet writers as the system of management whereby leadership is placed in a group of people (collegium) that deliberates and decides all basic questions of management. Decisions are made by majority vote. Usually, however, debate continues until consensus is reached. Once a decision is made, all members of the collegium commit themselves to its implementation. Collective leadership is applied in the Politburo of the Central Committee of the Communist party of the U.S.S.R., the Council of Ministers of the U.S.S.R., the U.S.S.R. Academy of Sciences, and a number of other important Soviet associations and institutions. A traditional problem with collective leadership has been that it encourages the tendency of managers to avoid personal responsibility by hiding behind collective decisions.

One-person leadership in the management of organizations is rooted in centuries of centralist traditions. The concept was borrowed from the army and introduced into Russian public administration by Emperor Paul I at the end of the eighteenth century. Lenin first established one-man leadership in 1918 as a key management system in Soviet administration.[4] As articulated by Lenin, one-man leadership institutionalizes at one stroke top-man power and autonomy of parts.

Collectivism goes as far back as Russian history. The tradition of tightly integrated collectives is one of the most powerful latent elements of Russian culture. Throughout Russian history, leaders have sought to strike a balance between centralized leadership and collective management methods. The search for this combination is reflected in the central Soviet principle of party and state management known as democratic centralism. The concept of democratic centralism was first introduced in 1906 as an organizational party statute of the Russian revolutionary movement. According to its original formula, it comprises four elements:

1. The application of the elective principle to all leading organs of the party, from the highest to the lowest.

2. Periodic accountability of party organs to their respective party organizations.

3. Strict party discipline and the subordination of the minority to the majority.

4. The absolutely binding character of the decisions of the higher organs upon the lower organs and upon party members.[5]

Lenin considered the principle of democratic centralism as the foundation of the economic system of socialism. He showed this principle to be "a combination of centralized direction of the economy by the state toward the solution of the key task of development, so as to guarantee the public interest, together with the initiative of the people, allowing for local conditions and the development of democratic principles in management."[6]

Before *perestroika,* the gap between practice and policy was enormous and the democratic element of democratic centralism was hardly ever applied. The frequent abuses of power have associated democratic centralism with Stalinist autocracy, and the term has fallen into ill-repute. A fundamental aim of *perestroika* is to restore the latent culture of the self-energizing coexistence of grass-roots participation with the STU leaders' authority for decision making. Gorbachev writes in his book *Perestroika,* "The aim of this reform is to ensure . . . the transition from an excessively centralized management system relying on orders to a democratic one, based on the combination of Democratic Centralism and self-management."[7] In this manner, the 1987 Law on the Soviet State Enterprise, while explicitly keeping one-person leadership in the administration of the enterprise, entrusts a great deal of decision-making power on important issues to the labor's collective, which is made up of the entire personnel of the enterprise, and to its elected employees' council. In the Soviet plants we studied we witnessed these democratic mechanisms being used regularly in decision making. We observed that the centralization of one-person leadership and the decentralization of collectivism are not incompatible forms of management.

The Soviets resolve this apparent paradox by clearly *alternating* these forms in distinct phases of an integrated system of decision making. The system combines top-down power and bottom-up power into an integrated system of management. We found that unless both powers function, any decision is very difficult to implement. It is hard for Westerners to see both forms of power as being real, but by alternation they are.

We observed six distinct decision-making phases:

- *Phase 1: Top-down goals.* The leader poses the issue for subordinates and clearly specifies the targets to be attained.
- *Phase 2: Deliberation.* Wide and open participation at selected levels of the STU, at times including the workers.
- *Phase 3: Bottom-up proposal.* Submission of proposal to the leader.
- *Phase 4: Deliberation.* Careful review of the proposal by the leader.

- *Phase 5: Top-down Decision.* Clear instructions issued by the leader.
- *Phase 6: Implementation.* Unified, committed, and disciplined action.

As we have observed, these alternating centralizing and decentralizing phases of the decision process take place at different times, and the switches from one phase to the next are signaled by social rituals. For example, the seating arrangements are informal during deliberation meetings, but for command meetings subordinates line up along a rectangular table by rank with their STU leader at the head. It needs to be understood that all phases of this delicate process are inseparable parts of a balanced and integrated whole. This means that if any one of its phases is ignored or exaggerated, the effectiveness of the system is weakened. However, if the system is practiced consistently, it can produce well-considered decisions that can be implemented.

These two important features of the Soviet management system were apparent from our research observations of actual Soviet decision-making procedures and day-to-day management methods. We have selected a few case examples that clarify how these features work.[8]

Our first evidence of the workings of the STU system comes from a review of a typical daily agenda of a Soviet plant manager:

Plant Manager's Day

7:30–8:00	Plant tour: stops to talk briefly with workers and supervisors; becomes active in finding solutions to problems
8:00–8:30	In office preparing for intercom broadcast
8:30–9:00	Intercom transmission of production numbers from plant manager, chief engineer, and production manager to all plant management down to foremen
9:00–9:30	Informal meetings with individuals from supply and construction departments
9:30–11:00	Plant tour (see above)
11:00–1:00	Informal meetings with individual shop managers and specialists
1:00–2:00	Lunch with staff and any visitors
2:00–5:00	Regularly scheduled formal meetings with different groups for each day of the week
5:00–5:30	Intercom transmission of second shift production numbers
5:30–7:00	Plant tour and informal meetings with night shift personnel
7:00–8:00	Desk work, answering mail
8:00	Leave for home

Also, once a week the plant manager holds open office hours to receive workers, their family members, and others from outside the plant.

The story of securing production equipment for a redesigned engine cylinder provides several additional examples of how STUs work.

In accordance with a national quality improvement element in the five-year plan, the enterprise head engineer issued an order to redesign the engine to reduce fuel consumption by 6 to 7 percent. The engine designers proposed changes that required a different configuration of the casting and machining of the cylinder head. This was a major project costing 500,000 rubles, of which 100,000 were earmarked for the engine plant. Because the benefits of the new engine were calculated at the enterprise level (headquarters) and several units in the enterprise were involved, the project was coordinated at the enterprise level by the chief engineer and the chief technologist, who set deadlines for the major phases of the work. The order for new equipment and tooling was included in the consolidated capital investment plan of the enterprise. The engine plant needed new equipment to machine the new engine block and to perform additional operations.

The engine plant experienced several problems in introducing the new equipment. One problem involved getting the cooperation of the enterprise's tooling shop and illustrates the problems of lateral decision making among the peer STUs of the plant and of the enterprise's tooling shop. Initially the tooling for the new equipment needed by the engine plant was assigned to the tooling shop and included in its plan. The chief engineer of the engine plant explained that the engine plant initially designated the tooling as an expense item rather than a capital investment in order to speed up the project. However, because the interplant transfer prices made the project unprofitable for the tooling shop, its workers were not interested in doing the job and held it up in every way possible.

The matter was put before a dispute settlement commission of the enterprise chaired by the deputy director general of the enterprise for new technology. Members of the commission were from different levels of the enterprise: the deputy director for production preparation of the engine plant, the deputy manager of the tooling shop, and four specialists involved in the development of the new engine block. The manager of the tooling shop explained that it was more profitable for the group to manufacture the equipment itself rather than the tooling that it required. The shop would do the tooling provided it was designated as equipment so that it would be charged as a capital item. The tooling shop's negotiators were so adamant in their position that the dispute settlement commission decided not to argue with them. Engineers rewrote the order as requested and the shop produced the tooling. It was clear in this instance that peer STUs can develop major conflicts that even a top level dispute commission does not easily resolve.

The tooling shop's workers also resisted when the production people in the engine plant pressed them to make the new tooling compatible with adjacent equipment. This would take more time, and the shop workers wanted to finish the job quickly. The chief engineer and the equipment designers finally persuaded them to make the equipment to the designers' specifications with the results to be monitored by the chief technologist and the chief engineer of the enterprise.

Another difficulty arose when the tooling shop began installing the tooling in the engine plant. In order to meet their deadline the tooling specialists did their work quickly and left. But the engine plant management wanted the tooling specialists to stay until everything was working properly. Again the peer STUs were deadlocked. After the intervention of enterprise headquarters, their common superior, the engine plant finally agreed to accept the tooling shop's work as long as it was approved by the equipment designers. Again direct lateral decision making between STUs was not possible.

The installation of new equipment was to be done without interrupting engine production because of the chronic difficulties of meeting production targets. Installation crews, accordingly, worked primarily on the weekends. Still some production stoppages were needed to keep up with the installation schedule. In such cases the deputy manager of the mechanical repair shop determined on the spot what would be done to meet the deadline. In addition, the project manager, the deputy chief of tooling, the deputy chief of maintenance, and sometimes the chief engineer of the engine plant would work on the job site on Sundays to solve problems on the spot. All of these managers were having to bypass the command ladder to perform in this way.

As a final example of STUs at work we will turn to a new product decision and its aftermath. This case also highlights some of the costs of central planning.

The electrical equipment ministry assigned plant A responsibility for producing a new model motor. In this connection the ministry authorized its technical institute to investigate new equipment to assist plant A with the production of rotors for the new motor. The plant's design office provided specifications of the new motor to the institute. The institute studied the situation and selected automatic rotor lines from Eastern Europe as standard issue for plant A and all other relevant enterprises.

When the new equipment was finally delivered it quickly ran into technical and financial problems. The Eastern European manufacturer claimed to have no space to set up the line and test it before shipment, so the manufacturer sent specialists to set the line up and test it on site. The specialists found they could not get the equipment working because, they said, they had not been informed of the plant's relevant specifications. As a result, the new automatic line had been sitting idle for several months and the rotor shop manager had to make do with the old equipment, which was constantly breaking down. The contract for receiving spare parts from the manufacturer had expired and the plant's adjusters were unable to repair the equipment. The manager of the rotor section explained that there was a shortage of skilled adjusters to maintain the equipment. "It takes years of experience to do the job and the adjusters are in great demand throughout the plant as well as throughout the country. It is difficult to attract workers to the job because it is hard work and the adjusters don't earn much more than regular, less skilled workers."

Faced with this situation, the director general of the enterprise decided to intervene by sending a task force of specialists from the main plant to repair the old equipment. He selected eight of the most skilled adjusters and sent them to work full time to plant A. After three months they succeeded in getting the old equipment operating properly.

To compound the technical problems, the electronics on the new equipment was not designed to function as expected. Unfortunately the equipment was incompatible with three other machine tools on the rotor line which would be difficult to modify. The plant was faced with the choice of not accepting the equipment and having nothing, or accepting it and substituting a manual production process in place of the three incompatible machines. The second alternative required 15 people to make what 2 people had done previously.

There were also financial difficulties relating to costs and a change in financial responsibility. The newly delivered model was three times more expensive than similar equipment that had been purchased a decade earlier. Costs had recently become an important issue to plant A, as a result of its becoming subject to *perestroika*'s self-financing requirement. Indeed, the chief technologist said costs had become their primary concern. To make matters worse, the plant and the import organization, a department under a different ministry, were at odds with each other because they are evaluated according to conflicting targets. According to the chief engineer, the plant management wants to buy the most suitable equipment as cheaply as possible to keep costs down, but the import organization wants to buy equipment that will minimize hard-currency expenditures. The upshot was that the plant's manager decided not to pay for the equipment, asserting that the money was not available, and that never again would the ministry make a buying decision.

The process of choosing the model of *khozraschet* (self-financing) at plant B was an interesting example of the alternation between centralized and democratic decision making.

Plant B had a good track record. The plant had been an early adopter of motor improvements and a part of an early *perestroika* experiment. The plant had met its plan targets consistently. It was generally within its cost budget, although it had occasionally failed to meet delivery targets.

In mid-1987, plant B had to decide which *khozraschet* model it would formally chose. Model 1 was closest to the traditional way of accounting and planning. It offered less risk but little favorable potential. Model 2 was the "face of the future," offering a new, more demanding method of accounting. Model 2 did involve a risk that the plant might not meet its wage and salary obligations and would have to borrow from the bank to cover its costs: the ministry would not fund shortfalls. However, under model 2 the firm would get to apply any savings directly to its material incentives and to employee fringe benefits. Thus, there was a meaningful possibility for the workers and managers to increase their income.

Initially, the plant manager had proposed that the plant follow the more traditional model. The ministry, however, urged the plant to reconsider model 2 because of the plant's strong performance. Plant personnel and management were most concerned with how funds for wages, salaries, and material incentives would fare under model 1 or model 2. Accordingly, the chief accountant's office began making calculations to compare performance under each model. The early analysis suggested that model 2 might be favorable. The chief accountant concluded, "Based on our calculations, we could be able to meet our salary obligations and possibly achieve quite a big improvement. However, we saw that this would be quite a bit more work for the accounting department and we did not know how to handle this." An important thrust of the second model was to push the efficiency incentives lower in the hierarchy. Cost accounting was supposed to be broken out by shops, so each shop could become, in effect, its own responsibility center. Rather than the plantwide cost figures used in the old model, the accounting group would need to develop and track figures for "local" costs. Thus, every shop would have its own internal "customers" and "suppliers." The amount of cost tracking the accounting department would have to do would increase dramatically.

Based on these studies, the plant manager had an open meeting with all his deputies, all the shop managers, all the staff department chiefs, and the chief accountant. During this meeting, the staff questioned the chief accountant. Generally, since the second model was more flexible and offered the possibility of greater income, there were no serious objections. However, there was a 45-minute discussion on how the new costing system might work, and about the need for a computer system to support it.

In the meantime, negotiations with the ministry had proceeded. When they were first asked, plant B's managers declined to chose the second model on the grounds that payments to the ministry were too high. The ministry wanted the plant to pay 24 percent of its net income (virotchki) to the ministry. The plant suggested paying the ministry 12 percent. At the end of the negotiations, the figure of payment to the ministry was 18.7 percent. Also, the ministry agreed to soften somewhat its targets for cost reductions.

With the ministry's concessions and the calculations favoring model 2 in hand, the management brought the proposal to the workers' collective. Prior to this meeting, the training department as well as the trade union, the Komsomol, and the plant's party office had been holding information meetings so that most of the workers were familiar with the options. After a short introduction by the plant manager, he and the chief economist answered a lot of specific questions. Most of the questions revolved around how the second model would affect individual wages. Primarily, the calculations suggested that if current performance continued, workers would receive the same wage and bonus, but if performance improved, they could receive an increase. The decision to try model 2 for the coming year was approved by the workers' collective at that meeting.

By that fall, the decision appeared to be working well. Because working performance had improved, the plant was 1.5 million rubles above its income targets for the first seven months. This was primarily because product was being shipped on time and up to plan specifications. This equated to a 2 percent growth of average total wage and bonus income. The improvements were spread out more or less equally between the different shops.

The combination of centralized and democratic methods are well illustrated by the way Soviet managers are selected by inputs from both subordinates and superiors. We witnessed this process in connection with the selection of a foreman.

In the machine shop the senior foreman was unpopular with the workers because of his authoritarian management style. He did not listen sympathetically to their problems or address their needs effectively. For example, he refused a worker permission to get off early to meet her son after his first day of school. The shop party secretary accumulated this information and became concerned about the social climate of the shop.

In late 1987 a general guideline of the ministry urged enterprises to abolish the position of senior foreman in all the shops. In the past a staff reduction would simply have been announced by management. But with the advent of *perestroika,* the shop party secretary and the shop manager informed the deputy director of personnel that they would like to hold an election for the two positions of foreman in the machine shop. The shop party secretary also felt it would be best for everyone concerned if the problem of the unpopular foreman were solved at the same time through the democratic process, rather than by the administrative means of the plant manager's punishing or dismissing him. The manager of the machine shop, the plant manager, and the party secretary gave their approval for elections to be held in December 1987.

There were four candidates for the two positions: the former senior foreman of the machine shop, the two incumbent foremen, and a white-collar worker from the shop's technology section who nominated himself.

The shop's party secretary presided over the election since it predated the formation of the employee's council. Ninety-five percent of the shop workers attended. One worker suggested that the shop manager speak. He described the vacancies and read statements about the candidates provided by the personnel department. This was followed by a five-minute speech by each of the candidates in which they described their plans for the shop. Candidates then answered questions.

After a short discussion of what voting procedure to use, the group decided to have a secret ballot, to give each voter two choices, and to appoint a five-person commission to supervise the balloting. The commission counted the ballots in front of the group, and the chairman of the commission announced the results. Of the 74 people present, 11 voted for the senior foreman. He was defeated by the technologist, who received 60 votes. Of the two incumbent foremen, the workers chose the one who was considered most principled and consistent. The chairman of the voting committee and the party secretary signed a special election protocol, and the election winners were approved and appointed by the plant manager two weeks later.

All four candidates have found a place in the organization. The senior foreman took a job in the production control office and no longer is in a management position. The technologist who became foreman is doing well, as is the incumbent foreman who was reelected. The other foreman who was not reelected took a job as a worker with no loss in pay.

As a final example of the practice of combining centralized and democratic methods we will turn to a more complex case of managerial selection.

Igor Bandura had been plant manager at plant C for 10 years. Until the last few years the plant had enjoyed a good reputation. As a manufacturer of small industrial motors the plant had been touted in the press for quality work and had successfully completed experiments in quality control. However, conditions deteriorated with the onset of several changes. First, the transition was made to a new series of motors. Second, equipment upgrades were delayed. Third, the state quality control commission, Gospriemka, increased quality requirements. Fourth, the economic reform of self-financing and cost accounting put an additional strain on the plant.

The problem became serious in 1986 when production was short by 100,000 motors, for which the plant paid 1.2 million rubles in fines to customers for nondelivery. The situation continued into 1987, when they paid 1 million rubles in fines in the first six months. The ministry and the general director decided to dismiss Bandura, and the party committee was in agreement. Bandura submitted his letter of resignation.

Meanwhile, the newly promulgated Law of the State Enterprise required that dismissal of a manager must be done with the approval of the employees' council. In April 1988 representatives from the ministry came to the plant to get the employees' council to approve the dismissal and consider other candidates for the position. A meeting was held, consisting of the ministry representatives, the employees' council, the party committee, and the plant manager. The chief of personnel administration from the ministry said the ministry was very unhappy with Bandura's performance and proposed to dismiss him on the grounds of not meeting the standards to be a plant manager. This was a very severe punishment that would ruin his career. The secretary of the party told the ministry officials that the party would agree to dismiss Bandura but on a less severe charge. The ministry officials agreed to the compromise.

The party committee and the employees' council decided on the procedure to announce Bandura's dismissal to the employees' collective. At the beginning of an employees' meeting, the party secretary was supposed to have explained the situation. Instead he gave the floor to Bandura to make the first statement. Perhaps the party secretary felt uncomfortable performing this unpleasant task and wanted to give some dignity to Bandura. The party secretary may also have been following the new policy of diminished party interference under *perestroika*. Although Bandura was aware of the agreement that he would be dismissed on less severe grounds, he announced that the ministry had come to punish him and dismiss him according to the more severe article. The director general believed that Bandura used this tactic to elicit employees' sympathy. Bandura talked about his long service at the plant and claimed that the ministry had not given him help when he had asked for it. He said that it was not fair for the ministry to blame everything on him and dismiss him. He then made an appeal to the employees for their support in helping him get the plant to move forward.

Upon hearing Bandura's version of the story and yet unaware of the compromise that had been reached, the employees' collective felt that the ministry was using Bandura as a scapegoat to cover its own irresponsibility. Consequently they decided to fight the unfairness of the ministry by holding an election for the plant manager's position. They said they had known Bandura for 10 years and that they would be the judge of his abilities. They posted notices and set up a box for nominations for one month seeking internal candidates. No one applied other than Bandura. The chairman of the workers' collective told the general director that he felt Bandura was not strong enough to turn the plant around; he was disappointed with Bandura's plan for the coming year and the future. The general director said he had another candidate from outside in mind, but he had not nominated him because he wanted to let the workers' collective try its wings without his interference. They decided in any event to proceed with the election.

On May 12 the election was held with the 400 delegates representing the employees' collective; the general director of the enterprise; party and union officials; and Bandura in attendance. Bandura spoke for half an hour about his "self-critical" plan for the plant for the next five years, outlining both positive and negative aspects. A dozen others made statements and asked questions. They criticized him on a number of counts and warned him that he had to improve and get the plant running smoothly. They then decided to call an open vote. Bandura was elected with 326 in favor, 2 opposed, and 2 abstentions. The meeting concluded with a 15-minute speech by Bandura. The workers' collective submitted written notification of its decision to the ministry for confirmation.

The chairman of the workers' collective admitted that the reelection of Bandura was the collective's way of exercising its authority against the ministry. Without that provocation the chairman was convinced the collective would have dismissed Bandura.

Five months went by, and the situation in the plant had not improved. In accordance with the law the director general had the right to raise the question about Bandura's performance before the employees' council; accordingly, he proposed dismissing Bandura and holding an election one month later. The employees' council agreed in a vote of 26 to 2. A selection board was organized and seven candidates applied—four internal and three external. The external candidate proposed by the director general won with a majority of the votes. One month after the new plant manager started work the plant fulfilled the plan. Bandura took a position in city government.

These case examples clarify the basic role of STUs and centralized leadership with grass-roots democracy to Soviet management. These two features significantly condition how Soviet managers use hierarchies and make decisions. U.S. managers need to understand these features in depth; in particular, they need to reach some accommodation with them to manage joint ventures successfully. The needed accommodation can take different forms in each joint venture. Some will choose to adopt primarily Soviet practice and others mainly U.S. practice, but agreement on the issue is essential. Only one set of ground rules should prevail, and social rituals will help in signaling when switches are made between systems.

The comparable U.S. practice that the Soviets need to understand in depth and come to some accommodation with is the use of networking or lateral decision making. Soviet managers have a great deal to gain from learning and practicing essential aspects of the U.S. system of lateral networking. It can facilitate effective work directly between functional departments, within cross-functional project teams, and also directly with suppliers and customers. This feature of U.S. practice is not only foreign to Soviet managers but violates the customary way of operating STUs. To use these U.S. practices Soviets will need to learn to work effectively in relationships that cut across the traditional STU boundaries. This will not be easy. It will require patient coaching and repeated practice.

The management system of each country has evolved from very different political and economic histories. However, one of the most important insights of our study is that their main strengths are *complementary*. The Soviet enterprise management practice of STU along with centralized leadership and grass-roots democracy can strengthen the *vertical* aspects of decision making, and U.S. networking can strengthen the *horizontal* aspects. Fitting these two decision systems into a harmonious single system will be a challenge, but we see no major obstacle to a joint venture's utilizing both systems in a single joint venture enterprise. To the contrary, we see a potential for real added strength in their careful combination. The STU system offers clear, strong leadership while the Soviet decision-making method can generate considered decisions with full commitment to back them up. This can serve to integrate decision and action up and down the hierarchy. It represents a particular form of employee participation and involvement that many U.S. firms are moving toward. The U.S.

practice of lateral decision making can both speed up the decision process and add significant value.

For joint ventures between U.S. and Soviet enterprises to be successful, they must clear a number of hurdles. They must, of course, make strategic sense to both parties. They must deal with the regulatory bureaucracy of both countries. They must be negotiated with care and patience to overcome the many, many hurdles—of which currency convertibility and the shortage of domestic sources of supply are the most conspicuous. This chapter has focused on the final and probably least understood hurdle of achieving effective joint operating management. We believe that U.S. and Soviet managers can manage together successfully if they study each other's system and take advantage of the complementary strengths of each.

CHAPTER 6

Corporate Experience in the Soviet Union

James L. Hecht

How much can knowledge of the past help us understand the future? In 1775, Patrick Henry wrote, "I have but one lamp by which my feet are guided, and that is the lamp of experience. I know no way of judging of the future but by the past." Sixteen years later, Edmund Burke observed: "You can never plan the future by the past." These famous quotations are as meaningful today as they were two centuries ago. Although they appear to conflict, they complement each other. The experience of the past cannot be assumed to predict the future. On the basis of World War I experience, the French relied on the Maginot Line to protect their country from an advancing German army, but the Maginot Line did little to contain the Germans during World War II because of changes in weaponry. Today technological changes are occurring at a far more rapid rate than in the period between 1918 and 1940, and technological changes in telecommunications and information systems have greatly increased the pace of social change. However, knowledge of the past remains a great advantage in planning for the future as long as a distinction is made between those elements of the past that will continue to shape events and new forces that will alter past patterns.

Thus, a company that is investigating opportunities in the U.S.S.R. cannot help but benefit by an overview of the experience of companies that have already done business in the Soviet Union. However, until recently not much was known, and much of that information was anecdotal. Studies had been made of technology transfer from the West which concentrated on the length of time required to bring in a new plant in the Soviet Union; this work is covered in Philip Hanson's *Trade and Technology in Soviet–*

Western Relations.[1] On many other questions of importance to business there was no reliable information.

In many ways that is not surprising. Even in a good year, U.S. exports to the Soviet Union were worth only about $2 billion, and U.S. imports were far lower. However, when in 1987 the Soviets enacted legislation that permitted joint ventures with Western partners, the need of such information was greatly increased, and James K. Oliver and I initiated a program at the University of Delaware to study the experience of U.S. companies in the Soviet Union.

This chapter covers the results of two studies that were carried out as part of this program. The first focused on the experience of 106 American firms that had significant sales in the Soviet Union.[2] This was followed by a study of the experience of 19 firms that had sold technology to the Soviet Union and the performance of 35 manufacturing plants in the U.S.S.R. that were built using the American technology.[3] The study on technology utilization by the Soviets will be particularly helpful to companies exploring joint ventures. Because this study was cosponsored by the Licensing Executives Society, a professional organization of lawyers and technology managers involved in technology sales, information was obtained which normally would not have been made available.

The most important findings of these two studies are the following:

- The Soviet Union has been very reliable in business dealings.
- Soviet trade has usually required greater marketing costs than other foreign sales, particularly for initial sales.
- It has taken much longer to build and start up a plant in the U.S.S.R. than in the West.
- Once in operation, most of the plants built in the Soviet Union under licensing arrangements with American companies have performed well. Product quality has usually been the equivalent to that of similar plants in the West—and occasionally better.
- The key to successful operation of a plant in the Soviet Union—in addition to such factors as insuring proper equipment and training personnel, which customarily are part of a technology sale—is an adequate supply infrastructure.
- The Americans who have been involved in technology transfer, particularly those involved in plant start-ups, have found the experience difficult.

The 106 American firms with significant sales to the Soviet Union reported that, on an overall basis, the U.S.S.R. was about average in desirability among their foreign customers. As shown by the data in Table 6-1, the Soviet Union was placed in the top half of their foreign customers

Table 6-1 Overall Rating of the
Desirability of the Soviet Union
among Foreign Customers

Quartile	Percent
Top	21
Second	33
Third	23
Bottom	23

SOURCE: *Columbia Journal of World Business* (Winter 1983): 44–50.

by 54 percent of the respondents. Generally favorable trade experience was further shown by the fact that, in reply to another question, 87 percent of the respondents indicated that their company would like to do more business with the Soviet Union and only 1 percent indicated that they did not want to do more business. Of the others, 9 percent responded, "It depends," and 3 percent had no opinion.

American firms that have done business with the U.S.S.R. give the Soviets very high marks with respect to reliability, as shown by the data in Table 6-2. Only five firms indicated having had experience with the Soviets' failing to meet agreements, and two of these commented that the failures appeared to be a result of inefficiency rather than intent. In their comments, many respondents praised the Soviets for reliability.

It should be pointed out that the Soviets would not have done as well on reliability if this study had been carried out in the summer of 1990 instead of late 1987 and early 1988. Starting at the end of 1989, the Soviets failed to make payments for a large number of purchases—a good example of how the past can fail to predict the future. Whether this failure to meet contractual obligations will be the pattern of the future or is only temporary remains to be seen, but I would guess that it is temporary—the product of a combination of the confusion caused by decentralization, an acute shortage of hard currency, and a cultural reluctance by the Soviets to borrow excessively or dig into certain types of reserves. Years of past experience tell us that it is part of the national culture to consider signed contracts as binding obligations.

Table 6-2 Rating of Soviet Compliance with Contract Agreements

Response	Percent
Very good	71
Meets agreements, but exploits loopholes and gray areas	24
Sometimes does not meet agreements	5
Does not meet agreements	0

SOURCE: *Columbia Journal of World Business* (Winter 1983): 44–50.

The need for a greater marketing effort in the U.S.S.R. than in other foreign countries was reported by almost three-quarters of the 106 respondents. A summary of the data is in Table 6-3. However, only 35 percent of the respondents reported that the high level of marketing was required on a continuing basis; 38 percent indicated that, once a product had been established, repeat business could be obtained with either normal marketing efforts or less than that required in other foreign markets.

One problem of getting into the Soviet market has been that the Soviets have often required extensive participation by a senior executive—probably because of the great importance of supplier reliability to the Soviets because alternative sources usually are not available. The involvement of a senior executive signifies that the supplier is committed to the Soviet market and will continue to sell to the U.S.S.R. even if the product is in short supply.

These overall findings were frequently echoed in comments made by company executives about their own experiences. A sampling of such comments make the statistical data more meaningful:

- "It is a challenge to get products established. Once established, repeat orders are relatively easy."—*Machinery company executive*

- "[It is] difficult to work with end users to develop new business."—*Chemical company official*

- "There is no problem in stimulating demand. The difficulty [is] getting product into the country."—*Consumer products executive*

- "Experienced companies bid a higher price because they expect to make concessions and know it costs more to do business."—*Chemical company executive*

- "Negotiations are lengthy, but once finished Soviets live up to the bargain."—*Electrical company official*

- "[A] plus is high reliability; [a] negative is [the] long incubation time of projects."—*Chemical company official*

Table 6-3 Marketing Effort Required to Sell Products in the Soviet Union

Response	Percent
Less expensive marketing effort is required than for most foreign customers	14
Level of required marketing is about the same	13
Initial sales require more marketing effort, but repeat sales do not	38
Much more marketing is required than for average foreign customer	35

SOURCE: *Columbia Journal of World Business* (Winter 1983): 44–50.

Perestroika may eventually result in allowing foreign companies to market products in the Soviet Union for costs comparable to elsewhere. However, because of recent changes, marketing in the Soviet Union is probably even more difficult now than when the survey was taken. But the organization of the economy is only one factor; traditions and culture, which cannot change as rapidly as organizational structures, are also important. I recently was trying to get official approval for a meeting that everyone involved had agreed should take place. But the letter requesting the meeting had not been received by the minister involved three weeks after it was sent, and a copy of the original, which had been sent to Moscow by fax, was not considered sufficient because it was not the original. So, to avoid further delay, I sent another original by courier.

The 106 respondents were asked a question to determine the amount of effort required for the business obtained from different socialist countries. While experiences differed, there was a clear overall trend: selling to the Soviet Union required more effort than selling to a typical Eastern bloc country, but less effort than selling to the People's Republic of China.

Respondents were also queried about their attitude toward joint ventures. The summary in Table 6-4 shows that 34 percent of the companies with experience in Soviet trade were interested in such ventures. This includes 12 percent who had reservations about joint ventures with foreign organizations but viewed joint ventures with the Soviet Union as a way of becoming established in the Soviet market. On the other hand, the complex problems of such a venture and the unknown factors discouraged many companies, although most of these were willing to explore possibilities. Only 17 percent of the companies indicated little interest in a joint venture with the Soviet Union.

Sufficient replies were received from a number of industry groupings to allow an analysis of the desirability of the Soviet Union as a customer by industry type. As can be seen from the data in Table 6-5, chemicals and

---

Table 6-4   Attitudes toward Joint Ventures in the Soviet Union

Response	Percent
Willing to participate	22
Have reservations about joint ventures with foreign organizations, but anxious to explore possibilities with the Soviet Union to become established in the Soviet market	12
Willing to explore, but have reservations about participating with foreign organizations	8
Willing to explore, but have reservations about participating with the Soviet Union	37
Little interest in joint ventures with foreign organizations	4
Little interest in joint ventures with the Soviet Union	17

SOURCE: *Columbia Journal of World Business* (Winter 1983): 44–50.

Table 6-5   Experience with Soviet Trade by Industry Segment

Industry	Number	Magnitude of Average Soviet Business, $MM/Year	Average Desirability of Soviet Union as Customer[a]	Ease of Marketing in Soviet Union[b]
Chemicals	18	17	1.9	1.3
Machinery	17	11	2.1	0.8
Food	8	10	1.6	1.5
Drugs	10	3	1.1	1.0
Electronics/ instruments	16	4	1.0	0.8
Entire sample	106	9	1.5	1.1

[a]Based on 3 for Soviet Union in top quarter of foreign customers; 2 for top half; 1 for bottom half; 0 for bottom quarter.

[b]Based on 3 for less expensive to sell than average foreign customer; 2 for about the same; 1 for Soviet Union requires high initial costs, but not after initial sales; 0 for much greater selling costs.

SOURCE: *Columbia Journal of World Business* (Winter 1983): 44–50.

machinery were rated above average; drugs and electronics/instruments were lower than average. The average desirability of the U.S.S.R. as a customer appears to be related to the size of sales by that industry. A statistical analysis of the data indicates that the probability is greater than 95 percent that there is a correlation. Another significant factor is export controls. Of the industries listed here, export controls would have the most impact on the electronic/instrument companies, and probably accounts in part for the lower rating given by this group.

Incidentally, Table 6-5 gives a good overall picture of the types of manufactured goods that the Soviets have been buying from American companies. Agricultural sales have constituted the bulk of U.S. exports to the U.S.S.R., but the sale of manufactured goods is greater than generally realized since many of the products sold by American companies are manufactured in European plants and therefore are not U.S. exports.

Viewing the results of this study more broadly, two conclusions with broad implications can be drawn. The first is that, despite the many problems of doing business in the Soviet Union, firms that have engaged in trade with the Soviets are more anxious to increase trade with the U.S.S.R. than companies that have little or no experience with the Soviet Union. As previously mentioned, 87 percent of the companies with Soviet trade experience indicated they would like more Soviet business, and only 1 percent (i.e., 1 company) indicated no interest in additional business in the U.S.S.R. On the other hand, 13 companies that had no experience in Soviet trade also answered this question; of these, only 38 percent were interested in Soviet trade and 15 percent indicated they were not interested in such trade. This much lower level of interest in doing business with the Soviet Union among companies with no Soviet experience also is consistent with the findings of two Boston College researchers. In a 1983 study, Hisrich and Peters found that only 51 percent of about 100 companies that were not trading with the Soviet Union were interested in such trade.[4]

The other broad conclusion which can be drawn is that, even when two nations have a poor political relationship, there can be trade which is mutually beneficial economically, and can lead to better political relations. The ability of American companies to engage in trade with the Soviet Union at times when relations between the two countries were very strained is consistent with the findings of scholars who have studied cooperation between adversaries. In his book *The Evolution of Cooperation,* Robert Axelrod presents a convincing case that satisfactory cooperation can take place with an adversary—even an enemy—as long as the relationship is durable.[5] Past history, as well as social theory, leave little doubt that American companies need not delay economic initiatives with the Soviets until the many remaining political differences between the two countries are resolved.

The 35 plants that constituted the technology utilization study represent roughly half of the plants that were built since 1969 under licensing agreements with American companies.[6] As shown by the data in Table 6-6, the plants were located throughout the Soviet Union, and the distribution roughly parallels the Soviet population. The data in Table 6-7 show the products manufactured by these plants. The strong bias toward chemical-type plants probably is the result of U.S. technological strength in this nonstrategic area, plus the raw material resources the Soviets have for such plants. Two of the plants were joint ventures. The other 33 were technology sales—all of which were for cash. In about 40 percent of the technology sales there was a third party involved, usually an engineering firm that constructed the plant.

The data summarized in Table 6-8 show that about one-third of the plants were built using only imported equipment, and almost 80 percent

Table 6-6 Location of Plants in Study

Location	Percent of Sample
Russia	37
Siberia	11.5
Ukraine	20
Caucasus republics (Armenia, Azerbaijan, Georgia)	11.5
Central Asian republics	17
Other	3

SOURCE: *Les Nouvelles* (September 1990): 101–5.

Table 6-7 Products Produced in Plants Studied

Product	Percent of Sample
Chemicals, petrochemicals	51
Plastics	17
Machinery, instruments	11
Glass, metals	9
Consumer products (including food)	12

SOURCE: *Les Nouvelles* (September 1990): 101–5.

Table 6-8 Extent to Which Equipment Was Imported for Plant Construction

Amount of Imported Equipment	Percent of Sample
100 percent	32
90 to 100 percent	28
80 to 85 percent	19
About 70 percent	9
50 to 60 percent	9
Less than 50 percent	3

SOURCE: *Les Nouvelles* (September 1990): 101–5.

of the plants used at least 80 percent imported equipment. Only one of the plants in the survey—an assembly plant—was built with less than 50 percent imported equipment. The use of imported equipment for most of the plant is usually specified to ensure reliability.

Proper training of personnel as a means of transferring know-how always is of great importance in the sale of technology. The data in Table 6-9 show that while training most frequently has been done in the United States and the Soviet Union, European plants similar to the one being built

Table 6-9 Where Soviet Personnel Were Trained

Location	Percent of Sample
United States	53
Soviet Union	62
Another country	21

NOTE: The total exceeds 100 percent since some companies trained personnel in more than one country.

SOURCE: *Les Nouvelles* (September 1991): 101–5.

in the Soviet Union often have been used for training. An interesting finding of the study was that in a number of instances training was done at both a Western site and in the Soviet Union. One company that used this practice considered it essential to success. The desirability of training both in the Soviet Union, where all personnel can be trained, and at a Western plant, where selected people can get more intensive training, is illustrated by the experience of a company that completely relied on the training of selected Soviets in the United States, but found that this training was not transferred to the other Soviets in the plant.

The information obtained in the study is consistent with previous work, which had shown that plant construction times in the Soviet Union are much longer than in the West. The data in Table 6-10 show that in no case was a plant in the U.S.S.R. constructed more rapidly than would be expected in the United States or Europe, and that equivalent plant construction times occurred in only 6 percent of the survey sample. On average, construction times were almost twice as long. Yet this is slightly faster than Hanson's finding that in the 1960s and 1970s construction times were two to three times longer. Moreover, an analysis of the data summarized in Table 6-10 indicates that construction times may have been slightly shorter in the period 1978 to the present than in the period 1969 to 1978. Construction times since 1978 have averaged 80 percent longer, compared with 100 percent the previous decade, but this small difference may not be significant.

Start-up times in the Soviet Union are more consistent with experience elsewhere and average only 50 percent longer than in the United States and Europe. For 41 percent of the plants covered in the survey the start-up time in the Soviet Union was equivalent to U.S. and European experience. However, several of the Soviet plants had long delays in start-up. In two of these instances the delay resulted from the unavailability of raw materials.

An analysis was made as to whether project delays were related to the

Table 6-10 Times Required for Construction and Start-Up in the U.S.S.R. Compared with Times in the United States and Europe

Soviet Union Takes:	Construction	Start-Up
About the same as the U.S. and Europe	6%	41%
25 to 50 percent longer	36	25
75 to 100 percent longer	43	22
About three times longer	9	12
Over three times longer	6	0

SOURCE: *Les Nouvelles* (September 1990): 101–5.

location of the plant. Some people feel that because the Central Asian republics are less developed than the rest of the Soviet Union that plant construction there will take longer. The information obtained does not provide support for that hypothesis, but because the sample size is small, and most of the plants built in Central Asia were different from those built elsewhere, this study cannot rule out that plants in Central Asia may average slightly longer construction times. The study did indicate, as a result of both data and comments, that a plant in Siberia will take longer to construct and start up because of delays resulting from the cold weather.

The long times required to construct plants have resulted from two distinct causes. One is the efficiency of construction. The Soviets do not have the equipment to match construction rates in the West. However, the greatest delays result from organizational problems inherent in the Soviet system. Hewett points out that 26 different ministries and departments are involved in construction work in the western Siberian oil fields. One ministry builds the roads, another provides electric power, another is responsible for piping, and there is no one on the scene with authority to coordinate.[7]

The information summarized in Table 6-11 shows that the capacity and yields of the plants built in the Soviet Union with American technology closely parallel the performance of such plants in the West. Less than 10 percent of the plants had production levels or plant yields considerably lower than similar plants in the West. Moreover, the two plants that had low yields were two of the three plants with disappointing capacities, and both problems resulted from a high rate of rejects. Since both these plants are labor-intensive operations, the poor performance probably can be attributed to the fact that in the past the expectation for labor usually has been to produce a quota without regard to quality. In addition, Soviet plants traditionally have been overstaffed, and little attention has been paid to increasing productivity.

The most important finding of this study is summarized by the data on product quality given in Table 6-12. Although a lack of technology and know-how cause most products made in the Soviet Union to be of such poor quality that they cannot compete in global markets, three-quarters of

---

Table 6-11 Soviet Plant Capacity and Plant Yield Compared to the United States and Europe

	Plant Capacity	Plant Yield
Soviet Union Does:		
Slightly better (10 to 20 percent)	6%	3%
About the same	79	81
Slightly poorer (10 to 20 percent)	6	10
Considerably poorer	9	6

SOURCE: *Les Nouvelles* (September 1990): 101–5.

Table 6-12   Soviet Product Quality
Compared to the United States and Europe

	Percent of Sample
Soviet Quality Was Judged:	
Slightly better	12
About the same	64
Slightly poorer	9
Considerably poorer	15

SOURCE: *Les Nouvelles* (September 1990): 101–5.

the plants in the study group produced quality that was at least equal to the quality achieved in the West, and four of these plants produced quality that was better.

Given technology, know-how, and training, Soviet industry clearly can compete in many areas of manufacturing. But not in all: five of the plants give product of poor quality compared to what is being made elsewhere. These five plants all produced plastics. Discussions with two of the U.S. companies involved suggest that the quality problem results either from impurities in the raw materials or the inadequacy of a catalyst used in the process.

To increase our understanding of what it takes to make high quality products in the Soviet Union, I spoke with executives of three of the companies that reported higher quality than in the West. In one case the higher quality was obtained by installing more expensive purification facilities than would be specified for a plant in the United States. Investment in the plant was increased to ensure that the product from the plant could be sold outside the Soviet Union, since product was being used as payment for the plant. The other two companies indicated that the superior quality resulted from having access to a "better" raw material source than is usually available to their plants elsewhere.

Thus the actual performance of Soviet plants that use U.S. technology and know-how is probably better than is generally believed in the Western business community. However, our study also indicates that the problems associated with these projects confirm the perception in the business community that doing business in the U.S.S.R. is difficult.

The problem mentioned most often was how difficult the project had been for the people involved, particularly the technical people who participated in a plant start-up. Most first-time business travelers to the Soviet Union voice complaints about the accommodations and food in Moscow, but Moscow is paradise compared with the industrial cities where most plants are located.

But forlorn living conditions have been only one of the many problems that people have had to face when working in the Soviet Union. Getting the job done required tremendous patience. To the usual problems encountered in the construction and start-up of a plant were added such additional burdens as: difficult communications with the Soviets; delayed decisions due to bureaucratic red tape; and complicated communications with the home office because of the inadequate telephone system.

The director of licensing of a large corporation put these problems into perspective when he wrote: "These projects . . . were good from a commercial standpoint once the tedious negotiations were done, but they were a difficult experience for the technical personnel. Depending on the location, working on-site in the Soviet Union can be tough. It takes a special kind of person to handle the isolation and the primitive conditions."

What characteristics make for "a special kind of person"? One man, who was bothered by frequently being without transportation, bought himself a bicycle. Another, who missed not being able to buy catsup, had the problem solved by his wife, who was with him for the plant start-up: she made catsup from tomatoes, corn syrup, vinegar, and spices. Another man had most potential problems solved before he got to the U.S.S.R. Because he was the mayor of his small Illinois town, the mayor of the Soviet town in which the plant was located accorded him special treatment—even though he was only a technician and was the lowest ranked member of the start-up team from the United States.

Some respondents were not as positive as the director of licensing quoted earlier. One wrote, "Because of the cultural shock, there were no volunteers for doing the same thing again . . . if it ever came up . . . which it did not." While the situation today is better than when these plants were put into operation, the selection and motivation of personnel to work in the Soviet Union will continue for some time to challenge companies doing business there.

Another type of problem widely reported was the inadequacy of the entire supply infrastructure. Experience with spare parts has been particularly bad. Spare parts almost always had to be supplied from outside the Soviet Union and, in addition, precautions had to be taken to ensure that spare parts were not used for other purposes. The experience of many of these companies was that nothing could be taken for granted. Machinery and tools regarded as generally available often were not.

The performance of the labor force also was a problem for some of the plants. Workers are well educated and, if properly motivated, will work hard to please, but the Soviet system has not socialized them to be effective in their jobs. The study indicates that in order to take advantage of the potential for an effective, low cost work force, foreign firms will need to use management techniques and training to make workers conscious of the need for high quality and high productivity.

Past experience clearly indicates that to operate successfully in the Soviet Union foreign firms must exercise patience. That is not likely to change soon.

CHAPTER 7

Joint Ventures: A Practitioner's View

Roman Pipko

In the summer of 1980, a popular Soviet joke quipped that communism in the Soviet Union had been temporarily suspended in favor of the summer Olympic games. At the end of that summer, as one of a few Soviet citizens allowed to emigrate to the West, I stood at the railway station in the city of Brest, on the Soviet border, waving goodbye to the country of my birth, to my father, and to my friends. Going through a demeaning customs search and rows of soldiers with bayonets on their guns, I abandoned any hope of ever seeing my home again. With a crisis in Poland and a war in Afghanistan, there seemed to be little doubt that the "temporary suspension" of communism in the Soviet Union would bring about continued political repression, economic decline, and military adventurism. I was sure that I would not have either the opportunity or the desire ever to set foot on this land.

Although I never saw my father again, after seven years I did come back to Moscow to discover a country transformed. The policies of *glasnost* jolted the nation from submissiveness and fear. They also exposed the horrors and misery of Soviet life and created an atmosphere of hopelessness and ambivalence toward the changes taking place in the country; these feelings were rivaled only by a previously unknown entrepreneurial fever permeating all layers of Soviet society. As a result, and because of my background and training, I became a frequent visitor to the U.S.S.R., now as an American citizen and American lawyer representing companies drawn to the Soviet market by the same forces that permitted my own return.

Amid signs of the colossal failure of the Soviet economy trumpeted daily in newspapers and television programs—now relieved from the constraints of censorship—the Soviet government has once again turned to the West for economic assistance.[1] On January 13, 1987, a Soviet version of the "open door policy" was promulgated in the form of new regulations permitting formation in the Soviet Union of joint venture companies with foreign capital participation. This consisted of three new laws which remain the foundation for joint venture activity in the U.S.S.R. These laws, commonly referred to as the Soviet Joint Venture Law, created a framework for the establishment of joint ventures with socialist and capitalist countries. The key elements of the 1987 measures, as they apply to relations with capitalist countries, were as follows:

1. The Soviet partner must hold at least a 51 percent share in the authorized capital of the joint venture (Article 5).　Many Western business managers viewed this provision of the law with apprehension, fearful of surrendering control over their investment in the joint venture to the Soviet side, and cited this provision as a major obstacle to investing in the Soviet Union. From the very outset these fears were not well founded, because—unlike in Western countries—under the Joint Venture Law majority ownership did not automatically translate into control over the joint venture's management. At any rate, this requirement has been lifted and now foreign investors may theoretically hold as much as a 99 percent equity stake of a joint venture. In reality, few joint ventures have crossed the 50 percent threshold, although it gradually becomes more acceptable for Soviet authorities to approve joint ventures with foreigners holding a 50 percent or greater equity interest. In this respect, I remember a long discussion with a senior Intourist official regarding a hotel joint venture. I insisted on a 50 percent interest for my client, and although at that time the law permitted such joint ventures, Intourist wanted to preserve its majority position. At the end of our conversation, this official admitted that he feared that had he conceded, and that if political circumstances in the country were to change he might be asked to "surrender [his] party card because [he] had sold out to capitalists."

2. The chairman of the board and the director general of the joint venture must be citizens of the Soviet Union (Article 21).　This provision had also discouraged some potential investors from venturing into the Soviet market out of concern that control over day-to-day activities of the joint venture would be in Soviet hands. Despite initial reservations, this limitation has not been a serious constraint on foreign investment, because the Soviets eagerly turned management responsibilities over to foreigners, while few Westerners could lead an enterprise inside the Soviet Union without the participation of Soviet officers. In addition, the Soviets accepted from the outset the principal of unanimity for all major management decisions. This principle has now been incorporated into the Joint

Venture Law. Its terms were also revised to allow the chairman of the board or the director general of a joint venture to be a foreigner.

3. All foreign currency expenditures of the joint venture must be covered by proceeds from sales of the joint venture's products in foreign markets (Article 25).   Many Western business executives perceive this as a critical stumbling block to joint venture opportunities in the Soviet Union. American commentators often assert that this clause defines the conflicting objectives of the parties—the Soviets' interest in enhancing export potential as opposed to Western desire to penetrate the Soviet market. In my experience, in order to relieve chronic shortages Soviets usually agree to earn a major portion of their share of profits in rubles from sales in the internal market. McDonald's is the prime example of such a joint venture. Foreign investors, on the other hand, usually expect joint ventures to generate at least sufficient hard-currency earnings to compensate for their investment in the Soviet Union. Some foreign investors, counting on the early convertibility of the ruble, have invested in joint ventures aimed primarily at domestic consumption. Their gamble may ultimately pay off, especially since the introduction of hard-currency auctions where joint ventures may exchange their ruble profits for hard currency.

4. All sales of products in the Soviet market and all supplies to the joint venture from this market must be paid for in rubles and effected through the relevant Soviet foreign trade organization (Article 26).   Initially, this provision of the law limited joint ventures to ruble sales in the Soviet Union, thereby ensuring that any hard-currency profits to be repatriated had to be earned abroad. Its flip side—that all purchases in the Soviet market had to be effected in rubles—committed Soviet enterprises to selling Soviet goods and services to joint ventures for rubles. Several companies tried to take advantage of this provision. For example, Rank Xerox contemplated an equipment manufacturing joint venture in the Soviet Union that would finance its activities by purchasing paper in the Soviet market for rubles and then exporting it to hard-currency markets. The Joint Venture Law, however, was changed before many similar arrangements were consummated. It now permits purchases and sales in the Soviet market by joint ventures in convertible currency or in rubles, thereby theoretically (and in practice for some joint ventures, like one established by Combustion Engineering) enabling joint ventures to sell their products for hard currency to Soviet enterprises, while at the same time purchasing goods and services on the Soviet market for rubles. It also authorizes Soviet enterprises to charge convertible currency for their sales to joint ventures. The Joint Venture Law was also revised to allow transactions between joint ventures and Soviet enterprises to be carried out without the participation of Soviet foreign trade organizations. This change was a logical step in an effort to decentralize the domestic economy, and it simplified relations between joint ventures and Soviet entities.

5. Tax provisions of the Joint Venture Law provide for a 30 percent income tax (Article 36) and a 20 percent tax on transfer of hard-currency profits abroad (Article 41).   The amount of these taxes under the law could be lowered by the Ministry of Finance upon application by the joint venture. The law also provided initially that joint ventures could enjoy a tax holiday for the first two years of their activities. This provision has since been relaxed and now provides for tax holidays during the first two years of *profitable* operations of joint ventures with foreign participants' interest of over 30 percent, except for ventures operating in certain areas of the Soviet Union, which enjoy more favorable tax treatment. In addition, Soviet tax legislation reduced from 20 to 15 percent taxes on profits distributed to joint ventures' participants, unless otherwise agreed in relevant international treaties.

6. All joint ventures must be approved by the Council of Ministers of the U.S.S.R. (Article 1).   In order to expedite and simplify the approval processes, U.S.S.R. ministries, the councils of ministers of Union republics, and local government bodies have been authorized to approve joint ventures.[2]

By and large, changes in the Soviet Joint Venture Law thus far have been in favor of foreign investors, and many concerns expressed by them regarding the shortcomings of the original text have been addressed by Soviet legislators.

Joint ventures, or joint enterprises as they are called in Russian, have become catchwords in the Soviet as well as foreign business communities for improved bilateral trade relations. In the minds of Western entrepreneurs, these two words signify access to a market of almost 300 million people longing for Western lifestyles and consumer goods. Many Soviets see joint ventures as a panacea for pervasive shortages, which would magically flood the country with Hilton hotels, Sony Walkmans, and Fiat cars.

The new regulations were received with optimism and excitement by the West, but initially prompted little practical activity. After two years, fewer than 200 joint ventures had been registered and very few were operational. However, particularly as a result of the 1989 changes in the Joint Venture Law allowing majority ownership of joint ventures by foreign investors, the gradual introduction of market reforms in the Soviet Union, and support extended by industrialized nations to the Soviet government, the number of joint ventures surged to almost 3000 by the end of 1990.[3] Previously shunned by foreign investors, Moscow was suddenly transformed into a mecca of enterprising entrepreneurs in search of profitable joint venture opportunities.

Until very recently, the concept of joint ventures with foreign entities was hardly known in the Soviet Union, and then only to a few Soviet foreign trade officials; it was thoroughly alien to the vast majority of government bureaucrats and directors of state enterprises.[4] Yet, within a short period of time, joint ventures with foreign companies have become the aspiration and a measure of success for Soviet managers. The explanation for the sudden elevation of joint ventures to such prominence in the Soviet economy and foreign trade may be found in almost forgotten legislation that predated the January 1987 decrees on joint ventures, but which in many ways foreshadowed their adoption, as well as many other reforms taking place in the Soviet Union.

Until 1987, almost the entire foreign trade of the Soviet Union was conducted by or through the Ministry of Foreign Trade, which served as an agent for all Soviet enterprises in their dealings with foreign companies. In August 1986, the Central Committee of the Communist party of the Soviet Union and the U.S.S.R. Council of Ministers adopted a joint resolution, "Measures to Improve the Management of Foreign Economic Relations." The joint sponsorship of this resolution was intended to indicate the importance attached to this law, as well as the unity of the Soviet government and the Communist party—in 1986 still the guiding force of Soviet society under the constitution—on certain provisions which at that time provoked tremendous controversy.

The new resolution allowed for the first time a few Soviet industrial ministries and enterprises to independently communicate and enter into business transactions with foreign companies. Although a timid step in terms of its reach (only 20 ministries and 70 enterprises were granted the right to bypass the Ministry of Foreign Trade and conclude direct trade agreements with their foreign counterparts), its significance lay in the demise of a myth taught to every Soviet schoolchild—the superiority and efficiency of a central planning system. Overnight, this resolution abolished one of the pillars of the Soviet state and its relationship with the outside world: the government's monopoly on foreign trade.

The statute was motivated not only by the desire to gradually phase out one entity's monopoly over the entire country's foreign trade but also to shake up the inherently corrupt and inefficient Ministry of Foreign Trade. To accomplish this task quickly, instead of gradually replacing the personnel of the Ministry of Foreign Trade with new appointees, as President Mikhail Gorbachev's government had done with many other ministries, a new umbrella entity—the State Foreign Economic Commission—was created, and in many respects took over the responsibilities of the Ministry of Foreign Trade. The latter was renamed the Ministry of Foreign Economic Relations, its authority was significantly diminished, and its personnel decimated by dismissal, prosecution, and incarceration.

Many observers correctly saw these changes as a first step toward complete decentralization of Soviet foreign trade, when all Soviet enterprises would be permitted to enter independently into trade agreements with foreign entities, and possibly the entire economy would have to be revamped. At the same time, senior Soviet government officials realized that years would pass before managers of Soviet enterprises, who had never been abroad, and in many cases had never seen a foreigner, would be able to negotiate and perform trade agreements without the oversight of the now incapacitated Ministry of Foreign Economic Relations. While more Soviet enterprises were gradually receiving permission to conclude trade agreements directly with foreign companies, few of them could take advantage of this opportunity because of inexperience, lack of access to foreign markets, and the pervasive controls of government agencies. Sensitive to these concerns, astute foreign entrepreneurs recognized that joint ventures would soon become a principal acceptable form of doing business in the Soviet Union. In anticipation of the new law, which would expressly authorize the establishment of such entities, adventurous Western companies—including Archer Daniels Midland, Combustion Engineering, and Pepsico—dispatched representatives to Moscow to start joint venture negotiations.

Joint venture legislation outlining precise terms on which Soviet enterprises could enter into cooperation agreements with foreign companies and entrusting control over supervision and implementation of these agreements to central ministries appeared, at that time, to be an ideal solution for addressing Soviet needs as well as wishes of foreign companies. Such legislation provided a relatively quick vehicle by which Soviet enterprises could acquire modern Western technology and management expertise without large convertible currency outlays. It invited foreign investors into the Soviet economy, gave leeway for cooperation with them to individual Soviet enterprises, and yet kept their activities within Soviet borders under the authority of government agencies. The adoption of the Joint Venture Law was designed to achieve these purposes.

Unlike the 1986 decree authorizing only a few entities to pursue all forms of cross-border trade, the Joint Venture Law permitted *all* Soviet enterprises to enter into joint venture agreements with foreign companies, albeit only on the terms contained in the law and only following approval by various government bodies. Despite these limitations, in 1987 joint ventures were catapulted into prominence as the only legally available outlet for the multitude of Soviet enterprises and organizations to enter into business relationships with foreign companies and to gain access to foreign markets. Many foreign companies, in turn, could now enter into commercial arrangements with any Soviet entity without conducting duplicative negotiations with the Ministry of Foreign Economic Relations and without ascertaining whether the entity was authorized to conduct independent foreign trade activities.

In this early period, I was commonly asked whether I was sufficiently familiar with Soviet joint venture laws to draw up the necessary agreements. It was assumed that joint ventures were the only game in town and the surest way to gain a foothold in the new market. Likewise, during my trips to the Soviet Union, I would receive up to 10 business proposals daily, all of them joint ventures. These offers were extended in an informal atmosphere by almost every Russian who learned that I was an American working in the field, and they covered a range of industries from medical equipment and hotel construction to food processing and computer software. In a country where contact with foreigners had often been considered a crime, joint ventures quickly became the only sanctioned way beyond government sponsored activities to forge economic ties with the West.

For a few years, joint ventures continued to be the only type of business arrangement between Soviet enterprises and foreign companies having the Soviet government's stamp of approval. As long as the heading "joint venture" was present on the document, Soviet enterprises were willing and also legally authorized to negotiate any form of economic cooperation without the interference by the Ministry of Foreign Economic Relations and in full compliance with Soviet laws. Because the parties often did not need a true joint venture—a new, separate company formed by the partners—to accomplish their business purposes, by the time many joint venture agreements were signed, they resembled traditional coproduction agreements, marketing contracts, or barter arrangements.

Unlike these other types of agreements, however, Soviet managers quickly recognized that joint ventures provided benefits usually unattainable through other structures. As a general rule, the joint venture format does not require Soviet entities to incur any convertible currency outlays. Quite the opposite, since the foreign investor has to make a contribution to the capital of the joint venture, it usually gets an immediate infusion of convertible currency without comparable expenditures by the Soviet partner. Even though the Soviet entity also makes a contribution to the joint venture fund, it consists either of rubles or has no market value and is priced at an inflated official exchange rate, resulting in a windfall to the Soviets. This is why, even when a transaction other than a joint venture is legally permissible, Soviets usually insist on a joint venture format. Although foreign investors often have no choice but to accede to these demands, they try to keep their contributions to a minimum—the majority of joint ventures are capitalized at below $1 million, and foreign contributions often consist of equipment transfers rather than cash.[5]

Although framing a transaction as a joint venture was indispensable to get the agreement approved, Soviet officials felt more comfortable with simpler and more traditional trade agreements. Foreign investors also could have frequently achieved their business purpose through more straightforward arrangements, but often had to veil their activities in the guise of a joint venture because of constraints imposed by Soviet law.

Gradually, the list of Soviet enterprises with direct access to foreign markets expanded, and beginning in April 1989 all Soviet organizations were allowed to enter into commercial contracts of any type with foreign entities. New legislation permitting foreign companies to establish wholly owned entities in the Soviet Union and to acquire equity interests in Soviet "joint stock companies" further broadens the choices of potential investors. With the adjustment of the ruble exchange rate to more realistic levels and continued introduction of market reforms, the advantages of the joint venture format, and the comfort of having the project approved by the government, may also lose their appeal.

Foreign executives planning commercial transactions in the Soviet Union should not be influenced by the headlines of earlier joint venture projects. Instead, they should carefully evaluate the optimum structure from a business standpoint. A company's success in the Soviet Union will depend less on the express provisions of the law than on the company's skill and imagination dealing with Soviet bureaucracy, adapting to the fast-changing environment, and identifying profitable business opportunities in the volatile Soviet market.

In any country joint ventures have common advantages over other forms of commercial transactions. As a general rule, joint ventures provide:

- Greater control over production, management, and quality
- An opportunity to obtain otherwise unavailable technology or natural resources
- Greater access to potential markets
- More firmly established long-term relationships with local authorities and enterprises
- Availability of less expensive and qualified labor.

Thus far, the most successful joint ventures in the Soviet Union have been those least dependent on the Soviet consumer market. Most of these joint ventures belong to one of two groups. The first group includes joint ventures offering their services primarily for convertible currency, mostly to foreign diplomats, businessmen, tourists, and, significantly, other joint ventures. They account for the large number of joint ventures in the service sector, such as restaurants, communications, business centers, consulting, hotels, and so on. These joint ventures are relatively insulated from Soviet consumers as well as Soviet producers, importing most of their supplies from abroad. The second group includes joint ventures aimed at the exploration or processing of Soviet natural resources where the products of the joint venture are sold outside of the Soviet Union for convertible currency. The number of projects in these sectors will likely continue to grow as opportunities for foreign investment expand.

Problems encountered by Western investors in the process of operating joint ventures in other fields stem largely from fundamental tensions in the

Soviet economy reflected in the Joint Venture Law and not cured by subsequent revisions or new legislation. The laudable goal of the Joint Venture Law—to facilitate foreign trade through independent activities of individual Soviet enterprises—is crippled as long as joint ventures have to operate within the confines of a centrally controlled, planned economy. Although under the law joint ventures became exempt from Soviet central planning, they are expected to operate in a system in which the distribution of resources and the supply of raw materials, energy, and labor are coordinated by and dependent on centralized planning. The situation is further exacerbated by the disintegration of the state-controlled economy without an evolution of adequate market substitutes; joint ventures are left in a vacuum, unable to rely on either central planning or fledgling market mechanisms. As a result, the joint venture initiative cannot produce the results anticipated without corresponding reforms in the domestic economy, which lag behind the new demands of foreign investment.

With one master stroke—elimination of the Ministry of Foreign Trade's monopoly—Gorbachev removed the most significant obstacle to the healthy development of the nation's foreign trade. It is taking much longer and proving to be much more difficult and controversial to remove the brakes on the domestic economy, arrested by a multitude of ministries, entrenched bureaucrats, and ingrained dogmas of socialism.

Since 1987, a major task of the Soviet government has been to bridge the gap between the pace of domestic economic and foreign trade reforms primarily by pushing for more liberalized domestic structure, but also by cutting back on decentralization of foreign trade. The dichotomy between the structure of the domestic economy and foreign trade remains the single most formidable obstacle to the success of joint ventures in the Soviet Union; inconvertibility of the ruble is the most apparent manifestation of this dichotomy. But while this dichotomy continues, it nevertheless presents foreign investors with opportunities that otherwise would not have been available.

One of the key advantages of the joint venture structure in the Soviet Union is not commonly available in other countries. This advantage is embodied in the legal status of joint ventures, which in the Soviet Union acquire a dual legal personality.

On the one hand, joint ventures become Soviet legal entities, just like any other Soviet enterprise. On the other hand, because of the participation of foreigners, joint ventures enjoy certain privileges that are denied to other Soviet enterprises and are unavailable to foreign entities. The possibility to utilize the joint venture format as a vehicle to attain results not obtainable through other structures is a major factor in comparing the joint venture with other forms of commercial transactions.

As the Soviet government introduces new legislation to bring the domestic economy in line with foreign trade regulations, some of the initial advantages of joint ventures are gradually diminishing while new benefits are emerging. In the beginning, joint ventures offered an opportunity to defeat government restrictions against individual enterprises entering into foreign trade transactions without the supervision of the Ministry of Foreign Economic Relations. The first transaction I negotiated in the Soviet Union was a typical example of such an approach. It involved an American company that planned to invite Soviet actors to perform in the United States. At that time all direct agreements with Soviet actors were still controlled by Goskoncert, a Soviet intermediary organization with a monopoly on representing Soviet performers abroad. Consequently, in order not to deal with a government monopoly, we had to form a joint venture company in the Soviet Union, which as a joint venture—a Soviet entity— was authorized to hire Soviet actors. Instead of having a direct agreement with the American company, the Soviet actors were retained by the joint venture, which in turn had an agreement with the American impresario for their performances in the United States. It took four months to negotiate and register this joint venture agreement with the Ministry of Finance. Such joint ventures were common in almost every field during the early days of Soviet reform and resulted in the creation of many nonproductive enterprises. Their use became obsolete in April 1989, when all Soviet entities were allowed to trade directly with the West, but these joint ventures created a pattern which is still followed in many transactions.

The joint venture structure, however, continues to serve a useful purpose in many areas. Joint ventures are allowed to enter into contractual relationships inside the Soviet Union on the terms agreed upon between the joint venture and the Soviet entity. Contracting parties are free to choose the currency for discharging their contractual obligations—either rubles or any convertible currency. Unlike any foreign company, joint ventures can purchase products in the Soviet Union for rubles, which is a privilege otherwise accorded only to Soviet enterprises, and then sell those products on foreign markets for convertible currency. Soviet enterprises may be willing to sell their products for rubles (or for a partial hard-currency payment), especially with a markup. Despite the constantly growing acceptability of foreign currency in the Soviet Union, the ruble remains legal tender throughout the country (except, at times, in Moscow taxis), and, therefore, can be utilized by these Soviet entities for purchases on the Soviet market. Soviet entities are prohibited from engaging in so-called intermediary operations, which involve purchases of goods for further resale. Joint ventures, on the other hand, under certain circumstances, may receive permits to engage in such transactions. This is a simple example of how a joint venture format could be used to a foreign investor's advantage.

Joint ventures performing functions solely as an intermediary have become a rarity. With the ruble's purchasing power falling precipitously, barter is gaining popularity not only in foreign trade, but also domestically. Instead of selling products for rubles, Soviet enterprises often exchange them for other goods in high demand directly with their manufacturers.[6]

In addition, as the Soviet population has become increasingly opposed to exports of raw materials or other products in short supply, stricter legislation has been passed prohibiting most exports without an appropriate license.

In contrast, many Soviet enterprises often agree to proposals for export of their products in exchange for a transfer of technology, know-how, and management skills. Joint ventures may be formed to engage in manufacturing activities, in addition to intermediary operations, when exports of the joint venture's products or raw materials are used to recoup the foreign partner's investment in the Soviet Union. Some foreign companies have formed manufacturing joint ventures primarily to obtain certain materials which could later be utilized (in effect resold) in their production facilities abroad.

Real estate is another area in which joint ventures have become a useful approach. Severe shortages of facilities meeting international standards in the Soviet Union have led many Western firms to negotiate hotel, office, and other real estate–related projects which would primarily cater to the Soviet Union's expatriate community. No Western company can yet buy a piece of land or a building in the Soviet Union. Soviet entities, joint ventures in particular, have much broader opportunities to acquire land or buildings in the Soviet Union and to put them to the desired use. In fact, many Soviet entities having no apparent connection with the real estate industry may become the best partners in such joint ventures. Artistic organizations, research institutes, and even museums frequently control centrally located plots of land which they are ready to contribute for joint venture use. For them the arrangement provides the surest way to earn convertible currency from the profits of a completed project. Several foreign companies now participate in such ventures. This may remain a fertile ground for new joint ventures, at least until real estate in the Soviet Union can be bought or leased by foreigners.

Until the establishment of viable capital markets, joint ventures also represent a unique instrument for the acquisition of productive Soviet assets. The Soviet Union has a strong industrial base which has been wasted by mismanagement, an underpaid work force, and misuse of assets. The efficiency of many Soviet industrial enterprises could be significantly increased by modest infusions of capital, Western-style management, and incentive programs for employees. While neither stock nor asset acquisitions, as they are known in the West, are yet possible in the Soviet Union, joint ventures are the only mechanism for "taking over" Soviet enterprises and converting them to more efficient operations. Western industrialists will surely discover "jewels" in the Soviet economy which could become centerpieces of profitable joint venture projects. Such joint ventures may be taken public if and when the Soviet Union develops a modern capital market. Moreover, few foreign investors would be willing to invest in Soviet enterprises without meaningful control over their management, marketing, production quality, and other functions. Hence, the joint venture structure, probably in a somewhat modified form, will survive even after Soviet privatization takes hold.

For many companies benefits accorded by joint ventures are insufficient to offset the shortcomings and costs of organizing a new enterprise in the Soviet Union. Difficulties often cited by foreign investors include opening an office in the Soviet Union, relocating personnel, getting through prolonged approval procedures, negotiating for long periods, and preparing complex documentation—all of which consume more time and resources than many companies can afford to commit.

Imaginative investors have started to pursue new opportunities by structuring joint ventures with Soviet companies outside the Soviet Union. As a rule, these transactions involve a marketing component that may be a final stage of a more complicated arrangement that includes technology transfer, licensing, or a turnkey project. A simple structure involves a foreign-based joint venture which receives products directly from the Soviet Union and then markets them for hard currency, splitting the profits between the Soviet and foreign participants. Before the marketing stage, however, offshore joint ventures may supply factories in the Soviet Union with technology or licenses to manufacture the product that would eventually be marketed in the West. Proceeds from the sale of products manufactured in the Soviet Union and sold in the West may subsequently be used to repay credits advanced to such joint ventures to purchase Western technology or licenses.

Over time, many investors have become discouraged by the hurdles of establishing and operating a joint venture in the U.S.S.R. Many Soviet managers, especially in the nongovernment sector, have also realized that despite many benefits they could derive from a joint venture, its establishment is too cumbersome and time-consuming and places them at the mercy of the state bureaucracy. Therefore, many proposals from Soviet enterprises now expressly request an agreement *other* than a joint venture, because it can be concluded quicker and with less interference and oversight by the government. Like joint venture agreements, these transactions may provide Soviet entities with the intangible benefits—such as foreign trips, access to hard-currency payments, and so on—which are so critical to motivate Soviet entrepreneurs.

The Soviet Union has a history of concluding non–joint venture agreements with Western companies long before joint venture legislation was passed. In the past, successful business agreements were reached by such companies as Pepsico, Occidental Petroleum, International Harvester, and Dresser Industries without creating a joint venture. All those agreements, however, were negotiated by or with the assistance of the Ministry of Foreign Trade, rather than individual enterprises. With the sudden relaxation of the Soviet foreign trade rules, uncontrolled Soviet plants and factories, giddy from the newly acquired freedom but with little or no practical experience, were left at the mercy of foreign entrepreneurs and domestic speculators ready to capitalize on the opportunities of the new regime. In their eagerness to acquire foreign currency, several Soviet enterprises sold oil, coal, lumber, and other natural resources to the West at well below market prices, while others contracted to buy Western goods without the hard-currency reserves to cover their purchases. This buying and selling spree turned the country into a chaotic bazaar. In response, the Ministry of Foreign Economic Relations was again asked to regulate Soviet foreign trade indirectly by licensing Soviet entities wishing to participate in foreign trade transactions and approving specific exports of raw materials and other commodities.

The lack of convertible currency and the Ministry of Foreign Economic Relations' new "police" powers significantly curtail the freedom of Soviet enterprises. Nevertheless, a foreign company entering the Soviet market will find many Soviet companies willing and able to consider agreements other than joint ventures. Indeed, if a business objective can be achieved without a joint venture, it is only logical to pursue such a contract first. Later, if necessary and if the Soviet partner proves to be desirable, this relationship can be upgraded to a joint venture. Many types of transactions overshadowed by joint ventures, including barter, licensing, cooperation agreements, and concessions, may now be brought to prominence again. A well-structured package of such agreements may permit companies to achieve about the same goals as a joint venture, while avoiding many of the associated hurdles.

Following the adoption of the Soviet Joint Venture Law, foreign investors who wanted to establish a foothold in the Soviet market had little choice but to enter into a joint venture agreement. Now, having determined that the Soviet market is too important to be neglected, a Western company has a number of alternatives to pursue, including joint ventures. If the business objective can be achieved without a joint venture, it is up to foreign executives and their counsel to structure such transactions and propose them to the Soviets. On the other hand, a creative investor should not overlook promising joint venture opportunities when other arrangements fall short of the desired result.

The Joint Venture Law authorized partial ownership of Soviet enterprises by "capitalist" firms on Soviet territory and employing Soviet workers. After 70 years of socialism this was a hard pill to swallow for Soviet citizens, including many reform-minded economists.

I overheard the most accurate expression of popular sentiments about the introduction of market reforms in the Soviet Union in a conversation between two older women at a newspaper stand in the center of Moscow. One of the women was recounting a statement made on television by Nicolai Ryzhkov, then the Soviet prime minister, that the biggest mistakes the government had made during the years of *perestroika* were the antialcohol campaign and the introduction of cooperatives (a new type of Soviet private enterprise). The other woman quickly shot back, "We would have to wait another 70 years before they'd admit that their biggest mistake was in 1917." This dialogue exemplifies today's tensions in Soviet society between resentment over the lack of consumer goods, rising prices, and a newly emerging class of private entrepreneurs, on the one hand, and a recognition of the total failure of socialist economy over the last 70 years, on the other. Just like cooperatives, many joint ventures catering to the foreign community or privileged Soviet elite breed resentment and humiliation in the Soviet population, which is still denied access to most of those establishments. Others, like McDonald's, Pizza Hut, and Baskin-Robbins, which sell their products for rubles, leave hope that some benefits and, ultimately, higher living standards, may trickle down to ordinary Russians despite the high prices and long lines.

The attitudes of ordinary Soviets are an important consideration, not only because they define the atmosphere in which joint ventures have to operate, but also because they often bear directly on the feasibility of the joint venture itself.

A Soviet newspaper publicized a story describing a potentially significant joint venture which ostensibly failed because the plant workers were accustomed to a leisurely work pace and hours and refused to work in a more rigorous, profit-driven, capitalist enterprise.[7] As real as this concern may be for many joint venture partners who rely on the Soviet work force, it has been successfully addressed by incentive pay, a better work environment, and other "sweeteners." It appears that the true reason for this joint venture's failure was the employees' fear that if the joint venture cured shortages of products manufactured at the plant, the employees would no longer be able to privately exchange these products for other goods in short supply. This example illustrates that foreign investors negotiating joint venture agreements in the U.S.S.R. must always consider the impact of the project on the people involved, and must develop ways to foster the favorable attitudes of those affected.

By the same token, Soviet officials frequently have hidden motives that may bear on their negotiating position. I remember a meeting with Ivan Ivanov, a deputy chairman of the Foreign Economic Commission and one of the most enlightened and well-disposed senior Soviet officials. Notwithstanding his responsibility for attracting foreign investment into the U.S.S.R., at this meeting he discouraged us from making investments in the Soviet Union because, according to him, the country was not prepared to absorb them. After the meeting I realized that he was not only a genuine well-wisher, but was also trying to push through a more radical foreign trade law and needed examples of dissatisfied foreign investors for internal political reasons. In fact, after we went ahead with the joint venture, he helped us obtain approval for it. At the other end of the spectrum, many Soviet officials appear overly anxious to sign on to any joint venture deal.

In many instances their eagerness is owed not to business considerations but to a desire to convert their considerable political influence into lucrative employment as managers of joint venture companies. Similarly, a transfer of government property to joint ventures is seen by some officials as a more stable and legitimate way to ensure continued control of these assets.

Many of the Soviet officials, including those with whom foreign investors have to negotiate commercial agreements, are ill-informed about Western culture, business practices, and economy. Despite the expanding travel and business opportunities, even the better educated economists and lawyers have confused notions of the market economy and the role of joint ventures in the Soviet economy. Many senior officials, sometimes those in charge of joint venture approvals, believe that joint ventures amount to Russia's selling out its resources to the West. In fact, in the wake of rising Russian nationalism "selling out" has become a popular slogan. During elections to the Leningrad City Council, for example, almost every candidate started his speech with an attack on the then-planned hotel and entertainment park joint venture in Lisiy Nos (a swampy area 20 kilometers from the city center), because it would be tantamount to the exploitation of Russian land by capitalists. Although this project was ill-conceived from the outset, popular opposition was one of the reasons it never took off.

The emergence of new, more progressive Soviet leaders who work in support of projects with foreigners does not always guarantee smooth negotiations. Many foreign investors still view the U.S.S.R. as a country in which any agreement should be negotiated at a political level to ensure its performance. The current fragmentation of the country into several, often adversarial, administrative and ethnic units; the decentralization of the economy; and the establishment of many private enterprises are creating new complexities for those who deal with the Soviet Union. While in the past an agreement at the top would usually set in motion all entities necessary for its completion, today any agreement requires an approval of every territory and every organization that has any relationship with the transaction. Moreover, if such a transaction cuts across the jurisdictional authority of different administrative units or several ministries, it may require protracted negotiations with all of them, each reluctant to yield ground to the other. Several joint venture projects were derailed because of the inability of different ministries or republics to come to terms over their implementation. Consequently, it is prudent, when possible, to confine activities of the joint venture to a single region and to avoid reliance on competing government entities, which may ultimately undermine an otherwise sound project.

Finally, the recent proliferation of cooperatives and other non-state-owned enterprises means that foreign investors must carefully ascertain the legal authority, background, and reliability of their partners in the Soviet

Union. Many foreign investors were drawn into business relationships with privately controlled Soviet enterprises, which are often more dynamic, flexible, and understanding of the foreign investors' needs. Yet, since many such enterprises have not crossed the threshold of acceptability and legitimacy in the Soviet Union, several of these agreements did not live up to the foreign investors' expectations. A senior Soviet official recently asserted that no cooperative in the U.S.S.R. was established in full compliance with Soviet laws. Although this statement should be taken with a grain of salt, it would be prudent before making any legal commitments to ascertain the capabilities and legitimacy of such companies. That said, it should be recognized that private enterprises are becoming more resourceful and skillful, and they may offer business opportunities that are unavailable in the government sector. Depending upon the character of the Soviet entity, the structure of any transaction should reflect the different constraints and advantages that would result from a relationship with such an enterprise.

After accounting for these divergent factors it seems that certain common negotiating strategies may be helpful in facilitating any type of a transaction with any entity in the U.S.S.R.

A common assumption, often repeated at various conferences on doing business in the Soviet Union, is that Russians are tough negotiators. I have found that this belief not only leads to the formation of stereotypes, but is also misleading. Although negotiations in the Soviet Union may often be more difficult and tedious than in some other places, problems result more from linguistic and cultural differences than from Russian "toughness." As reported in a Soviet newspaper, a majority of foreign investors suspended their negotiations in the Soviet Union because "the partners speak different economic languages."[8] These differences should be bridged by trying to understand the Soviet counterparts' language as well as their attitudes, and by carefully explaining your own reasoning to them. These are critical elements of negotiation in the Soviet Union.

Although many Soviet officials speak English, and would gladly practice with you at a dinner table, they will seldom agree to conduct formal negotiations in that language. As a rule, the Soviets will bring in a well-trained English-speaking interpreter to participate in the talks. Although interpreters' language skills are often superb, their understanding of the business concepts is not, and, therefore, usually leads to distortions of the foreign party's position. Not only must the resulting confusion be painstakingly retraced and cleared up, but misunderstanding also breeds mistrust between the parties. If there is no one to oversee the negotiations and notice mistakes in time, the outcome could be more painful. On several occasions I was asked by foreigners to review English and Russian versions of agreements concluded by them in the Soviet Union. Very often, the English version, prepared by foreigners, and the Russian version, prepared by the Soviets, did not match and the negotiations had to start anew to determine whose document was accurate. Sometimes the parties may not discover that they have different business objectives or that they disagree on key elements of their project, until after they have spent much time and effort to promote their relationship. It is therefore hard to overstate the importance for a Western investor who is going to the Soviet Union of bringing at least one person with strong Russian language skills and an understanding of the business side of the transaction. This will make both parties more comfortable at the negotiation table and will avoid delays and confusion that could spoil an otherwise amicable atmosphere.

In general, negotiations should deemphasize the adversarial nature of the relationship, becoming instead educational sessions. As stated earlier, much of the difficulty in negotiating with the Soviets stems from misunderstandings and suspicion that they will somehow be deceived. Often a simple explanation of the reasonableness of a foreign investor's position and its acceptability in international practice will overcome resistance and the Soviets will gladly subscribe to it, particularly if the Westerner does not appear paternalistic, but rather fair and competent. Fairness and competence seem to be so appealing to Soviet negotiators because of the prevailing perception in the Soviet Union that the country's economy has been ruined because in the past these qualities always took a backseat to ideological qualifications.

Even when the Soviets fail to question some of your positions, either because they overlook their importance or because they do not want to show their ignorance, it is important to raise and explain these points to them. For example, in a lengthy and complicated joint venture agreement we included a so-called squeeze-down provision, which provided that when the joint venture was short of operating capital either party could put up its own funds and the other party's interest in the joint venture would be reduced by a certain percentage. Although the Soviets did not question that provision, it was clear to us that they did not fully appreciate its importance, especially because they would likely be the party that was unable to contribute convertible currency to the project. Therefore, before signing the agreement, we carefully explained the consequences of this provision. Our counterparts had not understood it and asked us to revise it, in a way that was less advantageous to us. At the same time they were appreciative of our openness and impressed with our experience in handling such projects; these perceptions cemented our overall relationship.

Sometimes, explaining certain concepts may not be sufficient to win your partners over, especially when the provisions involved are alien to them or run counter to some deeply ingrained beliefs. In these instances, the most effective method is to try to locate an authoritative *Soviet* publication advocating your own point of view, or at least another agreement approved by the government containing the same terms. I once spent hours explaining a buy-out provision in a draft joint venture agreement. Despite the ingenuity and fairness of our arguments, the Soviets could not comprehend why after 20 years of operations a foreign company that had recouped its investment and made a profit had to be bought out in case of dissolution. I succeeded only after I found a Soviet, Russian-language publication on joint ventures that advised that such buy-outs were acceptable, and indeed common in international practice.

Often the hardest arguments to counter are assertions that certain provisions violate Soviet laws. But sometimes the Soviets are not aware of their own legislation. Indeed, few could keep up with the numerous recent changes. Nevertheless, in these circumstances it is important to know the applicable law and to show the text of it to your counterparts; they will then tend to adhere to it without objection. It is much more difficult to prevail when the Soviets claim that a certain provision runs counter to some unpublished regulation. Under these circumstances, it is imperative to request that they furnish this legislation (in my experience such a request was denied only once) and to carefully read and understand it. The existence of such unpublished internal regulations or instructions is well known, but sometimes the Soviets themselves either might misunderstand them or may wish to use them to mislead uninformed foreigners. I remember how negotiations were deadlocked for several months because our Soviet partners insisted that an unpublished regulation by the Moscow City Council might result in limitless rent increases on the land to be contributed by the Soviet partner to the joint venture. We ultimately convinced them that the regulation was inapplicable to our joint venture, but only after Soviet officials allowed us to inspect the text of this regulation in its entirety and consulted with their legal department regarding our conclusion.

Last, as in any foreign country, the Western investor should keep its business objectives in focus and learn how to say *nyet*. It is probably unavoidable for foreigners to rely on their Soviet partners for connections, logistical support, and advice on the Soviet system. However, when Soviet entrepreneurs wish to explore too many opportunities at the same time, Westerners should be careful not to be drawn into areas outside their business competence.[9]

It is undeniable that Soviet business practices have improved considerably over the last several years due to the influence of reforms, internal competition, and the experience of international business transactions. But as one Soviet official once very candidly pointed out to me, "Soviets are the unreliable party." Although they are often well intentioned, they are not accustomed to standard Western business practices. Preparing your own documents in English as well as their translation into Russian, although initially more expensive, is far more expedient than relying on the Soviet party. It is always a good idea to send all documents in advance to the Soviet Union for review, but do not be surprised when these documents lie untouched until your arrival. Do not expect timely responses to all your telexes, but do try to establish a system whereby each telex is numbered to discipline each party to answer promptly. Expect much of the work to stop between your visits to the Soviet Union, but do not hesitate to ask your Soviet partners to send periodic progress reports on the project; this often prompts them to continue working in your absence.

There is little doubt that Soviet joint venture regulations were motivated by the Soviet government's intention to facilitate the transfer of Western capital, technology, know-how, and management skills to the Soviet Union. As of this writing, few of the original hopes associated with joint ventures by the Soviets have been realized. Similarly, Western fears often likening Soviet joint ventures to the proverbial "sale of the rope with which it will be hanged" also proved unfounded. Clearly, joint ventures have transgressed the strictly set parameters of government policy. Along with other effects of *perestroika,* they have paved the way for the sudden exposure of many Soviet citizens to Western markets, business practices, and consumer goods denied them for many years. Joint ventures have played a significant role in Soviet economic thinking by pushing Soviet planners toward more radical domestic reform. Joint ventures have also become an outlet for thousands of Soviet managers, both government and private, to express a long-suppressed spirit of entrepreneurship. Once unleashed, this spirit may permanently erode the gripping controls of Soviet central planning. While joint ventures clearly steer the Soviet economy in a more market oriented direction, whether the goal of a free market system will ultimately be realized depends largely upon the success of broader reforms now taking place in the Soviet Union.

CHAPTER 8

Operating in Moscow

Tom Laurita

Moscow in 1991 resembles a boom town. With *perestroika* in full stride, the lure of fast money draws an array of entrepreneurs, salespeople, returning émigrés, and speculators. At the same time, the Soviet Union has been sold as perhaps the last frontier for multinational corporations, and it is rare to find a Fortune 500 company that has not put together a Soviet-Eastern European team, or at least a U.S.S.R. task force. As U.S. companies intensify their recent descent on Moscow, they find that their European competitors often have well-established trading relationships and that the World Trade Center in Moscow is populated largely by big Japanese trading companies. The Soviet foreign trade bureaucracy has reacted to the sudden influx of would-be partners with a typical bunker mentality, mixed with an ill-hidden pining for the wonders capitalism can produce.

Despite the apparently short-term orientation of Soviet foreign trade officials, who frequently propose joint ventures or mergers during the first meeting, the reality is that any company wishing to enter the U.S.S.R. market must do so with a long-term orientation. The Soviets, and especially Russians, place a high premium on stability, which in commerce translates into a long relationship developed cautiously and gradually. Also, the business culture in the U.S.S.R. is so alien to Westerners that it takes considerable time and effort to acquire sufficient expertise in Soviet ways of operating. It is impossible to create a substantial, ongoing business in the U.S.S.R. without cultivating an extensive network of contacts that includes Soviet foreign trade specialists, scientific and academic officials, factory or end-user representatives, and a few well-placed *tolkachi,* or "pushers"—individuals who eliminate snafus. For a large firm, government sponsors are also essential. These are middle and high level insiders within the Council of Ministers, the State Planning Board (Gosplan), the

State Committee for Science and Technology (GKNT)—or the successors of these and other organizations—who can lobby the firm's interests when key decisions are being made.

In Russian, many European words have been adopted, but their meaning has a specific Soviet shading. The word *serious* is one. In trade lingo, a company is *neserioznaya* (not serious despite its own serious intentions) if it bumbles into town every other month with English language brochures, holds Western-style seminars that fail to address the questions plaguing its audience, never serves alcoholic drinks, and is naive enough to expect responses from prospective buyers to reach its Cleveland headquarters. After a year of such mutual frustration, either the American firm will pull out, in which case it probably had never made a commitment to crack the market, or it will look for help. The "not-serious" company suffers from two deficiencies: it lacks experts in doing business with the Soviet Union and it has no local presence.

With rare exceptions, expertise and presence are essential for establishing a serious trade relationship. The Soviet Union is a buyer's market, strange as that may seem in a country without a convertible currency or a fully discernible trading system. As discussed in Chapter 1, there do exist isolated, limited sellers' markets—as, for example, when emergency purchases of food or specialized equipment are executed. But even firms that have made huge, opportunistic sales have no guarantee of consistent business, and eventually Soviet expertise and a local presence need to be established.

Expertise can be rented, hired, found in-house, or developed over time. Many firms make the mistake of unleashing armies of technical and commercial staff on the Soviet Union. They often cannot communicate their message, have no idea to whom that message needs to be communicated, and—worst of all—do not have the right message. The dynamics of a given Soviet industry and the imperatives of Soviet decision makers are beyond the purview of uninitiated Western sales personnel. The ideal staffing structure is a technical team with experience in the nuts-and-bolts problems its Soviet colleagues face, guided by experienced Soviet specialists who understand the firm's products well enough to be able to discuss them intelligently and to know when to call upon technical expertise.

Without someone in Moscow, it is impossible to arrange basic logistics. The president of a midsized U.S. company once learned upon arrival in Moscow that, although he presented a hotel voucher purchased in New Jersey, he had no room at the Intourist hotel. His threat to sit in the lobby on his suitcase until he received lodging didn't raise any eyebrows, nor did his one-hour sit-down strike. Like Napoleon, he found he was unable to transform Russia by force of will, and eventually he joined the line to see the omnipotent "hotel administrator" in a somewhat more deferential mood. As usual, "no vacancy" meant "you haven't yet expressed your desires clearly," and a small bottle of perfume fetched him a room.

Room, board, communications, transportation, and setting meetings are all headaches in Moscow. A trip to the U.S.S.R. usually does wonders for a Westerner's appreciation of most of what he or she takes for granted. A hotel room for the business traveler can often be arranged through an agency with Moscow offices, but during peak periods even this route is uncertain, and many firms develop contacts at each hotel for the predictable emergencies. This tactic is especially relevant if one wants to avoid distant and undesirable hotels like the Cosmos or Mozhaiskaya.

Most foreign offices in Moscow include a kitchen and cook/maid. Lunch is generally served for the entire staff and visitors. Although this may sound frivolous, it is actually the most efficient way to proceed, as any restaurant will take two hours to serve a meal if reservations can be made (usually for hard currency); it is hopeless to expect the Soviet staff to feed itself at a restaurant and return before nightfall.

Westerners working in the U.S.S.R. are in unanimous agreement that the lack of a modern communications infrastructure is one of the most damaging results of the Communist obsession with secrecy. The Soviet Union is struggling to remedy the problem, but so far with limited success. International phone communication is spotty at best when one is lucky enough to have access to direct dial facilities—and maddening when one must attempt to order calls through the operator. Satellite communications are slowly making their presence felt, but they are very expensive. Calling within the U.S.S.R. is actually more difficult than calling abroad, and some places are entirely unreachable. Without a Moscow presence, efficient communication is impossible under these circumstances. Each office has at least one driver/gofer and car, since the taxi system is uneven, and since Moscow is poorly marked for drivers (maps were purposely inaccurate until about 1990, and few good ones have been printed since).

As a result of poor communications, obtaining meetings with appropriate people is difficult. The situation is compounded by the Soviet habit of doing things at the last minute. Especially during *perestroika,* when uncertainty reigns for trade officials, one needs both an established reputation and a local voice calling persistently to catch the sought-after party and arrange a meeting. (Soviets seldom set meetings through their secretaries, preferring to control this small aspect of their destinies themselves.)

A firm's image is enhanced by having local presence and this can be of great importance. Since most Soviets have had no opportunity to become acquainted with Western companies and business practices, even in their own area, they judge the reliability and level of *serioznosty* (seriousness) of a company by its presence in Moscow. This is clearly not the only criterion applied, but it carries inordinate weight. It is probably a useful standard, since expertise and a network can be cultivated only from within the Soviet Union, so some base is essential.

There are various degrees of presence, and the value associated with one or another option must be weighed against the costs, which are in most cases relatively steep. Many firms start out sending representatives to Moscow on a limited basis. Some work out of hotel rooms (at an average cost of $150 to $350 per night), but this option is generally unsatisfactory. There exist two umbrella organizations that offer some services and facilities for U.S. business in Moscow—the U.S. Commercial Office (USCO) and the U.S.-U.S.S.R. Trade and Economic Council (USTEC).

USCO, the Department of Commerce office located next to the U.S. embassy, provides limited logistical support (telephones, telex, fax, and mail service). Advantages are low cost and convenient location; disadvantages include association with the embassy, which frightens many Soviet partners, and the fact that no real commercial support is offered. Rather than promote trade, USCO gathers trade figures, and can be a good source of information on U.S. trade legislation and changes in Soviet law. It also serves as the principal liaison between U.S. business in Moscow and the embassy.

A relic of détente, USTEC is a trade office supported by member U.S. companies and the Soviet Chamber of Commerce and Industry. Any American company can join, as can Soviet organizations with foreign trade rights. For U.S. companies there is a sliding fee schedule based on the firm's yearly worldwide sales volume—the maximum is currently $15,000 per year—and membership confers use of some logistical support and an assigned project manager. USTEC has five or six project managers on staff—both Soviet and American—each of whom is assigned a portfolio of companies to handle. This service can include the transmission of information and messages for these firms, and attendance and translation at Moscow meetings. By charter, the council does not promote one member over another and should be quickly outgrown by any firm making progress. It has a New York office and a formidable bureaucracy. Yearly council meetings are held alternately in the U.S. and in Moscow, and are useful insofar as they are one of the few occasions when executives from both sides are in the same place at the same time. USTEC is seen to be dominated by big business and by the current chair. Membership has traditionally been considered a yearly expense for participation in the Soviet trade arena, and most active U.S. firms become members. Complaints directed at the council often arise from inflated expectations about what USTEC can do. As a trade forum it has value.

A more substantial and expensive presence is available in the form of companies that act as agents or representatives in Moscow. There is a wide spectrum of them. Some work out of the United States or Western Europe and are one- or two-person operations. Others share a Moscow office and have a limited staff there; a smaller group of firms has established offices and reputations of its own in the Soviet Union. A still finer distinction can be drawn between those that are present in the Soviet Union but not accredited and those that are accredited.

Accreditation is a term normally applicable to diplomatic activities, but law and tradition in the U.S.S.R. make it a significant aspect of life for foreign companies as well. Under Soviet law, there are several national organizations that have the right to accredit a company. They include the Ministry for Foreign Economic Relations, the U.S.S.R. Chamber of Commerce and Industry, the U.S.S.R. State Committee for Science and Technology, the Ministry of the Merchant Marine, Aeroflot (the state airline), Gosbank (the state bank), and several others. Republican organizations are also gaining this right. By accrediting a company under its auspices, an organization accepts a degree of responsibility for that company, and in effect acts as its sponsor in the U.S.S.R. This cumbersome system is under review, but it will probably operate for the foreseeable future.

Accredited companies and organizations bear a seal of government approval, a source of comfort to nervous and confused Soviet partners making initial forays into the foreign trade arena. In theory, accreditation carries with it a government commitment to providing office space and staffing, although in practice many accredited firms cannot obtain space, and some enterprising nonaccredited firms have offices.

The proliferation of firms offering agency, representational, consulting, and strategic or financial services to companies wishing to trade in the Soviet Union confirms that there is an acute need for Soviet expertise and market knowledge and that numerous new entrants are testing the waters. Many companies choose to enter or expand into the market via local representatives. Some U.S. companies with European divisions have chosen European agents, and some even work through Japanese trading houses, usually because these organizations have more experience in the U.S.S.R. A relatively recent phenomenon is the return of émigrés to the Soviet Union as trade consultants or agents. Émigrés have often been viewed as betrayers of the homeland by Soviet decision makers, but this opinion is softening.

The fee structure of agency and representation arrangements varies, but usually involves a sliding commission on sales (3 to 15 percent, depending on volume and type of product), and often a retainer of some sort. Smaller operations back-charge expenses, while more established firms tend to absorb their own costs. Other forms of cooperation include joint ventures (see Chapter 7) and consulting on a project or overall basis. In each case, one gets what one pays for, and a serious entrant into the market is well advised to shop around.

A company that either rushes into the U.S.S.R. because it has found someone who speaks Russian or decides to economize at all costs, can be burned. There are well-known cases of individuals and firms being declared unwelcome in the U.S.S.R. because of bribery, currency speculation, and even spying. A proven track record is important, since presence should include a network and a longstanding reputation. An agent's association with reputable, established firms is one of the best characteristics to look for in choosing a partner. Experience with Russian language and culture is necessary but not sufficient. Knowledge of the specific product area is needed: a company aiming for a substantial long-term presence should investigate the breadth of the contact network possessed by a specialized firm and try to determine the degree of high level acceptance it has achieved. Accreditation is one indicator, but it may denote length of time on the market rather than an active current presence. Some U.S. firms with solid reputations and substantial presence include the SATRA, Chilewich, and VITAS corporations.

The traditional path into the Soviet market for American and many European firms has involved a period during which the firm is represented by an agent (about two to five years), followed—assuming some sales success—by an interim phase while the firm seeks and obtains its own accreditation (itself a process demanding substantial expertise), and finally the establishment of its own office. There are between 40 and 50 U.S. firms and several hundred European companies accredited in Moscow. In the past, accreditation could take up to five years, and more than one Fortune 500 company has been befuddled by inexplicable delays. These were the result of extreme inefficiency on the part of the accrediting organizations and multitudinous cross-checking requirements within the Soviet system, and often were prolonged in order to send negative political signals to the firm's country. Under *perestroika,* this process has become somewhat more transparent and rational, but it still brings in layers of what would appear to be the uninitiated to be Kafkaesque bureaucracy.

The establishment of a Moscow office is a significant move. It generally demands the CEO's and board of directors' involvement because a good deal of high level political lobbying is expected of U.S. firms in the U.S.S.R. and because the costs are high. There is an additional consideration: namely, it is much easier to get into the U.S.S.R. than to get out. Any company that has undergone the difficult process of building a Soviet presence, and then leaves or closes its office, must reckon with the long Soviet memory. Such a move would be interpreted as a public slap in the face, which is suicidal according to Soviet protocol. To return after leaving would be extremely problematic. Most Western firms understood this and maintained their offices and a skeleton staff during the post-détente frost of the early 1980s, even though they could not trade under the embargo imposed by President Jimmy Carter after the 1979 invasion of Afghanistan.

Setting up an office in Moscow is costly, in terms of both money and the time of senior executives, who must demonstrate appropriate interest and make frequent trips to Moscow during and after the establishment of the office. Commercial space in Moscow has become almost as expensive as in Tokyo. Firms have paid five years' undiscounted up-front rent as high as $800 per square meter per year (almost $80 per square foot per year) to get office space. I can best describe the desperation of companies looking for space by recalling a visit in 1990 from the CEO of a Fortune 100 company, during which he implored me to try to pull strings and assure his firm first crack at space my firm was vacating. We were unable to help.

UPDK, the Main Service Bureau for the Diplomatic Corps, which also services accredited firms, is an organization that had until 1990 a virtual monopoly over the provision of all services to foreigners in Moscow, including internal travel, all staffing of offices, and all rental space. The bureau—which was created by Stalin—is not very effective. As this book went to press, UPDK had a waiting list of 150 accredited firms that needed space and could not be accommodated. The Sovincenter, or World Trade Center (also known as the Hammer Center, after one of its principal financiers) is a complex that includes the Hotel Mezhdunarodnaya, 15 floors of office space, and various stores. Opened during the 1980 Olympic Games, it is an alternative to UPDK. Despite its American design and fixtures, it is overpriced, poorly managed, and inconveniently located. Some see it as a monument to the ability of the Soviet system to make mediocre any attempt to transplant excellence from the West. Yet there has been a long waiting list to get into this complex; being there is better than being nowhere. Lately, those who have found other options have begun to flee. Moscow real estate has thus become a prime area for would-be entrepreneurs, especially considering that the deficit of residential space is at least as catastrophic as the shortage of commercial space. The practice of isolating foreigners and leaving them at the mercy of one monopolistic bureaucracy is changing, and alternatives are emerging. Still, that transformation is slow, and the effects of a system that has survived since the last days of the Revolution will long be felt.

Touring downtown Moscow, one is struck by the plethora of uninhabited, dilapidated structures, even within the inner city ring one or two miles from the Kremlin. These buildings may still hint at their former splendor, but they have not been maintained for decades. This situation is the result of the Brezhnevite obsession with output figures. The more urgent the housing and office space crisis became, the more heroically were faceless, crooked buildings constructed outside Moscow, often too far away for convenience. This fevered building activity further diverted the already meager resources available for rebuilding or maintaining the city center and resulted in a chaotic urban picture in the 1990s.

The obvious first step—to allow Western (and Soviet) firms in need of space to finance reconstruction and refurbishment in the city—has been taken, albeit not without formidable opposition. The basic hinderance to a real estate market is the problem of ownership. Nobody is quite sure who owns most buildings, not to mention the land they stand on. Mossoviet, the Moscow City Council, formally administers much city real estate and controls all the land in the name of "the people." It has traditionally been a bastion of inactivity. Mossoviet issues an "order" permitting occupancy for a period of time in one or another building. Since neither a system of real estate valuation nor a market existed, those bureaucrats who issued orders had great power. After the old Mossoviet was voted out in the first free citywide elections (1989–90), many orders were issued before the new council took office, reportedly for bribes of up to 1 million rubles. The new city administration, under the reforming and enigmatic mayor Gavril Popov, was forced to annul all existing orders and to review the entire situation. The continuing disorder makes office space a prime headache for newcomers.

The high costs of operating in Moscow, other than space rental, include expensive business gifts expected by clients; participation in near-mandatory and very costly exhibitions; frequent visits and "business trips" to the West by Soviet partners and buyers; retail prices on food, clothing, and auto service that run up to 50 percent and more above Western average costs; and many others. Local Soviet personnel, on the other hand, receive lower salaries than their Western counterparts. They are usually commensurately less productive, having been trained in the Soviet system, where, as the expression goes, "initiative is punishable." However, the Soviet people often possess great native talent and ability, and individuals can be found who develop into excellent employees.

Typically, a Moscow office will include several "engineers"—a catchall Soviet term for most specializations except president and coal miner. These are technically trained individuals who may approximate salespeople or technicians. They, like all Soviet citizens working for Western firms, have normally been employed through UPDK. The firm paid UPDK dollars, and until late 1990 the employee received rubles at the least favorable official rate, plus up to about 25 percent of the salary in kind as clothing, household goods, and the like. Since direct employment by firms became possible in September 1990, UPDK was forced to permit employees to receive up to 100 percent of their salaries in kind to remain competitive. Joint ventures can employ Soviet individuals directly, as a local organization would, but still face significant currency restrictions. A good engineer might cost a Western firm about $20,000 annually, while secretaries and translators receive the equivalent of $10,000 to $12,000, and cooks, drivers, and similar help about $10,000. It should be noted that in terms of real purchasing power, these are huge sums by Soviet standards.

A major concern to be faced early on is management and control. Many U.S. firms staff their Moscow operations through Western European subsidiaries. The obvious advantages of proximity and a large pool of Europeans with broad Soviet experience seems to make this the preferred option. However, some companies have switched from this setup to a U.S.-managed structure because the U.S.S.R. has become a high priority market and the filter of European management is judged counterproductive. In all cases, control is the key. Very few major firms have entrusted management of their U.S.S.R. offices to Soviet staff, owing to their lack of business background and the temptations involved. The case of one large multinational corporation that did is sadly instructive. The U.S.-based chief representative was forced to leave most operational decisions to his Soviet deputy because of his physical distance from Moscow. He was eventually summoned to the Foreign Ministry and informed that a currency speculation operation was being run out of his office. Irreparable damage was done to the firm's image in the U.S.S.R.

The market in Moscow for experienced expatriate managers is fiercely competetive. A compensation package for Americans normally includes a middle executive base salary with up to 50 percent added for cost of living and hardship, a company car, an apartment rent-free, one or two annual paid trips to the U.S. (for Americans) plus two or three to Western Europe for the entire family, and other extras. High salaries are justified because a newcomer needs a year or two to adapt, even with adequate language proficiency. Family problems often arise because of the hardships faced.

To do the job properly, a Moscow representative may need to spend most weekday evenings with clients and/or Western visitors. Consuming large amounts of hard liquor during these evenings is a prominent feature of the Moscow scene, expected by many Soviet partners. This activity is an integral part of establishing trust and rapport in the U.S.S.R. Many Westerners are not prepared for such heavy drinking, and they either need to decline the offer of alcohol—earning the label "party pooper"—or partake. In the former case, Westerners begin to feel rejected by Soviet society. This feeling of isolation can also arise when the individual speaks no Russian, or from a generally negative attitude that sometimes develops during long uninterrupted spells in Moscow. The Westerner may retreat in such circumstances to the embassy cocktail circuit or to their home video machine. At this point the purpose of coming to Moscow has been defeated. On the other hand, the Westerner who dives into Soviet society, and the drinking that accompanies acceptance, can develop alcohol-related problems. The best solution is to take part as much as possible in Soviet society while recognizing and respecting one's upper limit on alcohol consumption. Soviets' drinking does not necessarily have as its goal oblivion; rather it is a ritualistic transformation of bleak reality into a state of uninhibited communion.

To reside in Moscow is a challenge for the family of a representative. Soviet labor laws and a disjointed labor market make it difficult for a spouse to find satisfying work. And because the employed husband or wife may be absent often, the nonworking spouse can become isolated. Although several women's organizations are active in Moscow, such as the International Women's Association and the American Women's Association, no real community exists to lend support. Unless the spouse is able to make an adventure out of his or her stay in the Soviet Union, or happens to have a background in Russian language or culture, he or she can become bored. This phenomenon is particularly common when the gray, dull, extended Moscow winter sets in—as early as October.

Most foreign families send their children to international schools, of which there are several, including Anglo-American, French, German, Finnish, Swedish, and a Soviet-run international school. They are generally adequate although not outstanding. Some families do decide to send their children to Soviet schools, especially if one of the parents is a Soviet national. Most families find, though, that if children spend too long in local schools they have difficulties readjusting to life in the West. Some embassies provide basic medical care in Moscow, and a UPDK clinic and hospital are available. However, Soviet diagnoses seem to differ widely from Western ones, and for any serious illness evacuation to the West is recommended.

When recreation time is available, many families opt for trips to Western Europe or elsewhere. This adds to the transitory nature of the Moscow foreign community. In Moscow, some sports facilities are available: swimming, very limited tennis, and of course plenty of snow for cross-country skiers. Familiarity with the Russian language is important if one wants to attend dramatic theater or film. On the other hand, the ballet, symphony, and opera are excellent and tickets are quite cheap. Moscow is not a well-planned, bright urban center, and most foreign housing is uninspired. Combined with the weather and nature of the job, all this means a family needs to plan and be enterprising to avoid depression in Moscow.

Given the particular challenges of working in Moscow, selecting executives for a stint there is a sensitive issue, and some companies spend years in the search, or settle for interim solutions that drag on for long periods of time. Because of the many uncertainties connected with creating and developing a Soviet presence, firms often start in-house, hoping thus to retain maximum control. The obvious advantage of choosing a person with years of service is that that person will have a feel for the firm's political and cultural demeanor, as well as product knowledge. Many firms outgrow this stage quickly though, since the individual selected will be thwarted by a lack of Soviet expertise, unless he or she is very flexible and a rapid learner. So either a deputy or a replacement with a deep knowledge of Soviet culture and language, and experience both in Soviet trade and in the industry in question, is frequently sought. Ideally a candidate should be healthy enough to keep up with the frantic pace in Moscow, have a stable personality, have a family ready for adventure, and be willing to accept the Soviet Union as it is and to address it on its own terms. The key is to find this degree of flexibility balanced with the ability not to cross the line and become Sovietized, by which I mean accepting Soviet laxity and inefficiency as normal. The director for U.S.S.R. operations located in Western Europe or the United States must be attuned to the problems Moscow representatives face and provide outlets to aid them in maintaining their balance.

Soviet culture is decidedly unliberated: should a firm choose a woman to head its office, it will be taking on all the above-mentioned problems plus millenia of Russian male chauvinism. Russian society is traditionally segregated in terms of both sex and class. A narrow and brilliant layer of individuals—the "intelligentsia"—is set against the "masses" of workers and farmers. While the intelligentsia may be open to Western ideas of sexual equality, in commerce one deals mainly with groups and a mentality that will not take a woman seriously as a leader. This unpleasant reality is reflected in the structure of Soviet political and economic power—and also in Soviet academia.

Whoever is chosen will need substantial company resources in terms of both money and patience. To resolve the dilemma of whether to select a person with broad company experience or outside Soviet expertise, firms sometimes try to send one or more of both types, with one person serving as the principal liaison with the company and the other as the Soviet liaison. Other firms have sought to use employees of Eastern European or Slavic origin or nationality. Poles, Czechs, Hungarians, and Romanians are often quite well acquainted with the Soviet Union. This can be an effective route to take, although these individuals may face discrimination, or the firm may suffer a loss of prestige, as a result of the nationalistic competitiveness and mutual dislike among these nations and Russia. A talented and adaptable individual can overcome this problem, and there are cases in which this approach proved successful. Still, Soviet partners like to see what they consider *solidnost* (solidity), which translates into having an American or Western European at the helm. Such a statement may sound shocking and racist, but it describes reality.

Much of what I have written reflects the Soviet Union that *perestroika* is meant to reform. Yet in attempting to bring about change, *perestroika* must operate with existing mechanisms and mentalities. I personally do not expect such ingrained traits as xenophobia and disorganization to change rapidly. These can evolve slowly as individuals take advantage of newly available opportunities. In any case, the decentralization of Soviet commerce can only make local presence and expertise more important. It becomes similarly imperative to travel to end-users throughout the U.S.S.R., and even to open offices and representations in other key cities, such as Kiev, Leningrad, and Minsk. To be successful in business in the Soviet Union, a firm's representatives must engage the country and people on their own terms.

CHAPTER 9

Doing Business
Outside of Moscow

Elisa B. Miller

The six-seater plane took off from Nome, Alaska, with the president and the senior vice president of Alaska Airlines, two technicians, myself (the company's Soviet affairs consultant), and a crew of two. Nome is a small town on the northwest coast of Alaska. Two hundred fifty miles due west, across the Bering Strait, is Provideniya, a small town in the territory of Chukchi, U.S.S.R. (see Figure 9-1).

The flight to Provideniya was a technical flight, authorized by the Soviet government. We were to find out whether the airport in Provideniya would be able to accommodate a Boeing 737 the following month. Ours was the first authorized flight into this northern Soviet airspace since lend-lease airplanes flew the route during World War II. Except for an American who had made a swim from a U.S. island to a Soviet island in the Strait the month before, no Americans had been received in the region since World War II.

Alaska Airlines had received authorization from the U.S.S.R.'s Ministry of Civil Aviation and Ministry of Foreign Affairs to make the flight. The U.S. Department of State had given us the green light, saying all approvals had been received. Yet we had absolutely no information about the local situation. We had not been able to establish radio communications with the Soviet air authorities in the region.

On the morning of our takeoff we were not able to confirm either the location of the airport or the weather conditions. Our only sense of security as we crossed the international dateline and flew into Soviet airspace came from the phone call I had managed to make the evening before. Having reached the home of the mayor in Provideniya, and knowing that I had a very short time to talk (connections were always breaking unexpectedly),

Figure 9-1   The Soviet Far East

THE SOVIET FAR EAST

0 100 200 300 400
MILES

ALASKA
CHUKCHI SEA   Bering Strait   Nome

ARCTIC OCEAN
Wrangel Island
Chukchi Peninsula   Provideniya
BERING SEA

Cape Shelagskii
Pevek
Chaun Bay
EAST SIBERIAN SEA
Anadyr

LAPTEV SEA

CHUKCHI NATIONAL AREA

KORYAK NATIONAL AREA

Omolon R.

Gizhiga

Indigirka R.   Kolyma R.

Verkhoyansk

Arctic Circle   YAKUTIA

MAGADAN DISTRICT   Gizhiga Bay

Magadan

KAMCHATKA DISTRICT
Petropavlosk-Kamchatskii

Lena R.
Vilyui R.   Yakutsk
Aldan R.
Mirnyi

Okhotsk

SEA OF OKHOTSK

Severo-Kurilsk

KHABAROVSK TERRITORY

Nikolaevsk

SAKHALIN   KURILE ISLANDS

Chulman

Udokan
AMUR DISTRICT

Amur R.   Tatary Strait

Yuzhno-Sakhalinsk

Shilka R.   Amur R.

Irkutsk   Lake Baikal   Chita
Ulan Ude

JEWISH AUT. DISTRICT

Khabarovsk   La Pérouse Strait

MARITIME TERRITORY   JAPAN

MONGOLIA   Argun R.   Sungari R.   CHINA   Vladivostok   Nakhodka

SEA OF JAPAN

(Adapted with permission from John J. Stephan, *Soviet-American Horizons in the Pacific* [Honolulu: University of Hawaii Press, 1986].)

I asked one question: "Do you know we are coming tomorrow, arriving at eight in the morning local time?" The mayor's wife answered, "Yes, we know!" With that knowledge and the special bravado of Alaskans, we landed in Provideniya, a small harbor town tucked into a bay whose name reassures the Soviet icebreakers that ply the arctic routes.

We were greeted by the mayor. No one had a visa. Six of us had our passports; one of the pilots had only his driver's license. So began one company's remarkable adventure to establish a scheduled air service across the Pacific to the "back door" of the U.S.S.R. And so began a remarkable interaction between neighbors and the practical application of my experience working at the local level to develop and to facilitate business relations.

One month after that technical flight, in June 1988, 81 Americans boarded a Boeing 737 for the Alaska Airlines friendship flight to Provideniya—this time with the governor of Alaska, a U.S. senator, the editor-in-chief of *National Geographic* magazine, and many of Alaska's business and cultural leaders. Several months later, a friendship boat with Soviet counterparts docked in Nome. More than a year of intense work and communications had succeeded in breaking the "ice barrier." Players on both sides could be congratulated. On the U.S. side, these included Jim Stimpfle, of Nome. Stimpfle's vision was that useful communications could be established between Alaskans and their Soviet neighbors. After a symbolic first act of floating friendship balloons toward the U.S.S.R., he eventually garnered the active support of Alaska's governor, Steve Cowper, and a top assistant, Virginia Brelsford, who skillfully developed the necessary support and played a major role in organizing the U.S.-Soviet meetings that resulted. On the Soviet side, important roles were played by officials in Provideniya and the territory of Magadan and the Soviet ministries of Foreign Affairs and Civil Aviation.

The historical aspect of these endeavors—meetings between representatives of industry and government *on site, at the local level*—is easily forgotten now in these times of intense and rapid change. Yet as recently as 1988 none of these direct ties could have taken place. In business dealings, for example, as recently as 1988, if an Alaskan firm wanted to place an order to buy fish caught in Soviet waters of the Bering Strait, negotiations had to take place in Moscow. To make a deal for logs cut in forests near the Sea of Japan, negotiations again took place in Moscow. And so, too, for selling machinery and equipment for use in the Soviet Far East, the table of negotiation was about 6000 miles away in Moscow. Regardless of the nature of the business arrangement or the information needed, the first stop was always Moscow. After that, and only then with central authorities in the lead, a visit to the local site might be allowed. Trying to develop and negotiate a deal in any other way, such as talking with industry officials at the site, was prohibited. Rights to have contacts with foreigners were severely circumscribed and the majority of industrial personnel did not have these rights. Foreign manufacturers of equipment imported into the U.S.S.R. were seldom permitted in the factories that were using the equipment. Business dealings with foreigners at the local level were formal, approved, and recorded; in every case the final words were: "Talk to the authorities in Moscow."

The policy shifts of the Gorbachev years have created significant changes. Rather than being stiff and cautious, local officials extend a genuine welcome. New forms of business organization have been legalized as a substitute for, or in addition to, state activities and as an intermediary step between the state-run economy and a private market economy. "Come pay us a visit," we hear, from every corner of the U.S.S.R. "Come, consider these proposals; come, stay and learn. We can deal with you directly." Any serious visitor who spends time in the hinterlands of the U.S.S.R. will receive calls from dozens of people representing organizations ready to do business.

Dealing at the local level is becoming increasingly valuable. *Razgosudarstvlenie* is a word that refers to the dismantling of the state (i.e., denationalization). As *razgosudarstvlenie* proceeds, political power and the control of resources shifts from the center to the lower level republics, states, and provinces and their constituencies. Dealing directly with factory management in industry, agriculture, science, and technology means dealing at the local level with local partners. The problem then becomes one of sorting out—from a set of many and in conditions quite fluid and uncertain—who are these potential partners, what are their resources, expertise, and connections, both in Moscow and at the local level. It is a new game with new players, requiring new strategies.

The opportunities are abundant. Put 12 people in a room and there is a high probability that 2 will have the same birth date; so too, it is likely that if a dozen U.S. and Soviet business executives are brought together at least one pair will find a mutually interesting business arrangement. So, when Alaska and the Soviet district of Magadan (which administers the territory of Chukchi) held a first round of official visits in September 1988, business discussions were included. Out of 16 presentations by U.S. firms (each firm was limited to a half-hour for a presentation, and written material was standardized in a prearranged format) one project impressed everyone present: a proposal to produce sausage products out of reindeer meat.

The U.S. firm, Indian Valley Meats (Indian, Alaska), which had presented the proposal, was experienced in making prize-winning sausage products out of reindeer meat.[1] Its products are sent annually to the President of the United States as the representative food of the state of Alaska. Reindeer are raised in great numbers by the indigenous peoples of the Soviet Far North. Herds roam vast expanses and head counts run in the millions. Reindeer is a good source of protein. But the lack of adequate packaging, refrigeration, and transportation has prevented reindeer meat products from reaching the country's more populated areas. Sausage products, however, have a long shelf life even with minimal refrigeration. They are tasty and have long been a staple of the Russian diet. Indian Valley Meats was an ideal potential partner for the local agricultural committee in the Magadan region, which had plenty of reindeer but badly needed what the American firm could supply: equipment and know-how. So it was not difficult to put a proposal together for cooperation. The Soviets would pay for equipment, expertise, packaging materials, and spices with reindeer by-products such as horn and other animal parts. These products command good prices in hard currency in Asia, where they are used medicinally and considered aphrodisiacs.

Six months later, on a mild spring day, I was part of a group landing in an Aeroflot helicopter on the continental divide just south of the Arctic Circle between the Kolyma and Omolon rivers. We were there to gather data for the project's costs and feasibility. The Soviet side was pushing hard to create a joint venture because of the special advantages partners in a joint venture enjoyed. The local agricultural committee had chosen a state farm to be the proposed joint venture partner, not because of its expertise but because of its location near a concrete airstrip—the only one in the surrounding territory—and thus secure transportation. We were introduced to officials on every rung of the administrative hierarchy—the state farm, the local mayor, the county officials, the region's chief executive, and finally, in Moscow, "the central authorities."

Our purpose was to assess the resource, assess the project's feasibility, assess our potential joint venture partner. These were not easy matters, given that the project was without precedent and the partner was without experience. Nevertheless, despite incomplete information and doubts about the abilities of the local partner, the project went ahead: based on trust, on the project's strong potential, and because of the strong support from the governors of both regions. Indian Valley Meats and the local agricultural committee of Magadan formed a joint venture (MAGAL) and the first shipments of equipment and horn were exchanged in the summer of 1989 within six months of the signed agreement. Eighteen months later, instead of 1 state farm, the joint venture project had 13 participating farms and 2 more joint venture partnerships were in the works, 1 in neighboring Kamchatka and the other in the European north of the U.S.S.R.

After the success of the friendship flight in the summer of 1988, I led the first official state of Alaska trade mission to the Soviet Far East, a territory extending 2800 miles from ProvidUniya to Vladivostok. This was a milestone in my career, making practical use of my academic background as a specialist in the Soviet Far East economy. I had just returned from a four month research visit to the Soviet Far East as a participant in an academic exchange sponsored by the U.S.S.R. Academy of Sciences and the U.S.-based International Research and Exchanges Board. My objective was to report on the new rights of local enterprises to engage in international economic activities. The director of the state of Alaska's Office of International Trade asked me to prepare a study in conjunction with the professional staff at the University of Alaska on trade opportunities in the Soviet Far East. The resulting report was then used to define the purposes, and guide the selection of, the trade delegation. The trade mission was kept small and consisted of five carefully selected companies, each representing a market area that matched the economic needs of the Soviet Far East. These were mining, transportation, communications, fishing, and consumer goods. Where possible, the companies selected had some prevous experience with Soviet trade.

Two years later, all of the five companies reported active operations with Soviet partners in the Soviet Far East. In the fall of 1990, with a new U.S.-U.S.S.R. bilateral air agreement permitting trans-Pacific flights, Alaska Airlines acquired the legal authority to fly scheduled flights between Anchorage and the cities of Magadan and Khabarovsk. Magadan includes a major gold mining region, the Kolyma, and is known as the site of some of the worst of Stalin's labor camps; Khabarovsk is a major industrial city about 500 miles north of Vladivostok. Alascom, a communications company, in cooperation with the Magadan branch of the U.S.S.R.'s Ministry of Post and Telecommunications, has put in a direct telephone link between Alaska and Magadan and Khabarovsk (with plans to link the Kamchatka territory as well). From Alaska a long distance operator dials directly to an operator on the other side. As a result, telephone and fax service is better than between Moscow and New York, greatly facilitating business communication and management. Greatland Exploration (in conjunction with the Bering Straits Trading Company) has created a joint venture, Svzyal, with the major gold mining enterprise in the Magadan region, Severvostokzoloto. The joint venture is exploring the feasibility of mining operations in the far north with the participation of COMINCO, the Canadian mining conglomerate. The Alaska Commercial Company, a consumer goods retail chain serving rural Alaska, has a modest but stable trade exchange. The fifth company, Alaska Joint Venture Seafoods, in December 1990 concluded a joint venture fishing agreement with Dalryba (a large fishing conglomerate headquartered in Vladivostok) to fish in Soviet waters in exchange for food and other consumer goods.

Each company achieved results following its own unique path. Yet, for each, that path included developing relationships with the local authorities. For example, in a single year Alaska Airlines delivered two friendship missions. The second mission carried an American team with its equipment to the arctic city Anadyr to join up with a Soviet team and *walk* together 1500 miles across the Bering Strait. Greatland Exploration created a mechanism for accomplishing several exchanges of mining specialists. Alascom set up a transmitting disk in Providentiya to send, by satellite, live coverage of the historic friendship flight to U.S. audiences (including the Soviet embassy in Washington, D.C.).

These companies are playing the new game, dealing at the local level, making assessments and choices about local partners, and at the same time paying attention to the role of Moscow. Dealing at the local level is not easy. Denationalization has created several new forms of economic activity: leasing or renting arrangements, the joint stock company, the nonprofit association. The new forms of business organization are replacing the state enterprises, which (except for consumer cooperatives) until very recently had been the sole source of employment in industry. All of the new forms now have the right to do business with foreigners, either directly or by way of a foreign economic association.

Renting or leasing state-owned property is a transitional form of business halfway between state-owned and privately owned property. Use of the property is in the hands of the leasing organization, but control is limited. Thus, a group of five individuals has been given a lease for 50 years for a park in the city of Nizhny Novgorod (formerly called Gorky), which they will develop and sublease but will not own or be able to sell. The joint stock company is a new form of business in which control and ownership is in the hands of shareholders, thus making it similar to the Western corporation. A large number of shares are issued to cover the ownership of an enterprise. These shares can then be bought by individuals or other enterprises, including joint ventures and individual foreign investors. Shares also can be distributed to workers. Nonprofit associations, another new form of business, have been organized in an attempt to replicate some of the functions of the state but outside of its bureaucratic system. These bear a resemblance to nonprofits in the United States. A Soviet example is the Fund for Air Safety, headed by the former director of Air Traffic Control for the Moscow Airport.

The old and the new now exist side by side, but the old has changed as well. The state enterprises have made changes and practically all of them now operate on a self-financing, self-sufficiency basis. These firms, with their newly established "independence," operate with advantages and disadvantages. Their advantages include established facilities, skilled labor, research and development institutes, and established connections with suppliers. Their disadvantages are obsolete equipment and top-heavy bureaucratic management. Many of these enterprises must shift output because they were heavily involved in military production. For example, the Ulyanov factory in Nizhny Novgorod has been engaged in making electrical heating elements for naval ships. Now, using the same basic element, it is converting to new consumer products: coffee makers, electric kettles, grills, toasters, and so on. While formerly it would have marketed all its goods under direction from Moscow, it has now formed its own marketing arm which includes international sales. In addition, many state organizations can sponsor a small enterprise *(maloe predpriyatie)* which is yet another new form of business organization at the local level. These small enterprises, while connected to a larger, usually state, organization, operate more flexibly and with a different set of rules. They are part of the new system of business organization at the local level and are active players in the new scene.

In the West a potential partner can easily be assessed with respect to business structure, business fit, financial strength, marketing organization, technology base, and so on. A request to Dun and Bradstreet and the task is more than 50 percent accomplished! In the new business environment of the U.S.S.R. this task is formidable. Information is difficult to get and difficult to assess. As a result, the Western business often must settle for less information than is desired.

Sometimes a great deal can be learned easily because many well-known, well-established organizations have established branch offices or divisions at the local level and are open for business with foreigners. For instance, Komsomol (the communist youth organization) has an Association for Business with Neighboring Countries. *Komsomolskaya Pravda* (one of the country's largest newspapers) has a commercial firm ready to deal with foreign firms.

New organizations are the most difficult to assess. Some have already established their reputations, but many have not. One way to better understand these new organizations is to investigate their domestic affiliations. For example, Tiumeninterconsult is associated with the city of Tiumen's executive offices, and has close ties to the local officials. Prognostika is associated with the U.S.S.R. Academy of Sciences, an important power base in the Soviet Union.

A similar situation exists with Soviet associations, joint stock companies, and joint ventures. Knowing the participating companies either as contributing members, stockholders, or partners helps one better understand the organization. In their make-up many of these new Soviet organizations have no counterparts in the West. For example, executive committees at the city and state level (akin to the mayor's office and the executive branch of a state government in the United States), banks, and the Communist party are among those who are striving to be players in the new economic game. Two joint venture business centers located in the city of Khabarovsk serve to illustrate this point. One joint venture is partnered with the Khabarovsk regional executive committee (the equivalent to a governor's office); the other is associated with the local Institute of National Economy, part of a large and powerful educational ministry. Which network of influence is more suitable depends on the objectives to be attained.

Even the Communist party is now interested in forming partnerships and engaging in business activities with foreigners. During a trip to a large city near Moscow, the purpose of which was to discuss several project proposals with one particular enterprise, I was invited to a meeting at which a different enterprise offered a similar set of proposals and invited joint cooperation. I asked what kind of organization was making these proposals and what its affiliations were. I learned that it was a small enterprise and that its sponsor was the local party committee. The party holds control of many resources and considers itself a reliable business partner.

Besides affiliations, another factor in assessing new organizations is its key personnel. The reorganization and the liquidation of ministries create reasons for the movement of personnel, and professionals *are* voting with their feet. Key personnel bring to a new Soviet organization connections and networks that have been established in previous work posts. These connections are important as sources of information, as well as goods and services.

- Recently, a Western firm decided to set up business with a local Soviet organization. A deciding factor was that the director of the organization was formerly a deputy minister of domestic trade for the U.S.S.R. who had widespread connections and was therefore considered a partner with great promise.

- "Who is your Soviet partner?" I asked a business acquaintance engaged in a cooperative venture to refurbish a recreational facility into the first motel in Moscow. The answer was a deputy minister of Hydropower, a person of some influence and authority.

Business experience is another factor to assess in a local partner. Unfortunately, legal, economic, and technical expertise, as well as international market data, are usually absent at the local level. This is a legacy of a system in which all decisions were made in Moscow. With decision making now able to take place throughout the U.S.S.R., the shortage of qualified personnel with needed business expertise is acute. As a result a local partner may overstate skills.

When the local partner overstates skills, the Western firm ends up having to provide training. Even when skills are not overrated, training programs are of great importance. Indian Valley Meats has found that Soviet and American ways of doing business are so different that a good training program is required. This firm brings to its plant near Anchorage as many as 12 Soviets at a time for a period of three to four weeks, during which they receive instruction in both production activities and business practices. So far about 200 workers and managers have visited. The company has set up a classroom for the program, makes use of videotapes, and employs a Russian-speaking instructor.

The Alaska Commercial Company (ACC), one of the five companies who participated in the state of Alaska's first trade mission, has also faced the need for training directly. The ACC is a large retail consumer goods cooperative serving rural communities throughout Alaska. Its interest is to buy and sell consumer items with its Soviet partners. Its retail stores at Alaska's seaports already serve Soviet sailors when their ships dock. After establishing a business relationship with Soviet partners in Magadan, the company's management soon realized that progress was handicapped by the lack of understanding on the part of the Soviet partners as to what in fact doing business together entailed. Consequently, under the supervision of a Soviet manager who works full time at the company's headquarters in Anchorage, the ACC hosts a management trainee from the U.S.S.R. every three months. Prior to arriving at the ACC, the trainee gathers samples of native products to market in Alaska. With the assistance of ACC's staff, the trainee then spends the three-month internship promoting these products as well as keeping track of previous orders and deliveries. In this way, the Soviet manager-trainee is learning about promotion and selling at the same time as these activities serve the joint commercial interest: to develop two-way business and trade.

Western firms find that new Soviet enterprises often overstate their resources as well as their skills. The joint venture formed by Indian Valley Meats provides a good example. When initial negotiations were under way, the Soviet partner indicated that there would be no problem supplying enough reindeer horn to pay for the first shipment of machinery and equipment. "No problem" was the Soviet partner's position. But this did not turn out to be the case. In fact, there were problems to be overcome: tools for cutting the horn, appropriate methods of storage and shipping. As it turned out the Soviets lacked cutting equipment as well as refrigerated containers for transporting the valuable cargo. And, as a result, Indian Valley Meats had to get involved in an aspect of operations that was not originally foreseen.

Despite these surprises, Indian Valley Meats was still very fortunate, for it was not the resource itself that was overstated, simply the means for exploiting that resource. In many other cases, the access to the resource itself has been overstated. When such problems occur, the Western firm needs to determine the situation of the local partner. Several possibilities exist: (1) the local organization has simply overstated its case in the hope that with the help of the foreign firm resources will be found; (2) the struggle over resources is real, what belongs to whom is in question, and the outcome is not clear; or (3) the resources do belong legally to the local organization but are blocked by a regulatory agency.

The issue of property is closely tied to denationalization. The dismantling of state property and the transfer of these resources changes the ability of the local partners to provide resources. New types of property are being defined by legislation and the union, the republics, and the lower level states and provinces are all involved in the question of property rights. This is a very difficult issue. Not only are republics claiming greater independence and authority but so are lower level administrative units (*oblast* and *krai* are the Russian words for these units, meaning a state or province). Claims of independence are directly tied to control over resources. Thus, Amur Oblast, an administrative region in the Soviet Far East whose resources include minerals, coal, and timber, has announced that all property within its territory is its own—not the property of the Soviet state or the Russian Republic. Similarly, Yakutia has claimed control of the diamond mines within its area. The uncertainty over property rights will not be settled quickly. However, the expansion of the legal forms of ownership and the dismantling of state property will significantly aid the ability of local partners to garner and secure resources.

Affiliations, key personnel, resources, and skills are important factors to assess in a local partner. Equally important, and equally difficult, are subjective values: talent, drive, initiative, ingenuity, and integrity. Integrity can be especially difficult to assess because Soviet managers have been working in a system that is so very different from our own. Western executives who work directly with Soviet managers report that neither side is particularly successful in understanding the other's points of reference. In America, for instance, business is an honest activity where integrity can prevail and wealth is an honest reward for an honest activity. The Soviet manager, on the other hand, has been working in a society where to succeed required going around the system, working through the back door, "on the left," with the shadow economy. As a result doing business openly is more difficult. These differences are important. A Western manager describes his Soviet partner as "daring, entrepreneurial, and quick," but also "secretive and cagey." Yet where a Western firm complains of corruption and disloyalty, a Soviet partner sees only normal business behavior.

In this situation it may be naive to depend on trust. Top management at Indian Valley Meats has had the opportunity to use some of the experience gained with its first joint venture partner to do better a second time. In spring 1991, a second joint venture, KAMAL, was founded. KAMAL is located on the Kamchatka pennisula and is a consortium of 14 reindeer-producing farms in that region. The concept of the joint venture remains the same: reindeer horn and other by-products are traded for know-how, machinery and equipment for sausage production, and consumer goods for reindeer farmers. But in shaping the operations of the joint venture and the responsibilities of each side, the U.S. partner "will be more explicit. . . . I will ask the new consortium to choose the most honest, the hardest working, the best businessman to be its leader," said Doug Drum, owner of Indian Valley Meats. But because of the firm's concerns regarding differences in management practices stemming from different systems, and based on the experience of the first joint venture, the second venture will have a "much more detailed and tight set of internal accounting and financial procedures, as well as a structure for more participation by the American side in overall management decisions."

As the role of the local organization gains dominance in business deals with foreigners, the precise role of the supporting organization in Moscow becomes more difficult to assess. In the past *every* local organization was part of a hierarchy leading to Moscow: the local organization had no authority and always referred the question to the central authorities in Moscow. With decentralization the requirement of approval from an organization's "Moscow boss" should become obsolete. But practice does not always match theory. The situation may remain murky for some time.

When the local organization is part of a still-intact Moscow hierarchy, the Moscow organization can be aggressive and dominant or passive and acquiescent to a proposal coming from below. The relationship between the local partner and its Moscow connection accordingly can be competitive or cooperative. When it is competitive, a deal with a Western firm can be caught in the middle and, as a result, delayed until the local organization works out an agreement with its Moscow connection.

Instead of a still-intact Moscow hierarchy, a local organization may be caught with its Moscow connection in an active state of disintegration or reorganization. With the intense decentralization that is going on under denationalization, all central authorities are subject to being dismantled or dissolved. A local organization that is relying in one way or another on its Moscow connection may suddenly find that its Moscow partner is "unavailable" either because the institution is undergoing reorganization or liquidation or because the staff has changed jobs. This too represents delay. In 1988, when negotiations first began on forming a joint venture to make sausages out of reindeer meat, the question was who the local Soviet partner would be. Several possibilities existed: the local executive committee, the local branch of the ministry of agriculture, the local state farm, an association of local state farms, or a new organization. But the question also was who the Moscow authority would be. When the process started the Ministry of Agriculture (Gosagroprom), which traditionally was to give direction, was still intact but was soon dissolved, leaving the issue to the Russian Republic's Ministry of Agriculture.

I believe the role of Moscow will remain important, but will change. As denationalization proceeds, the Moscow connection will become less one of dictating decisions and more one of filling critical support functions for the local organization such as access to business and technical information and services not available at the local level.

The precise role of the Moscow connection in deals at the local level probably will not be settled for some time. But what is clear is that increased authority over foreign economic activities in the hands of local level administrative agencies adds another challenge to Western firms that work with partners at that level. Under the changing economic structure local authorities have been given rights to create enterprises and joint ventures in certain categories of industrial sectors and to approve and support industrial development in special economic zones. This decentralization is discussed elsewhere in this book: what is important here is that the new discretionary policy on the part of the local authorities means increased diversity in local policy and requires the Western firm to take into account these differences when considering a local partner.

Rules and regulatory policy can now come from three different authoritative units: the local territorial unit (at the level of the *krai* or oblast), the republic level organization, and the all-union level authority. Policies cover a wide range of areas in foreign economic activities and include, for example, taxation, export controls and licensing, and environmental regulations. For example, a forest project proposal from the South Korean firm Hyundai was opposed and finally defeated by local interests because of the perception that it would be environmentally damaging. For firms working at the local level, first there is the problem of determining exactly what the relevant prevailing policy is. Decrees and instructions from higher authorities are not always adequately communicated to the local level. Second, there is the confusion due to conflicting regulations issued by different agencies at different levels of jurisdiction. Entrepreneurs can spend a great deal of time keeping up with the new legal regulations in order to provide an adequate foundation for their activities if challenged. A U.S. joint venture partner was surprised by a reprimand from a branch office of the Ministry of Foreign Trade for having offered to pay a local organization in dollars for services rendered to the joint venture (this was before these rules were somewhat clarified). The Westerner in turn asked the representative why the ministry did not publish such prohibitions and asked how was he otherwise to know this was not legal. In another instance, a joint venture firm found that its account at the local branch of the Soviet Foreign Trade Bank had been debited without its authorization because "a state organization had presented to the bank an invoice for payment" and, in the banker's words, "state organizations' requests for payment from other state organizations occur automatically unless challenged." To its surprise, the joint venture's bank account was suddenly vulnerable to debits without its permission; much time was spent trying to clear the matter up, including the bank manager's request to Moscow for a final clarification. The point here is that rules are confused and clarification at the local level is not always easy to find.

The new opportunities available to Western firms to work with local partners introduce new difficulties and uncertainties. Choosing partners is not easy, nor, when necessary, is divesting. Information is never complete, yet mutually beneficial projects do proceed, as we have shown. The successful projects I have been involved in have had strong personalities as the main driving force—people who are determined and visionary. In my estimation, those who succeed in the present atmosphere are not unlike the Wright brothers: pioneers who launch their projects not because they have perfect information but because they have gotten far enough to believe the project will fly.

CHAPTER 10

The Pioneers

Gail Friedman

Constantin Ohanian, a vice president of Tambrands, Inc., had enough experience setting up business worldwide to know his way around international banking. That was until he had a firsthand look at financing, Soviet-style. In 1989, Tambrands's Soviet bank transferred 1.6 million rubles (about $2.5 million) from the multinational corporation's account to a municipality. Why? Because a local official asked for it.

The city had taken a property tax and rent dispute into its own hands. "The municipality presented us with a bill for 1.6 million rubles, which would make it more expensive than renting in the center of Manhattan, and we said, 'You guys must be joking.' So, as we were discussing it, they just took the money off our account," said Ohanian, who coordinated Tambrands's Soviet operations. It took about six weeks to recover the money.

That is just one of the episodes that has frustrated Ohanian. But the Soviet Union in many ways is a dream market for Tambrands, which manufactures feminine protection products in 9 countries and sells them in 135. The corporation targets 30 million Soviet women of childbearing age in the Soviet Union and sells all it can manufacture—with no advertising and no competition. Until it put tampons on the market, Soviet women had little choice but to buy cotton in pharmacies and fashion their own sanitary napkins.

Tambrands's experiences illustrate the lures and pitfalls of the Soviet market: opportunity so great that capitalists salivate at the thought, and a system so unpredictable that many throw up their hands and go home.

Talk to the pioneers of Soviet-American joint ventures, the executives who entered the Soviet Union before the crowds arrived, and most will remember the formidable hurdles, memories they'd rather not conjure up. But those who have had success—and they are few—are first in line to take advantage of future opportunities.

Four of the companies that are succeeding with joint ventures in the Soviet Union are Tambrands; McDonald's; Asea Brown Boveri, which bought Combustion Engineering, the first American company to register a joint venture in the Soviet Union; and Zeiger International, a smaller business that owns interests in an American-style restaurant, a pizza truck, and a Nathan's hot dog outlet. These businesses have shown the persistence, patience, and sensitivity needed to weather a market that has in some ways become more challenging since the end of the cold war. Increasingly assertive republics have compelled foreign executives to deal with extra layers of bureaucracy as they try to get a handle on the shifting set of business rules.

Few of the businesses that explore a Soviet joint venture ever begin one. Many bow out after lengthy investigations; others register joint ventures but never get them off the ground. Those who succeed not only manage to understand the Soviet psyche and work through an intimidating bureaucracy, they also learn to make a venture worthwhile in a system whose currency is worthless on world markets.

"You can't go in and think in terms of folding green U.S. dollars," said Eugene Madara, the lawyer who has negotiated Combustion Engineering's joint ventures, including the first American-Soviet venture, which manufactures process-control equipment. "You have to throw out all the ideas about how you do business in the West and start concocting other ways to get paid. If you can't satisfy the question, How do I get paid? you don't do it."

Until rubles are easily convertible on favorable terms, Western businesses must find ways to collect hard currency or take out goods that they can sell for hard currency. Some are investing ruble earnings within the Soviet Union, betting on a long-term payoff once the currency is worth converting.

Asea Brown Boveri takes out profit from its six joint ventures in exported products, raw materials, and hard currency. The corporation generates hard currency by supplying projects financed by Western banks and by working with ministries or other enterprises that have hard currency, such as the Oil and Gas Ministry, which collects hard currency from exporting resources. When deals cannot be struck for hard currency, exports including pulp, metals, and minerals are the company's payoff. In some bartering arrangements, a joint venture sells goods to a foreign company, which then pays Asea Brown Boveri directly in hard currency.

Tambrands takes out profit in cotton. Ohanian said the Soviets agreed to the arrangement because a tampon uses 10 to 12 fewer grams of cotton than a woman otherwise would use on a homemade sanitary pad. Although Tambrands executives would not discuss the specifics of their arrangement, Ohanian said there is a correlation between the amount of cotton saved through tampon use and the agreement that allows the company to take out cotton and expand its operations. "The concept of the business is that by using tampons instead of making homemade pads they save enough cotton to pay for that industry to be there in the Soviet Union," he said.

The Soviet McDonald's invested $50 million and 12 years of planning and negotiations before it earned its first ruble. McDonald's did reap a public relations bounty when it opened—the kind of attention that is not as important to a company selling industrial goods—and quickly became the best-known Western business in the Soviet Union.

The venture, between McDonald's Restaurants of Canada, Ltd., and Mosrestaurantservice, the food service of the Moscow City Council, seems an ideal arrangement. While many products are needed by the Soviet people, none is more desired than food. When the chairman of McDonald's of Canada, George A. Cohon, was walking through the long lines of people waiting to get into the Moscow McDonald's, Soviets frequently asked him if there would be food left when they finally reached the counter.

In a country where food processing was primitive, McDonald's could furnish world-class technology and know-hòw. But it couldn't make a ruble valuable. The Moscow McDonald's, an enormous store on Tverskaya Street (formerly Gorky Street) at Pushkin Square and near Red Square, serves 1.2 million people monthly. But the joint venture agreement allows for 20 stores, including a hard-currency store in Moscow, near several tourist hotels. The corporation has arranged to take out profit from the hard-currency store based on revenues from all its branches in the Soviet Union.

Some businesses earn both rubles, to pay salaries and overhead, and hard currency, which leaves the country as profit. Trenton, New Jersey, importer and entrepreneur Shelley Zeiger opened an American-Soviet joint venture in 1988, a truck that sold slices of pizza and soft drinks. At first it stopped at popular Moscow spots and collected rubles four days a week; twice a week it parked near a hotel that was popular with foreigners and collected hard currency. Now it sells pizza for hard currency 25 days a month, parking outside the arena where foreign exhibitions are held; 5 days a month Soviets can buy a slice for rubles outside the Gorky Park subway stop. While industrial joint ventures may find it difficult to earn hard currency and therefore arrange to take out profit in manufactured goods or raw materials, those businesses that can cater to foreign customers have a direct way to generate profit in hard currency.

A former liquor distributor, Zeiger originally went to the Soviet Union in 1973 to try to get the rights to Stolichnaya vodka—a deal that Pepsico had negotiated. Instead, he began importing Soviet perfumes and dolls. In 1989, Zeiger—a Ukraine-born Holocaust survivor—opened the first American restaurant in Moscow, named TrenMos after the cities he loves to boost, Trenton and Moscow. (He likes to blend names: a subsidiary of his company, Zeiger Enterprises, is Shelmar Imports, named for himself and his wife, Marion.)

Zeiger's third eatery in the Soviet Union is a joint venture between a

Soviet partner and Nathan's, the New York hot dog chain. Hot dogs and paper goods are imported to maintain Nathan's standards, but other food items, such as potatoes, beef, soda, and juice, come from local sources. Hot dogs are sold to foreigners most of the month for hard currency and to Soviets for rubles about one week a month. While the rubles generated by Zeiger's operations pay for local goods and salaries, the entrepreneur said he is counting on eventual convertibility for the rubles he is accumulating. He is considering using the rubles to invest in Soviet property; for now they sit in a bank earning about 3 percent interest.

TrenMos generally serves 25 percent of its meals to ruble-paying customers and 75 percent to diners with hard currency, though those percentages fluctuate. The restaurant originally seated hard-currency customers in a separate room from those paying with rubles, but Soviets and foreigners now mix. When reservations are taken, the type of currency that will be used is noted. A typical foreigner spends about $40 at TrenMos for dinner, while a Soviet diner spends 100 rubles. There are two separate menus, one in English with prices in dollars and one in Russian with prices in rubles; both offer the same dishes. The ruble prices are based in part on how much of a dish is made with imported ingredients, while the dollar prices are based on what a similar dish would cost in a good American restaurant. For example, a New York strip steak, served with potatoes and a vegetable, costs $21 on the English menu and 35 rubles on the Russian menu. Business is brisk.

TrenMos is a step into the good old U.S. of A., complete with apple pie and Dixie beer. There's a huge picture of George Washington crossing the Delaware; red, white, and blue decor with brass railings; and letters and photos on the walls—including a shot of the American city some Soviets must by now know as well as New York and Washington: Trenton.

TrenMos has turned Zeiger's son and manager, Jeffrey, into a sudden celebrity, catering parties for Moscow-based diplomats. When Raisa Gorbachev wanted a Western-style working luncheon for a cultural organization, Jeffrey supplied Caesar salad, roast beef sandwiches, potato salad, coleslaw, pickles, and apple pie. Jeffrey grew up in suburban Moorestown, New Jersey, and was at one time reluctant to travel with his father to the Soviet Union; he has now been on several TV and radio shows in Moscow and has been featured in newspapers. Both Zeigers speak Russian.

The younger Zeiger has found local sources for meat, vegetables, and virtually all the other foods used in the restaurant. Unlike the average Soviet citizen, he can afford to pay premium prices to farmers' markets and individual dealers—10 to 15 times more than the prices charged in state stores. The menu is written daily, after two trucks—one refrigerated—are loaded with the best that the market can offer. For TrenMos, finding local food sources was the key to profit, which Zeiger believes has been greater than the amount he would have earned from a similar venture in the United States.

Ohanian also stressed the importance of finding local sources of goods—a process that took him 2½ years. In some cases, Tambrands set up joint ventures with suppliers so they could meet the tampon's specifications. Still, Ohanian said, Tambrands is importing about 10 percent of its materials into the Soviet Union, based on the total cost of the goods used.

Combustion Engineering initially imported most components and slowly tapered off the amount as it trained Soviets to manufacture them. Anticipating such limits of the Soviet supply infrastructure has been essential to Western investors.

The Soviet McDonald's is the only McDonald's worldwide that supplies its own food; Soviet food processors were not capable of meeting the restaurant's specifications. McDonald's $40 million food production and distribution center, outside Moscow, is no small accomplishment in a food-starved nation. Each week it can process 55 tons of local beef, 1 million buns, 71 tons of potatoes, 24,000 gallons of milk, 128,000 cheese slices, 10 tons of fresh vegetables, 18,000 gallons of special sauce, and 5,300 gallons of pickles, among other products.

When McDonald's could not find local sources for the ingredients it needed, it created local sources. For example, suitable potatoes for McDonald's french fries were not available, so McDonald's brought in the seeds as well as an agricultural expert from the Netherlands to help Soviet farmers cultivate the potatoes. When potatoes were rotting throughout Soviet fields, Cohon, the colorful McDonald's chief, personally led 200 employees to one of the restaurant's farms to harvest the vegetable.

To provide all the ingredients in a "Beeg Mek," McDonald's also helped a local farm grow iceberg lettuce, which was not available in the Soviet Union. McDonald's did not find or create local sources for a few goods, such as mustard and spices, and is importing the ingredients. It intends, however, eventually to find local sources for all of its ingredients.

Success for these joint ventures took more than know-how and local sources for raw materials. Each of these companies' executives have learned to understand the Soviet psyche. And all have learned that patience is not only a virtue but a prerequisite to business success in the U.S.S.R. Combustion Engineering's meetings sometimes started at 8 A.M. and continued until 2 A.M. the next day. "It depends on who can sit the longest, and he who sits the longest wins. I've been known to sit for a long time," Madara said. "I think you have to keep redescribing the issue until something finally hits."

Such patience is necessary not only during touchy negotiations, but also during mundane business routines, such as placing a phone call or photocopying a document. In the U.S.S.R. photocopy machines are guarded like gold. According to Madara, these machines, which are considered potential printing presses, are locked; one person has the key. Making a copy entails finding that person, persuading him or her to unlock the machine and bring in the paper, then running the copy while he or she watches. If you need another copy a few minutes later, you repeat the whole process.

It can take hours to get an international phone line. And it can take months or more to get a telephone installed in your office. Direct lines are rare, and there are no phone directories. "All the Westerners go around with these little pieces of paper with penciled phone numbers on them," Madara said.

While the opportunity is enormous, profit also requires patience—a longer wait than a corporation might normally endure. Michael Rae is president of Argus Trading, Ltd., a firm that consults with and represents about 100 Western companies that do business in the Soviet market. According to Rae, who has been negotiating business with the Soviets since 1973, most companies have to operate for two to five years before they make a profit.

However, Combustion Engineering was able to turn a profit on its first joint venture by the end of its first year. But it took many months to teach Soviets to produce goods up to Western standards. Until the locally made products met specifications, Combustion Engineering imported components; even today, some components are imported. "There was a lot of scrap at the beginning," said Madara. "We sent components in until they learned the technology. At first the Soviets only assembled imported components, then they started to make some of their own components using our designs and drawings and training. Gradually, the local manufacturer took over larger and larger pieces."

Tambrands burned everything produced the first week. "That made a major impact," said Ohanian. "It wasn't up to spec and we burned it, and we made sure that the employees knew."

Getting the notion of quality through to the Soviets can mean bridging not only the language barrier, but cultural and psychological barriers as well. Soviets simply think differently than Westerners might expect. One example is a story Rae likes to tell about a Soviet shovel manufacturer. (Argus Trading primarily sells Western products to Soviets, but the firm also markets Soviet products.) One day a shovel manufacturer told Rae he was interested in exporting his goods to the U.S. When Rae asked for samples to show potential customers, he was given shovels with cracked handles and chipped paint. "These are supposed to be examples," Rae told the man, "not factory rejects." The manufacturer replied that he has to sell the good shovels, and that if potential customers wondered about the quality, "You tell them that they won't be any worse than these."

How can a Westerner develop the patience to work around such an enormous cultural chasm? You try to understand the Soviet and put aside the feeling that you know how to do things much better than your Soviet colleague—even though that may be true. Madera warned:

> Don't go in as the ugly American and say, look, I know how to
> do this and I'm going to show you. That's a stupid attitude. I

taught my team to put themselves in the Soviet person's shoes. Recognize the culture and the history and the background.

I sat in one meeting with one fellow who kept referring to the Soviets as Russkies. That's asinine behavior. People forget where they are, they forget what they're doing, they have no sensitivity to the culture. It's the same sort of boorish American who'd put his feet on the table in front of an Arab. That American typically will lean back, put his feet up on the desk and cross them. He doesn't realize it but he has just killed his deal. It's very easy to kill your deal.

Madara grew to understand the Soviet culture as he spent time in the country and paid attention to details of everyday Soviet life. When he learned that young couples routinely visit a war memorial right after they are married and listened to a colleague relate that she had survived the siege of Leningrad, he began to recognize that a wartime mentality persists and shapes Soviet attitudes—and the way they do business.

The attitude in the U.S.S.R. is that the West has always been preying on it—the opposite of what we were always taught. Disregard all that propaganda from both sides. Recognize that they probably think you're the aggressor. You're trying to cheat them out of something. So you've got to explain, this is what I'm doing, and this is how it benefits me. Obviously the joint venture benefits me or I wouldn't be doing it. And this is how it benefits the Soviet Union. The discussion then changes from my side versus your side to this is a joint venture. It's going to be our company, so problems are our problems.

Rae warned of executives "with business school educations and clean fingernails" who are not prepared for business styles that were never broached in a textbook. They may be frightened by the ponderous way decisions are made or by the elaborate Soviet contracts, which tend to be loaded with penalty clauses and open to little modification.

Successful executives have realized they could not go to the Soviet Union expecting to direct operations as they did in France, Brazil, or elsewhere. They recognize that the system is supply-driven, not demand-driven; the manufacturer who is asked to produce certain goods will generally first push products that the factory already produces, even if they don't meet the Westerner's specifications.

When Combustion Engineering was looking for a manufacturer to produce valve castings—giant metal bodies that hold the valve's mechanism—one Soviet businessman insisted that an existing product would meet the company's needs. In such an instance, "you walk away," advised Madara. In recent years, he added, Soviets have become more and more likely to call you back provided you have not made the mistake of giving them an either-or ultimatum. Hardball, in general, is not popular.

Corporations must modify their internal structure to work with the Soviets, who are not used to delegating authority. Madara described how all decisions had to go through the Soviet director general. In one Combustion Engineering venture, when a Western deputy director gave instructions, a Soviet subordinate would listen but would not act until the Soviet director general gave the order.

The successful joint venture has Western leaders who realize that approaches that often work elsewhere can kill a deal in the U.S.S.R. Executives experienced in Soviet trade warn novices not to sit down with a stranger and get right to business. Small talk—about family, music, any benign topic—is an important icebreaker, a small way to begin earning the confidence of someone whose instinct may be to mistrust you.

Something as simple as offering alternatives doesn't work because the Soviets are not used to such choices. "They've had one product to choose from; there's no brand competition," said Madara. "That is changing—but in the early days, if you said, we can do it this way or we can do it this way, there was no psychological way that they could decide between two. So you discuss this one to death, then you say, how about this instead? But if you say, either or, up to you, and sit back, that's it for the day, you might as well go fishing."

The Soviet on the other side of the table often has little understanding of capitalism. Two successful strategies for improving that understanding are to give the Soviets firsthand experience in the West and to teach them a crash course in basic economics.

For the McDonald's joint venture, four Soviet managers received 1000 hours of training both on the job in McDonald's restaurants and in the classroom at the McDonald's Institute of Hamburgerology in Toronto. A Russian-speaking manager helped them at the restaurants where they trained. The Soviets also spent two weeks at McDonald's Hamburger University in Illinois. Later, another 25 Soviet managers came to Canada for training.

During its first year in the Soviet Union, Tambrands brought 17 Soviets to the West, primarily to England, for between three weeks and three months of training in technical and supervisory skills. Combustion Engineering brought Soviets to the U.S. and England, usually for a month of technical training. Asea Brown Boveri continues to bring Soviets to the West when new training is necessary, but also relies heavily on Westerners who are on site at Soviet plants.

Madara essentially taught his Soviet colleagues a crash course in basic economics, explaining the meaning of gross margins, operating expenses, and other simple items on a balance sheet.

Economics is not the only subject Western executives have taught. Zeiger found himself teaching American-style manners to a college student who was collecting money in his pizza truck. He suggested she thank each person as they paid. "But you don't have to," she replied, wise to the fact that the pizza would still sell if she continued to scowl. When she relented, she began thanking people meekly, then gained confidence and thanked more loudly. Suddenly, Zeiger said, customers started thanking her for thanking them. A huge smile was on her face, he said, "as if America had arrived."

The practiced American smiles on McDonald's Soviet hamburger sellers have been well publicized. In a country with severe food shortages, happy faces may not be needed to sell hamburgers, but they are an important component of the company's fine-tuned image.

Whether the message is about how to greet people or how to make plastics, getting through to the Soviet worker can be difficult. He or she may have been taught for years to produce goods without regard for quality. But workers respond well to incentives.

All of the joint ventures studied pay well above the average Soviet salary. Tambrands employees earn 50 to 100 percent more than the average Soviet. But just as important, Ohanian said, are the working conditions. When a local union was trying to organize the Tambrands factory, "One of the ladies turned around and said, 'Look, you know, for the first time I've been working somewhere that people don't shout at me. I can talk to my boss. And there's no way I'm going to let you guys in here.' " In addition, Tambrands employees have access to an in-factory store and to programs that help them get housing, education, and necessities.

McDonald's would not discuss its salary structure or incentive plan, but said that Soviet workers' incentives include pay, food, and other goods.

At TrenMos, the 60 staffers who wait tables, wash dishes, peel a half ton of apples weekly for pie, and perform other chores earn about the same as a government minister—500 to 800 rubles a month, Zeiger said. While they don't receive the perks of a minister, the young Zeiger devised a way for them to receive tips even when it was illegal to give them hard currency. He'd tally up the tips earned by each of the waiters; at the end of the month, he would either take the waiters to a hard-currency store and buy things for them or hand them a Sears or J.C. Penney catalog and order for them. TrenMos has virtually no employee turnover.

Salary and benefits are just part of what makes a job attractive to a Soviet employee. Besides a generous salary, Combustion Engineering's employees' benefits are not substantially different from the average Soviet worker's. However, working for a Western company—just having access to a computer—can be a perk in Soviet society. Some savvy Soviets try to work for an international firm in the hope that someday they will earn bonuses in hard currency.

Such incentives can help make Soviets loyal and productive employees, despite the fact that for years they may have been conditioned not to care much about their work. On the other hand, while Western employees may have a cultural work ethic, they can be just as much of a management challenge in the U.S.S.R. as the Soviet workers.

To help them function, expatriates generally receive frequent vacations. Westerners working for Tambrands receive a month's vacation each year plus one week off every three months. At Combustion Engineering, Western employees might receive a month of vacation yearly, plus a week outside the Soviet Union every 90 days if they live in Moscow or two weeks every 60 days if they live in a remote town. Simple tips, such as information about European stores that will ship in food—Stockmann in Helsinki, Marks & Spencer in London—can help ease the transition to Soviet life.

Madara said that Asea Brown Boveri uses a service to evaluate whether employees and their families will function well in the Soviet Union. The British often adapt better than the Americans. Both Madara and Ohanian said that people who are used to life in Third World countries are excellent candidates. In addition, a good candidate, Ohanian said, "burns with ambition to get somewhere and sees this as a stepping stone."

The Westerner who survives happily in the Soviet Union is exceptionally strong, with few emotional or material needs. Anyone with alcoholic or depressive tendencies is a poor candidate, said Rae, who knows of a few Westerners who committed suicide in the Soviet Union. Single people tend to succeed, as do stable families—although families may end up costing companies substantially for private schools, larger living quarters, and other benefits. Rae described an active social life among expatriates, but said that Westerners must be suspicious when Soviets strike up a friendship. They actually may want access to Western goods or medical supplies.

Living conditions can be especially trying for Westerners used to spacious surroundings. Waits are so long for apartments that executives may spend weeks or months in dreary hotel rooms. At one time these hard-to-get apartments were in buildings full of foreigners, said Madara, with strict security out front. Now Westerners are scattered, which means they are better integrated into Soviet society but are not as safe from crime. Most apartments have one bedroom; families have an extremely difficult time getting more than one, Madara said. The apartments generally are well below Western standards and need to be refurbished.

Still, most Westerners prefer their own apartment to extended hotel stays. Madera explained:

> The hotels range from average by Western standards to not pleasant—roaches and dirt. By and large, the hotel people are friendly; they're just disorganized. Checking in can be a 45-minute to an hour process because your reservation typically is written down in a looseleaf notebook. It's not alphabetical. They flip through until they find the day on which your reservation was made. It could be an hour; it could be longer.
>
> You just have to learn not to get discouraged. You've been flying for 12 hours, you're dirty and tired, you fought your way through immigration and customs and got a taxi that actually

brought you to your hotel. You're in a totally alien culture with a different language, you can't read the street signs, and it's snowing and it's dark and you get to the hotel and they say, no, there's no reservation. You just have to persist. The line builds up behind you and people are angry. If you don't move, the desk clerks tend to find the reservation.

Like many other Western firms, Asea Brown Boveri now pays a premium to book hotel rooms through a Western travel agency that has access to blocks of Soviet rooms. Two of these agents are Barry Martin Travel, Inc., in New York, London, and Moscow, and the Soviet American Travel and Trade Association, Inc., in Gonzales, Louisiana. They can reduce problems dramatically, but do not guarantee a smooth check-in. Tambrands's agreement with the Soviets allowed the company a long-term lease on a guest house in Kiev, so the firm's executives frequently bypass hotels.

In addition to coping with poor accommodations, Western executives face difficulties that stem from the Soviet republics' battle for power, which has made it hard to determine who's in charge. Some executives have seen the ministries that they were dealing with dissolve, then have shuttled back and forth between the republic and Moscow, looking for an authority.

"Any contract that you sign today may not be valid next week," warned Ohanian. "A person with whom you may have signed it today may not be there tomorrow. We completed an acquisition for our joint venture in the Soviet Union in Leningrad and the municipality that approved the deal was dissolved the next week and the office where the deal was made has been dissolved. So we had to start the whole thing all over again."

Besides dealing with dissolving ministries, companies may also have to deal with a governmental bureau that hasn't gone away: the KGB. Tambrands has had at least three KGB investigations that were designed to determine whether the joint venture's activities would conflict with Soviet interests. In addition, Tambrands has invested considerable time responding to questions posed by various deputies on a variety of subjects. "The next thing you know, you've got seven commissions from different ministries investigating a certain aspect of your business because somebody has asked a question," he said.

Zeiger believes small businesses have an easier time with the bureaucracy, dealing one-to-one more than by committee. He sometimes proceeded with business despite bureaucratic obstacles. He essentially gave his Soviet partners half interest in TrenMos even though they contributed little capital to the deal.

TrenMos did not have a particularly smooth opening. Construction that should have taken six to eight weeks took nine months, Zeiger said, in part because workmen did not have proper tools. "We had parquet floors but we had to wait three to four weeks to get the glue. Then we couldn't get the expert who lays the tile. It was two weeks before opening, so we said, the hell with it, we're going to go with a brown carpet. It's a red, white, and blue decor, but we went with a brown carpet just to get it open."

Given another chance, Zeiger said he would send in a Western architect, interior designer, engineer, and two or three supervisors who are electricians and plumbers, as well as all materials, including items as small as nails. Sending in foreign experts is not uncommon, although such experts tend to be technical people, such as the McDonald's agronomist or the technical and financial experts who consulted in the Soviet Union for Combustion Engineering.

Three days before Trenmos's opening, the restaurant was in turmoil, partly because the Soviet manager was building more hurdles than he knocked down. Zeiger wanted the manager replaced, but expected the board's vote to split along Soviet and American lines. His confidence in the Soviet system soared—despite the chaos—when the vote for dismissal was unanimous. The manager was out. To Zeiger, that was a significant signal that his Soviet partners understood the *joint* in joint venture, and were placing the welfare of the business above the machinations of a rusty system.

Zeiger is working on several other joint ventures and is considering opening additional restaurants throughout the Soviet republics.

Tambrands has no immediate plans for expansion, though the corporation is poised for new ventures when the time is right. Ohanian is cautious. He is quick to warn Western firms that the Soviet Union is a difficult market, one that will challenge them with problems they may not have faced before.

Then he reflects, "There is no problem-free business. In some markets we have a competitive problem. We don't have that problem in the Soviet Union, but we have some other problems. All of them are solvable, but they do take a lot of effort, a lot of time, a kind of almost fanatical commitment."

CHAPTER 11

A Soviet View

Yevgeniy Y. Pompa

Victor Hugo once wrote, "There is one thing stronger than all the armies in the world, and that is an idea whose time has come." My 15 years of experience in Soviet foreign trade and in international economics convince me that the international business community is being challenged by a vast new economic idea—the Soviet Union. That conclusion is not based only on theory; international business activity has always pursued new resources and new markets. The Soviet Union represents 16 percent of the earth's land, 14 percent of global industrial production, and 300 million potential consumers. The international business community will expand into the Soviet Union just as the ocean will expand into a coastal bay after a seawall that was keeping it out is brought down by an earthquake.

No corporate development strategy can be complete without addressing the question of doing business with the Russians. American business's underestimation of this market, unique in its dimensions, might well put the Soviet driver behind the wheel of a Toyota in place of the Fords that have enjoyed prestige in the U.S.S.R. ever since World War II. For the Soviets, foreign economic cooperation is needed now to assist in the economic reforms and the transition to a market economy which will make both the U.S.S.R. and the partners who collaborate with us richer. President Mikhail Gorbachev expressed this clearly in June 1990: "Those who are with us now cannot lose. But those who turn their backs on us will stay where they are."

It was once believed that a good bargain was a transaction in which one person got the better of another. We now understand that a good contract is a transaction that is good for both parties. This principle is followed in the fundamental restructuring by the Soviet Union of its foreign economic relations—opening up the Soviet economy to foreign capital, technology, and expertise, and paving the way for mutually beneficial long-term cooperation.

Until recently, the development of Soviet foreign trade was defined to a significant extent by factors of a political nature. The concept of economic sovereignty resulted in the formation of an isolationist stereotype for development of the U.S.S.R.'s external economic relations. This led to the fact that, after the last concessions to foreign capital were closed in the 1930s, commodity exchange became essentially the country's only official form of participation in global economic relations (Table 11-1).[1] Exports, for the most part of raw materials, were considered to be instruments for exerting political influence on importers, and imports were viewed as a desperate measure to which a country would turn only if it had no other choice.

The Soviet civilian machine-building industry did not enjoy the same level of priority and investment as did the military branches of the economy. Only about 14 percent of the machines, equipment, and transportation facilities exported by the U.S.S.R. meet world standards. The result (see Table 11-2) has been a decrease during the last 20 years in the share of high value-added goods in Soviet exports. Machinery and equipment exports to the industrially developed countries have made up only 3 to 4 percent of total exports over the last few years.

Almost 60 percent of the U.S.S.R.'s exports come from fuel, minerals, and other raw materials and metals. The Soviet Union's specialization in

Table 11-1 Soviet Foreign Trade

	Trade in Billions of Dollars		
	1970	**1980**	**1989**
Total trade turnover	24.6	147	224
Exports	12.8	78	109
Imports	11.8	69	114
Socialist countries	16.0	79	138
Exports	8.3	42	67
Imports	7.7	37	71
Developed countries	5.2	49	59
Exports	2.4	25	26
Imports	2.8	24	33
Developing countries	3.3	19	27
Exports	2.0	11	16
Imports	1.2	8	11

SOURCE: Official U.S.S.R. foreign trade statistics for 1970–89.

Table 11-2   Structure of Soviet Foreign Trade

	Percent Exports		Percent Imports	
	1970	1989	1970	1989
Machines, equipment, and transportation infrastructure	21.5	16.4	35.6	38.5
Fuel and electrical power	15.6	39.9	2.0	3.0
Ores, concentrates, metals, and goods made from them	19.6	10.5	9.6	7.3
Chemical products, fertilizers, rubber	3.5	4.0	5.7	5.1
Timber and cellulose-paper products	6.5	3.5	2.1	1.2
Unfinished and half-finished textiles	3.4	1.6	4.8	1.6
Food products and the raw material for their production	8.4	1.6	15.8	16.6
Manufactured consumer goods	2.7	2.6	18.3	14.4
All other products	18.8	19.9	6.1	12.3

SOURCE: Data from official U.S.S.R. foreign trade statistics.

raw materials is especially high in trade with the developed countries, where about 75 percent of exports consist of raw materials. Oil and gas deliveries to the world market provide about 70 percent of the U.S.S.R.'s receipts of hard currency. The Soviet Union lost about $60 billion in the years 1986–88 because of decreased prices for petroleum and other raw materials.

The U.S.S.R. approached the beginning of the 1990s with an import structure formed during the years of "petroleum euphoria." Petrodollars transformed imports into a means of covering up weaknesses in the economy.

Thus, although the Soviet Union produces more steel than any other country, the U.S.S.R. has become the world's largest importer of pipes. Food imports remain a sore point, having grown swiftly in the 1970s and 1980s, despite the fact that the Soviet Union has more arable land per capita than the United States or the countries of Western Europe.[2]

The priority of political factors in the development of the U.S.S.R.'s foreign economic complex likewise led to an unjustifiably high share of trade with the socialist countries. At present they account for more than 60 percent of the U.S.S.R.'s trade, while producing (without the U.S.S.R.) only 15 percent of world income. Trade with developed market economy countries accounts for 25 percent of the U.S.S.R.'s total, although these countries account for 57 percent of world income.

The cumulative effect of foreign trade problems has led to a worsening of the foreign trade balance. In 1989 the foreign trade balance became negative for the first time (about $7.8 billion), and the trade deficit with the industrialized developed countries reached $5.9 billion, as opposed to $1 billion in 1985.

Perestroika is being called upon to radically change the situation in the U.S.S.R.'s foreign economic complex. Our task is to make the foreign economic complex an active assistant of reform, a factor for developing the economy, for increasing its level of competitiveness, liquidating its chronic shortages, and raising the standard of living of the Soviet people. An important place in these plans will be allocated to foreign companies. It is considered that their financial and technical resources—and their organizational, managerial, production, and marketing experience—could be important factors in the development of the Soviet economy. Therefore, the striving to attract foreign companies to the U.S.S.R. is part of a long-term strategy based upon economic reality.

When appraising the business possibilities opened up by the U.S.S.R.'s new foreign economic strategy, Western entrepreneurs need to understand that reform of the Soviet Union's foreign economic complex is part of a fundamental change toward market principles and integration into the world economy. In addition, the aspiration for business cooperation with other countries is not just a product of a series of decrees from the Soviet government.[3] The new economic environment is based on a genuine change in the way Soviet people think about business and entrepreneurship.

The rapid development of the cooperative movement in the country can serve as one example of this. In 1988 alone the number of active cooperatives grew 2½ times and reached 193,000. Almost 5 million people work for cooperatives, and the volume of their yearly sales is the equivalent of about $60 billion. A new guard of Soviet business people is interested in making use of whatever opportunities for mutually advantageous business undertakings exist—from the organization of business schools to prospecting for natural resources.

To do business with the Soviet Union is far from simple. It is not easy to succeed in business in any foreign country. Cooperation with the U.S.S.R., like that with any other country, must be based on a strategy that takes into account its various unique characteristics as a business partner. The skill of the foreign entrepreneur should consist of correctly evaluating business potential in relation to the Soviet market and finding a way of combining the interests of the foreign company with those of the Soviet side.

As a first step in this direction, it is crucial to define the nature and extent of the company's interest in the Soviet market. The opportunities in the U.S.S.R. are countless; the current state of the U.S.S.R.'s economy is such that we can speak of huge production resources, and also of demand for trade in essentially all conceivable areas (Table 11-3). But exactly which opportunity will bring success to each individual firm, and what its scale

Table 11-3   Comparisons between the U.S.S.R. and the
United States (1988)

	U.S.S.R.	United States
Gross national product (GNP), in billions of dollars	2,500	4,862
GNP per capita, in dollars	8,700	19,800
Population, millions of people	289	248
Production per capita		
Electric power, kilowatt-hours	5,967	11,868
Steel, kg.	571	372
Synthetic resins and plastics, kg.	16	112
Grain and leguminous cultivation, kg.	683	842
Meat, kg.	69	122
Milk, kg.	374	268
Railroads, thousands of km.	146	270
Highways, millions of km.	1.6	6.4
Number of TV sets in use, millions	85	150[a]
Number of radios in use, millions	162	495[a]
Number of installed telephones, millions	35	183

[a]1982

SOURCES: *National Economy of the USSR in 1988* (Moscow: USSR Gos-komstst, 1989), 678–79. *Statistical Yearbook of the Member-Countries of Comecon, 1988* (Moscow: Finances and Statistics, 1988), 303. Central Intelligence Agency, *The World Factbook, 1989* (Washington, D.C., 1989), 273–75, 308–10.

will be, depends on each firm's overall approach to organizing its cooperation with the U.S.S.R. The main question is whether to simply trade with the U.S.S.R. or to build relations on the basis of investments. Both approaches have their advantages. Approaching the Soviet market within the framework of traditional commodity exchange can give foreign firms the opportunity to understand the Soviet side better, to familiarize themselves with business practices and customs in the U.S.S.R., and to verify the reliability of their partner without putting a major investment on the line. This can be especially important for American companies that have no experience working with the U.S.S.R. However, a few important points should be kept in mind.

In the United States, there is a widespread tendency to view opportunities for cooperation with the U.S.S.R. primarily through the prism of developing American exports. Such a one-sided approach, from our point of view, is hardly viable. The Soviet economy is in need of further development of foreign trade, but that trade must be balanced and of mutual benefit. Imports are planned to increase in the future, but they will cease to be the slave of shortages and will be oriented toward the solution of the Soviet Union's needs through modernization, replacement of expensive production facilities, and expansion of the products available on the Soviet market. Likewise, exports will cease to be a means of selling what is left over after satisfaction of internal demands and will, instead, be based on comparative advantage and become the instrument for meeting import needs. When planning business operations in the U.S.S.R., foreign companies should take into account not only the huge capacity of the Soviet market but also our need to expand exports so that we can earn the money to increase our imports.

In this respect, foreign entrepreneurs, particularly Americans, will have to overcome yet another widespread misconception: "The Russians have nothing to sell." This is not so! Besides oil, gas, wood, minerals, vodka, and caviar, the Soviet Union has at its disposal huge intellectual resources, an enormous scientific and technical capability, and competitive production in a number of areas. The Achilles' heel of the Soviet economy has been the inability, with the exception of a few branches, to make use of innovation on an industrial scale. Lack of new ideas was never the problem. For example, Soviet mathematicians have been the leaders in this century. Soviet technologies that are world-class include rocketry for launching commercial satellites, airplane building, computer software, medical diagnostic methods, radiation dosage tracking, metal-forming techniques, coating technologies that greatly extend the life of cutting tools, and many others. Among the manufactured products that the Soviet Union could export in volume are chemicals and metals.

The conversion of military production now going on in the U.S.S.R. offers many new commercial possibilities. For example, the advanced technologies developed during the Energy-Buran space project are available to foreign buyers. During work on this project, the highpoint of which was a successful unmanned space mission, including a flawless landing by a reusable spaceship, Soviet scientists and engineers developed dozens of new materials, 240 production processes, and 130 types of advanced equipment, all of which are now available for use in shipbuilding, medicine, and other fields.

The use of Soviet intellectual resources can yield large profits to foreign companies. Foreign firms can use the experience of Soviet specialists to great advantage in developing software for specific projects. For example, there are many qualified and talented computer programmers in the U.S.S.R. The original version of the computer game Tetris, so popular in the United States, was developed by the Soviet programmer Aleksey Pazhitnov, who now works in one of the Soviet-American joint ventures. Intelligent Resources International, Inc., of Baltimore, Maryland, has set up a U.S.S.R. operation with 15 Soviet programmers, and the company intends to increase the number to 200. According to the president of the firm, the move has represented an opportunity to significantly reduce labor expenses. Programmers with a Ph.D. and four or five years of experience can be engaged for a salary equivalent to $500 per month or less. On one of its projects, the firm managed to reduce expenses from the $1.5 million it would have cost in the United States to $250,000.

Many Soviet goods other than high-technology manufactured products have export potential. For example, the agro-industrial complex Siberia in Novosibirsk has exported sauerkraut to Western Europe. The Siberians have dozens of techniques for making sauerkraut, and with proper marketing they could build a large business.

A Russian proverb says, "He who seeks shall always find." Foreigners can "find" by visiting the U.S.S.R., participating in or attending exhibits, and advertising in the Soviet press. Americans have made many contacts with Soviets in Moscow, Leningrad, Kiev, and other major cities. But in Siberia, the Far East, and Central Asia representatives from Western Europe and Japan visit much more often than Americans.

When considering the possibilities for exporting to the U.S.S.R., foreign entrepreneurs should take into account the Soviet Union's import priorities. I have already mentioned that it is a principle of the U.S.S.R.'s foreign economic relations to achieve stability in the country's balance of payments, and to contain external debt within dimensions that do not threaten the Soviet Union's status as a dependable and solvent borrower. This, together with the Soviet Union's limited hard-currency resources, force us at present to approach any increase in imports with great caution. However, some products are being given priority to meet the needs of the Soviet people. These include consumer goods, food products and the raw materials for their production, textile raw materials and half-finished textile products, medical equipment, pharmaceuticals, computers, and equipment for the food industry and light industry. In 1989 the import of these goods grew almost 22 percent (overall imports grew 11 percent) and reached $40 billion. These imports included 87 million pairs of shoes, 138,000 sewing machines, 40,000 vacuum cleaners, 143,000 television sets, 317,000 tape players, and 157,000 videocassette players.

A foreign exporter wishing to market goods in the U.S.S.R. inevitably runs into the problem of payment since the ruble cannot yet be freely converted into the currencies of Western countries. But that problem can be resolved if the foreign company develops creative trade management. There are various options. If the Soviet Union is unwilling to purchase using hard currency, a foreign exporter can sell for rubles and then use the rubles to purchase and then ship out of the U.S.S.R. Soviet goods or services that are in demand on the world market. Finally, the exporter can exchange foreign goods for Soviet goods by means of countertrade. A good understanding of the latter can be an important component of success in trade with the U.S.S.R.

Countertrade is widely used in world markets. For the Soviet Union, as for other countries that have limited hard-currency resources, counter-trade offers an opportunity to partially resolve the problems connected with the financing of imports. For a company wishing to export to the U.S.S.R., countertrade is an instrument for competing in an unfamiliar but promising market. According to Dan West of the Monsanto Company, the chairman of the American Countertrade Association, American compa-nies are letting their rivals best them in the area of developing countertrade, and if Americans want to succeed in the Soviet market, they should change their approach of "Just give me dollars" and learn "to listen to the cus-tomer and help him with currency needs."[4]

The trade agreement concluded with Pepsico in 1990, for instance, will give that company the opportunity in the 1990s to almost double the number of its factories in the U.S.S.R. (from 26 to 50), and to increase Pepsi sales severalfold from the 40 million cases sold in 1989. Because of its skillful use of countertrade, Pepsi dominates the Soviet market even though Coca-Cola far outsells Pepsi in most countries. Coca-Cola cur-rently sells only 20 million cases a year in the U.S.S.R.

In the 1970s, countertrade with the U.S.S.R. was accomplished pri-marily by a type of cooperation known as the buy-back transaction. Such transactions were generally on a large, industrial scale and were planned out over an extended period of time, perhaps 15 or 20 years. A good example of this type of transaction was the cooperation between Occidental Petroleum and the Soviet Union. Occidental helped the Soviet Union construct chemical plants and supplied equipment and superphosphoric acid, in exchange for which chemicals produced in the plants (carbamide, ammonia, and potassium chloride) were shipped back to Occidental.

Then, in the late 1980s, many Soviet enterprises became increasingly interested in exporting the output they had left over after fulfilling their government plan so that they could countertrade for goods their workers needed. This provided the impetus for further development of counter-trade. In just the first half of 1990, Soviet enterprises engaged in about $2 billion of countertrade.

The practice of countertrade in the U.S.S.R. is still in the process of development. This has its pluses for American firms. They can decide for themselves what form, or combination of forms, of countertrade will be the most mutually profitable and best suited to their needs. Medium- and small-sized exporters might choose simple barter, the exchange of goods of approximately the same value within the framework of one contract. In such transactions, it is crucial to work out the mechanism of exchange of goods so as to minimize unnecessary delays and risks. The advantages of this form of trade are its simplicity, which is important for firms just beginning to engage in countertrade, and also, as a rule, its relatively short duration.

Compensational transactions also still take place, similar to those of the 1970s, though not always on such a large scale or over such a long period of time. These transactions are similar to simple barter in that they are based on one contract that provides for deliveries of goods from both sides. The differences are that the compensational transaction may involve payment in currency as well as exchange of goods, and the deliveries of goods by each side may not take place at the same time.

Compensation and, especially, simple barter are being used ever more widely by Soviet organizations for export and import of relatively small batches of goods. For example, in 1989–90 Soviet enterprises supplied American companies with fabrics, scrap metal, and crystal in exchange for equipment, clothing, perfume, and other goods. In 1990, 67 percent of Soviet countertrade exports were of fuel and raw material commodities.

Major corporations and trading firms often make use of more complex forms of countertrade and combinations of them. Counterpurchase is one example of these more complex forms of countertrade. Counterpurchase usually involves the signing of two contracts, one for export of goods from the Soviet Union, the other for purchasing goods for import to the Soviet Union. The purchase contract may be independent of the export contract. Deliveries, calculations, and payments are carried out according to the separate contracts, independently of each other and often with the mediation of a third party. These transactions are often planned out for a period of five to seven years, and are usually linked with large projects, such as infrastructure or factory construction. Often there will be an overall agreement signed about the intent to develop countertrade, and then there will be many individual contracts to cover the actual details of the various transactions involved. Various characteristics of counterpurchase may be observed in the new agreement between Pepsico and the U.S.S.R., according to which, in oversimplified form, Pepsi concentrate and food industry equipment are being exchanged for Soviet vodka and ships.[5]

Whatever form of countertrade is chosen, the foreign exporter needs the advice of a legal firm with experience working with the U.S.S.R. and a familiarity with the Soviet system of regulating external trade by export licensing. Just as the United States defends its economy from destructive dumping, the U.S.S.R. defends its internal market from shortages. Export licensing is used to prevent the excessive export of goods that are in short supply in the U.S.S.R., and this applies both to goods exported directly for hard currency and to goods exported within the framework of countertrade agreements. As the Soviet economy improves, this will change, but for the moment the U.S.S.R. licenses approximately 70 percent of export goods and only 5 percent of imports.

For the optimal corporate strategy, foreign firms should pay special attention to the prospects offered by joint ventures for long-term cooperation with the Soviet Union. The Soviet Union is moving toward full inclusion in the world economy and toward transferring its economy to a market and free enterprise basis. "The aim of restructuring the Soviet economy," said President Gorbachev while visiting the United States in 1990, "is to make sure that the Soviet Union enters the twenty-first century as a law-governed, democratic state and as an integral part of the world economy. The key task here is to raise the degree of compatibility of our economy with the laws and nature of the world market." Reforms of this scale cannot be completed overnight. But the changes that are being made have begun to modify the face of the Soviet Union as a trading partner, making its economy more comparable with the economies of other countries.

The advantages of entering the Soviet market by means of investment-production activity are the same as for the gold prospector who stakes his claim on time. By participating in the development of the Soviet economy, foreign companies guarantee themselves a long-term presence in the Soviet market and receive access to resources of production that are less expensive than those in the West, as well as to many millions of consumers who are fed up with shortages. Considering that Western markets are mature and that the level of competition in them is high, this can have a very positive effect on the competitiveness of the foreign investor.

The Soviet Union wants to attract foreign investment as a source for modernizing the economy, for up-to-date technology and management experience, for the development of hard-currency exports, and for the replacement of imports. It is important to note that this interest exists not just at the governmental level. It would be very hard now to find a factory or *kolkhoz* (collective farm) in the U.S.S.R. that would refuse joint enterprises. Investment-production cooperation and the creation of joint ventures are the most promising avenues of cooperation, for both Western and Soviet firms.

The picture of the U.S.S.R. as an investment opportunity would not be complete without a few facts of life that foreign businesses need to recognize. Economic and organizational conditions in the U.S.S.R. are such that it will be some time before most investments, which include the time and personal efforts of busy executives as well as money, produce a return. Western European and Asian investors appear more willing to invest under these conditions than Americans. That could result in missed opportunities for American business.

Foreign business executives interested in long-term cooperation should decide not only what business to invest in but where to invest. In that connection I would like to suggest some of the opportunities opening up in the Soviet Far East. The Far Eastern economic region (see Figure 9-1 on page 126) consists of a territory in the east of the country with an area of 2.4 million square miles (28 percent of the U.S.S.R.'s territory) and a population of about 8 million people (3 percent of the country's population).

The rich and essentially untapped economic potential of the Far East is an enormous reserve for the entire Soviet economy. In addition, development of the Far Eastern economic region will provide the Soviet Union with opportunities for more active cooperation with the Pacific Rim, one of the most dynamic parts of the global economy.

From the Soviet side, prospects for international cooperation in this area are linked with development of its rich natural resources and of the industries that process those raw materials. In order to encourage foreign firms, the region has an advantageous tax regime: exemption from income tax for the first three years after declaring a profit (in comparison with two years in the rest of the U.S.S.R.), with subsequent payment at a rate of 10 percent (30 percent in the rest of the country).

Forty percent of the territory of the Far East is covered with forests. Timber reserves are approximately 23 billion cubic meters (that is, 30 percent of the total reserves of the whole country). They consist for the most part of larch and birch, but also spruce and pine, all of which can be converted into commercial products for use in the U.S.S.R. or for export. The region has the potential of becoming a major producer of paper and paper products, furniture, finished wood, and other wood products.

Consider the case of paper. In 1988 the U.S.S.R. produced 22 kilograms of paper per person, as opposed to 143 kilograms in the United States, and the U.S.S.R. spent the equivalent of $380 million importing paper. The shortage of paper is so severe that it impedes the process of *glasnost:* there is not enough paper to meet the needs of publications. Thus, foreign companies that participate in the paper industry will be producing products for the huge domestic demand that will also be very competitive for export.

Forty percent of the U.S.S.R.'s catch of fish and fish canning comes from the Far East. There are good prospects for cooperation in connection with a growing shortage of fish-processing plants and storage facilities, as well as opportunities for better packaging.

Another good opportunity for joint business ventures in the Far East, where the fishing industry and the fishing fleet make up huge complexes, is ship repair. The Soviet ship-repair industry in the region is obsolete; as a result, ships are idle for long periods. Joint enterprises in this sector should be able to expand from a base of a large Soviet business and also service foreign shipping.

Yet another opportunity arises from the fact that a significant number of ships in the Far East have served out their term and are earmarked for scrapping. The region lacks specialized factories for utilizing old ships. Joint enterprises could be organized with relatively low capital investment for the preparation and sale of ferrous and nonferrous scrap and other production from worn-out ships.

The Far East also has rich deposits of coal, oil, and nonferrous metal ores. Another resource is the unique landscape, which, coupled with low population density, offers possibilities for tourism. Yet another opportunity would be to organize a consortium to create a joint enterprise zone in the Far East on a strip of Soviet territory near the borders of Korea and China, which would include the port city of Nakhodka. A U.S. group might find this project particularly attractive, since Americans are experienced in land development in sparsely populated regions.

This approach to the creation of a joint enterprise zone in the city of Nakhodka can be extended to other similar zones, more than 20 projects for which are currently being developed by local authorities. Among them are the city of Vyborg (near Leningrad), the cities of Tallinn and Tartu in Estonia, and the cities of Odessa and Yalta on the shore of the Black Sea. A U.S.S.R. law is being prepared on joint enterprise zones based on the concept of creating maximally favorable conditions for the activity of foreign firms. These would include freedom from customs duties for goods brought into the zone, freedom from export and import licensing, an advantageous taxation regime, and a provision for fully foreign owned enterprises.

Much has been written earlier in this book about the problem of securing necessary raw materials and equipment in the Soviet Union; this problem is totally unfamiliar to foreign firms. In the U.S.S.R. opportunities to purchase what is needed are extremely limited. The wholesale market is just being organized, and it will take time to function fully. Raw materials and other materials and equipment currently are divided up among Soviet organizations by government organs (Gossnab), based on enterprises' requests. Thus it is very important that a joint venture become enrolled in this system of allocation. To do that, the foreign firm needs to find a participant on the Soviet side that can take on the supply function. For that purpose, the most dependable partners for joint ventures are the large- and medium-sized enterprises, plants, factories, and associations. This supply route will become more effective in the near term. In my opinion, cooperatives will be less dependable.

Especially important in the planning of a joint venture in the U.S.S.R. is to correctly understand the possibilities for repatriation of profits and of one's initial investment. Many foreign firms are put off by the Soviet requirement, stemming from the ruble's inconvertibility, that a joint venture must earn enough hard currency to cover its own initial and on-going expenses. They interpret this principle to mean that the joint venture has no choice but to export part or all of its production from the U.S.S.R. They then begin to doubt whether it is worth investing in a new and poorly understood market, with all the attendant risks, only to end up selling in the Western market, with all its well-known problems. Such doubts result from an incomplete understanding of the diverse opportunities offered by the Soviet market and from a lack of flexibility and ingenuity in approaching work there.

By Soviet law, joint ventures may choose in what currency (rubles or hard currency) they wish to sell their services and production in the U.S.S.R. That gives the joint venture the opportunity to organize "hard-currency export" within the borders of the Soviet Union.

The demand for goods and services in hard currency is growing quickly in the U.S.S.R., linked with the increase in the numbers of enterprises, as well as of Soviet and foreign citizens, that have hard currency. Primary among these are Soviet enterprises, organizations, and cooperatives that export their products to the West. In addition to meeting their industrial needs, these companies may, by law, use almost a third of their hard-currency income on the acquisition of consumer and durable goods for their employees. Moreover, in many cases these enterprises would rather make their import purchases from joint enterprises than from abroad, aware of the advantages that come from cooperating with the partner next to you, as well as of the competitive level of prices. In 1989 Soviet enterprises had almost $800 million of disposable hard-currency income.

From 1991 on, according to a government resolution, all enterprises and organizations that are legal entities by Soviet law will be able to sell and buy foreign currency for Soviet rubles at the market rate. The latter will be determined on the basis of supply and demand for currency within the territory of the U.S.S.R. In the same year an all-union currency exchange will open in Moscow, as will republic and regional exchanges, all of which will expand the access Soviet enterprises have to hard-currency resources.

Soviet citizens who have worked abroad or received an inheritance from abroad add several hundred million more dollars to the currency figure cited above. Inheritances, incidentally, add up to $40 to $60 million a year. It is important to note that in 1990 several rules for bringing currency into the U.S.S.R. were liberalized. In particular, a Soviet citizen will henceforth be able to open a hard-currency account in a bank without presenting a declaration about its source. Another important source of hard currency is foreign tourists traveling in the U.S.S.R. The number of tourists from countries with developed market economies grew from 1.43 million in 1985 to 1.74 million in 1988.

Some joint ventures in the U.S.S.R. already are familiar with the practice of organizing internal exports. One example is the joint Soviet-Italian enterprise Logovaz, which sells secondhand American cars in the U.S.S.R. for hard currency. Cherokee, Wrangler, and Wagoneer Jeeps are very popular because 25 percent of the roads in the U.S.S.R. are unpaved. These vehicles cost $8000 to $8700 for 1983–85 models. The automobiles are guaranteed for six months or 10,000 kilometers.

A joint enterprise, of course, will do much of its business in rubles. Salaries, rent, and other operating expenses will be paid in rubles. Therefore, the most viable joint venture model is one that uses all the methods of sales: sales within the country for hard currency, export from the

U.S.S.R. for hard currency, and sale of goods and services within the country for rubles. In 1989 joint ventures—to which the system of export licensing generally does not apply—exported more than $200 million in goods, 85 percent of which went to the developed countries of the West. The tax on transferring profits outside the country (20 percent in the absence of an international agreement specifying otherwise) is not levied on whatever part is carried out in the form of goods.

Ruble sales are of value beyond paying bills, since there are now good opportunities for ruble investments.[6] The most promising are investments in development of infrastructure and real estate in the regions of the free enterprise zones and in shares of enterprises that are going over to the joint stock company form of organization. Incidentally, the development of joint stock companies in the U.S.S.R. is proceeding at a rapid pace, and foreign investors can participate. By the middle of 1990 Soviet enterprises, mostly medium- and large-sized enterprises and banks, had issued shares making up a sum equivalent to almost $200 million. Among those transferring to the joint stock company form is the huge KAMAZ automobile factory.

A combined approach to the currency problem has been one of the components of success for Dialogue, one of the first Soviet-American enterprises. Specializing in computerization and computer programming, Dialogue was founded in 1987 by the American firm Management Partnership International and KAMAZ, Moscow State University, and other organizations on the Soviet side. Dialogue currently employs 750 workers and has offices in many cities around the country. In its first two years, it sold over 7000 computers in the Soviet Union. Approximately 60 to 70 percent of the sales have been hard-currency sales to Soviet organizations. Dialogue also sells its own software in the U.S.S.R. and distributes that of Western firms such as Microsoft.

Dialogue has sold more than $600,000 worth of software in Western markets. The joint venture has signed an agreement with Systat, Inc., of Evanston, Illinois, which will sell Soviet software, either separately or together with general utility programs, in the United States and other countries.

The joint venture's revenue so far has come to about 120 million rubles ($190 million). With ruble profits Dialogue has joined in a hotel venture and in the construction of individual homes, and intends to invest in other development, including the reconstruction of the port in the proposed free enterprise zone in the city of Nakhodka. Dialogue has even formed its own bank.

American firms entering into business contacts with the U.S.S.R. will now encounter completely different Soviet partners than in years past. Since 1988 all Soviet enterprises that put out a competitive product were granted the right to enter foreign markets. This change has significantly enlarged the availability of potential partners on the Soviet side; by the middle of 1990, they numbered almost 15,000. Among them are not only foreign trade associations with significant experience working in the foreign market, but also novices in the area of foreign trade, including small- and medium-sized government enterprises, cooperatives, research institutes, and public organizations. While the large industrial enterprises may continue, for the most part, to turn to the services of foreign trade associations in their export-import operations, the novices are very active in independently developing foreign trade. The novices' share in the U.S.S.R.'s foreign trade was already 12 percent by the end of 1989, and that percentage is likely to grow in the future. They conduct negotiations with Western partners themselves; relying on self-financing, they resolve the practical questions of cooperation independently and fairly smoothly. Getting ready to trade with the West and to survive in the emerging Soviet market, they display a high level of receptiveness to modern management concepts. These new enterprises create for foreign firms a new niche for business activity in the U.S.S.R.

Specialists will be needed to help orchestrate the Soviet economy's transition to market principles. It is certain that there is going to be a very promising market in the area of training managers, and also in the rendering of consulting and information services. Future Soviet managers need modern experience in operating and managing production in a competitive environment; they need information services; they need education in the "marketing culture," including its foreign trade aspects. The scale of the Soviet economy will determine the volume of demand for such services. Its managing apparatus now includes almost 15 million people, including 5 million in industry, 2 million in construction, 1 million each in agriculture and transportation, and so on. Just as Italian consultants assisted in the rise of huge Soviet industrial associations, so can other Western firms sell their experience in organization and management.

The economic reforms in the U.S.S.R. will result in rapid organizational changes. Because the poor information infrastructure in the U.S.S.R. may make it difficult for Western firms to find partners and to analyze investment opportunities, it may be desirable to establish contacts with Soviet organizations in the United States.

Based on my personal experience, contacts with the trade representation of the U.S.S.R. in the United States can be very useful. The U.S.S.R. has similar representation in 110 nations. Trade delegations are manned by highly qualified officials who devote themselves to, among other tasks, helping foreign firms with information on commercial opportunities and economic conditions in the U.S.S.R. and on Soviet legislation and foreign economic practices. The experts at the trade representation can help you find partners in the U.S.S.R. and to get into contact with them. One example of the many projects that have developed on the basis of such contacts is the creation by the Chicago firm Market Knowledge and the Moscow World Market Research Institute of a data bank in the United States that lists several thousand Soviet enterprises interested in establishing business contacts with foreign firms. The first edition of this directory was published in fall 1990, and is available in both a bound edition and on a computer diskette, with periodic updates to both versions. On-line services will be developed later as well.

Another organization that can help American firms with both advice and actions is the Amtorg Trading Corporation. Founded in 1924, this company works on concrete foreign trade deals and cooperative projects. Its staff includes specialists in the most important areas of Soviet foreign trade, as well as lawyers and experts in transportation, financing, and insurance.[7]

I would like to conclude with an issue that no serious examination of prospects for cooperation with the U.S.S.R. should skip.

Goods with the label "Made in the U.S.A." are very popular and highly valued in the Soviet Union. Yet Soviet enterprises, choosing a partner for years of cooperation, exhibit a certain restraint with relation to American firms. And there is not a bit of anti-Americanism in this.

The issue here is another. Soviet-American economic cooperation, unfortunately, carries to this day part of the burden of the days when our countries opposed each other uncompromisingly. Business contacts were highly politicized. Fundamental damage to the business relationship resulted from such U.S. policies as strict export controls, the lack of most-favored-nation status for goods from the U.S.S.R., limits on government credits, prohibitions on delivery to Soviet enterprises of oil and gas equipment and computer technology, prohibitive duties on the import of Soviet products, and the grain embargo. As a result, Soviet managers formed the idea that the American market is not for us, just as Americans excluded the U.S.S.R. from their field of vision. The volume of trade between our

Table 11-4   Trade between the U.S.S.R. and the United States (Millions of Dollars)

	1980	1989
Total trade turnover	1503	3394
Exports to U.S.	151	530
Oil and oil products	13	191
Fertilizers	38	40
Precious metals	1	205
Imports from U.S.	1352	2865
Machinery and equipment	311	167
Grains	747	1893
Superphosphoric acid	11	175

SOURCE: *Vneshnay Torgovlay SSSR 1989–1990,* (Moscow, Finansy i. Statistika).

two countries which, together, produce approximately one-third of the world's gross product, has remained of little significance—in the vicinity of 2 percent of each country's trade (Table 11-4).

We have entered a new era. The stereotypes connected with the past must be changed. Cooperation should be the order of the day. The U.S. business community should take a more active role in developing U.S. trade policies vis-à-vis the U.S.S.R. It would be in everyone's interest. As Benjamin Franklin said, "No nation was ever ruined by trade."

CHAPTER 12

Financing Joint Ventures

Lawrence J. Brainard

The financing strategy for any prospective joint venture must aim to strike a balance between the business risks and the financial rewards borne by each partner. Unless each partner feels the risks and rewards are adequately balanced, there will be an incentive for one party to shirk its responsibilities in one way or the other. In the context of today's Soviet economy, however, the balancing of such risks and rewards is neither straightforward nor clear.

A major problem derives from the lack of convertibility or standard measure of value of the ruble. Soviet joint ventures typically require both ruble and foreign currency financing to meet the venture's working capital and investment requirements. The Western partner, for example, may find itself asked to guarantee its share of the venture's ruble loans. On one side, the firm's potential financial risk—the ruble guarantee—can be met only by converting Western currencies, most probably at an overvalued official ruble exchange rate. On the other hand, the firm's potential rewards will likely be ruble earnings, which are difficult to convert into Western currencies or to use for purchases of export-quality goods.

Although the ruble risks and rewards may be balanced in purely financial terms, the Western partner will undoubtedly perceive an imbalanced risk/reward structure. The reasons are the ruble's overvalued official exchange rate and the near impossibility of securing export-quality goods for rubles unless such exchanges are a part of the original joint venture agreement.[1] Thus, to secure a workable balancing of risks and rewards the Western partner must look beyond the financial projections of any deal to the conditions of the Soviet economy that create risk and reward. In addition, the Soviet partner may find itself in a similar situation, being asked to provide guarantees for the venture's Western borrowings while earning its rewards primarily in rubles.

A second difficulty in balancing risks and rewards is presented by the current upheaval in Soviet institutional arrangements. Even the best financing strategy may be radically affected by future economic reforms that alter the ability of Soviet institutions to meet existing commitments. Reforms, for example, could affect the ability of existing firms or ministries to earn and use foreign exchange and to transfer real property to other entities. A particular concern is the possibility that controls over certain resources, such as foreign exchange, raw materials, commercial buildings, and land, may be granted to the republics or municipalities as centralized controls on resource allocation are relaxed.[2] Price or tax reforms, in turn, could turn projected profits into losses overnight.

Financing strategies, therefore, must go beyond a simple accounting of risks and rewards in ruble or foreign currency terms. A strategy must address the way the institutional structure of the Soviet economy alters the risk/reward structure for each partner. The challenge is to construct a financing strategy that is realistic in its balancing of the actual risks and rewards for each party, while at the same time retaining flexibility with regard to possible changes due to future economic reforms.

In assessing the influence of the institutional structure of the Soviet economy on alternative financing strategies, the best place to start is with the banking system. Each joint venture will encounter its own unique array of firms and ministries relevant to its specialized branch of the economy. But all ventures must deal with the Soviet banks. Perhaps the most important lesson for potential Western joint venture partners to bear in mind is that Soviets banks have very little in common with banks in the West.

Traditionally, bank lending has been a state monopoly. Gosbank, the state bank, handled both the functions of a central bank and most commercial banking activities. In 1988 Gosbank's commercial banking monopoly was ended and most lending and traditional commercial banking activity was handed over to five specialized banks:[3]

- Agroprombank for agriculture and agrobusiness
- Promstroibank for industrial construction
- Zhilsotsbank for housing and municipal services
- Sberbank for consumer savings
- Vnesheconombank, the Bank for Foreign Economic Affairs (BFEA).

A second stage of the banking reform in late 1988 permitted the formation of new commercial and cooperative banks. More than 100 banks have been formed by Soviet organizations, including firms, ministries, research institutions, cooperatives, and municipalities.[4] Most of these new banks are seeking to take business away from the established, state-owned commercial banks by providing better service to potential clients; the banks also offer higher returns on deposits and charge higher rates on loans than the state banks. Despite accounting for less than 2 percent of total banking assets, these new banks have attracted considerable attention because of their ability to take advantage of the enormous inefficiencies and distortions of the state-run banks.[5] A new banking law creating a semi-independent central bank along the lines of the U.S. Federal Reserve System was adopted by the U.S.S.R. Supreme Soviet in December 1990.

Each of the five specialized state banks is authorized to provide ruble and foreign currency loans to joint ventures, either short-term working capital or trade financing or longer term financing for capital expenditures. The banks may also take equity holdings in joint ventures. Foreign currency financing, however, is subject to special controls of the BFEA. Several cooperative banks are also advising on the establishment and financing of joint ventures.[6]

The BFEA is the successor bank to the old Foreign Trade Bank (Vneshtorgbank). The BFEA is represented by a number of branches, subsidiaries, and representative offices in all the major Western financial centers. It also continues to exercise administrative control on foreign borrowing by the Soviet government, and it regulates other aspects of Soviet international payments. A prospective joint venture would, therefore, negotiate ruble financing with the bank responsible for its particular sector of the economy and foreign currency financing with that bank and the BFEA. Assistance from the Soviet partner is an essential part of such negotiations.

The purpose behind the banking reform was to achieve greater economic efficiency by having the Gosbank focus on monetary control and by decentralizing lending decisions to the new banks. However, since each of the specialized banks continues to enjoy a monopoly in its sector of the economy, no real competition has been created. Furthermore, there is little prospect that these banks could create the core of a capital market structure similar in any way to sound banking institutions active in Western capital markets. It is important, though, for Western joint venture partners to understand the actual role played by these banks in the economy.

These five banks were created or expanded by transferring existing loans from the portfolio of the Gosbank. The banks thus started life under the reform with an inherited legacy of troubled assets, highly concentrated by enterprise and industry.

At this stage of the reform, the specialized banks should be viewed more as fiscal agents of the Finance Ministry than as banks in their own right. They collect a large part of the government's inflation tax on enterprise cash balances (on which no interest is paid), and they redistribute resources to enterprises through interest rate subsidies (i.e., negative real interest rates on loans). Given such implicit subsidies, the competition for loans from the banks is intense, and the ability of a prospective Soviet partner to access such financing is a valuable resource.

The bulk of such loan subsidies, however, goes to firms unable to service existing loans. Faced by the refusal and inability of loss-making firms to service existing credits, the banks have simply refinanced such loans and provided new ones on top of the old ones in order to pay the interest. Neither the government nor the banks have been willing to push companies into bankruptcy. In extending new loans, therefore, the banks are not putting their own capital at risk, since any losses will accrue in one way or another to the government.

Given the situation of the domestic banks, Western partners should not expect an easy time in arranging ruble financing, especially for longer term capital expenditures. Western partners should bear this in mind if their venture requires substantial ruble financing. At the same time, future reforms will undoubtedly further transform conditions in financial markets as the banking reform progresses. One change incorporated in the December 1990 banking reform bill tightens regulations on the activities of the private and cooperative banks.[7] Another likely change is the elimination of loan subsidies by means of substantial increases in interest rates on loans to create positive real lending costs.

Each foreign currency financing structure presents a different mix of risks to potential creditors. Before alternative financing structures are outlined, it is necessary to highlight the risks that would concern a potential creditor bank.

Any foreign financed project presents two related kinds of risks to the creditor bank. One is *credit risk,* the risk that the project or venture will not perform as projected, i.e., will fail to generate the stream of earnings necessary to service the project's debt. Foreign currency financings also create *country* or *transfer risk,* the risk that the host country will not possess or will not permit sufficient foreign exchange to be transferred abroad to meet debt service requirements.

In recent years, for example, a number of foreign-financed ventures in Latin America have operated profitably in domestic currency terms, but found themselves unable to purchase foreign currency with such domestic earnings because the central bank of their host country was unable or unwilling to sell them foreign currencies. In such cases country risk acts to override the credit risk of a given venture. In the case of potential Soviet ventures, therefore, even the best credit risks will fail to find foreign financing unless the banks are willing to assume Soviet country risk.

In practice, credit and country risk are often closely intertwined. Deteriorating country risk—characterized by high inflation, balance of payments deficits, and a mounting probability of currency devaluation—will act to increase the credit risks of ventures in that country. Such macroeconomic instability may also derive from inefficiencies associated with the provision of critical goods and services to a venture from state-owned entities, such as raw materials, electricity, and transport.

Country risk may also be perceived differently by different groups of creditors. A number of countries that have rescheduled their foreign debt in recent years discriminate in their allocation of scarce foreign exchange, giving preference to multilateral institutions, foreign governments, and bondholders over commercial bank creditors. This fact has made commercial banks increasingly wary of assuming new country risks.

As a general rule, therefore, the level of Soviet country risk will act to put a cap on a venture's overall creditworthiness as perceived by potential lenders. When country risk is seen by lenders to be deteriorating, financing strategies must find ways to mitigate the country risks. The most common ways to do this are with third party guarantees and project financing techniques.

Alternative financing structures represent different ways of managing and transforming the credit and country risks presented by any venture. The appropriate structure for a given financing package in the Soviet Union will depend on the nature of the project's inherent credit risk and the perception of Soviet country risk on the part of prospective lenders.

A financing structure for any given venture may choose to focus on reducing a venture's credit risk, or it may seek primarily to mitigate country risk. Efforts to reduce a venture's credit risk, however, will prove ineffective if banks are reluctant to take on additional country risk.

The most common way to reduce credit risks is by means of outside guarantees, either from the partners themselves or from outside parties in the Soviet Union or abroad. Efforts to reduce Soviet country risk typically focus on obtaining insurance or guarantees from official Western export credit agencies (ECAs) and in applying project financing techniques that segregate a venture's hard-currency cash flow or capital assets for the benefit of the lenders.

Four idealized financing structures which have been applied to Soviet joint ventures are outlined below. A combination of these structures may be applied in specific cases, especially for large, complex ventures.

1. Stand-alone financing.   Financing in this arrangement is provided to the venture without additional credit enhancements. This structure may be appropriate for a venture that has already established a sound track record of profitability and enjoys preferred access to foreign exchange by virtue of its critical importance to Soviet authorities.

2. Soviet financing guarantees.   This financing structure seeks to mitigate a venture's credit risk by securing foreign currency guarantees or loans from Soviet institutions, e.g., from the Soviet joint venture partner, its ministry, a governmental authority (municipality or republic), or the BFEA. It should be recognized that this structure does not affect Soviet country risk; the creditworthiness of the guarantor will still be subject to the scrutiny of the lenders.

3. Western financing guarantees. This structure utilizes guarantees (insurance in certain countries) primarily to reduce Soviet country risk. Most Western export credit agencies (ECAs) and related investment guarantee agencies provide guarantees or insurance on financings for capital goods exports and on certain types of investment risks, such as expropriation, inconvertibility, and so on. In nearly all cases Western ECAs will refuse to bear any credit risk, necessitating a Soviet guarantee (usually from the BFEA) on the venture's borrowings. Since most ECA programs limit coverage to 85 percent of the export values and do not cover local costs (e.g., construction), the Western joint venture partner may also be asked to guarantee any remaining portion of the venture's credit and country risk.

4. Project financing techniques. These structures seek to segregate and consolidate a venture's foreign currency cash flow in the hands of the lenders. Proceeds from the venture's export sales would typically flow through a foreign bank account controlled by the lending banks. The legal structure of the financing would stipulate that the banks would be paid amounts owed before the funds would be allocated to other uses. This approach is best suited to export-oriented projects involving raw materials or semiprocessed resources. A variation on this structure, which may become feasible in the future, seeks to create a security interest for the lenders in a venture's movable capital assets, such as aircraft, ships, oil rigs, and the like. This approach requires that such property or associated property rights (e.g., leases) pass freely to the lenders in the case of nonpayment.

Since only rare joint ventures can expect to secure stand-alone financing, potential Western partners should anticipate that both Soviet and Western credit support will be essential to a successful financing strategy.

Soviet guarantees are possible because a number of Soviet institutions are now authorized to provide guarantees on borrowings by joint ventures. Examples include banks, ministries, republics, municipalities, and enterprises. The primary concerns of Western lenders with such guarantees are their validity and enforceability. If the guarantee has to be called, will the guarantor be able to deliver the necessary foreign currencies? Given the current turmoil associated with economic reform and changes in institutional arrangements, a prospective lender would find it difficult to evaluate whether, in the future, a given Soviet guarantor will have the legal status and financial ability to perform under a guarantee signed today.

Potential problems that a Western creditor would likely have in mind when evaluating such guarantees are amply illustrated by recent Chinese experience. In recent years, many Chinese enterprises and ministries granted guarantees in order to secure foreign financing. Faced with rising claims by foreign banks, the Chinese government is now dragging its feet in honoring loan guarantees issued by state enterprises. The government is arguing that the guarantees are invalid, having been issued without central government approval in the first place. In one case cited by the *Wall Street Journal,* lenders reasoned that a high degree of central and provincial support on a given project would enhance its credit. When the project defaulted, the banks discovered that not only did the guarantor not have any foreign currency to honor its commitments, but the company had undergone a restructuring that severed its ties to the central government, thus removing any chance that it would come by foreign currency in the future.[8]

The ability of a Soviet enterprise or ministry to perform under a guarantee could easily be hampered by changes in regulations that restrict its ability to earn and use foreign currency. For example, STIM, a Soviet-U.S. joint venture specializing in children's toys, was expecting to earn hard currency by means of countertrade. When a new Soviet regulation was implemented banning countertrade for joint ventures, the venture found itself dead in the water.[9]

For these reasons, most foreign banks and Western ECAs require a guarantee from the BFEA, which is the only Soviet institution with a credible track record as a sovereign borrower.[10] As already noted above, the BFEA is responsible for administrative controls on Soviet borrowings by all Soviet organizations. In exercising this role under the current economic circumstances, the BFEA is primarily concerned with maintaining its credit standing and is, therefore, very reluctant to provide guarantees to any joint venture borrowings. Only projects with a significant impact on foreign currency export earnings are likely to be considered.

Lacking a BFEA guarantee, a prospective Western joint venture partner should expect to be asked to provide a corporate guarantee to any loans to its venture. The only other option is to structure the venture with project financing, which introduces a new set of problems, as will be seen.

The Soviet Union has generally enjoyed an excellent credit rating among Western banks. The Soviet net-debt-to-export ratio—a common measure of relative indebtedness—has historically ranked among the lowest in Eastern Europe and was far below similar data for a group of major developing countries (Table 12-1).

The ability of the Soviet Union to avoid the problems encountered by many Latin American countries in the early 1980s impressed the banking community and resulted in gradually improving conditions for Soviet borrowings from the West during the decade. By 1987, the Soviet Union was able to borrow eight-year bank credits at ⅛ percent over LIBOR (London Interbank Offered Rate). Another reflection of the banks' confidence in Soviet creditworthiness is seen in the share of Western bank credit in total

Table 12-1   Net-Debt-to-Export Ratios for Eastern Europe, China, and 15 Highly Indebted Countries

	Net Debt to Export Ratio[a]		1988 Gross Hard Current Debt ($ Millions)	1988 Net Hard Current Debt ($ Millions)
	1981	**1988**		
U.S.S.R.	0.36	0.66	43,000	28,195
Bulgaria	0.63	1.56	7,810	6,032
Czechoslovakia	0.76	0.62	5,520	3,848
G.D.R.	1.54	0.60	20,730	7,572
Hungary	1.16	1.80	17,349	13,880
Poland[b]	4.61	4.21	35,470	37,497
Romania	1.21	0.12	1,931	1,122
Yugoslavia	1.16	0.89	18,683	14,296
Eastern Europe	1.03	1.04	150,493	112,442
China	−0.20	0.24	35,020	10,929
15 highly indebted countries	1.77	2.73	470,700	437,200

[a]Debt to Export Ratio is defined as: Net Hard Currency Debt divided by Hard Currency Current Account Receipts.

[b]Poland ratios actually 1982 and 1987 respectively.

SOURCES: PlanEcon, *Trade and Finance Review* (July 1989); IMF, *World Economic Outlook* (October 1989).

Soviet foreign debt, which rose from 29 percent in 1981 to 62 percent in 1988.[11] Banks in France, Germany, and Japan accounted for the top three positions in lending activity (Figure 12-1).

Beginning in 1988, the enthusiasm of the banks for Soviet loans began to wane. One reason was the growing level of individual bank exposures. A second factor was the evidence of a deterioration in Soviet economic performance, which accelerated during 1988–89. Preliminary data for 1990 indicate that the Soviet net-debt-to-export ratio worsened noticeably, moving from 0.66 in 1988 to approximately 1.10 in 1990. Although this ratio is still far below the experience of other highly indebted countries, the emergence of widespread arrears on commercial payments in early 1990 led to a sharp decline in Soviet creditworthiness.

Most of the payment delays may be traced to large state trading companies, whose longstanding business practice was to import under "open account" or "payment against documents" agreements with Western suppliers. The emergence of these problems caused a sharp slowdown in imports as Western suppliers canceled deliveries or demanded payment by means of irrevocable letters of credit. The size of the arrears is unknown,

Figure 12-1   The Soviet Union's Foreign Debt, 1981 and 1988
Billions of dollars

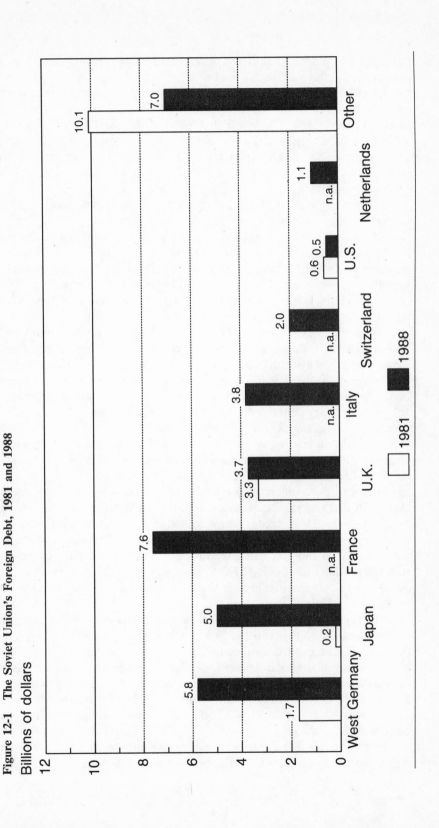

but estimates suggest that at the peak in mid-1990, arrears built up to 10 percent of Western imports, or over $3 billion.[12]

In an effort to deal with the payments crisis, emergency financing estimated at $2.5 billion was raised in mid-1990 using gold and diamonds as collateral.[13] Reports indicate that payment arrears leveled off during July. Thomas Alibegov of the BFEA reported in an interview with Reuters that more than half of a 5 billion mark ($3.3 billion) credit arranged in July with the West German government was used to clear arrears with West German companies.[14]

The use of the West German credit for preferred payments to German companies raises a troublesome precedent of politicized payments. Companies domiciled in other Western countries must contemplate the risk that they could come at the end of the payments queue after other companies whose governments are more forthcoming with such financings not tied to specific reports to the Soviet Union.[15] The West German willingness to provide such financing was seen as tied to Soviet political concessions that paved the way for German unification.[16]

Since the BFEA continued to meet all of its foreign obligations throughout 1990, most banks did not experience any arrears on their Soviet exposure. Only a handful of banks extended loans to Soviet entities without the guarantee of the BFEA. Nonetheless, it is clear that the willingness of banks to extend new credits to the BFEA has been adversely affected by the country's payments problems and continuing economic turmoil associated with economic and political reforms.

Future bank lending policies will undoubtedly take their cue from the success of domestic economic reforms and developments in the country's balance of payments position. Banks will also seek to tie a greater percentage of new loans to official export credit programs from their own governments. In early 1991, for example, Deutsche Bank (the leading German bank financing Soviet trade) announced that no new financing would be made available to the Soviet Union unless it was backed by a 100 percent guarantee from the German government.[17] These developments indicate that the availability of official ECA cover will be a critical ingredient that influences the competitiveness of Western companies seeking investments in the Soviet Union.

Most major Western countries provide assistance to their companies' exports and investments in the Soviet Union. European ECAs typically provide guarantees or insurance on exports up to a maximum, usually 85 to 90 percent of the total value of the shipment. Several countries' ECAs provide direct financing to the Soviet borrower, e.g., the Japan Export-Import Bank. Some of these countries also provide insurance for the coverage of certain investment risks, such as expropriation, war risk, and inconvertibility.

In the United States, legal constraints continue to affect trade and official financing by the U.S. Export-Import Bank. The Jackson-Vanik restrictions, which are tied to Soviet emigration policies, deny official credits for U.S. exports to the Soviet Union as well as most-favored-nation (MFN) treatment to imports from the U.S.S.R. Even though President George Bush temporarily waived these restrictions at the end of 1990, MFN status continued in abeyance pending ratification by Congress of the June 1990 U.S.-Soviet Trade Agreement. In addition, the Stevenson Amendment limits Export-Import Bank's total credit exposure to $300 million, and for energy projects to a maximum of $40 million per project.

Each country's ECA has a different set of regulations outlining which types of exports may qualify for cover. Several countries offer short-term cover for exports of semifabricated goods, and all provide cover for exports of capital goods. The usual procedure to obtain cover is for the exporter to negotiate payment terms with the Soviet importer and then to apply for cover to its respective ECA and pay the applicable premium.[18] Such supplier credits, along with the guarantee (insurance), are usually then discounted with one or several local banks. The uncovered portion is either carried as the exporter's risk or it may be assumed by the bank that discounts the paper. In rare cases, the importer may pay the 10 to 15 percent uncovered amount as a down payment. The exporter, obviously, must include the costs of the guarantees and related bank fees in its export price.

The attractiveness of ECA financing to the exporter lies in longer maturities on the loans and more attractive interest rates than available with commercial financing. More important, official cover permits banks to spread their financing risks over a larger number of projects, thus enhancing their overall returns, since they are able to charge fees for arranging each deal and they may receive other banking business from the company as part of the overall banking relationship.

Official cover, however, cannot solve all financing problems. With rare exceptions, ECAs require a guarantee on their financings from the BFEA. As already noted, the BFEA is reluctant to provide such guarantees unless the project has a demonstrated export potential or is accorded high priority for other reasons. ECAs also typically restrict their financings to export shipments; local costs, such as construction, are usually not covered. Official insurance for noncommercial investment risks, in turn, is seen by many companies to be rather expensive. In seeking to structure financing packages, banks have found the ECAs in Italy, Belgium, Austria, and Finland to be relatively more flexible than their counterparts in other countries.

The prospect of Soviet membership in and/or association with the IMF, World Bank, and European Bank for Reconstruction and Development will bring new financing possibilities. Even though such financing may not be available for specific joint venture projects, the increased availability of foreign financing may help ease the strain on other financing sources, making them relatively more accessible to prospective private financing packages. In addition, the EBRD must allocate a substantial portion of its lending to private sector projects. It is possible that the bank may be able to direct new funds to financing joint ventures, especially those involving privatization of existing firms.

Given banks' caution in new lending to the Soviet Union, the availability of official cover has now become an essential component of most financing packages. And even where official cover is available, companies may still be asked to provide a guarantee on the uncovered portion of the financing. For some of the very large projects, such undertakings may prove an unmanageable burden for the exporting companies. The only viable option in such a case is to apply project financing techniques, in order to reduce risks to levels acceptable by the banks.

Project finance involves the creation of security that provides the basis for credit enhancement for the lending banks. In Western countries the project's fixed assets are typically used to secure project financings. In the Soviet Union it has so far been impossible to create such security.

There is, first, no possibility under existing Soviet law for foreign lenders to obtain an enforceable security interest in fixed or movable assets located in the Soviet Union. Second, even if the law were to change to allow foreign ownership, the valuation of fixed assets located in the Soviet Union poses enormous problems in the absence of private property rights, a convertible ruble, and a free capital market to establish values.

Banks take assets as security, not because they want to own or manage the assets, but because in the case of default they can sell the assets to another buyer and recover their loans. The security value to a bank of a chemical plant in Siberia is what it could sell the plant for to another buyer. Most banks today would assign a low valuation to such an asset, given the evident lack of alternative bidders offering hard currency for such a plant. It may, however, become possible to structure financings for movable assets, such as aircraft, ships, or oil rigs, since their value can be determined by reference to prices in Western economies. A critical assumption is that future changes in Soviet law would permit a lender not only to own such assets, but also to export them without restriction for sale abroad in the case of default.

Given these legal problems, project financing in the Soviet Union has focused on creating a security interest for the lenders in a project's foreign currency cash flow. This approach seeks to segregate the receipts from a project's exports sales into a single account under the control of the lending banks. Thus, provided exports occur as projected, the banks have first call on the use of the export proceeds for servicing their commitments. Such an arrangement requires special permission from the BFEA. The major cash flow financings to date are shown in Table 12-2.

Cash flow financing provides banks with a prioritization of specified cash flows associated with the given project. This approach to financing is best suited to projects that generate a large and stable flow of export earnings. If the project fails to perform as expected, the banks will face

Table 12-2   Major Project Financings for Joint Ventures

Palace Hotel, Tallinn

A financing package totaling 45 million Finnish markkas ($12 million) was arranged in January 1989 for this Finnish-Soviet joint venture. A Finnish travel agent with an equity involvement in the project provided commitments for foreign exchange by providing guarantees of tourist visits to the hotel; loan guarantees were provided by the City of Tallinn and Estonian Republic Council of Ministers; other commitments were provided by the hotel management company and the general contractor.[a]

Asetco

A $330 million financing package was signed in May 1989 for the expansion of two polyethylene plants. The Soviet Ministry for the Chemical and Oil Refining Industry guaranteed feedstock supplies on a "supply or pay" basis, and Britain's Exports Credits Guarantee Department provided partial cover for exports; project risk and polyethylene price risk were carried by Asetco and the banking syndicate. Financing was structured around a non-Soviet JV with an "offtake" commitment from Union Carbide at a discount from world market prices.[b]

Sherotel-Novotel

Signed in August 1989, the joint venture hotel project at Moscow's international airport involved a 42.3 million European currency units ($60 million) financing package guaranteed by the Belgian official export agency, Office National du Ducroire. Both the commercial banks and OND assumed project risk without other Soviet guarantees. Aeroflot, in its new status as an independent, self-financing enterprise, provided a contingent guarantee to the extent of its shareholding. This is the first example in which an Export Credit Agency has accepted and insured a significant element of straight project risk in the Soviet Union. Security for the lenders is provided by a hard-currency escrow account derived from credit card receivables.[c]

Sovbutital

Signed in December 1989, this joint venture with Press Industrial of Italy and the Tobolsk Petrochemical Kombinat and Neftekhimbank (both under the Soviet Ministry for Chemical and Oil Refining Industry) involves a financing package of 410 million German marks ($275 million). The joint venture is to produce butyl and halobutyl rubbers in Tobolsk. Unlike the other project financings, which utilized offshore cash flow arrangements, this venture utilizes Soviet guarantees, though cash flows were used to structure the guarantees; BFEA guaranteed 70 percent of the loan, while the ministry covered the rest. SACE, the Italian export credit agency, provided a substantial portion of the external financing.[d]

---

[a]"Curtains Up, Project Financiers," *Euromoney* (April 1990) 64; "Investing in the USSR" (available from the law offices of Cole Corette & Abrutyn, Washington, D.C.), 28.

[b]"Curtains Up," 62; "Investing in the USSR," 28.

[c]Moscow Narodny Bank, *Press Bulletin* (August 16, 1989) 31–32; "Investing in the USSR," 28.

[d]Moscow Narodny Bank, *Press Bulletin* (January 1990) 1–2; "Curtains Up," 62.

losses even though the Soviet Union continues to service all its nonproject debt.

The basic challenge of cash flow financing, therefore, is to mitigate the performance risk associated with the project—i.e., the risk that the project will be completed in a timely fashion, operate efficiently, and find a ready market abroad for its output. In order to manage a project's performance risk, therefore, the lending banks would seek the following provisions in the contract:

1. Construction and start-up of the project meet given deadlines.
2. Project operations meet quality and output targets.
3. Export sales meet targets with regard to price and quantity.
4. Other nonproject risks (expropriation, war/insurrection, revocation of export licenses, etc.) are covered by appropriate insurance contracts issued abroad.

The most difficult aspect of cash flow financing is that substantial Soviet performance risk is unavoidable. Potential lenders will find it difficult to evaluate such Soviet guarantees and commitments, given the present state of Soviet economic management and performance.[19]

For example, any Western contractor experienced in building Soviet projects will be reluctant to provide blanket performance guarantees, since construction and start-up targets will depend on work performed by Soviet construction firms. Credible Soviet completion guarantees on construction are difficult to negotiate.

Western operators, in turn, will seek to establish control over operations, maintenance, and quality control. But such efforts may be hampered, for example, by late deliveries of critical inputs or by labor restrictions in Soviet law, which govern the hiring and dismissal of workers. The Western operator will typically require Soviet "deliver or pay" commitments on raw material inputs critical to the project's operation. Input prices will often be linked to output prices from the project, thus increasing the Soviet partner's risk since it will likely not be able to pass on price declines to its suppliers or workers. Work rules may be negotiated as part of the joint venture contract, but the legal basis of such agreements may not be clear, particularly in the face of job action by the workers.

Export sales may be assured by means of "take or pay" contracts with established Western companies; in addition to quantities, such contracts frequently involve mechanisms setting minimum or reference prices. In some cases, a Soviet exporting firm may be asked to provide similar commitments.

Given the wide scope of a project's potential performance risk—ranging from construction to operations to sales, it is essential that an influential Soviet partner capable of providing commitments be engaged as the joint venture partner where cash flow financing is used.

The cumulation of all these considerations highlights an internal contradiction inherent in cash flow project financing. The complex list of commitments necessary to manage performance risk is costly to provide, both in terms of negotiating time and negotiating trade-offs (the Soviet partner will increase its commitments only for a quid pro quo). This suggests that such financing techniques are suitable only for large projects, where the financing costs may be spread over large volumes.

However, as the project size increases, the credibility of the various commitments to the financing package, especially the undertakings on the Soviet side, is increasingly strained. Although the original reason for project financing approaches is to get around dependence on a general Soviet guarantee, there is a point at which the project-specific commitments on the Soviet side come into question. And since the financing required from the lenders rises with project size, the risk/reward calculus is quickly overwhelmed by escalating risks. Until Soviet reforms bring greater stability to economic and political life, it may prove impossible in most cases to structure financing packages that reduce performance risks to acceptable levels.

With all the complexities surrounding current changes in the Soviet economy, the challenges facing any joint venture financing strategy are bound to seem daunting. At the same time, though, Soviet needs for infusions of Western technology and management skills will continue growing.

The transition to a market-based economy in the Soviet Union will be fraught with difficulties and will require years. Companies interested in the Soviet market must be prepared, therefore, to make a long-term commitment. If membership or association with the IMF and World Bank becomes a reality, there is the prospect of growing Western involvement in designing and executing economic reform through the involvement of these institutions. If this happens, Western official financial support for future Soviet reform efforts should increase.

These considerations suggest that commercial bank financing of joint ventures, by means of either direct loans or cash flow project financing techniques, will prove difficult to arrange. The most promising avenue for financing strategies lies in utilizing government-supported programs for export financing and investment guarantees.

If American companies are to avoid falling further behind in the competition for the Soviet market, changes in U.S. legislation to facilitate new lending by the U.S. Export-Import Bank and extension of OPIC insurance programs to the Soviet Union are critical. Unless such changes are enacted, U.S. companies will find themselves farther and farther behind in the competitive race to establish themselves in this important market.

CHAPTER 13

Legal Aspects of Doing Business

Richard N. Dean
(Part I)

James A. Forstner
(Part II)

PART I

The Changing Legal System, by Richard N. Dean

Foreigners conducting business in the U.S.S.R. today confront an aspect of Soviet society with which they are totally unfamiliar and about which they have always been somewhat suspicious: Soviet law. Such a confrontation has not always been necessary or even possible. However, understanding the dramatic changes taking place in the "new" Soviet legal system has become as important as knowledge of politics, history, culture, and language in preparing foreigners to conduct business in the U.S.S.R. today.

Companies that wish to operate in foreign countries need to understand local laws to do business successfully. An American financier cannot raise money in the United Kingdom without a knowledge of U.K. securities laws; a supplier of consumer products to France must work within French consumer safety standards and advertising regulations; a German industrialist operating in Australia must understand Australian environmental laws; a Japanese distributor with exclusive rights to market and sell a product within a certain geographical area in the United States must know the limits placed on such activities by federal and state antitrust and competition laws; an Italian firm seeking to establish a Japanese company to distribute its clothing products in Japan must become familiar with Japanese corporate laws. All of these companies are accustomed to looking to courts in the foreign jurisdictions in which they operate to attempt to enforce their rights under contracts entered into with parties in those jurisdictions. Such companies are aware that they face the sanctions of regulatory bodies for failure to comply with local laws and private lawsuits against them if their activities violate the rights of others. In short, in the West law heavily influences, if not governs, the planning, structuring, implementation, and enforcement of every business transaction.

By contrast, Soviet law has had little influence on foreign business transactions in the U.S.S.R. prior to the reforms initiated by Mikhail Gorbachev. This chapter will explain why the role of Soviet law has been so limited and to describe how that role has begun to change under the legal reforms which have formed a part of the Soviet policies of *perestroika, glasnost,* and *democratization.*

Certainly the U.S.S.R. has had a legal system throughout its more than 70 year history so that the commonly held view that "there is no law" in the U.S.S.R. is simply erroneous. Soviet law is a combination of its Russian antecedents and the peculiar ideological characteristics of Marxist-Leninist policies as they have evolved under Lenin, Stalin, Krushchev, and Brezhnev. Prior to the Russian Revolution of 1917, Russian law was closely linked to continental European "civil law" legal systems rather than the "common law" systems of England and the United States. Under civil law systems, codes of laws (rather than legal precedents developed by courts) are the primary sources of law.[1] Even within the absolutist monarchy of czarist Russia, the basic foundations of a legal system developed. Criminal and civil laws, including laws on property and inheritance, family laws, labor laws, and laws regulating commerce were enacted. By the end of the nineteenth century, a well-developed court system was in place which included trial by jury.

The Russian Revolution and its aftermath severely stunted the development of the Soviet legal system, as Soviet law became a hostage to ideological debate in the 1920s and a weapon in Stalin's arsenal of terror in the 1930s. The "antilaw" bias of many early Bolsheviks, who believed that law, as part of the superstructure of the state, would "wither away" under communism, emphasized the irrelevance of law, particularly as a foundation for guiding and administering relationships in society.[2] The abuse of the law under Stalin, who in 1936 promulgated a constitution that on its face was among the most democratic in the world while he simultaneously embarked on the arbitrary and horrible purges that resulted in the execution and imprisonment of millions, badly discredited the Soviet legal system. The hypocrisy of the Stalinist period remains a key obstacle to establishing a rule-of-law state in the U.S.S.R. today.[3] The ability of a dictator to fashion his own rules and clothe them in legality haunts Soviet legal reform today, as many reformers have expressed growing concern over the vast powers Gorbachev has amassed as President and as General Secretary of the Communist party.

Throughout Russian and Soviet history, there have been legal rules, standards, and sanctions that affect the lives of Soviet citizens. Administrative bodies impose penalties and courts enforce rights. Remarkably, however, none of this applied to foreign companies in any systematic manner until very recently. Soviet laws have always existed; they simply never had any material affect on commercial transactions and activities conducted by foreigners in the U.S.S.R.

The reasons for this anomaly are both cultural and political and reflect the great differences between relatively open, market-oriented Western societies and the relatively closed, highly controlled and centralized Soviet society. For centuries, Russians have held foreigners at arm's length, regarding them with a mixture of awe and fear. Western business people who live in the "foreign ghettos" of Moscow (apartment houses that are inhabited solely by foreign diplomats, business people, and journalists) are often surprised to learn that foreigners have been segregated from the general population since Peter the Great's reign three centuries ago. The movements and conversations of foreigners in the U.S.S.R. are carefully monitored, and any contact by a Soviet with a foreigner has been a "reportable event" with the KGB. With this background, it is little wonder that the legal system was also cutoff from foreigners. Indeed, foreign business people resident in Moscow who ran afoul of Soviet law, such as by engaging in illegal currency trading or black market activity, never faced the sanctions of Soviet law. The Soviet "sponsors" of those foreign business people (i.e., certain Soviet organizations responsible for the foreign companies that maintained offices in the U.S.S.R. and employed these business people) merely informed their employers that such business people should be "recalled to their home offices." Foreigners rarely saw the inside of Soviet courtrooms. The treatment of foreigners has contrasted sharply with the treatment of Soviet citizens for similar violations of Soviet law. For example, severe criminal sanctions can be imposed on Soviets who engage in black market activity, which in extreme cases remains punishable by execution. The criminal law punishes illegal currency trading by imprisonment for up to eight years at hard labor.

Foreign companies operating in the U.S.S.R. have only infrequently come into contact with Soviet law or Soviet courts, because any legal problems that arose in connection with their operations were also handled by the government organizations charged with responsibility for these businesses. Foreign companies that have regularly done business in the Soviet market have usually maintained representative offices in Moscow. Such companies have been permitted to open these offices through a process known as accreditation. Once a foreign company opened an accredited representative office, under Soviet law certain Soviet organizations have functioned as intermediaries, or interfaces, between the foreign company and the Soviet legal system. A foreign company's sponsoring organization (in the case of foreign commercial entities, usually the U.S.S.R. Ministry for Foreign Economic Relations or the U.S.S.R. State Committee for Science and Technology), and the Main Service Bureau for the Diplomatic Corps (known by its Russian acronym UPDK) monitored the activities of the foreign company and its employees based in Moscow and acted as intermediaries for the company with other organs of the Soviet government (such as by submitting foreign employee information to the Ministry of Finance for tax purposes). In circumstances where a foreign company may have violated Soviet law, the company's sponsoring organization would meet with the head of the company's Moscow office to work out a solution. Because of this arrangement, foreign companies have had few relationships with local Soviet organizations which required access to Soviet courts to enforce contractual rights. UPDK (and, more recently, the U.S.S.R. Chamber of Commerce and Industry) has had the exclusive right to provide office space, housing accommodations, and employees to the foreign company.

Clearly, the Soviet bureaucracy has kept foreign companies away from the legal system. There have been other reasons why foreign companies by their own choosing have avoided the Soviet legal system. Among the key reasons has been that Soviet laws have been generally unavailable. While it was possible through some effort to acquire copies of the civil codes of the Soviet republics, which, inter alia, set forth basic principles governing contractual relationships, such codes have not been widely available in the U.S.S.R. In fact, few Soviet attorneys have copies of, or even easy access to, these fundamental laws. More than 90 percent of what would be considered Soviet law has been internal, unpublished regulations of the all-union and republic-level ministries—those industrial behemoths, often having hundreds of thousands of employees nationwide, which formed the higher level of the Soviet centrally planned economic structure.[4] From this perspective, the Soviet legal system is best understood, as a practical matter, as an enormous administrative law system, with minimal obligation on the part of the authorities to publish the rules intended to govern the conduct of individuals and businesses. This practice contrasts sharply with the U.S. legal system. As one Soviet lawyer put it to me recently: "In the West the skill of a lawyer is measured by his ability to understand, interpret, and apply the law. In our system, a good lawyer is measured by whether he can find out what the rules are."

This problem of "unavailable" law persists today. When we opened our office in Moscow in February 1988, we attempted a simple task. We compiled a list of cross-references in the new Soviet joint venture decree to other pieces of Soviet legislation, such as labor laws, accounting rules, insurance regulations, tax rules, and the like. Then we set about trying to find copies of the laws referred to in these references. Our list numbered approximately 15 items. After trying for six months we had managed to obtain only 4 of those items.

Often laws have been unavailable by design. The Soviets have classified many laws as state secrets. The Council of Ministers frequently censors its decrees so that what is published is not, in fact, the complete version of the decree, although it may appear to be complete, since the Council of Ministers often renumbers the articles of the decrees to eliminate the appearance of censorship. Thus, the published version of a Council of Ministers' decree on export licensing, for example, does not contain information setting quotas on exportable items. The published version of a decree authorizing Soviet organizations to invest abroad omits provisions limiting compensation that can be paid to Soviet individuals employed abroad. Often the censored portions of decrees are provisions requiring KGB approval of transactions.

The Soviet penchant for secrecy is well known. For many years it has been a crime for Soviets to disclose data about Soviet economic performance without the approval of state authorities. Foreigners who have frequently visited the U.S.S.R. are aware of the strict prohibitions against photographing Soviet airports, bridges, and other "strategic" sites, including industrial plants and factories. Such restrictions prohibit Soviet enterprises from disclosing sales data and financial information to prospective foreign partners. These legal rules have seriously hindered the conduct of business with Soviet organizations because a foreign company is understandably concerned to obtain basic economic and financial data about its potential partner's business. However, no such information can be obtained. There is a well-known story in the American business community in Moscow about an American company that refused to take no for an answer on this disclosure issue. Its negotiator constantly and persistently pressed the Soviet organization with which it was working for a balance sheet so that the American company could assess the partner's financial wherewithal. Finally, the Soviet negotiator produced a single sheet of paper with a single number on it (having no label to identify what the number was or descriptive material to explain the number) and announced that this paper was the Soviet organization's balance sheet!

Soviet laws have not only been unavailable to foreigners but also largely irrelevant to foreign business transactions in the U.S.S.R. Given the Soviets' excellent record of performing their contractual obligations until early 1990, foreign business people paid little attention to legal formalities. One of our early experiences negotiating the sale of consumer goods in Moscow on behalf of an American client illustrates how the irrelevancy of Soviet law affected the contract. The Soviet purchaser was one of the traditional, large foreign trade organizations (FTOs) controlled by the Ministry of Foreign Trade. Its representative presented us with the FTO's standard for-purchase contract which, to an American-trained attorney, was almost incomprehensible. The document had originally been written in Russian and translated very poorly into English. The document contained inconsistent provisions and failed to deal at all with certain critical legal issues. Many provisions were so ambiguous as to invite disputes over their meaning. All of this was in a contract to sell goods in a country with no developed commercial code to assist in interpreting what the parties might have meant by certain provisions. We patiently explained these legal problems to the Soviet negotiators, who replied arrogantly that they bought and sold millions of dollars in goods every year using that standard form and were not prepared to alter the provisions at the "whim" of American lawyers. Although our client expressed concern about the contract, he relented and signed based on the belief that, notwithstanding the contractual problems, the Soviets would pay as they had always done in the past.

Nor was there any question in the past that Soviet organizations with which foreign companies dealt had the authority to complete their transactions and that the Soviets who signed the contracts had the authority to bind their organizations. Governmental approvals were handled by the Soviets, foreign business partners did not participate in the process of obtaining such approvals, and often were unaware of many of the approvals required. However, foreigners had some inkling that a variety of approvals were necessary for foreign trade transactions, not only from governmental organs but also from the Communist party apparatus and the KGB. Fear of dire consequences if one approval were missed meant that no Soviet official would sign a foreign trade contract without every approval imaginable. Soviet foreign trade negotiators were not risk takers. As one Soviet FTO representative hysterically explained to us when a contract he had negotiated with one of our clients appeared to be on the verge of failure: "Don't you understand the consequences to me if this contract fails? A few years ago I could have been shot!" What would have been taken as a joke among Westerners was a looming threat to our Soviet colleague.

Another factor that has contributed to the irrelevancy of Soviet law to foreign companies has been the efforts on the part of the Soviets to keep foreigners outside of the legal system. Special decrees have governed the presence of foreigners in the U.S.S.R., as well as their housing, office facilities, tax obligations, and use of Soviet employees. During the 1920s "concessions" granted to foreign companies to operate in the U.S.S.R. were special decrees outside of the normal Soviet legislative process.[5] Even the joint venture decrees enacted in 1987 provided especially for *foreign* participation. One set of decrees covered joint ventures with foreign participants from capitalist countries; another set, quite separate from the first, applied to joint ventures with foreign participants from socialist countries. The practice of treating foreign commerce outside of the legal system continues even today. In 1988 executives from five major U.S. companies—

Chevron, RJR Nabisco, Archer Daniels Midland, Eastman Kodak, and Johnson & Johnson—announced the formation of the American Trade Consortium, which intended to deal with key organizations within the U.S.S.R. to promote large-scale American investment in the U.S.S.R. Although the arrangements between the consortium and its Soviet counterparts were to be based loosely on the existing joint venture law, a special decree of the Council of Ministers was required to authorize particular aspects of those arrangements and to permit variances from the joint venture law. The decree, which has never been officially published, represented a modern equivalent of the special concessions granted in the 1920s.

Published and available Soviet law has lacked the specificity and detail necessary to form a proper body of law to govern commercial relationships from a Western standpoint.[6] General principles enunciated in Soviet laws to "promote the building of socialism" and other such ideologically and politically charged sloganeering also made foreign companies wary of agreeing to have their contracts with Soviet organizations governed by Soviet laws. The distinctive features of the Soviet legal system—such as the dominant role of the Communist party in making and enforcing laws, the lack of well-developed, independent courts and legislative bodies, the predominance of centralized planning over legal rules, and the criminalization of economic activity (such as the buying of goods and reselling them at a profit, which is not merely acceptable in the West, but is fundamental to the success of Western economic systems)—all served to deepen the aversion foreign companies have felt for the Soviet legal system.[7] In fact, in important transactions it has been common for foreign and Soviet parties to negotiate contracts that provide that the laws of a third country would govern the transaction and that disputes between the parties would be resolved in a neutral forum outside of the U.S.S.R. The most common set of neutral laws has been the laws of Sweden, and the most common site for dispute resolution has been Stockholm; in particular, agreements have specified arbitration proceedings under the auspices of the Stockholm Chamber of Commerce. Apparently, Sweden has been considered to be socialist enough for the Soviets but capitalist enough for Western companies.

Because the basic values of the Communist system were perceived to be inimical to Western, capitalist values, foreign companies were wary of having their business disputes with Soviet organizations resolved before a Soviet court or arbitration panel. Ironically, the Foreign Trade Arbitration Court (FTAC) in Moscow has had a fine reputation over the years for rendering fair, well-reasoned decisions.[8] However, the fact that the FTAC would not permit foreigners to act as arbitrators, with the result that a foreign company in a dispute with a Soviet organization would face an arbitration panel consisting of all Soviets, has made most foreign companies even more concerned about the possibility of a politically motivated decision adverse to them.

Even the basic goals of the Soviet legal system differ dramatically from the goals of Western legal systems, a perspective that contributes to the aversion foreigners have felt for the Soviet legal system. No concept of natural rights has undergirded Soviet legal theory. Human rights have been granted by the state (and could be taken by the state). Therefore, Soviet law did not attempt to protect the individual from the state in the way that Western, particularly Anglo-American, legal systems have done. Moreover, the chief goal of Soviet law has been to administer and control a vast, centrally planned economy. Such goals did not lend themselves to the establishment of a set of legal rules to permit parties to contract with each other with minimal transactional costs, including the provision of adequate enforcement mechanisms and meaningful remedies to protect the rights of contracting parties.[9]

The Soviets' approach to working with their own legal system also confounds foreigners. When approaching a problem, Soviets apply a very different perspective than is common in the West. In the Soviets' way of thinking—shaped by years of fear and uncertainty about whether their conduct might result in very severe consequences—unless something is specifically authorized, it is prohibited. Contrast this with our Western experience in which, particularly in the United States, our perspective is just the reverse: unless something is specifically prohibited we believe it is permissible. Soviet reformers have picked up on this distinction, and the "reversal" of Soviet thinking has become an important part of *perestroika*. However, my colleagues and I constantly run into this limited way of thinking in negotiating commercial transactions. This is particularly the case where we have advised a client that a particular project makes little commercial sense as a joint venture under Soviet law, and the much preferred route would be a simple contract. In the early days of our practice this idea met with very strong resistance from the Soviets, who claimed that unless one did business through a joint venture there was really no way to accomplish the transaction. Interpreting their position in light of the legacy of the legal system, it is clear that the problem was not that the simple contract route was illegal, but rather that such a route was not specifically mandated as the joint venture route was. Against a backdrop of suspicion and xenophobia, the joint venture law provided a relatively clear and politically safe way to engage in commercial transactions with foreigners, especially Americans.

With the remarkable thaw in East-West relations over the last few years, many of these concerns have been alleviated. But it is still important for foreigners to understand the cultural heritage they confront in negotiating a contract. In one negotiation we held in which a Soviet attorney objected to the simple contract approach, he defended his position by saying that the contract would require numerous special approvals and that the approval process would be far easier if the transaction were structured as a joint venture, even though that would involve a far greater commitment than the foreign company was prepared to make at the time. It was at this juncture that we reminded our Soviet colleague that Mikhail Gorbachev himself had stated that the Soviet Union must move along the road that leads to an outlook that if something is not specifically prohibited it is permitted. Our Soviet colleague responded: "Please understand that Mr. Gorbachev deals at the level of theory; we are dealing here at the level of reality."

The historical background set forth in the preceding pages lays the foundation for the key questions: How has *perestroika* changed the Soviet legal system for foreign companies seeking business opportunities in the U.S.S.R.? Can foreign companies expect this legal system, heretofore virtually irrelevant to the conduct of business in the U.S.S.R., to affect their business opportunities and transactions in the "new" U.S.S.R.? Gorbachev has clearly indicated his desire to transform the Soviet Union into a country governed by the rule of law:

> Democracy cannot exist and develop without the rule of law, because law is designed to protect society from abuses of power and guarantee citizens and their organizations and work collectives their rights and freedoms. . . . We know from our own experience what happens when there are deviations from these principles.[10]

Gorbachev goes on to point out that during the period of Stalin's rule, "The emphasis on strict centralization, administration by injunction, and the existence of a great number of administrative instructions and restrictions belittled the role of law. At some stage this led to arbitrary rule and the reign of lawlessness."[11] Alexander Yakolev, an eminent Soviet jurist, explains the challenge facing his country as follows:

> But most of all we need to face squarely our own destiny. Is it not a paradox: building the Rule of Law State in a country where the predominant ideology was that law (and the state itself) were doomed to die, to wither away? And this prophecy was realized in a specific manner: people's power was usurped by the undemocratic state, the state power was absorbed by the totalitarian Party, the Party power was concentrated in the Party's apparat, which became a tool in Stalin's hands, and now we have to transform this structure into the State based on law.[12]

The impact that Gorbachev's goal has had on foreign business in the U.S.S.R. is gradually being felt.[13] Slowly there is taking place a shift from conducting business primarily (and some would argue almost exclusively) on the basis of personal relationships, power, and influence. To be successful in the U.S.S.R. a foreign company has been required to cultivate relationships with key Soviet officials in the Communist party responsible for the industries in which the company was interested, in the State Planning Committee (Gosplan) and within the key, all-union ministries. While such relationships remain important, establishing access to the "new" Soviet lawmakers, such as the Congress of People's Deputies, the Supreme Soviet, republic-level authorities and even the local Soviets (i.e., city councils, such as Mossoviet and Lensoviet) in a more public and routine fashion more closely related to "lobbying" in Western democracies is also important. There are also indications that the long dormant, politically dominated Soviet judiciary may be developing a degree of independence.

Soviet legislation in the foreign trade area reflects this shift in emphasis. As the authority to conduct Soviet foreign trade has decentralized, and more and more Soviet organizations conduct business directly with foreign companies, the old heavily centralized, administrative control of the Ministry of Foreign Trade (recently reconstituted and renamed the Ministry of Foreign Economic Relations) has been abolished. In its place is a new system of registration and licensing under which Soviet organizations wishing to conduct foreign trade must register with, and obtain a permit from, the Ministry of Foreign Economic Relations. Exports and imports are now regulated by a licensing procedure. Although the arbitrariness and bureaucratic problems of the old centralized system have not entirely been eliminated, those new procedures represent an important step for the U.S.S.R. in laying a foundation for foreign trade to be conducted more in accordance with the rule of law than has been so in the past.

Consistent with this shift in emphasis to the rule of law, the foreigner attempting to conduct business in the U.S.S.R. today must be familiar with a variety of new Soviet (and republic-level) laws which have been passed in the areas of foreign investment, foreign trade, property and leasing, and taxation. These new laws have forced foreigners to become directly involved in the Soviet legal system as never before. While many problems remain in interpreting these new laws, in understanding how they fit into the Soviet legal regime, and in resolving conflicts between new and existing laws—and even between the new laws themselves—this recent legislation is forming the basis for the development of a more complete and sophisticated legal regime for foreign commercial transactions than has ever existed in the U.S.S.R. In addition to the Soviet joint venture laws, Gorbachev, under his emergency powers granted by the Supreme Soviet to implement economic reform, has issued a decree permitting foreign companies to establish wholly owned subsidiaries in the U.S.S.R. No implementing regulations have been issued, but it is expected that this matter will be addressed in a new foreign investment code currently under consideration in the Supreme Soviet. Other investment structures, such as joint stock companies, may also be available to foreigners in the near future.

In 1990, the Soviets promulgated an entirely new system of taxation which will have dramatic effects on foreign companies and their employees residing in the U.S.S.R. Under the former tax regime, separate decrees set forth rules for foreigners and Soviets. The new regime consists of a broad-based law, issued by the Supreme Soviet, which applies to both foreigners and Soviets. Under the old decree, which applied only to foreign companies, such companies were taxed at a 40 percent rate on profits earned from commercial transactions in the U.S.S.R. The new tax law lowers this rate to 30 percent but introduces several new forms of taxation, including an export-import tax, a turnover tax, a tax on dividends and distributions, and a tax on employee compensation. The new law also dramatically alters the taxation of joint ventures.

The personal tax law has changed dramatically as well. Previously, the Soviets had basically a flat tax rate system, under which Soviet citizens (and foreigners resident in the Soviet Union) paid income tax at a rate equal to approximately 13 percent on what amounted to gross income. There were very few deductions permitted. In addition, the collection system was quite poor for foreigners, who frequently resided in the U.S.S.R. for extended periods without paying tax. The new law introduces a graduated tax rate system under which the highest marginal rate is approximately 60 percent. Most foreigners resident in the Soviet Union would pay tax at the 60 percent rate because such rate applies if an individual's income exceeds 3000 rubles per month. These high tax rates may result in additional costs for Western businesses with expatriate employees resident in the Soviet Union to develop business opportunities, but to date this has not been the case. Because the tax is calculated at the official (artificially high) ruble to dollar exchange rate of 1 dollar equals 0.6 rubles, but the tax may be paid in rubles in cash, the effective tax rate is no more than 6 percent. This anomaly exists because a foreigner is permitted to buy rubles in cash at the tourist rate of six rubles to 1 dollar. Most experts do not believe that this anomaly will persist much longer.

In early 1990, the newly constituted Supreme Soviet began what has become a far-reaching reform of Soviet property law. Prior to this reform, the concept of property in Soviet legal philosophy was closely linked to Marxist-Leninist ideology. Private ownership has been anathema, and all the land and mineral wealth of the Soviet Union is (according to such theory) owned by all of the people. As a practical matter, and consistent with the Soviets' centrally planned economic structure, property has, in fact, been owned and administered by the state. It was made available to Soviet organizations for use, typically on an indefinite basis pursuant to simple administrative arrangements. However, the new legislation on land, on property, and on leasing represent a dramatic departure from prior Soviet philosophy on the use of property and mineral resources. Most significantly, for foreigners these laws provide a basis for long-term leases over land, equipment, and other assets in the Soviet Union. For example, the leasing law clearly provides that foreign organizations may be lessees of land, equipment, and other assets.

With the promulgation of so many new laws from at least three major sources—the Council of Ministers (newly reconstituted as the Federation Council), the Supreme Soviet, and Mikhail Gorbachev himself under the new emergency legislative powers granted to him by the Supreme Soviet—there is little wonder that there are problems of legislative interpretation, conflicts in laws, and uncertainty as to which laws take precedence and which older laws remain effective. This problem has been exacerbated by the insurgent legislatures of republics, which are now asserting their own legislative authority. A foreign businessman learned this lesson the hard way recently when he found himself caught in the struggle between the central authorities and the republics. Armed with approvals from the Russian Republic to convert rubles to foreign exchange, he appeared at the Soviet border to exit the country. Upon presenting his papers, he was arrested by the customs authority, an all-union organization, and detained several days for currency violations.

There are also significant problems in determining whether Soviet organizations—often organizations that typically have had no previous contact with foreign companies, let alone experience in international business transactions—have the legal power and authority to enter into and perform contracts and have obtained the necessary approvals within the Soviet bureaucracy to do so. Not surprisingly, often Soviets are at odds with one another over what authority and approvals are necessary. Many reform-minded Soviets will do almost anything to avoid having to seek approvals from what they perceive to be a Byzantine, corrupt, and dilatory bureaucracy!

Although the U.S.S.R. is making progress in establishing a better legal base for commercial transactions, the next several years are likely to continue as a transition period. Vestiges of the old system remain. The export-import legislation enacted in 1989 contained a prohibition on commercial intermediary activity, reflecting a longstanding Soviet cultural and ideological bias against "speculating." Under these restrictions, a Soviet entity (including a joint venture) may import only what it needs for its own production and export only what it produces. No intermediary activity—i.e., the distribution networks that have become so vital to ensuring broad product selection in the West for consumers—is permitted without special approval from the Ministry of Foreign Economic Relations. These restrictions may have a serious negative impact on the development of Soviet retail trade, particularly involving foreign investment. No one is certain whether Soviet organizations can import finished consumer goods for resale in the U.S.S.R. For example, one interpretation of these restrictions is that a joint venture specializing in automobile repair could import spare parts for use in servicing automobiles but could not import the same parts to sell over the counter to customers.

Major transactions are still carried out on the basis of secret laws that are not available to foreigners. Limited circulation of ministerial directives continue to appear mysteriously to thwart the proper planning and implementation of transactions. An American company recently negotiated a barter transaction in the Republic of Georgia involving the exchange of dyes for textiles only to learn when the company's representatives arrived in Moscow that recently enacted legislation at the all-union level imposed strict limits on barter transactions. These restrictions made the transaction illegal.

But while the "old" system continues to plague foreign businesses active in the U.S.S.R., there is hope as Soviet reformers struggle to reverse decades of legal stagnation. One example will help to focus these efforts. A major Soviet organization involved in the promotion and development of foreign trade recently contacted us to request that we help them develop a list of information that Western companies wish to know about their potential Soviet partners among state organizations. Our list included such items as financial data, operating history, management experience, and expertise and business plans. The Soviet organization that had made the request reasoned that, although current Soviet criminal law prohibited the disclosure of such information to foreigners, it might be able to collect such data itself and prepare a list of Soviet entities which, based on the data supplied, would be credible partners for foreign companies. This creative approach reflects a constructive attitude toward realistically dealing with difficult problems, an attitude that we have seen more and more as reform has progressed.

Whether the Soviet legal system is in transition or in chaos remains an open question. While many vestiges of the old system remain, many characteristics of a more developed legal system based on the rule of law are being added. Laws are becoming more important in a system where relationships, power, and influence have been paramount. No doubt law will continue to have an uneasy relationship with politics in the U.S.S.R. Lineal, consistent progress toward the development of a rule-of-law state is unlikely, as Gorbachev's efforts to limit the recently enacted freedom of the press laws to suppress media coverage of the crisis in the Baltic states indicates. Whether Gorbachev can achieve his goals of restoring the integrity and dignity of law in the U.S.S.R. and of transforming the Soviet Union into a state governed by the rule of law, and therefore a more stable basis for foreign investment, is simply not yet clear.

PART II

Intellectual Property, by James A. Forstner

Obtaining Soviet patents and negotiating agreements with the Soviets to license technology have historically been laborious processes.[14] Moreover, these activities will continue to be difficult for the foreseeable future since Soviets think differently from Americans and Western Europeans. Many

Soviets are eager to learn, but the old guard officials will be slow to change. To many of them, Western business methods are often immoral, not just part of another political system.

Those who are concerned with protecting and licensing intellectual property in the U.S.S.R. should know the following:

- Soviets are risk-averse.

- Nonbinding memoranda of understanding ("protocols") are useful during negotiations.

- Disclosures should be written in the language of the party selling technology.

- Agreements should specify that arbitration will take place in a neutral country.

- To obtain sound Soviet patent protection the patent applicant must submit more examples of the invention than is required in other countries.

- The U.S.S.R. is an attractive partner for technology transfer since the Soviets respect contracts once concluded.

Some additional points to consider in negotiating technology agreements with the Soviets have been given by William A. Finkelstein, Pepsico's counsel:

- To establish credibility with your Soviet counterparts, tell them you are there for the long haul, not merely for quick profits, and act like it.

- Be creative and flexible, not bound to any particular way of doing things.

- Identify the goals and objectives of the U.S.S.R., and try to meet them by finding goals for yourself that are compatible.

- Understand the Soviet legal system and government, the structures of the agencies you deal with, and Soviet law and regulations.

- Pay attention to personal relationships.

- Be persistent and patient.

- Get all details in writing before the final deal is signed, since the U.S.S.R. lacks the business environment Americans take for granted.

- Be firm, and be prepared to leave if the Soviets are unreasonable.[15]

If you must walk away from the negotiations, be prepared to return later. Don't adopt the attitude seemingly suggested by a sign on the nightstand in an Intourist hotel in Moscow: "If this is your first visit to the U.S.S.R., you are welcome to it." As with the sign, the problem may just be that better communication is needed—next time, communication may be better.

Chances of success are often enhanced by early, high level contacts between corporate executives and Soviet officials. Experience has shown that these high level contacts result in the conclusion of a nonbinding memorandum of understanding which sets out the principles upon which the Western company and the Soviets contemplate future collaboration. Such contacts and memoranda can be useful to both the Soviets and the Western company during the agreement approval process (the Soviets might be able to say, "I know that company, and I share its objectives for the U.S.S.R. market"). Moreover, such an understanding may blunt interference by Soviet entities who are not a party to the negotiations and who may view themselves as competitiors of the Soviet partner.

A memorandum of understanding should reference the high level meetings and mutual respect of the parties and provide a framework or umbrella agreement for other transactions. It should document the intent to seek commercial and/or technical relations in a particular field with a particular focus on a few subfields in the next two years. It might express the intent to explore the feasibility of joint ventures and invite a Soviet to the United States to deliver a symposium on Soviet business structures and an American to the U.S.S.R. to give a technical seminar. The memorandum should require confidentiality but allow disclosures to affiliates of the Western company and to other Soviet entities. The usual practice is that each party pays its own expenses under such an agreement.

It would seem axiomatic that the technology supplier should produce the first draft of the agreement, since the supplier knows what it has and what it can deliver. Often a first draft produced by a licensee reflects many unrealistic expectations. However, axioms, like many other things, often do not work in the U.S.S.R.

Most large Soviet entities already have their own form agreements, and the technology supplier can turn this into an advantage. The Soviet bureaucracy will be able to deal with a familiar form much more easily than with a typical Western contract. Therefore, early in the negotiation, the Soviet entity should be asked for its form agreement. Then the technology supplier can employ as much of the structure and wording of the Soviet form as is compatible with a mutually satisfactory transaction. Of course, the fact that the Soviets offer a form in the first year of negotiations may not prevent them from offering a different form in the third year of the negotiations.

As an example, the Soviet import company Techmashimport in 1988 offered us its 36-page form agreement. It included extensive sections on penalties, guarantees, preparing equipment for shipment to the U.S.S.R., and so on. Many of the provisions were oppressive, and the guarantees were so unreasonable that the contract could have been a financial disaster for us. We walked away from the negotiations for a period of time, later resumed negotiations, and ultimately agreed upon mutually beneficial terms.

Although historically the Soviets have been reliable in making payments, it is wise to provide for penalties if Soviet payments are late. When cash payments are specified, the best mechanism is to obtain irrevocable letters of credit guaranteed on a Western bank. This may not be possible unless the Soviets are very anxious to acquire the technology. However, there is a variant available to technology licensors. The Western company may enlist as a partner an international engineering company, preferably one experienced in dealing with the U.S.S.R. Such companies include Kobe Steel, Ltd., of Japan. The technology supplier and the engineering company jointly negotiate a contract to construct a plant based on the supplier's technical information. The technology is disclosed to the engineering company under appropriate secrecy restraints ("Use only for one U.S.S.R. plant in Irkutsk having a capacity no greater than X"). The engineering company obtains financing for the Soviets, takes some or all of its compensation in countertrade, and pays the technology supplier in hard currency. In this arrangement there will be contracts between the engineering company and the U.S.S.R. and between the engineering company and the Western technology supplier. In addition, the Soviets sometimes seek from the supplier direct confirmatory licenses under relevant technology and patents. This has not proven to be a problem once the engineering company-U.S.S.R. agreement has been negotiated. In fact, confirmatory agreements of only a few pages have been possible.

In a further variant, when the technology supplier wants to build the plant itself, it can involve a trading company in financing the transaction, accepting countertrade, and paying the supplier in hard currency. Of course, this arrangement increases the ultimate cost to the Soviets, but it reduces the administrative burden on the technology supplier and hard-currency demands on the Soviets.

The Soviets have been willing, where cash payments are agreed upon, to pay in lump sums and/or in royalties. The lump sum payments are usually made over a period of time and tied to the achievement of certain benchmarks, such as groundbreaking, mechanical test of plant, completion of test run, and first anniversary of test run.

A fundamental problem in negotiations has been to establish the intended scope of the license first, and then the magnitude of the payment by the Soviet licensee or the Soviet joint venture. If unlimited use of the technology in the U.S.S.R. is intended, a certain price is set. If use for a specific limited production capacity is intended, a lower price is specified. In fact, we have found the Soviets willing to negotiate a price for a specific production capacity, yet ask for free expansion rights. That is not fair, as the Soviets have agreed. However, the Soviets have not been willing to agree in advance on a fee for expansion rights. Therefore, many agreements provide a technical fee for a specified limited capacity and a commitment to negotiate expansion fees.

As with negotiations anywhere in the world, a comprehensive search for technology for trade by each side can enhance the chances of concluding an agreement with the U.S.S.R. One should try to identify Soviet technology for trade to non-Soviet parties.

The Soviets are typically even more risk-averse than most Western negotiators. In the typical technology-based agreement, the Soviets want to produce a product that is much the same as that produced by the Western technology supplier. They also want the supplier to guarantee that the highest quality specifications will be met every time, at high yield, using minimal utilities, with zero defects, and so on. The Soviets may also demand an indemnity against infringing any Soviet patent (for example, owned by another Western entity) and any patent outside the U.S.S.R. in the event of exports from the U.S.S.R. Any good negotiator would seek such guarantees. Since all these features of an agreement are elements of cost, the technology supplier should make a reasonable offer and then be prepared to walk away.

With regard to patent warranties, the technology supplier should at least be prepared to state that it is aware of no patent problems in the relevant market (the U.S.S.R., and other countries if exports are contemplated), or to describe any potential patent problems of which it is aware. As a larger concession, the supplier might conduct searches for relevant patents, then represent that the supplier has performed competent searches and has found no patent problems, but does not warrant that none exist. The third and most rigorous step is to warrant that there are no problems and to assume the defense of any patent suits, if properly notified and given cooperation by the Soviets, and to accept liability for any patent damages. It would be wise to limit such a warranty to Soviet patents. Otherwise the supplier might become embroiled in patent lawsuits in a dozen countries. It would be wiser yet to limit the supplier's dollar liability for patents to a percentage of the contract value. It is only fair that the sudden appearance of previously unrecognized patents should not make the supplier liable for more than the value of the contract. If the Soviets want across-the-board indemnities, they should pay more.

With regard to plant performance guarantees, it is reasonable to guarantee specific performance levels in the contracted U.S.S.R. plant, provided that the people trained by the supplier are available to run the plant, the starting materials are of the quality specified in the contract, the plant utilities are not interrupted, and so on. Still, it is unreasonable to warrant that the Soviets will consistently meet the technology supplier's best results. The supplier itself does not do this consistently.

In one case in which I was involved, events during the visit made the Soviet negotiators understand that their demands were unreasonable deal breakers. One of my co-workers left his hotel room for a negotiating session; after waiting 30 minutes for the elevator, walked down 10 floors to find the ground-level door locked. After beating on the door he was told that he must return to his floor because he was only authorized to exit on the tenth floor. That evening he tried for three hours to phone his wife without success. When the next day he was asked to guarantee that the Soviets would produce only first quality product, he said that if the Soviets cannot make the phones or elevators work, he could not guarantee first quality results in a technically sophisticated plant. A compromise was reached.

Any good compromise should include financial limits on the supplier's liability, related to the value of the contract, if the agreement is to be fair to both parties. Finally, the performance guarantees should not last indefinitely. They should relate to one or more tests, run without utility interruptions, over a finite period of time.

The language of agreements with the Soviets has been the subject of contention. It is logical that the language of the supplier of the technology should also be the language of the agreement. The Soviets often ask that Russian be specified as the contract language. However, English is preferable since the adequacy of technical disclosures is often the ultimate disagreement. Furthermore, sometimes the Soviet technicians involved in running the plant do not have Russian as their first language.

The Soviets may ask that the contract be prepared and be "equally effective" in both languages. However, the two texts are seldom identical, and often disagreements will result when the Soviets try to enforce the Russian version and we the English version. This two-version approach seems to be the most common at present. My own view is that using two equally effective translations is an inappropriate compromise, inviting trouble. I would suggest that when the Soviets supply the technology, the agreement and disclosure be in Russian, and when the Americans supply it, English be the language used. In each case there might be a contractual commitment by the supplier to work with the licensee to perfect the translation.

Disputes will arise under U.S.–U.S.S.R. technological agreements because both the agreements and the licensed technology are complex. It is important to have the dispute resolved promptly and effectively so that the contractual relationship can resume as soon as possible. Of course, both the U.S. and the Soviet parties distrust the national courts of the other party to resolve the dispute fairly. Indeed, there is some basis for the American view that Soviet courts have been subservient to the government.[16]

The Soviets would have us believe that their arbitration tribunals are impartial. However, the safest course is to provide for arbitration in a neutral third country such as Sweden, Switzerland, or Austria.[17]

The arbitration clause should provide that the language of the arbitration is English, since many of the underlying disputes will relate to technology that was disclosed in English. The arbitration clause should also specify which national law is to be applied in the arbitration, perhaps Swedish or that of some other neutral country.

It is often said that the Soviets do not like to assume confidentiality obligations with regard to technology. However, absent confidentiality restraints, the technology supplier's ability to license the same technology to other countries may be lost. It has been our experience that the Soviets are willing to accept obligations for 10 to 15 years to maintain the technology in confidence and use it only in the licensed plant.

Convincing the Soviets to grant a patent can be a lengthy and painful process. Furthermore, the resultant U.S.S.R. patent is often more narrow than the counterpart U.S. patent. However, the effort is worthwhile because of the respect the Soviets have demonstrated for U.S.S.R. patents and the risk aversion of Soviet managers.

For example, Du Pont obtained a Soviet process patent. A few years later the periodical *European Chemical News* reported that a plant using that process had been constructed for the Soviet Union by an international (non-Soviet) engineering company. Du Pont advised the Soviet managers of its patent. The Soviets eventually responded that it was not really their problem, since the plant had been constructed by a non-Soviet engineering company. Du Pont then responded that the process infringement was being carried out by the Soviets in the U.S.S.R., not in the country of the engineering company. Also, several years earlier, Du Pont had offered to that engineering company licenses under its patents for the engineering company's customers, and the engineering company had declined. The Soviets then advised the engineering company to resolve the problem with Du Pont or cease doing business in the U.S.S.R. Shortly thereafter Du Pont signed an agreement with the engineering company licensing the Soviet plant for a lump sum fee of hundreds of thousands of dollars.

The Soviets are operating under an antiquated patent law which is not modern, but are moving toward a revised law that is more in line with internationally accepted standards for patent protection. The present law provides for two kinds of patent property—inventor's certificates and patents of invention. Inventor's certificates are unlimited in time, but rights belong to the state, and the state has a 15-year exclusive right. The inventor is compensated if the invention is commercialized. This is of no interest to a Western company and will probably be eliminated when the law is revised. Patents of invention grant the inventor or the inventor's assignee an exclusive right (the right to exclude others).[18] The right is of limited duration, 15 years from the patent filing date in the U.S.S.R. These patents can be used to protect Soviet operations or to license Soviets. Unlike the United States, the U.S.S.R. demands what is called absolute novelty as a condition for obtaining a patent. That means the inventor should not disclose the invention or sell it commercially before filing the initial patent application,[19] even though under U.S. law there is a grace period of one year after disclosure to file an application in the United States.

Draft U.S.S.R. patent laws illustrate that the Soviet view of the world remains very different from that of the West. The draft Soviet laws are burdened by provisions regarding housing and annual leave for inventors. However, the draft laws would expand the classes of inventions that can be patented (e.g., to include chemical and pharmaceutical substances), and would also extend the patent term to 20 years from filing rather than 15.

Even though a meritorious technical argument will be much more important to a Soviet patent examiner than would be a legal argument, the process of obtaining Soviet patents can be protracted, involving perhaps five to eight interchanges with the Soviet patent office. Furthermore, since U.S. practice is quite different from theirs, the Soviet patent is often much narrower than its U.S. counterpart. Soviet patent examiners require many more working examples of the invention. Hence, before filing a patent application in the U.S.S.R., the applicant should add to U.S. patent applications additional examples to enhance the probability of obtaining reasonably broad claims.

Many Western patent applicants have in the past employed West German patent attorneys as intermediaries in negotiations with Soviet agencies. The Soviets insist that the use of an intermediary is not necessary, and can cause further misunderstandings and delays. I have, however, found the services of Germans useful in many cases.

Since the Soviets are risk-averse, only several of the reported U.S.S.R. patent infringement suits have been carried to their conclusion. The Soviets will try to arrange a license. Failing that, they will avoid the patent claims.

The June 1, 1990, trade agreement signed by Presidents George Bush and Mikhail Gorbachev commits the two countries to provide effective intellectual property protection and binds the U.S.S.R. to legislate to carry out that commitment. The political uncertainty in the U.S.S.R. in no way negates the desirability of filing important patent applications in the U.S.S.R. There is international precedent for extending the effect of patents to territories transferred between nations, as when the Saarland left France and rejoined Germany in the 1950s. In addition, there is a concept called patent of importation which might be used by a breakaway Soviet republic to give effect in that republic to Soviet or even non-Soviet patents.

Both the negotiation of an agreement with the Soviets and the process of procuring a Soviet patent are usually difficult and fraught with perils. Some excellent guidance is provided by a most unlikely source, a Tibetan prayer: "May you always hear the pack ponies' bells in time and only meet yaks in the wide part of the trail." In negotiations with the Soviets one must be attentive for warning bells indicating that one does not understand Soviet goals, and one must be flexible so that the trail to agreement remains wide.

CHAPTER 14

The Future of the Soviet Economy

Herbert S. Levine

To comprehend the future shape of the Soviet economy and the path it will have to traverse from where it is to where it is going, it is first necessary to comprehend the past. For, as with all societies, the future of the Soviet Union will emerge from its past.

A general pattern of economic development is discernible in the long sweep of Russian economic history. Emerging from Mongol domination in the middle of the fifteenth century, the small principality of Muscovy began a long process of territorial expansion, uniting under its control the land inhabited by Russian and other Slavic people and spreading beyond to forge a multiethnic empire of great size. During this process of expansion, the Russian state at times came into contact and conflict with more advanced and more powerful Western nations. Such confrontations forced upon the leaders of Russia the realization that they would not be able to attain their goals because of the backwardness of the Russian economy. In such situations, the Russian state took on the role of initiator of economic development, in particular the development of the industrial sector. The state, employing its coercive and fiscal powers, would accelerate the development of the internal economy.

This was the cause of the fitful movement of Russian industrial development: spurts of rapid industrial growth followed by long periods of relatively little growth. When the military needs of the state were compelling, the economy was pressured into rapid growth; when a degree of power parity was reached, the need for further rapid growth subsided and the state relaxed its pressure. Because so much growth was compressed into such short periods, the burden of sacrifice borne by the people living in Russia during those periods was enormous. To exact this sacrifice, oppressive means were applied through oppressive institutions. The intensity of pressure and the exaction of sacrifice were so great that they led to the exhaustion of the internal population. Consequently, a period of rapid growth was likely to be followed by a long period of little or no growth.

The pattern is clearly seen in the period of empire building under Peter the Great in the first quarter of the eighteenth century. It is subsequently observable in the period of rapid economic growth in the 1890s. And it is seen in the Soviet period, with the massive industrialization drive launched by Stalin at the end of the 1920s.

When Peter the Great came to power, the Russian economy was woefully backward. Because of the economic and social rigidity resulting from the czarist state's autocratic political and social control, its monopoly of nearly all the country's economic wealth and productive resources, and its ability to keep the country isolated from foreign influences, Russia did not share in the economic development experienced by the more flexible societies in the West. The Russian economy remained technologically and institutionally primitive.

Thus, to support his foreign policy military ambitions, Peter the Great pursued a program focused on bringing the Russian economy rapidly up to the level of contemporary Western economies. Some of his policies, aimed at forging a national economy, were similar to those pursued in the West during the mercantilist period. He was concerned with means of communication and transportation, and he inaugurated the construction of a number of canals and roads. He introduced a unified system of weights and measures. He encouraged the development of domestic industries. He imported foreign technology and technologists, offering high salaries and privileges.

There were, however, significant differences from the usual mercantilist pattern. The state under Peter performed much more of an entrepreneurial function than did the state in the West. The scale of industry was larger, illustrating the state's ability to command. The composition of output reflected a devotion of the economy to the needs of the state: little production of luxury goods, great development of mining and metallurgy for military hardware, and increased output of linen and wool for sailcloth and uniforms. He substantially reordered Russian society, harnessing both the nobility and the peasantry to the interests of the state. The nobility were required to give service to the state, and Peter vastly expanded serfdom (at a time when it was disappearing in the West), attaching whole villages of enserfed peasants to individual nobles to be used not only in agricultural production but also in manufacturing and mining. And finally, at tremendous cost in workers' lives, he had Saint Petersburg built as Russia's "window to the West."

A sharp confrontation of foreign policy and economic backwardness such as occurred at the time of Peter was not seen again until the 1850s with the defeat of Russia in the Crimean War. While the Russian economy had developed rapidly during the reign of Peter, growth dropped sharply after his death. As succeeding leaders withdrew state pressure for growth and as the stranglehold of serfdom intensified, the Russian economy languished, growing at only a slow rate after the first quarter of the eighteenth century into the nineteenth century. At the same time, Western economies, under the spur of the Industrial Revolution, were undergoing rapid development. Thus, by the middle of the nineteenth century, the Russian economy was again seriously backward compared with Western economies.

The shock of its defeat in the Crimean War led to a number of major reforms in Russia in the early 1860s, including the abolition of serfdom, but it did not lead to economic expansion until 25 years later. From the mid-1880s to 1900 Russia experienced a burst of industrialization. With the leadership of the Russian state, and the very active participation of foreign capital from advanced Western nations, the Russian economy moved ahead rapidly. One of the prime elements was the expansion of railroad construction. During the 1890s the total mileage of Russian railroads almost doubled; the great Trans-Siberian line was built then. The state encouraged the development of private industry by means of direct and indirect investment, state contracts and subsidies, and a policy of highly protective tariffs. It also pursued policies to attract foreign investment. Of critical importance was the program of currency convertibility that culminated in Russia's going on the gold standard in 1897. To a great extent this was accomplished through the forced exportation of grain and the maintenance of a surplus in Russia's balance of payments. The program was highly successful. In the 1890s, foreign capital accounted for almost one-half of all new capital invested in Russian industry. In 1900 foreigners owned more than 70 percent of the capital in mining, metallurgy, and machine building.

Despite the protective tariffs, foreign trade played a significant role in Russian industrialization. During this period, the trade of czarist Russia exhibited the characteristics typical of a developing economy. Russia exported raw materials and imported machinery and other industrial items. Its exports consisted chiefly of grain, lumber, and oil. At the turn of the century Russia was the world's second largest producer and largest exporter of oil. Its imports consisted mainly of machinery and equipment and certain materials that it did not produce: rubber and nonferrous metals. Imports also included some items it did produce in increasing quantities, but for which the domestic demand outstripped local capacities: rolled ferrous metals, copper, coal, and cotton. Of critical importance were the imports of machinery and equipment. From the middle of the 1880s to the beginning of World War I, these imports increased fivefold. In 1913 they constituted 75 percent of domestic machinery and equipment production.

Estimates of Russia's national product for the 1885–1900 period indicate that the overall economy grew at a rate of about 3 percent per year. Agriculture rose 2 percent per year, while industry rose more than 6 percent per year for the entire 1885–1900 period. In the 1890s the output of cotton yarn and sugar doubled, coal and oil almost tripled, and iron and steel more than tripled. During the general European recession that began in 1900, Russia experienced little economic growth, but from 1906 until the beginning of World War I, industry grew at more than 6 percent per year and agricultural crop production grew more than 4 percent per year. By 1913, though its national product per capita was far below that of the leading industrial nations, its total national product was the fourth highest in the world and its total industrial output was fifth in the world. In the production of such raw materials as grain, oil, and timber, Russia was second only to the United States.

Significantly, this renewal of growth after 1905 was accomplished without the leadership of the Russian state. Something new was occurring in the Russian economy. Private economic activity had been developing and had reached significant levels. From the great reforms of the 1860s until World War I, private sector institutions expanded. Between 1861 and 1873 about 350 new companies were formed, but in the 1890s almost 700 were established. Active development of private institutions in the banking sector also occurred; by 1900, 40 commercial banks with some 200 branches were doing business. The credit generated domestically was substantially augmented by foreign credits. Initially, foreign credits were acquired primarily as a result of government loan guarantees. As confidence in the Russian economy grew, unguaranteed private sector foreign investment in Russian industry increased in importance.

After 1900, cartels developed to a marked degree. The cartels found themselves more and more dependent on the banks after the direct role of government in the economy diminished. As the investment role of the government receded, Russian banks moved into the void. The Saint Petersburg banks dominated activity in the major industries and in Russian financial relations with foreign countries. Entrepreneurship, after the turn of the century, became more and more Russified. Between the mid-1880s and 1900 foreign capital and management were a moving force in Russian industry. But after 1900, investment in Russian industry was done increasingly through Russian banks, which foreigners could invest in but not control. Russian banks and syndicates even began to float the stock of purely Russian companies on West European exchanges, and Russian managers came to occupy more important positions within companies that had earlier been dominated by foreign managers.

In agriculture, state policy toward the peasant commune changed after the turn of the century as a result of mounting peasant uprisings. The Stolypin reforms, introduced in 1906, encouraged the establishment of large private farms by permitting peasants to consolidate the strips of land they were working and withdraw from the peasant communes. In a brief span of time, almost 25 percent of the peasants left the communes to set up their own farms.

Thus, on the eve of World War I, Russia was becoming for the first time in its history a part of the world economy. This was true with regard not only to the interrelations of commodity trade but also to the interactions of contemporary economic and financial institutions. Furthermore, given the appearance of nascent democratic political institutions in Russia before World War I, added to the judicial and municipal reforms of the 1860s, it could be said that Russia was showing signs of developing into what is now called a civil society—one in which authority and power are substantially decentralized and in which people and groups across the entire society play a significant role in its governance. The collapse of the czarist government and the subsequent assumption of power by Lenin and the Communist party ended this movement toward civil society.

The Russian Revolution of November 1917 was followed by a counter-revolution in the summer of 1918. The period that followed, known as the period of War Communism (1918–21), was marked by the chaos of civil war and the attempts by the Communist government to gain central control over the economy in order to prosecute the war. Much of industry was nationalized and private trade was abolished. Moreover, workers were drafted into labor armies and, due to the hyperinflation that took place, were paid in terms of physical goods (food, clothing), with preference given to workers in priority industries. Farm output was requisitioned from the peasants, often forcibly.

The Communist regime succeeded in solidifying its military position by the end of 1920. The crisis under which the economy of War Communism came into existence had been overcome, and the dangers of continuing that economic policy were growing more apparent. The trade unions were revolting against the crippling centralization of industry and the conscription of labor. The alienated peasant population was reducing grain output and calling for the abolition of the state grain monopoly. Industrial workers were restive, the military was in a rebellious mood, and the government was in danger of falling victim to internal discontent. The industrial labor force was down 50 percent, and industrial output had fallen to about 20 percent of its prewar level. The Communist leadership moved quickly to dispel this discontent by replacing War Communism with the New Economic Policy (NEP) in March of 1921.

The most striking feature of NEP was its attempt to combine a market economy with socialism: agriculture remained in the hands of the peasant, and the management of industry was substantially decentralized. Market links replaced state control of production and distribution. Private activity quickly began to dominate retail trade, restoring the market link between consumer and producer. By 1922–23, nine-tenths of all retail trading outlets were private, and they handled over three-quarters of the value of all retail trade turnover, with state and cooperative outlets handling the balance. The private trader, or *nepman,* was less strongly entrenched in wholesale trade, which remained dominated by state and cooperative organizations.

In agriculture, a proportional tax replaced requisitions, giving the peasants an incentive to increase output. The state granted the peasants commercial autonomy to sell their output to the buyer of their choice, be it the state, a cooperative, or a private dealer. This measure required the legalization of private trade, which was permitted to compete with state and cooperative trade organizations. Now the peasants could market their after-tax surplus at terms dictated by market forces, not by a state monopoly. Moreover, since they no longer faced a state supply monopoly rationing out industrial products to them, the resurgence of private trade provided a further incentive for the peasants to market their surplus. Finally, they were allowed to lease land and to hire farm laborers, both of which had been forbidden under War Communism.

In industry, the majority of enterprises were permitted to make their own contracts for the purchase of raw materials and supplies and for the sale of their output. During War Communism, the state had performed these functions. Small enterprises employing 20 persons or fewer were denationalized, and some of them were returned to their former owners. Others were leased to new entrepreneurs, thereby re-creating a class of small-scale capitalists. The state even granted a limited number of foreign concessions. The lessee typically signed a contract of several years' duration obligating the enterprise to sell a prescribed portion of its output to the state.

While most of large-scale industry remained nationalized, decision making throughout industry was decentralized to a substantial extent. Nationalized enterprises were divided into two categories. The "commanding heights" of the economy—fuel, metallurgy, war industries, transportation, banking, and foreign trade—were not separated from the state budget and remained dependent upon centralized allocations of state supplies. The rest of the nationalized enterprises were granted substantial financial and commercial autonomy from the state budget. They were instructed to operate commercially, that is, to sell to the highest bidder, be it state or private trade. Most important, they were not obligated to deliver output to the state according to production quotas, as they had been under War Communism.

The use of money, which had been virtually eliminated during War Communism, was reintroduced. The State Bank was reopened in 1921, and both state and private enterprises were encouraged to deposit their funds in the bank. Limitations on private bank deposits were removed, and safeguards were established to protect such deposits from state confiscation. A new stabilized currency, the *chervonets,* was issued by the state bank in 1921, a balanced budget was achieved in 1923–24, a surplus obtained in 1924–25, and the old depreciated paper ruble was withdrawn from circulation in the currency reform of May 1924. Thereby a stable Soviet currency was created, which for a time was even quoted on international exchanges. Money transaction between state enterprises replaced earlier barter transactions.

NEP also witnessed an attempt to reestablish relatively normal trading relations with the outside world. Although a state monopoly over foreign trade established shortly after the revolution was retained under NEP, Soviet leaders pursued a strategy of learning from the enemy without becoming dependent upon capitalist markets. Thus the state trade monopoly aimed at the importation of capitalist technology and foreign experts, and of equipment that could not be produced at home. Foreign concessions were granted and credits from the capitalist world were sought. While foreign trade did recover somewhat during NEP, it remained well below half that of the prewar level, credits from the capitalist nations were not forthcoming, and the concessions program accounted for less than 1 percent of the output of state industry. Even so, in such sectors as coal mining, electrical equipment, communications, and motor vehicles the concessions program appears to have had considerable impact.

Just as War Communism provided the means for waging the civil war, NEP provided the means for recovery from the war. In 1920, industrial production and transportation were at only one-fifth of their prewar level. The shortage of fuel threatened to paralyze industry and transportation, and industry was living on dwindling reserves of metal. Agricultural production was one-third below its prewar level. The food shortage led to the exhaustion and demoralization of the labor force. In 1928, after eight years of NEP, industry and transportation had reattained their prewar levels. Agricultural output was above its prewar level, though—of critical importance—the level of agricultural marketing was only half of what it had been before the war.

These rapid rates of growth, however, were associated with the recovery of the economy from the devastation of the world war and civil war. Once the economy had grown back into its preexisting economic shell, it became much more difficult to maintain such high rates of economic growth. What was now necessary was a major program of new investment to expand the economy's productive capacity rather than the restoration of existing capital. An intensive debate took place among various groups of Soviet leaders and economists about how this industrialization program was to be organized and financed. A major focus of the debate was on the peasantry and how to raise the rate of marketing of agricultural output to support the increased movement of labor from agriculture to industry. Essentially the issues were how fast should growth be and who was to bear the burden of the saving required by the enhanced level of investment.

The debate was settled by Stalin. The solution he chose called for a very rapid rate of economic growth through the suppression of the market and the introduction of centralized planning and control of the economy. Through forced collectivization of agriculture with the obligation of collective farms to deliver to the state planned quotas of farm products, direct control over the distribution of food was acquired. And through the institution of centralized planning, direct control over the allocation of labor and capital resources was acquired.

As were previous industrialization drives, Stalin's program was derived from the sharp conflict between the perceived military security needs of the Russian state and the backwardness of its economy. In a speech in 1931 Stalin pointed to the numerous times in its history that Russia suffered beatings at the hands of its enemies because of its backwardness—the Mongol Khans, the Turkish beys, the Swedish feudal lords, the Polish and Lithuanian gentry, the British and French capitalists, and the Japanese barons. He concluded: We are 50 to 100 years behind the advanced capitalist nations; we have 10 years in which to catch up; either we do it or they will crush us.

The objective that Stalin established was survival and the means of attaining it was rapid industrialization and structural change aimed at building the industrial base to support the military needs of the state. Under such conditions, centralized control of resource allocation appeared attractive, as it would to the United States and other nations during World War II. For it offered the Soviet state a means of directly concentrating economic efforts on high priority sectors and diverting the impact of mistakes onto low priority sectors, as well as a means of transmitting pressure and urgency to the economy.

In Stalin's hands, centralized control was used in cruelly oppressive ways to exact severe sacrifice from the Soviet people—high production, low consumption. Stalin's use of collectivization, for example, was in many ways the equivalent of Peter the Great's use of serfdom. The Soviet people paid a high price for the rapid economic growth and the development of basic heavy industries that were achieved in the 1930s. These contributed to the Soviet Union's success in repelling the German invasion that came almost exactly 10 years after Stalin's 1931 speech.

The Soviet economy recovered fairly rapidly from the devastation of World War II and grew at a rather quick pace through the 1950s. By the end of the 1950s, the original goal of achieving military parity with the leading capitalist nations was achieved, the symbolic evidence of this being the Soviet launching of Sputnik. Other goals, including that of increasing consumer welfare, began to compete with the military for economic resources.

In such an environment, the coarse resource-allocation instrument of centralized planning became less appropriate. No longer was there a single high priority activity, with all other activities regarded as low priority and available to absorb the costs of the inefficiencies of the centrally planned system. In the new environment of multiple priorities, the inefficiencies of the centralized system began to fall upon activities that were now regarded as important. This brought to the fore the basic economic issues of choice and price—the price of choosing A is how much of B has to be given up, where both A and B are deemed important. In such an environment, an economic mechanism that can effectively calculate the relative costs and benefits of different activities becomes appropriate. This is not a strength of centralized planning. Furthermore, the very growth of the Soviet economy made central planning more difficult. For as the number of firms and the number of specialized products increased, the interrelationships in the economy that had to be planned and controlled centrally increased enormously complex. By the beginning of the 1960s, the stage was set for economic reform.

Given the goal of rapid growth, the Soviet economy had been operating under the constant pressure of excess aggregate demand at the macro level, and of taut planning and little slack in regard to outputs, inputs, and inventories at the micro level. Planning was output-oriented—ever increasing levels of output were achieved through substantial infusions of labor and capital inputs—rather than stressing efficiency, higher productivity, and quality.

The Soviet economy has been described as a command economy. Commands, in the form of obligatory annual plan targets, were issued by the central leadership and were communicated down through an administrative hierarchy, organized primarily by sector of production, from the ministry at the top, down to the basic producing units (enterprises) that were responsible for their fulfillment. Lines of authority were strictly delineated. Orders were issued by superiors in the hierarchy to their subordinates, while information about production possibilities flowed up the hierarchy. The Soviet economy was thus administered by means of a massive bureaucracy.

Roughly speaking, all the enterprises producing a certain type of product were subordinated to a single branch ministry (ferrous metals, petroleum, chemicals, machine tools, and so on). These ministries possessed significant power, since they controlled large groups of production enterprises, often including production facilities for some of the material inputs required by their enterprises. Ministers and their deputies were essentially senior business executives or civil servants, rather than politicians in the Western sense. They were often former managers with engineering or technical backgrounds.

Soviet enterprises did not differ much in physical form from firms in the West, except that they tended to be much larger in size. For example, in the 1960s, fully 25 percent of Soviet enterprises employed more than 500 workers, whereas in the United States and Japan only about 1 percent of firms were of that size; in addition, only 15 percent of Soviet enterprises employed fewer than 15 workers, whereas in the United States and Japan, the number was about 90 percent. The managerial structure of the Soviet firm resembled that of Western firms. The chief executive officer was the director. This executive bore full responsibility for the fulfillment of all the plan directives set for his enterprise. He was appointed to his position by his minister and high Communist party officials, and he retained his position as long as his performance was considered satisfactory (that is, he fulfilled his plan targets) or until he was moved upward in the bureaucracy. The director was assisted by a chief engineer, who served as a deputy director, and by a managerial staff of functional and line officers.

Since the dominant objective of Soviet planning was rapid, dynamic growth rather than the smooth, harmonious operation of the economy, Soviet workers and managers were subjected to pervasive pressures to meet performance targets. Soviet workers were paid largely on the basis of piece rates, and managers derived a substantial part of their total income from bonuses given primarily for the fulfillment and overfulfillment of production targets. These incentives probably led to greater output in the priority sectors than would have been forthcoming in the absence of rewards tied to performance. And in encouraging a successful enterprise in a given branch to surpass its output target, planners were able to compensate for a shortfall in the production of an unsuccessful enterprise in that branch and thus contribute to the maintenance of interbranch balances, a major concern of Soviet planners.

However, the incentive system also had negative effects. Since managerial rewards were a function of performance relative to target, managers were concerned not only with output but also with getting low targets; for that reason, they distorted the economic information sent to the planners. The managers limited their overfulfillment because of the ratchet principle—today's performance was the floor for tomorrow's plan. And they resisted technological innovations, especially in production processes, because the rewards were short-lived; any change in production processes might cause a failure to meet plan targets, which could mean the loss of managerial status and all the privileges that went with it (good apartments, access to special stores, medical service, travel, and so on). Moreover, because of the dominance of the output target, managers were concerned solely with their own production problems and not with the needs of those who used their products. Thus, product innovation suffered, as did quality, assortment, delivery schedules, and so forth. Further, the unit of account, often a physical unit, in which the output target was stated caused problems. No physical unit can measure the various attributes of a product that comprise its worth. If the output of nails was measured in terms of weight, then a small number of large nails were produced; if in terms of number of nails, then many small nails were produced. And the situation was not greatly improved when the output of an enterprise was valued in terms of price. Since Soviet prices were just the sum of labor and material costs with an arbitrary profit margin, and were not adjusted by market forces, they were poor indicators of relative value.

Finally, the implementation system suffered from the ills of overcentralization. The center gave detailed instructions to peripheral units without having detailed knowledge of the units. The set of detailed instructions received by an enterprise on various aspects of its activity was frequently not only inappropriate for it but also internally contradictory (insufficient funds to pay the labor it was commanded to employ, and the like). And the massive bureaucracy retarded decision making and adjustments to the unforeseen developments that take place in all economies, including centrally planned ones.

The period beginning in the mid-1960s witnessed a series of economic reforms, primarily in the plan implementation system, with the aim of improving managerial performance and the efficiency and growth of the economy. Essentially, the number of targets given to an enterprise was reduced and some increase in the decision-making power of managers was granted. In the Kosygin reforms of 1965, the main incentive criteria established for managers were volume of sales and level of profitability (profit related to capital stock). In the early 1970s, the criteria of labor productivity and quality of output were added.

There were, in addition, some changes in the organization of enterprises in the attempt to bolster technical change. But these reforms, primarily because of their partial nature and the entrenched position of the economic bureaucracy, failed to have any lasting effect on the performance, growth, and efficiency of the Soviet economy. From the middle of the 1970s, a sharp economic slowdown set in, accompanied by widespread disillusionment with the Soviet system, and continued more or less steadily to Gorbachev's rise to power in March 1985. However, it was not until two years later that discussions of serious, radical economic reform began.

Fundamental economic reform consists of two elements:

- The design of a new economic system.
- A strategy of how to get there.

The idea that the market will play a major role in the future Soviet economy has become generally accepted. The question is what the nature of that system will be.

One approach is based on the NEP experience. This is what Soviet leaders and economists have in mind when they speak of a socialist or a regulated market economy. The vision is of an economy with a certain amount of private ownership, but with key industries, the "commanding heights," owned by the state. Current economic activity and decision making of both private and state enterprises are to be decentralized and mediated through markets so as to be able to handle the enormous information and incentive problems of a modern industrial economy. But the central planners will play an important role in investment policy with regard to long-term directions of growth and technical change.

A second approach draws on the pre-1917 experience of Russia in the movement toward a civil society and the development of private, capitalist economic and financial institutions. This approach calls for a return to the path being pursued at the end of the nineteenth and beginning of the twentieth centuries, in effect treating the Soviet experience as a 70-year diversion. It does not speak of a socialist or regulated market system, just of a market system. It stresses the dominance of private ownership and institutions in all markets, with the state both maintaining proper monetary and fiscal policy and providing an extensive social safety net. Particular attention is paid in this approach to democratic political institutions—a federal state based on the republics possessing substantial political and economic sovereignty—so that a credible commitment is shown to the rule of law, which is the indispensable backdrop for the effective functioning of a market system. By 1990 this approach appears to be gaining in acceptance. Even Gorbachev has droped the terms *socialist* and *regulated* when speaking of the future Soviet market system.

The other major issue facing Soviet economic reform today is the problem of transition from a centralized to a decentralized economic system. Even if the design for a new economic mechanism were perfect, and accepted by all, a dominant problem would still be: How do you get there from here? While there is abundant Western theory to help Soviet economists design a market system, there is no available theory of transition from a centralized arrangement of economic institutions to a decentralized one. Western economists have not been concerned with this issue, since the development of decentralized economic mechanisms in the West took place slowly over more than a century. And, since previously radical market-type reform could not be openly discussed, Soviet economists themselves have only recently begun to work on the issue. Hence there are no theoretical guides, either Western or Soviet, that Soviet leaders and economists can draw upon as they attempt to deal with the problems of transition.

At the base of the transition problem is the interrelatedness of an economic system. One element of the system cannot be changed without changing other elements if true change in economic behavior is to be achieved. Thus to give Soviet managers decision-making power over what they are to produce, they must also be given the power to decide what inputs they will use: materials, labor, and machinery.

First, if managers are to have the power to decide what materials they will use, the centralized system of material supply, introduced in the 1930s, has to be abolished and a system of wholesale trade put in its place. But given the widespread nature of material shortages in Soviet industry, there is a fear that the removal of the centralized materials rationing system will exacerbate these shortages and cause massive disequilibria in the economy. Supporters of reform, however, argue that the rationing system itself contributes to the appearance of shortages, because managers, operating within the administrative centralized supply system, order an excessive amount of inputs to protect themselves against the inefficiencies and uncertainties of the command system.

Second, Soviet managers have to be given increased power over the hiring and firing of workers. If managers are to be encouraged to seek out and adopt advanced technology in the pursuit of the reform's goal of economic modernization, they have to have the right to adjust their labor force to the quantity and quality levels appropriate to the new technology. This means giving managers the right to fire workers: not only those who are loafing, but also those who are performing well but who are made redundant by the new technology. Thus the extensive job security enjoyed by Soviet workers, especially during the Brezhnev period, will be diminished. But as many Soviet economists argue, the Soviet guarantee of full employment should guarantee the Soviet worker *a* job, not guarantee *his or her* job. Institutional arrangements will have to be expanded for handling unemployment and for the retraining and redistribution of labor.

Third, managers must have the power to acquire the capital equipment that they decide they need. This change again involves the abolition of the centralized system of materials and equipment supply and its replacement with a market system of wholesale trade. It also, however, involves the question of investment and credit. If managers are to have the power to acquire capital equipment on their own, then they have to have access to the financial means to acquire this equipment. Moreover, to maintain the goal of decentralization, the banking institutions that decide on the allocation of investment credit must also be decentralized and should base their decisions on the commercial creditworthiness of loan applicants rather than on any centralized investment plan.

If this freedom for Soviet managers to acquire the inputs they decide they need is not to lead to rampant inflation, their demands must be constrained. With the removal of centralized control over supplies and labor, the constraint that must be instituted is a hard budget constraint. That is, managers must be required to cover the cost of their inputs out of the revenues they earn. If they fail to do so, the process of bankrupcy must be enforced. Without vulnerability to bankruptcy, the freeing up of managerial decision making will not work.

Furthermore, if managers are to make their own output and input decisions, independent of central planners, they will need meaningful signals with regard to economic costs and benefits so that the pursuit of profit will lead to the efficient use of resources. Otherwise, decentralized decision making will lead to substantial inefficiency and waste. This means the Soviet price system will have to undergo radical reform. Not only will subsidies have to be removed, but the system for setting prices will have to be changed. Buyers and sellers must be given the right to negotiate their own prices in a free and flexible way so that prices adequately reflect the conditions of supply and demand in the economy.

The reform of the Soviet economy is, in essence, a monetization of economic transactions and decision making. The target planning of the command system is to be replaced by producer and user decision making involving magnitudes calibrated in monetary terms. Therefore, monetary stability becomes critical. Issues of macroeconomic policy and control— the size of the money supply and of the government deficit—become of great importance. If the required monetary control is not exercised and if reasonable monetary stability is not achieved and maintained before and along with the introduction of the reforms, then the resulting surge of inflation will seriously weaken or destroy the effectiveness of the reform.

Finally, the reforms described so far may not work in the absence of competition. Without buyers being given a choice among competing suppliers, decentralization may lead not to the meeting of customer's demands, efficiency, and technological dynamism, but instead to monopoly and the danger of continued technological stagnation and price inflation. Therefore, an additional element of the required set of reforms may be the introduction of a Soviet antitrust policy.

What all of this means is that in light of the interrelatedness of any economic system, a number of reforms must be introduced more or less simultaneously in order for economic reform to begin to have any effect. In other words, to get the rocket of economic reform off the launching pad, an initial bundle of simultaneous reforms is required. If one had a theory of transition, it might be possible to calculate a bundle of "minimum simultaneity," i.e., a minimum bundle of simultaneous reforms required to launch the transition to a market system. This is particularly important in the Soviet Union, for under conditions of extensive market disequilibria, an abrupt shift from a centralized system to a full market system would produce chaos.

In the process of transition, it is necessary that the destabilization produced by the introduction of institutional changes be constrained to a level that allows the economy to continue to function. Certainly this is a policy constraint demanded by political leaders. Central planners and the economic ministers have been criticized for continuing to operate in the old ways. But at the same time, they have been held responsible for the performance of the economy. The only way these officials know how to carry out this responsibility is by means of the old planning and control methods.

The main problem here is that the leaders want reform, but they want to bring it about without acutely destabilizing the economy. The maintenance of some of the old forms of planning and control is necessary to prevent destabilization. Thus, the transition process initially involves the introduction of new forms alongside the old forms, rather than immediately in place of them, with the idea that the new forms are to grow and in time replace the old forms. This growth and replacement process is, however, not well understood. To what extent does the maintenance of old forms inhibit, or even prevent, the development and growth of new forms, and what is the nature of the replacement process if it does take place?

There is, in addition, another underlying tension. An effective economic mechanism is one that produces rapid adjustment to changing conditions, to changes in technology and changes in people's desires. But adjustment involves the pain of dislocation. It reduces people's security. It affects rewards and penalties and the distribution of income. A socialist system politicizes the allocation of pain. A capitalist market system tends to depoliticize it. Though people in all countries look to their governments for protection against pain, in socialist countries this feeling is particularly strong. Thus there is the danger that the political pressure for government protection and intervention will prevent the economy from adequately adjusting to change, thus inhibiting the progress of economic reform or limiting its effectiveness.

When Gorbachev came to power in March 1985, his initial economic program was focused on the reinvigoration rather than the reform of the economy. He called for economic modernization and an acceleration in growth based upon sharp increases in investment directed toward machine building and energy, plus extensive changes in administrative and management personnel. It was not until June 1987 that discussion of serious economic reform began. At a meeting of the Central Committee of the Soviet Communist party, a resolution calling for the radical restructuring of the Soviet economy was adopted. The resolution recognized that the interrelatedness of an economic system required a bundle of changes to be made for any real change in the functioning of the economy to result. It did not, however, appear to recognize the difficulties that would be involved in the transition.

The June 1987 resolution was accompanied by a new law on the state enterprise. Together they formed a program that promised a substantial move toward economic decentralization. The program called for the virtual abolition of the annual state plan and its obligatory targets, significant independence of enterprise managers from control by the central planners and the industrial ministries, enterprise incentives based on the pursuit of profit and financial responsibility, flexibility in the payment and allocation of labor, the reform of prices and the system of price formation, the loosening of controls on foreign trade, and the permitting of joint ventures with capitalist countries on Soviet soil. The new system was to be in place by the beginning of the 1990s. Until then, some aspects of centralization were to be retained, e.g., the so-called state production orders fulfillment of which was obligatory for the enterprises.

A year later, in June 1988, Gorbachev launched a radical political reform affecting both central and local governments. An elected congress of people's deputies was created, which in turn elected a president and a legislative parliament (Supreme Soviet). And local councils (Soviets) were to be directly elected by the people. Gorbachev appears to have recognized that political reform is a necessary precondition for economic reform. In order for economic reform to succeed, decision makers must have the information they need to make decisions and they must be free of arbitrary government intervention in carrying out their decisions. Leaders in government and in the economy must be accountable for the results of the actions they take. They must have credibility in the eyes of the people. Thus, *glasnost* and *demokratsia* are prerequisites for successful economic reform.

In the period from June 1987 to December 1990, little progress was made in the reform of the Soviet economy. And there have been a number of very serious and troublesome developments, in particular the growth of inflationary forces, the spreading shortages of consumer goods, and the decreasing levels of output. A thick cloud of crisis hangs over the economy, and the people's expectations for the future are bleak.

Among the major causes of the present crisis was the Soviet economists' and leaders' insufficient understanding and appreciation of the macroeconomic factors involved in the transition to a decentralized economic mechanism. Wage inflation (and through it, price inflation) has been a direct function of money creation resulting from (1) the government deficit, which has been substantial (even when account is taken of the fact that in the Soviet Union most of the investment in the economy is on the government budget) and (2) enterprise managers' pressure to increase money wages far beyond increases in productivity, given the flexibility of the incentive wage system accompanying the reform. Much of the current problem of empty shelves and shortages in consumer goods is demand-related, a consequence of the sizable increases in money wages which would not have been possible without excessive printing of money and the growth of the monetary overhang in the economy.

There has, however, also been a slowdown in the growth of output. This results from the fact that while some of the glue of the old command methods of management that held the economy together has been removed, new economic methods of management have not developed fast enough to replace it. The first element of the economic mechanism to be affected has been that of the coordination mechanism. The flow of materials from producing enterprises to using enterprises has been seriously weakened, leading to a slowing down of growth—in 1990 there was an actual decrease in output.

A further critical flaw has been the postponement of price reform. The maintenance of below-market-clearing prices, often through the payment of subsidies, contributes to the government deficit and to the prevalence of goods shortages. And the maintenance of the centralized system of price setting means that prices are not flexible signals of the relationship between supply and demand.

Thus the simultaneity problem in the transition to a decentralized economic system has proved to be a formidable barrier to the progress of Soviet economic reform.

In light of the failure of economic reform to get started and the growing sense of crisis in the country, several important developments have occurred with regard to both an increased understanding of the economic issues and the working out of proposed programs for economic reform, particularly for the handling of the issue of transition.

First, there has been a growing understanding among Soviet economists of the principles and importance of macroeconomic policies. Fiscal and monetary policies are discussed in a clear and straightforward manner, with the stress placed on the role they will play in the reformed Soviet market economy, particularly their role in managing inflation. Much attention in the public discussion of economic reform has been given to the monetary overhang and to ways of stopping its growth and of decreasing it: taxing increases in wages above a certain level, and sales of stocks, bonds, and apartments to the public.

Another important development in economic discussions over the past year has been the increasing focus on property rights and the creation of different forms of non-state-owned property. "Destatization" of property ownership has become a rallying cry. There is a growing perception that a profit incentive is not enough to give enterprise managers the needed sense of responsibility for the economic assets under their control. An ownership relationship is also necessary. Ownership brings with it not only an interest in an increase in the flow of profit (income) but also an interest in an increase in the value of the property (wealth), which leads to the protection and nurturing of society's assets.

In addition to the progress in understanding of economic issues, there have been several major programs put forth for the transition to a market economy. First there was a report issued in October 1989 by the State Commission on Economic Reform, headed by the economist Leonid Abalkin, a deputy prime minister in the Ryzhkov government. The report outlines a design for a future Soviet market economy and discusses in some detail the measures that have to be taken to move the Soviet economy through the transition from a centralized structure to a decentralized market structure. Three possible approaches to the transition issue are discussed. What are termed the conservative and radical approaches are dismissed; the first because it will never produce any progress in reform, and the second because it will lead to chaos. What is called the radical-moderate approach is the one preferred. In essence, it is a step-by-step approach of preparing and then introducing a bundle of simultaneous reforms which include a well-developed set of government fiscal and monetary controls. These will be used to manage the inflation that is inevitable with the introduction of markets in an environment of shortages. Extensive attention in the report is paid to the protection of the people from some of the pain of adjustment. This protection will help people adapt to a market system. Included here are the indexation of incomes and pensions. The report is clearly aimed at reviving popular support for the economic reform and the movement to the market.

The report also sketches out a schedule for the transition to the reformed economic system. Four stages are described, covering the periods 1990, 1991–92, 1993–95, and 1996–2000, by the end of which a new market system will be established.

Conservatives attacked the Albalkin report's plan for the conversion of the Soviet economy to a market economy. The radicals attacked what they considered to be the excessive protection of workers from the economic adjustments which, they argued, would be necessary for the success of economic reform, i.e., for the creation of an economic mechanism that could respond flexibly to changes in technology and consumer demand.

In December 1989 Prime Minister Ryzhkov stated that he supported the Abalkin program, but he called for a two-year delay in its introduction, during which period heavy centralized priority would be put on increasing the production of consumer goods to eradicate consumer shortages. This echo of the command approach was not well received. It was followed in May 1990 by a formal government plan put forth by Ryzhkov, which was similar in some ways to the Abalkin program but which called for beginning the transition to a market economy with an immediate (July 1990) doubling of basic food prices, coupled with indexing of wages and pensions. This was rejected by the Soviet parliament, which called upon Ryzhkov and Abalkin to submit a revised program.

In the interim, dramatic changes were taking place in the Soviet political scene. Power was shifting from the Communist party to the elected government bodies and from the Kremlin to the republics. In June 1990 Boris Yeltsin was elected president of the Russian Republic. He made clear his intention to assert the Russian Republic's sovereignty over its own economy and his intention to move the republic quickly—in 500 days—to a market economy. In July, at the end of the Soviet Communist Party Congress, Yeltsin left the party, solidifying his position as an independent political force.

Gorbachev thus faced a serious challenge, particularly sharp in the economic sector. He responded with a compromise approach. A joint Gorbachev-Yeltsin working group was set up at the end of July, under the direction of the respected economist Stanislav Shatalin, a member of Gorbachev's Presidential Council, with the task of drawing up a program for the transition to a market economy. The working group met during the month of August; at the beginning of September the group submitted a lengthy report, including drafts of over 20 laws, which comprised a program for the transition to a market economy in 500 days.

Shatalin's transition program was quite different in essence from those of Ryzhkov and Abalkin. The heart of the program lay in the rapidity of the transition process and in the dominant role it gave to privatization and to stabilization, and in its recognition of the sovereignty of the republics as the foundation for the creation of an economic union.

First, the rapidity of the transition process was symbolized by the phrase "500 days." This time frame was not to be taken literally, but it represented a commitment to move ahead resolutely with a tightly sequenced bundle of reforms, recognizing the simultaneity problem. Such a commitment was critical in establishing the credibility of the reform program, which in turn was crucial to the program's success. Furthermore, the Shatalin group made clear that they were talking about the transition to a market system, not the full development of such a system. The latter, it was generally acknowledged, would take several decades.

Second, the transition to the market was to be built on the basis of privatization rather than on the decentralization of state enterprise management. Privatization was to proceed from the top (turning state enterprises into joint stock companies) and from the bottom (helping individuals to set up small- and medium-sized firms, with credit and access to space and materials). Financial institutions necessary for privatization (stock markets, commodity exchanges, etc.) were to be set up.

Third, stabilization policies were to be introduced immediately. Investment financed through the state budget was to be cut sharply, as were the defense and KGB budgets. Tight monetary policy was to be initiated. Monetary reform through confiscation was to be avoided. Rather, the monetary overhang was to be absorbed through the increased supply of consumer goods (production and imports) and sales to the public of apartments and a range of state assets. The prices of up to 150 basic consumer goods were to remain fixed for the entire period of 1½ years. Reform of other prices was to start as soon as the stabilization program began to take hold. The aim of the stabilization program was to make the ruble the accepted, totally fungible, legal tender throughout the Soviet Union. As some members of the Shatalin group put it, the aim was to make the ruble "real money."

Fourth, the Shatalin program began with the fundamental recognition of the sovereignty of the republics and it tried to create institutional arrangements that would encourage the republics to delegate some of their sovereignty in order to share in the benefits of these arrangements. A good example of such an institution was the proposed central bank, which was designed along the lines of the American Federal Reserve System. The board of governors of the bank consisted of a chairman and representatives from each of the republics. Thus each republic that joined the system would have a voice in the setting of monetary policy for the entire economic union.

The battleground is now in the political arena. As the old economic, social, and political structures are being destroyed and new structures are slow in developing, instability is increasing. To deal with the situation, it is necessary for Soviet political leaders, primarily Gorbachev and Yeltsin, to reach certain agreements. First, they must agree on the nature of the new Soviet political union and the level of sovereignty of the republics. Without this, the political power to implement economic reform is lost. And second, they must agree on a program of economic reform, one that addresses the major problems of transition—minimum simultaneity, property rights, and macroeconomic balance, and one that stresses the stimulation and protection of private investment and entrepreneurial activity from below at the level of small- and medium-sized business. Two different approaches have already been proposed and more may come along. If the political leaders come to an agreement soon, then there is a chance that by the turn of the century the Soviet economy will look substantially different from what it was and is today: it will begin to show signs of becoming a market economy with economic, financial, and legal institutions resembling those of the advanced industrial nations.

If, on the other hand, there is great delay in the political acceptance and introduction of significant transition measures, then the disequilibria and instability in the economy will intensify and the reimposition of economic controls will be likely. Where this path will lead is not clear. However, since recentralization will not solve the problems facing the Soviet economy, it can be argued that in 5 to 10 years another cycle of economic reform will be initiated. In the successor to *perestroika,* Soviet leaders and Soviet people, with the experience they have gained, may be more successful in dealing with economic reform and its transition problems, and a Soviet market economy may begin to take shape toward the end of the first decade of the twenty-first century.

CHAPTER 15

The Future of the Soviet Union

Lawrence E. Modisett

I will begin this hazardous chapter with the prediction I am most confident will come true: however history judges Mikhail Gorbachev, the currents his leadership has set in motion will prove fundamental and irrevocable.* Recognizing that change was necessary and inevitable, and bold enough to try to manage it, he allowed powerful nationalist and populist forces suppressed or coopted for 70 years to emerge and achieve a momentum that cannot be reversed. Near-term setbacks notwithstanding, the tide of grass-roots political activity that has arisen with his relaxation of controls will dominate Soviet politics and society for the foreseeable future. It will have a profound impact on the prospects for doing business in the U.S.S.R. and on the environment in which business will have to be conducted.

Gorbachev's first six years in office guaranteed him a major place in Soviet history. In external policy, he dispelled the traditional image of the U.S.S.R. as an aggressive, militarist power by disavowing confrontation; retrenching in the Third World; reducing Soviet military forces both unilaterally and through arms control agreements; and, most dramatically, allowing the dismantlement of the Soviet empire in Eastern Europe, the democratization of former satellites, and the reunification of Germany. In domestic policy, he took major steps toward democracy and engineered the transfer of power from party to state institutions. His support of *glasnost* opened the door to an airing of ideas and challenging of authority unprece-

*The author is a senior analyst in the Central Intelligence Agency. This chapter has been reviewed by the CIA to ensure it contains no classified information, but that review neither constitutes CIA authentication of material nor implies CIA endorsement of the author's views.

dented in Soviet history. The speed and magnitude of the public response was remarkable among people long indoctrinated with an authoritarian ideology and unaccustomed to the toleration of dissent.

On the negative side, Gorbachev's goal of economic reform remained unachieved in the face of bureaucratic opposition, public misgivings, and his own caution and apparent lack of clarity over how to proceed. The growing perception that his efforts not only had failed to deliver promised benefits but had made things substantially worse led to dramatic declines in his popularity and public confidence in his leadership. Economic hardship resulted in public protests and contributed to a surge of interethnic fighting and secessionist movements.

The centrist position Gorbachev sought to maintain proved increasingly untenable. The support of the public and many of his own advisers shifted to rivals who favored more rapid steps toward reform, particularly Boris Yeltsin, president of the largest republic in the U.S.S.R., the Russian Soviet Federated Socialist Republic (RSFSR). At the same time, the prospect of continually worsening living conditions and a further breakdown of order fueled conservative demands for a return to authoritarian methods. And the growing assertion of power by individual republics threatened to make whatever action Gorbachev took increasingly irrelevant.

Faced with growing challenges to his leadership, and evidently fearing that accelerated reform could bring political and economic collapse, Gorbachev apparently decided late in 1990 to ally himself with the conservatives, at least temporarily, and use the military, the KGB, and his own enhanced powers as president to restore stability. This decision prompted his close political associate, Foreign Minister Eduard Shevardnadze, to resign in December 1990, warning of impending dictatorship. Shortly afterward, a military crackdown in the Baltic republics and a call by Gorbachev for reimposition of censorship seemed to give credence to Shevardnadze's charges.

Nonetheless, there are good reasons to believe *perestroika* will continue, with or without Gorbachev as leader and despite setbacks resulting from his decision to crack down. Many of his reforms have achieved a viability of their own and simply represent the belated adaptation of institutions to changes that have taken place in Soviet society as a result of increased urbanization, education, and communication. Citing the sweeping changes since Stalin's day, S. Frederick Starr has observed that Gorbachev should be credited not so much with "creating change" as with "uncorking it."[1] Freedom of expression has taken root in the media, the arts, and a range of grass-roots political organizations. Attempts to repress it would arouse massive resistance, divide the authorities themselves, and risk plunging the country into chaos. Although economic reform has not proceeded as far, here, too, changes are under way at the grass-roots level and within individual republics that could not be reversed without dangerous disruptions. Moreover, the long-term need for economic restructuring is virtually undisputed; even conservatives more often question the pace than the principle.

The external environment also favors reform. With Eastern Europe free and Germany reunited, Soviet security and the prospects for economic growth depend more than ever upon the cooperation of the West, and every Soviet leader knows that Western cooperation stands in jeopardy if reform is abandoned.

Moreover, beyond institutional reforms lie the powerful political currents Gorbachev has let loose. For the first time, mass movements reflecting the popular will on national self-determination and other deeply felt issues have arisen thorughout the U.S.S.R. These movements will shape Soviet political, economic, and social developments for the foreseeable future and determine how the U.S.S.R. interacts with the rest of the world. It is to these long-term forces, and their implications for U.S. business, that we now turn.

Nationalist forces have surged to the forefront of Soviet political life with breathtaking swiftness, not just among minority nationalities but among Great Russians as well. Nationalist fervor has been fed by frustration over the economy and encouraged by the new freedom of expression, the party's weakened grip on Soviet life, and the Eastern European example.

Within the various Soviet republics, nationalism has taken two principal forms: resentment over domination by Moscow and animosity toward ethnic rivals. The outpouring of nationalist sentiment has expressed itself in many ways, including renewed emphasis on traditional languages, culture, and religion; public demonstrations; calls for economic autonomy; declarations of sovereignty; secessionist movements; and interethnic violence bordering on civil war.

A third form of nationalism, xenophobic opposition to foreign influences, also is experiencing a revival in some circles, particularly in the RSFSR. Its adherents, traditionally known as Slavophiles, hold Russian culture to be superior to that of the West and blame Russia's problems on foreign influences. Opponents of this view, traditionally known as Westernizers, hold that Russia is historically backward and must look to the West for intellectual models and up-to-date technology. Gorbachev has followed the eighteenth-century example of Peter the Great in embracing the Westernizers' view. Nonetheless, the strength of present-day Slavophiles is evidenced by Gorbachev's appointment to his short-lived Presidential Council of one of their leading representatives, the Russian nationalist writer Valentin Rasputin. The exiled writer Alexander Solzhenitsyn is another influential exponent.

What does nationalism portend for the future of the U.S.S.R. and the prospects for U.S. business there? Writing in 1969, the Soviet dissident

Andrei Amalrik predicted that when the breakup of the Soviet empire came, it would take one of two forms. Either power would pass to extremist elements and the country would "disintegrate into anarchy, violence and intense national hatred," or the end would come peacefully and lead to a federation like the British Commonwealth or European Common Market.[2]

Now, more than 20 years later, the U.S.S.R. seems increasingly likely to follow one of the scenarios Amalrik described. A number of trends appear to favor the gloomier alternative: public discontent, loss of confidence in the central authorities, and resurgent nationalism have fanned disintegrative tendencies, while rising crime and ethnic violence seem to bear out Amalrik's warning that "anarchy, violence and intense national hatred" could become endemic.

On the other hand, it would be a mistake to assume that dissolution of the U.S.S.R. is inevitable or that violence will become pervasive. Some apocalyptic forecasts reflect the natural propensity to fear the worst in times of uncertainty. Secessionist rhetoric and separatist measures passed by legislators at the republic and subrepublic level are not inevitably harbingers of the future; to some extent they represent political posturing and a relatively easy way to vent nationalist emotions long suppressed. On occasion, these symbolic acts could even reduce the pressure for more drastic steps toward independence.

Moreover, it is important to note that the U.S.S.R. already has weathered enormous political changes and economic stress without massive disorder. The violence that has occurred, while tragic, pales in comparison with the calamities that swept the country during its first three decades. Viewed in that perspective, Soviet society has shown remarkable stability in reacting to the dislocations associated with *perestroika,* and this fact in turn suggests that prophets of gloom underestimate the degree to which today's Soviet society is more cohesive and politically mature than that of the past.

There are further reasons to challenge the assumption that the dissolution of the U.S.S.R. is inevitable. The strength of secessionist sentiment in a republic and its prospects for achieving independence depend upon a number of variables, including a tradition of independence, the proportion of minority populations within the republic, the prospect of remaining secure from attack, and economic viability. With the possible exception of the RSFSR, no republic scores high on all four counts, and most score low on two or more.

A collective memory of previous independence is a powerful source of secessionist sentiment. The more recent the experience, the more intense that sentiment is likely to be. It is particularly strong in the Baltic republics, which lost their freedom in 1940, and Moldavia, which Stalin seized from Romania the same year. Even in republics that fell under Russian hegemony much earlier, such as Georgia, annexed in 1801, the tradition of independence remains strong.

Not all republics have such a tradition, however, and even where one exists other forces may work against it. As Table 15-1 shows, Soviet republics vary widely in the percentage of the population represented by the ethnic majority. Minorities within a republic may oppose secession in the belief that their rights will be better protected within a larger union, or they may harbor strong secessionist sentiments of their own that could threaten to dismember the parent republic if it sought to stand alone. The 1990 law on secession accords these minorities a significant voice that could enable them to block legal secession in many republics.

Another consideration weighing against the establishment of new independent states will be the inability of most republics to guarantee their own security if faced with a powerful and acquisitive neighbor. Every republic of the U.S.S.R., including the RSFSR, has had repeated experience of foreign invasion and occupation. Were the union to dissolve, only the RSFSR would be likely to retain sufficient forces to enable its people to feel confident of deterring any potential aggressor. Lack of such forces, the absence of defensible borders, and the proximity of historic foes will argue for caution on the part of republics contemplating independence.

The argument raised most frequently against separatism is economic. Moscow's policies have created what one scholar calls an "intricate web" of mutual dependencies.[3] In some republics, particularly in Central Asia, this interdependence of markets and supplies is reinforced by dependence on subsidies from the center. Among the smaller republics, even the most developed would find it difficult to establish and maintain an independent financial structure, ensure an unbroken supply of energy and other essential resources, and undertake the many other tasks necessary to maintain a functioning economy, while dealing simultaneously with the accelerated social and political changes independence would bring.

Therefore, although independence movements may prove strong enough in one or more republics—particularly in the Baltic region or the Caucasus—to sever all political ties with Moscow, various forces will work to keep the majority of republics in some form of union. The form most frequently discussed is a confederation, with individual republics enjoying considerable autonomy but reserving certain key responsibilities for the central authority. As envisioned by Gorbachev and other Soviet leaders, those responsibilities would include monetary, credit, currency, and tax policy; preserving an all-union market; managing the power industry and major transportation and communications systems; ecological policy; foreign economic policy; and strategic defense.[4] Individual republics have proposed more limited powers for the center, especially in the areas of economic policy and taxation. Any agreement will require compromise on both sides, but over time the alternatives to such compromise are likely to appear increasingly unattractive.

Many Soviets cite the Europe of 1992 as a model that would allow sufficient autonomy for member republics while providing a common eco-

Table 15-1 Comparative Data on Soviet Republics

Republic	Population in Millions (1989)	Area in Thousands of Square Miles	Percentage of Ethnic Majority	Major Economic Activities	Principal Resources
RSFSR	147.0	6,593	82	Industry; agriculture	Coal; copper; diamonds; gold; iron; natural gas; petroleum; platinum; timber
Ukraine	51.4	233	73	Industry; agriculture	Coal; manganese; mercury; natural gas
Uzbekistan	19.8	173	71	Agriculture (cotton)	Natural gas; petroleum; sulfur
Kazakhstan	16.5	1,049	40	Agriculture (cotton)	Chromium; coal; copper; iron; lead; nickel; petroleum; zinc
Belorussia	10.1	80	78	Agriculture; industry	Flax; peat; timber
Azerbaijan	7.0[a]	33	83	Agriculture	Aluminum; fisheries; cobalt; iron; petroleum
Georgia	5.4	27	70	Agriculture (citrus fruit; tea; tobacco; wine)	Coal; manganese; steel
Tadzhikistan	5.1	55	62	Agriculture (cotton)	Aluminum; uranium
Moldavia	4.3	13	64	Agriculture	
Kirgizia	4.3	77	52	Agriculture	

Republic				Economy	Natural resources
Lithuania	3.7	25	80	Agriculture (dairy and meat products); industry (appliances; chemicals; electronics; food processing; machinery; shipbuilding)	
Turkmenistan	3.5	188	72	Agriculture (cotton)	
Armenia	3.3[a]	12	93	Agriculture; industry	Basalt; copper; gold; iron
Latvia	2.7	25	52	Industry (agricultural machinery; appliances; buses; electronic equipment; food processing; machinery; railroad cars; steel)	
Estonia	1.6	17	62	Agriculture (dairy and meat products); industry (agricultural machinery; chemical fertilizer; mining machinery; processed foods; textiles)	Oil shale; phosphorites; timber
Total	285.7	8,649[b]			

[a]Accuracy may have been impaired by conditions resulting from the 1989 earthquake and civil disorder in Nagorno-Karabakh.
[b]Includes the White Sea (35,000 square miles) and the Sea of Azov (14,000 square miles) which are not included in any republic.

nomic structure. However, the European Community as yet makes no provision for common security, deferring that responsibility to NATO, or for a common foreign policy.

The Swiss Confederation provides another possible model, with its history of independent, multilingual states superseding their differences to create a thriving joint economy and provide for a common defense and foreign policy. The Swiss Confederation, however, was 700 years in the making and arose primarily through voluntary accessions in the face of common external threats. It is questionable whether such an arrangement could be transplanted to the U.S.S.R., where the history of unity is much shorter and many republics were incorporated against their will. It also is unclear whether the majority of Soviet republics would be willing for Moscow to retain as much power as the central authorities exercise in Switzerland.

The U.S.S.R. is entering uncharted territory as it seeks to develop political institutions appropriate to the unique conditions it faces, and the political arrangement that finally emerges may have no equivalent elsewhere. The republics that remain within the union may differ from one another in their internal political structure and relationship with the center, and whatever structure emerges is likely to reflect the sharp variations among republics and regions in geography, history, demography, and economic development. It is also likely, however, that economic ties will remain close.

As the Communist party and other unifying institutions become weaker and individual republics pursue their separate courses, they are likely to differ increasingly in the strength of democratic institutions, levels of economic and social development, and openness to foreign influences. Regional differences will also intensify. Business risks, such as market disruptions, work stoppages, and supply interruptions, will vary depending on the locations of plants and suppliers.

The Baltic republics—Lithuania, Latvia, and Estonia—were the first to translate their newly awakened nationalism into formal moves toward secession. Lithuania has taken the most sweeping steps toward independence and, despite periods of intense military and economic pressure from Moscow, seems likely eventually to achieve its goal. The likelihood of independence for the other two republics is less certain. While Lithuanians represent 80 percent of the population in their republic and Russians only 9 percent, the proportions in Latvia are much closer—52 percent Latvians and 34 percent Russians. Estonia lies between, with Estonians comprising 62 percent of the population and Russians 30 percent.[5] The larger Russian minorities in Latvia and Estonia will make the independence process more complicated and may block it altogether.

Whether the Baltic republics are inside or outside the U.S.S.R., Western traditions and experience with parliamentary democracy will enable democratic institutions to take root more readily there than in other regions. There is no recent history of interethnic clashes, and civil disorder is unlikely.

Western traditions will also ensure an easier transition from a controlled to a free economy. Economic success will be facilitated by the high education level and strong work habits of the population and by a level of industrialization and an economic infrastructure that are advanced by Soviet standards.

The Baltic republics will offer a hospitable environment for Western business partners, particularly Scandinavian and German, with whom commercial ties extend back to the medieval Hanseatic League. At the same time, economic ties with the East are likely to continue, particularly the import of energy supplies from the RSFSR. These ties could help maintain economic stability in the Baltic republics and aid Western businesses in penetrating the much larger markets of Belorussia and the RSFSR.

The Slavic republics of Belorussia, the Ukraine, and the RSFSR comprise nearly three-fourths of the population of the U.S.S.R. The RSFSR alone has nearly 150 million people and occupies three-fourths of the total Soviet territory (see Table 15-1).

These republics, like their non-Slavic counterparts, have provided fertile ground for resurgent nationalism. Although no strong secessionist movement has arisen in Belorussia, separatist movements have gained ground steadily in the Ukraine and RSFSR.

Ukrainians have a strong sense of national identity, although most of their history has been spent under the domination of others. In the words of a leading historian, "The frustration of the Ukrainians' attempts to attain self-government is one of the key aspects of their historical experience. Therefore, the Ukrainian past is largely the history of a nation that has had to survive and evolve without the framework of a full-fledged national state."[6] Nationalist resentment has focused primarily upon Russians, who have dominated the Ukraine for most of the past three centuries and whose rulers have attempted repeatedly to suppress Ukrainian political activity, language, and religion.[7]

It is not surprising that the Ukrainian parliament passed one of the U.S.S.R.'s most sweeping declarations of sovereignty in July 1990. It not only asserted the precedence of Ukrainian laws but called for independent armed forces and currency. Moreover, support for outright independence has grown. At the Second Congress of the nationalist organization Rukh in October 1990, for example, an overwhelming majority voted for full independence, hardening Rukh's previous stand.[8]

On the other hand, some major factors weigh against independence for the Ukraine. The historic inability of the region to sustain itself as an independent state has been due largely to its lack of natural frontiers and resulting vulnerability to invasion. Also lacking are clear boundaries between Ukrainians and other ethnic groups. In particular, the presence of a large Russian minority in the eastern half of the republic creates a strong constituency for continued ties to the RSFSR, although even the Russian-dominated areas favor greater autonomy.

Whatever political arrangement emerges, the Ukraine seems bound to remain linked to the RSFSR economically. While strong in agriculture and industry and endowed with considerable resources, including coal, natural gas, iron ore, and manganese, the Ukraine depends upon the RSFSR for petroleum and markets. The next few years are likely to bring a proliferation of agreements governing economic ties between the two republics.

In the RSFSR, nationalist sentiments have also found new vehicles of expression. Slavophiles and advocates of Great Russian nationalism have assumed prominent political roles. Their appeal rests in part on popular perceptions in the RSFSR that the republic, richly endowed with petroleum, natural gas, coal, timber, and other resources, has "subsidized" other republics by investing heavily in their development. More recently, resentment has grown over the human and financial costs of trying to maintain order in republics beset by ethnic violence. The RSFSR issued its own declaration of sovereignty and reinforced it by asserting the right to have the final say in any agreement involving sale of its resources. Moreover, as Gorbachev temporized on economic reform, Yeltsin sought to press ahead on his own and to remove the economy of the RSFSR from central control.

The RSFSR is unlikely, however, to adopt a go-it-alone strategy. Yeltsin himself has never advocated dismantling all central authority, but he favors a pluralistic federation bound together primarily by horizontal ties among republics rather than controls extending from the top down. Even Russian nationalists disagree among themselves, with some favoring severance of ties to non-Slavic republics, as Solzhenitsyn advocates, while others seek to preserve Russian hegemony.

Considerations involving minorities also weigh against an independent RSFSR. On the one hand are the substantial Russian communities within other republics, whose position would become less secure in the absence of a central authority. On the other hand are the 27 million members of minority groups within the RSFSR, some of whom already are agitating for independence. The dissolution of the U.S.S.R., by underscoring the weakness of Moscow's control, would encourage these secessionist movements as well.

Security is an important consideration. Although the RSFSR is the only republic likely to retain large military forces in the future, to abandon its ties with republics on the periphery would violate the longstanding principle of seeking as much friendly territory as possible between Russia's borders and any potential invader. Ties with the Baltic and western Slavic republics are of particular importance in the aftermath of Eastern Europe's emergence from Soviet control and the dissolution of the Warsaw Pact.

Economic needs also weigh heavily. Although the RSFSR is well endowed with resources and possesses a massive industrial base, it depends upon other republics for critical imports, particularly agricultural products. The difficult process of converting to a market economy would place it in even greater need of the goods and services other republics can provide. Recognizing this interdependence, Yeltsin has moved quickly to negotiate economic agreements at the republic level.

The variety of parties and political movements that has arisen in the Slavic republics could lead to a less settled political environment, with frequent changes of leadership and shifts in policy. If economic conditions continue to deteriorate, public protests will increase and may on occasion be directed against foreigners and Soviet minorities traditionally associated with commercial activity, such as Armenians, Georgians, and Jews.

Anti-Semitism remains deeply rooted, and *glasnost* has allowed it to be expressed more openly. The Russian nationalist organization Pamyat (Memory) has even revived the notion of a Zionist-Freemason conspiracy first popularized in the 1905 *Protocol of the Elders of Zion.* [9] Because Jews traditionally have been linked in the popular mind with economic exploitation and subversive international movements, they easily could become targets of resentment if economic hardship accompanies marketization and foreign penetration of the economy. Anti-Semitism could be directed against both native Jews and Jewish representatives of foreign firms. [10]

Tension between Ukrainians and Russians also could flare up, although it has been reduced in recent generations by intermarriage, experience in mixed communities, and shared hardship, particularly during the Nazi occupation. The greatest danger of conflict will arise over the disposition of religious property, as Ukrainian Catholics, or Uniates, act to recover churches and other property transferred to the Russian Orthodox Church when Stalin banned the Uniate religion. [11]

Economic prospects in the Slavic republics are mixed. Levels of development vary widely, from highly urbanized, industrialized communities to primitive rural areas and populations. Recent decades have brought rapid growth in the number of skilled, educated workers, but as earlier chapters have discussed, poor work habits, including absenteeism and alcoholism, are widespread and have contributed to the current economic malaise.

The transition to a free economy will be hampered by lack of an entrepreneurial tradition in the RSFSR and the persistence among some of the population of what Geoffrey Hosking calls "sullen egalitarianism"— the resentment of those who profit from private enterprise, even when their efforts provide goods and services otherwise unavailable. [12] Gorbachev himself has criticized this "levelling out psychology." [13] Some scholars trace it to the egalitarianism of medieval peasant communes, and Communist ideology and Stalin's campaign to eliminate the wealthy peasants reinforced it. The presence of this attitude among even a small number of malcontents provides a handy tool for conservative opponents of marketization, and Hosking suggests it could make private enterprise less successful in the RSFSR than in the Baltic region, the Caucasus, or Central Asia.

The political scene in the Caucasus—Georgia, Armenia, and Azerbaijan—is likely to remain turbulent. Diversity of language and culture between republics is the greatest of any region in the U.S.S.R., and sharp ethnic divisions exist within republics as well. Georgia and Armenia have traditions of political and cultural independence that predate by centuries their absorption into the Russian empire. (Georgia was annexed in 1801 and Armenia in 1920, after a previous Russian occupation from 1828 to 1878). Personal and political loyalty in all three republics centers upon networks of relatives and friends, a tradition conducive to shifting alliances and a volatile political life.[14]

In keeping with their traditions of independence, Georgia and Armenia appear to have embarked on separatist paths. Georgia was one of the first republics to proclaim its sovereignty, and some Georgians even advocate a return to monarchy. Although Armenians traditionally have regarded Russia as a protector against their Moslem neighbors, Armenia's Supreme Soviet declared independence in August 1990, and separatist sentiment has fed on the belief that Moscow is siding with Azerbaijan in the ongoing quarrel between the two republics.[15]

Azerbaijan, on the other hand, has no history of independent existence and harbors considerably less separatist sentiment than Georgia and Armenia. Mindful that the mingling of ethnic groups across its borders could lead to stormy relations with both Armenia and Iran if it pursued an independent path, Azerbaijan appears inclined to cast its lot with Moscow.

Ethnic strife, more than independence movements, is likely to threaten the future stability of the Caucasus and negatively affect commercial activities in crisis-prone areas through work stoppages and property destruction. The most bloody dispute so far, a virtual civil war between Armenians and Azerbaijanis, has centered upon the autonomous region of Nagorno-Karabakh, a largely Armenian enclave within the republic of Azerbaijan. Azerbaijani blockades of Armenia periodically have severed that republic's ground transport links with the rest of the U.S.S.R., highlighting its vulnerability. Potential for conflict also exists between Georgians and the Abkhazi, who occupy an autonomous republic within Georgia and have their own tradition of independence dating back to the eighth century, and between Georgians and the Ossetians, who occupy an autonomous oblast within the Georgian republic.

On the other hand, certain developments could moderate tensions over the next few years. One proposal would raise the status of Nagorno-Karabakh to that of an autonomous republic, a move that might defuse the issue as a source of contention between Armenia and Azerbaijan, although this is far from certain. Continued migration could reduce friction as members of minorities flee communities where they feel vulnerable and resettle among their ethnic kin. The concerns of the Abkhazi and Ossetians could be alleviated by guarantees from Tiblisi to respect the rights of minorities. Improvements in the economic situation could reduce the frustration that has fueled ethnic animosities throughout the region.

Economic prospects for the region offer some cause for optimism, in part because of the skills of the population. Transition to a market economy would provide a growing outlet for the legendary commercial and entrepreneurial talent of Armenians and Georgians, a quality that has enabled many from those republics to prosper within the U.S.S.R. as well as overseas. High birth rates have produced what one expert calls a "pool of reserve labor," which could attract investors, and the quality of the work force is high.[16] Among Soviet republics, Georgia and Armenia enjoy the highest and second highest proportion of the population with a secondary education, and according to 1980 figures Azerbaijan had the highest level of industrial labor productivity in the U.S.S.R.[17] Moreover, the cosmopolitan cultures of Armenia and Georgia will help create a favorable climate for foreign business activity.

The Central Asian republics—Kazakhstan, Kirgizia, Turkmenistan, Uzbekistan, and Tadzhikistan—have elements in common with the Caucasus. The culture is predominantly Moslem, unemploment is high, and recent years have seen massive outbreaks of interethnic violence. Conservative Communist party officials have been more tenacious here than elsewhere in holding on to power and resisting reform, and democratic institutions have been slower getting started. The future operating environment for foreign business is likely to share many characteristics with that of the Middle East and of South Asia.

Nationalist feelings run high. The first popular upheaval in the U.S.S.R. under Gorbachev's rule occurred in Alma Ata, the capital of Kazakhstan, in December 1986, when the replacement of longtime party leader Dinmukhamed Kunaev by an ethnic Russian sparked three days of rioting. Recent years have brought efforts throughout the region to revive cultural awareness through renewed emphasis on languages, ethnic history, and national monuments.

Along with their separate national identities, peoples of the region share a common cultural identity as Moslems, whether or not they actively observe Moslem religious practices.[18] Iran and Pakistan have sought to reinforce this Moslem consciousness by radio broadcasts, taped messages, and other means of cross-border communication, and Saudi Arabia has provided financial support. If the sense of Moslem identity continues to intensify, separatist tendencies could increase in the Central Asian republics in coming years.

Nonetheless, despite heightened national and cultural awareness, the path toward independence may well hold greater obstacles here than in any other region. Like European colonial powers in Africa, czarist and Soviet rulers established administrative boundaries among the conquered territories of Central Asia with little regard for traditional groupings, and in the years since their incorporation into the U.S.S.R. these republics have seen a large influx of nonnatives. As a result, their populations are among the most mixed in the Soviet Union. The 1989 census shows Kazakhs comprising less than 40 percent of the population of Kazakhstan, the second largest republic after the RSFSR, and Kirgizi numbering just over 52 percent in their republic.[19] Also weighing against independence is the undeveloped state of the region's economies, particularly their overreliance on the production of cotton. While part of the nationalist program is to restore a more balanced economy, continued dependence upon external subsidies, investments, and markets will remain a deterrent to secession.

Continued outbreaks of interethnic violence are likely in some areas, such as the fighting between Uzbeks and Kirgizi over the fertile but overpopulated Fergana valley. The scarceness of vital resources, especially water and grazing land, historically has aggravated interethnic tensions.[20] More recently, growing unemployment has raised the level of frustration and increased the propensity for violence, while contributing to higher instances of alcoholism, drug abuse, youth gangs, and other social ills.[21]

With the highest rates of population growth in the U.S.S.R. and a labor force that is largely rural, unskilled, and immobile, Central Asia can look forward to no early abatement of the conditions that give rise to conflict. Moreover, there is no certainty that central authorities will be able or willing to maintain order in the future. With memories of Afghanistan still fresh, resistance is growing in the Slavic and Baltic regions to sending young soldiers to risk their lives policing Moslem nationalists. Opposition to using draftees in this role has been an issue around which Russian women have successfully organized, and politicians at the republic level, including Boris Yeltsin, are asserting the right of republics to determine where their draftees serve.

Despite the potential for civil strife, the republics of Central Asia enjoy a number of assets conducive to foreign business activity. These include cheap labor, large potential markets, and natural resources, particularly in Kazakhstan, which has coal, petroleum, and nonferrous metals. The region's location and Moslem culture may prove particularly attractive to Middle Eastern investors, and improved economic opportunities over time would ameliorate the sources of ethnic strife.

Along with nationalism, Gorbachev's relaxation of controls has allowed the rise of grass-roots political movements that transcend ethnic groups and focus on issues that are countrywide. Like nationalism, these movements will profoundly affect the environment for future business activity, introducing new risks as well as opportunities. Two such movements—unofficial labor organizations and environmental groups—are already well established and will grow stronger in the years ahead. Movements representing consumers and women are also likely to emerge and have a growing impact.

The rise of independent labor unions in the U.S.S.R. will have an effect on the future business environment of the U.S.S.R. no less profound than that of awakened nationalism. The birth and growth of an independent labor movement is all the more remarkable coming after 70 years of repression, during which the only unions permitted were official organs intended to serve as "transmission belts," in Lenin's phrase, for imposing decisions of the party hierarchy.

The political potential of labor in a democratized U.S.S.R. first became apparent during the elections of March 1989, when the strongest antiestablishment votes came in areas with the highest concentration of workers.[22] A dramatic demonstration of workers' ability to organize and exert their strength came with the miners' strike of July 1989, which focused upon issues involving safety and working conditions and won concessions on every demand. A second, one-day strike in July 1990 underscored the miners' unity and may have aided Gorbachev in his victory over conservatives at the party congress that month by demonstrating grass-roots support for democratization.

On the other hand, despite its reformist bent, the workers' movement includes conservative strains that could become politically significant. While supporting democratization, workers tend to oppose economic reforms that threaten the social security network to which they have become accustomed. An end to price controls and guaranteed employment are fearful prospects to Soviet workers, who have come to depend upon a guaranteed subsistence in exchange for accepting a standard of living well below that of their Western counterparts.

A right-wing coalition of workers' groups, the United Workers Front (UWF), has become established throughout the U.S.S.R. with the help and encouragement of conservative party officials. It not only opposes economic reform but favors a return to centralized party rule and the suppression of dissent. Although the UWF represents only a minority of workers, its ranks could swell if prolonged economic hardship led to increased sentiment for a return to the old ways. Gorbachev acknowledged the potential power of this organization by appointing its cofounder and spokesman, Veniamin Yarin, to his Presidential Council in 1990.

Whether their political outlook remains reformist or takes a turn toward conservatism, Soviet workers of the future are likely to be well organized and active in pursuing their demands. The successes of Solidarity in Poland throughout the 1980s, and the more recent successes of the Soviet miners, have demonstrated how quickly workers can learn to organize despite decades of enforced passivity. As in Poland, even the official unions—or the conservative UWF—will have to become more representative if they are to retain any influence. The experience of Solidarity and the dramatic effects of the miners' strikes have demonstrated to Soviet workers the potential impact of labor actions. Soviet workers are likely to flex their muscles often as they strive to consolidate their economic position in the years of uncertainty that lie ahead. They may also follow the example of counterparts in Europe and the Third World by using the threat of strikes as a political weapon to influence debate on national issues.

A paramount concern of union members will be job security, although working conditions will attract increasing attention as well. The prospect of losing their jobs has been practically unknown to several generations of Soviet workers and has been largely responsible for their compliance with a system that otherwise provided meager benefits. Even the tentative beginnings of economic reform caused severe dislocations and widespread anxiety. Further implementation of reform in the years ahead is likely to produce at least intermittent hardship and insecurity, if not panic. These conditions will be a strong incentive toward militancy among workers if the state-provided safety net dissolves and they come to view unions as the primary protector of their well-being.

One implication for foreign firms operating in the U.S.S.R. will be the need for caution in determining initial levels of staffing, since subsequent efforts to cut back could spark strong union opposition and even strikes. Moreover, because workers represent a substantial part of the Soviet electorate, they are likely to enjoy considerable support from lawmakers and other elected officials. This influence undoubtedly will give workers some say in shaping the environment in which foreign business activity, including labor negotiations, is conducted.

On the other hand, foreign-operated enterprises are likely to be preferred employers, and this may reduce their vulnerability to labor action. The most highly skilled and motivated Soviet workers will be attracted by the prospect of cleaner, safer, technically advanced working environments; more sophisticated and effective management styles; greater opportunities to advance on the basis of performance; and possible fringe benefits such as access to scarce goods and better than average housing. The ability to offer such inducements could provide foreign firms leverage in developing a loyal work force and avoiding strikes.

Another grass-roots movement that has had a dramatic impact on Soviet political life and that will be a major influence on the future business climate is the environmental movement. As early as the 1960s, there were protests over despoliation of the environment and the threat industrialization posed to natural resources such as Lake Baikal. Until the advent of Gorbachev, however, organized protest was not allowed.

Glasnost made possible a proliferation of unofficial environmental groups and brought environmental issues into the mainstream of Soviet political life. The disaster at the Chernobyl nuclear power plant in April 1986 raised awareness throughout the U.S.S.R. that disregard for the environment posed a direct threat to the life and health of present and future generations.

The intensity and rapid spread of the movement also reflect its close link to nationalist issues; indeed, environmental concerns have acted as the trigger for nationalist demonstrations in all regions of the U.S.S.R. Chernobyl, the Ignalina nuclear power plant in Lithuania, and the effects of the cotton industry on Central Asia are prominent examples, but others abound and encompass many fields of manufacturing, processing, and extraction. Most environmental damage has been caused by intensive development decreed by Moscow without regard for local concerns or economies. Often, oversized projects have been imposed on the republics; these have distorted their economies required importing large numbers of Russians to supplement the local labor force, and ignored the effects of pollution and ecological damage.

Health problems resulting from these projects have prompted some nationalists to charge that Moscow's policy of developing the outlying republics amounted to "ecological genocide."[23] Those harboring such feelings have been unmoved by counterarguments that Moscow sought to strengthen local economies and integrate them more fully into that of the U.S.S.R. as a whole, or by the fact that many Russians consider the money invested in distant republics an unfair burden on themselves.[24]

The rise of environmental consciousness in the RSFSR itself has shown little sign of defusing the issue as a source of conflict between Russians and non-Russians. One of the leading Russian environmentalists, novelist Valentin Rasputin, is an extreme nationalist who, along with the Pamyat group, has decried the expenditure of resources on behalf of the outlying republics. Moreover, Russian environmental concerns may clash with those of other republics, as in the dispute over proposals to divert Siberian rivers south to replenish the waters of the endangered Aral Sea.[25]

Among the most remarkable accomplishments of the environmental movement has been a string of victories against the military establishment. These victories have included cancellation of plans for chemical weapons destruction at a plant in Chapayevsk in the Kuybyshev oblast of the RSFSR, a halt to construction of a large radar facility in the western Ukraine, and agreement by the government to phase out nuclear testing at the Semipalatinsk site in Kazakhstan. The effort against nuclear testing, spearheaded by the Nevada-Semipalatinsk movement, is noteworthy not only for its success on an issue of particular military sensitivity, but as a rare example of binational cooperation between Russian and Central Asian activists.[26]

The Soviet environmental movement will continue to grow and make its influence felt at all levels of government. Environmentalists are likely to be particularly strong in the legislatures of the republics as the latter achieve increased autonomy or independence from Moscow, and they will seek to augment their influence by appealing for support from the global environmental movement. On the other hand, Soviet public support could diminish on issues that threaten to worsen an already precarious economy. The absence of such a backlash so far has been noteworthy, as environmentalists repeatedly forced the closing of facilities that provided energy and jobs, but public priorities could shift as hardship grows.

Foreign firms operating in the U.S.S.R. will need to be at least as conscious of environmental safeguards as in the West and may find— because the U.S.S.R. has experienced some of the worst environmental catastrophes in the world—that regulation and enforcement will be even more stringent. The political environment will be particularly sensitive, because any environmental protests over foreign business activity will provide xenophobic nationalists a pretext for attacking the foreign presence generally; there already has been grumbling over despoliation of the environment for the sake of profits that end up overseas.

On the other hand, Soviet environmental concerns also offer opportunities for foreign business. Economic backwardness helps cause environmental problems by promoting the use of outdated and destructive methods in an effort to increase near-term productivity without regard for long-term consequences. Many foreign firms have the advantage of extensive experience in harmonizing environmental interests with industrial efficiency. Some firms will also be able to take advantage of the strong and growing Soviet demand for up-to-date techniques and equipment to deal with environmental problems.

If current trends in Soviet society continue, other grass-roots movements are likely to join the labor and environmental movements in shaping the climate in which foreign business operates. Movements representing women and consumers, in particular, are likely to show increasing strength in the years ahead.

Glasnost has opened the door to frank discussion of the problems, some new, some centuries old, confronting Soviet women. Despite the nominal equality accorded women under Communist rule, and a proportion of women in professional and semiprofessional jobs that dwarfs that of Western countries, the Soviet system generally has denied them access to positions of leadership within their professions.[27] Moreover, the traditional priority accorded heavy industry has resulted in a dual wage structure whereby female workers, while earning the same pay as men doing the same jobs, are concentrated in sectors of the economy where wages are lower than those in fields where men dominate.[28]

In addition, women have been saddled with the dual burden or double shift of jobs, many of which are physically exhausting, and the bulk of household and child care responsibilities. One classic study using Soviet sources found that while men and women spent approximately the same amount of time each week on their jobs, women spent almost 2½ times as many hours as men on housework and had barely half the free time. The study found women spent 6 hours a week on shopping and house cleaning, 6 hours on laundry, and 10 to 12 hours on cooking.[29] Adding to the burden are a dearth of consumer goods and services and a lack of reliable household appliances and convenience foods like those that help many women in the West cope with the competing demands of job and family.[30]

Certain religious traditions also have contributed to women's inferior status. In Central Asia and parts of the Caucasus, women are subject to the traditional restrictions of Islam, which severely curtail their ability to achieve positions of responsibility or to attain equal social status with men.

Russian Orthodox tradition has also embodied values hostile or disparaging toward women, associating them with sin because of their sexual attraction. One scholar has traced these views back to Scythian and pre-Christian Slavic society, where sexual attraction could be literally enslaving since a free male who married a slave acquired her status.[31] As the current resurgence of religious activity and influence continues, the need to counter traditionally negative attitudes toward women is likely to become of ever greater concern to women's rights advocates.

Alongside this negative legacy, there is a more positive tradition in which women have occupied positions of strength and leadership. The Amazons of antiquity are said to have lived in what is now southern Russia, and legends about them continue to captivate the popular imagination.[32] Women have played significant roles in Russian history from the time of Catherine the Great through the reformers and revolutionaries of the late nineteenth and early twentieth centuries to prominent advocates of *perestroika* like the economist Tatyana Zaslavskaya and Supreme Soviet Deputy Galina Starovoitova.

Moreover, advocacy of women's rights is part of the revolutionary tradition. The freeing of the serfs in 1861 was followed shortly by the appearance of Nikolai Chernyshevsky's *What Is to Be Done?* a revolutionary tract that addressed women's issues and was much admired by Lenin. The new Soviet state pursued policies that promoted women's rights until the 1930s, when Stalin's decision to emphasize economic and military development brought a shift in priorities that worked to women's disadvantage. Khrushchev, in pursuing de-Stalinization, sought a return to the earlier policy and revived the official women's councils, or *zhensovety.* Although they relapsed into dormancy under Brezhnev, Gorbachev again sought their revival, and by April 1988 they numbered 2.3 million members.[33] An important milestone in the discussion of women's issues was the All-Union Conference of Women in January 1987, where the first woman astronaut, Valentina Tereshkova, presided over a candid airing of complaints on such topics as unequal conditions in the work place, the burden of homemaking, male alcoholism, the position of women in Moslem communities, problems in health care, infant mortality, and the dearth of women in leading Communist party roles.[34] At the Twenty-eighth Party Congress in July 1990, Gorbachev appointed Galina Semenova to full membership on the Politburo with responsibility for women's issues, providing women a full-time advocate within the party leadership for the first time since the 1920s.

The existence of serious grievances, a tradition of female activism, and new freedom to seek political remedies favor a growth in the women's movement in the 1990s. One indication of women's potential strength has been their mobilization to protest the mistreatment of recruits and the use of conscripts in areas of ethnic conflict. Local grass-roots groups have formed countrywide links through umbrella organizations like the All-

Union Committee of Soldiers' Mothers. A Soviet specialist on women's issues predicted in the summer of 1990 that there would be an "explosion of women's movements" arising out of dissatisfaction over the inefficacy of official women's organizations and the general failure of *perestroika* to improve the situation of women.[35]

A large portion of womens' activism undoubtedly will focus upon the work place. Probable demands include equal access to positions offering higher pay and responsibility and measures to ease the double burden of job and family. Because many women would like to spend more time in the traditional roles of mother and homemaker, future demands may include extension of paid maternity leave (already generous by U.S. standards), greater opportunity for part-time or flex-time employment, and access to child care facilities at the place of employment.[36]

In recent years, U.S. firms have begun to accumulate experience in dealing with a mixed work force of men and women at all levels of responsibility and in responding to women's needs for programs to ease the burden of balancing family and career. The experience gained will be of great help in attracting and retaining female Soviet workers, whose reputation for skill and reliability represents a valuable resource.

The Soviet economy has been less oriented toward consumers than that of almost any other country; until *glasnost* arrived consumers were able to express their dissatisfaction only through the time-honored practice of using barter, bribes, and the black market to obtain goods the system failed to provide through legitimate channels. The simultaneous occurrence under Gorbachev of growing consumer frustration and new freedom to voice discontent has created conditions favorable to the rise of a consumers' movement.

The failure of such a movement to appear thus far may be due largely to the public's preoccupation with the day-to-day challenge of acquiring sufficient provisions to survive. Under such conditions, the most likely vent for frustration is spontaneous outbursts like the "cigarette riots" of August 1990. Concern over a possibly violent backlash undoubtedly has contributed to Gorbachev's reluctance to implement radical economic reforms such as removal of controls on prices.

Nonetheless, the birth of an organized consumers' movement is likely once the economy stabilizes and the public no longer has to expend so much energy meeting daily needs. Even if the variety and selection of goods increases in coming years, a "revolution of rising expectations" is likely to set in, with public concern focusing on product safety and reliability. Increased activism among women will reinforce this trend, since women in the U.S.S.R., as in the United States, make most purchasing decisions.

The future of the U.S.S.R. will be subject to great uncertainty for at least the next several years, with political and economic developments unfolding rapidly and unpredictably. This uncertainty will continue, as uncertainty always does, to foster apprehension and even fear. In such an atmosphere, the risks of doing business in the U.S.S.R. will loom large in the thinking of Western firms.

At the same time, the risks must be kept in perspective so as not to obscure the opportunities the U.S.S.R. offers. Apprehension over the future must be weighed against the fact that the U.S.S.R. in recent years has undergone momentous changes without the cataclysmic results many observers would have predicted, if they had acknowledged the possibility that such changes might occur.

Moreover, as I noted earlier, even the political fragmentation of the U.S.S.R., in whatever form it may occur, would be unlikely to result in permanent economic dismemberment, since economic and commercial interdependence among the republics is deeply rooted. For the foreseeable future, it will be in the interest of all republics to maintain the free passage of goods and services across borders and to coordinate economic, financial, and commercial policies.

It is also worth noting that the population of the Russian Republic alone is 147 million, nearly twice the population of united Germany, and that the three Slavic republics together have 209 million people, nearly two-thirds the population of the European Community. Even the loss of all non-Slavic republics, therefore, would leave significant economic entities intact.

Finally, it is important to bear in mind that foreign business activity can itself play a role in influencing developments within the U.S.S.R. Creating jobs and developing depressed areas will moderate the economic conditions that have contributed to political instability. Supplying goods and services now lacking will confirm to the Soviet public and policy makers the correctness of "new thinking" and the benefits of seeking cooperation rather than confrontation. And creating a marketplace of ideas as well as products will help ensure favorable long-term prospects for Soviet reform.

CHAPTER 16

Action to Take

James L. Hecht

The picture that emerges from the previous 15 chapters is consistent and clear: the Soviet Union offers many good opportunities for foreign investment, but to take advantage of the opportunities requires detailed knowledge, enormous patience, and a willingness to take risks.

Risk taking is unavoidable. For example, the most compelling reason to invest in the U.S.S.R. is the size of the market but, as discussed by Lawrence E. Modisett in Chapter 15, that large market could fragment as a result of nationalist fervor. However, Modisett's analysis indicates that the risk of market loss is far less in some parts of the Soviet Union than in others.

The place to invest with the greatest likelihood of retaining a large market is in the Russian Republic (RSFSR). By itself the RSFSR provides a market of almost 150 million people, and there are good reasons for many of the other republics to stay in some type of union with the Russian Republic. Conversely, since Lithuania at this time is the republic that appears most likely to sever ties with the Soviet Union, it makes little sense to locate a venture there if the objective is to tap a very large market. Incidentally, if not only Lithuania left the U.S.S.R., but also Estonia, Latvia, Moldavia, Georgia, and Armenia, the population loss would be only about 7 percent, and there would be no change in the economic advantages based on market size which were discussed in Chapter 1.

However, even if the investment is made in the RSFSR, there is a chance it will not provide access to a large market. As noted in earlier chapters, the Russian Republic is divided into subunits such as autonomous regions, and there is a possibility that ethnic nationalism and battles over resources will balkanize the RSFSR. But such fragmentation is not likely to occur.

In many ways investing in the Soviet Union is similar to investing in a new product. Both are aimed at developing a substantial new business in which profit margins will be high, but which usually will require waiting at least several years before profitability is achieved. Also, both offer a way of increasing market share but involve a higher level of risk than certain other investments with potentially lower payoffs.

Another risk that must be taken by a foreign company that invests in a joint venture in the Soviet Union is that the potential advantage of a low cost, well-educated labor force will be wiped out as a result of inefficient labor utilization. Much has been said in this book about how Soviet labor has been socialized so that little attention is paid to productivity and quality. But there also is good evidence that it can be advantageous to have a Soviet work force if a joint venture is properly managed.

The experience of McDonald's demonstrates what seems like a reasonable assumption—that a foreign joint venture can have its pick of employees. When McDonald's wanted to hire 630 employees, the company received more than 27,000 replies from this small ad in a Moscow newspaper: "If you want a job where you get paid based on productivity and you want a chance to stay and grow with an organization, then come to work at McDonald's."

McDonald's subsequent success with employee performance has been front-page news. George Cohon, the chairman of McDonald's Restaurants of Canada, has said that the employees in the firm's Moscow restaurant are among the best workers in the McDonald's system. However, as discussed in Chapter 6, some other companies with labor-intensive operations have had problems. Success appears to require careful attention in each of three areas: employee selection, employee training, and incentives based on performance. Although McDonald's needed a relatively large number of employees, they were recruited in an area with a very large population. A firm setting up a large plant in a sparsely populated area could not be as selective, nor could a joint venture whose work force would be drawn from employees of the Soviet partner.

Problems caused by inadequacy of the supply infrastructure have been discussed in earlier chapters and constitute another problem. A foreign company should not participate in a joint venture unless it has assurances of the availability of inputs such as raw materials and necessary manufactured components. As discussed in previous chapters, particularly Chapter 9, the decentralization process that is currently taking place in the Soviet Union makes this risk greater than before. Risks with respect to inputs can be minimized by negotiating appropriate agreements with several levels of government (e.g., the state, the republic, and either an autonomous region or a city government).

A different type of risk is the potential ineffectiveness or loss of a key employee as a result of the problems faced by foreigners living in the Soviet Union. As discussed in Chapters 6 and 8, an executive who sparkled as a plant manager in the United States or as a country manager in Western

Europe may be completely inappropriate for an assignment in the Soviet Union. Working in the U.S.S.R. takes a special type of person.

But many exist. Because I feared that the hardships of assignments in the Soviet Union might rule out certain types of business arrangements, I once asked a senior vice president of a large oil company if his firm would be willing to send U.S. employees to work on a joint venture project in northern Siberia. The answer—without hesitation—was yes. He pointed out that his company had people working in northern Alaska, where it was just as cold, and they also had people on an oil rig just off the coast of Iran at a time when relations between the United States and Iran were very strained. For these people the handling of stress and difficult living conditions was just a part of successfully doing their jobs.

Joint ventures in the U.S.S.R. also face risks arising from political turmoil (including violence) and mass strikes. Strikes could result in plant shutdowns beyond the control of the management of the joint venture; the unavailability of raw materials or manufactured components produced in the turbulent area; or even the destruction of the facilities of the joint venture. However, these risks also can be minimized because, as pointed out in Chapter 15, violence is more likely to occur in the republics of the Caucasus and Central Asia than elsewhere. For example, if the joint venture obtains inputs from these areas, the enterprise should either develop another U.S.S.R. source or maintain a stockpile. Direct investments in such republics—which, as pointed out in Chapter 15, may be advantageous in certain respects—can be made judiciously and in ways that minimize the risks.

Probably the most frustrating risk of all that faces a Western firm considering a joint venture in the U.S.S.R. is the uncertainty of the economic future of the Soviet Union. While some potential joint ventures will give acceptable levels of profitability even if the Soviet economy does not improve, others will require that the Soviet economy improve.

As discussed in detail by Herbert S. Levine in Chapter 14, the future of the Soviet economy will not be clear for some time. The great majority of Soviet economists and many political leaders favor a market economy and increased privatization. However, as Levine points out, a rapid transformation from a centralized economic system to a decentralized one is a formidable task without precedent, and will require both a painful transition and "minimum simultaneity"—a large number of simultaneous reforms to counterbalance the destabilization produced by individual reforms.

But the difficult transformation outlined by Levine is only one of the problems blocking Soviet economic success. If the Soviet economy is to prosper, many of the cultural traditions discussed in Chapter 2 by Mario R. Dederichs must be abandoned. As long as Russians feel like the fisherman who said, "I want him to lose all that"—a story I have heard many times in different variations—the Soviet economy cannot prosper. Nor will it prosper as long as vital economic functions (e.g., matching products to markets) are considered immoral speculation and the realization of fair returns on risk capital is viewed as exploitation. Incidentally, as also pointed out by Modisett in Chapter 15, the egalitarian traditions that will work against business success are strongest in the Russian Republic.

Another challenge that the Soviets must meet if there is to be economic prosperity—a challenge that can directly affect negotiations with potential joint venture partners—is the need for the Soviets to exercise discipline and to use their sources of hard currency to encourage joint ventures with Western firms. As decentralization has taken place, Soviet organizations with access to hard currency, such as those selling petroleum, often use part of this hard currency to purchase consumer goods for direct use by their employees or to barter with other Soviet organizations for consumer goods. However, as discussed in Chapter 1, if the Soviets are willing to defer gratification for several years, they can use the hard currency from the oil to allow foreign investors to repatriate profits from joint ventures that would make consumer goods which the Soviets now are importing for hard currency. This change would allow the Soviets to convert natural resources into anywhere from three to ten times the amount of consumer goods they would obtain by purchase or barter. Thus Western companies interested in developing Soviet resources, such as oil, might do well to seek other Western firms for such partnership arrangements as a way of countering a Soviet reluctance to export natural resources. A type of economic growth could take place in the Soviet Union similar to that which has taken place in Japan where a large number of enterprises are often tied together. In Japan the relationship revolves around a large bank; in the Soviet Union the relationship might consist of a series of joint ventures tied to a Western oil company and its Soviet counterpart.

To what extent the Soviets are willing to defer an increase in the availability of consumer goods is, of course, another question. After all, Americans—who have a far higher living standard—have been unwilling to defer their desire for consumption in order to reduce huge budget deficits or to match the capital spending of the other industrial nations in the West. In the U.S.S.R. there is a great deal of talk about economic reform, but not about economic discipline—such as increasing savings and increasing work.

Thus there are many reasons to be pessimistic about the economic future of the Soviet Union. But there also are facts that suggest a more optimistic outcome. As frequently mentioned in earlier chapters, the U.S.S.R. has great wealth in natural resources. Also, thanks to modern communication systems, cultural traditions that run contrary to economic growth can change quickly. Moreover, some cultural traditions may work in favor of economic growth. For example, the Russian tradition of group cooperation should make Soviets good team players, a desirable characteristic in a large organization in which cooperation between conflicting interests is important to success.

The history of Russia is another reason to voice optimism. There have been desperate times, but the Motherland has always prevailed. Both Napoleon and Hitler, after conquering most of Europe, sent powerful armies to subjugate Russia, but were defeated. What the Russians lacked in equipment and trained manpower they made up in something that could not be tabulated—what Clausewitz called Will. Now, in a very different world in which economic power is replacing military power, that quality may appear again and surprise those who have ridiculed Soviet economic prospects. It should not be forgotten that only 40 years ago Japan was viewed as a poor nation that could compete only where it could capitalize on its cheap labor. The Soviets are disciplined and used to making sacrifices—useful qualities for a nation seeking rapid economic growth. When properly motivated, Soviets have repeatedly proved to be world-class performers. For example, they have consistently won more Olympic medals than the athletes of any other nation. And, despite mediocre incentives and an inadequate infrastructure, Soviet scientists in many fields are given very high marks by their Western counterparts.

Although the problems and risks involved in a joint venture in the U.S.S.R. will vary, in most cases these will be greater than for a similar business in one of the industrial nations of the West. Consequently, for a Western firm to make an investment, projected returns need to be greater than in countries where the risks are less and management does not have as many problems to deal with. This need for a joint venture to be able to project high profits greatly decreases the number of joint ventures that can command private funding in the absence of government assistance.

That is, of course, precisely why the governments of a number of industrial countries have given economic aid to the U.S.S.R. by aiding companies from their country that seek to do business in the Soviet Union. Such aid transforms unacceptable joint ventures into acceptable ones. For example, investment guarantees decrease risk and therefore allow investments to be made for lower returns; low cost loans increase earnings, turning ventures that are not profitable enough into ventures that are. Government policies such as these have the dual affect of helping the Soviet economy and, if wisely done, also helping the economy of the country giving the economic aid. However, the U.S. government, as of this writing, has no such policies; as pointed out by Lawrence J. Brainard in Chapter 12, if American companies are to avoid falling farther behind in the competition for the Soviet market, government programs must be instituted by the United States.

It clearly is in American interests to increase U.S.-Soviet trade. Besides helping U.S. companies, trade serves as an instrument of peace (see Chapter 1). Increasing Soviet economic growth also serves the interests of the

United States by helping to create political stability in the U.S.S.R. Political turmoil in a nation armed with thousands of nuclear weapons is a danger to the entire world.

In addition, properly administered economic aid can play a critical role in moving the Soviet Union toward a democratic, market-oriented society. Since that is what virtually everyone in the United States and other industrial nations wants to happen, why not make it happen by the method that experience has shown is the way to make things happen—the use of incentives? Without economic assistance the chance that reform will be successful is greatly diminished. The Soviets need both the know-how and the capital that Western companies can provide through joint ventures. Economic aid is needed also to reduce the pain of the transition to an acceptable level.

Economic aid has, of course, been given to many countries and can take a variety of forms. These include investment guarantees against political risks, tax breaks on profits, and low cost loans.

There are, unfortunately, undesirable aspects to the methods used in the past to increase private investment in a foreign country. Often aid is given not to the best investment but to the one whose sponsor has the most political influence in Washington. Another problem is that aid is given for an investment that would be made even if aid were not available—with the result that there is no increase in the investment going into the country, only an increase in the profits of the company making the investment. Thus new concepts to encourage foreign investment need to be developed and tried.

A plan that takes into account these undesirable aspects is to give aid in the form of a tax rebate on U.S. earnings to companies that have made approved foreign currency investments in the Soviet Union, and to base the approval process on an auction in which those ventures that request the lowest percentage of U.S. government support are given approval. For example, suppose that up to $2 billion would be available in a fiscal year to encourage U.S. investment in the Soviet Union. Each quarter there would be an auction to award at least $500 million in tax rebates to the low bidders (more would be awarded if the full amount available had not been awarded the previous quarter). Companies interested in investing in the U.S.S.R. would put in a bid for the amount of rebate they would require to make an investment—and could make their bid for rebates anywhere from 5 percent to 50 percent of the total they would invest. Naturally, every company would bid as high as practical; the difference between a 20 percent rebate and a 30 percent rebate on a $50 million investment would be a savings of $5 million in future taxes on earnings. But if a company bid above what became the rebate cutoff point, that company would not be awarded any rebate and would have to try again the following quarter— in the meantime, putting the project on hold.

This concept has many advantages. The United States could decide exactly how much aid it wished to give the Soviet Union, and then give that amount;[1] the ventures getting the aid would be determined by market conditions rather than government bureaucrats; and, while some ventures that would have been funded without the aid program would get some money, these ventures would probably get less than if there were an aid program without an auction. Also, certain potential abuses would be eliminated by the provision that the government aid would be a tax rebate on corporate profits from U.S. operations. Although that would restrict participation to profitable companies, the limitation is a reasonable one: if a company is not profitable, it probably should not be investing in the U.S.S.R. Most important, considerable U.S. investment, accompanied by American technology and management know-how, would be pumped into the Soviet Union quickly, despite the many problems we have discussed, because the aid program would reduce the risk and increase projected profits by a large amount. Subsidies are required for many of the joint ventures now being considered because, compared with other investment opportunities open to Western companies, these ventures are not attractive enough without some type of government aid.

There is another type of economic aid that the United States and other Western countries should offer the Soviet Union, in addition to incentives used to encourage corporations to invest. We have already mentioned that for the Soviet Union to transform its present economy into a market economy will be a monumental task that will require minimum simultaneity and entail a painful transition. Consequently, in order to increase the chances that this transition will be successful and that the Soviet people will not rebel midway through the transition and set the clock back, Western nations, led by the United States, should offer substantial economic assistance in the form of consumer goods, including food, on a one-time basis during the critical period of the transition. This type of assistance, however, would be given only if the Soviets adopted, and then started to execute, a plan to go to a market economy which embraced the basic concept of minimum simultaneity.

A final type of economic aid that should be given to the U.S.S.R. is management training. As discussed in Chapter 5, Soviet managers are skilled, but Soviets are unprepared for a market economy. One example that illustrates just how unprepared they are is given by Robert D. Schmidt, who, when he was a vice president of the Control Data Corporation, was trying to negotiate an agreement in which the Soviets would partially pay Control Data with greeting cards made in the U.S.S.R. The problem encountered by Schmidt was that the Soviets insisted they receive the price for which the cards would sell in the store.[2] While management training will be most cost effective if conducted primarily in the U.S.S.R. with visiting lecturers, there is much to be said for having as many trainees as possible spend some time in the West for additional instruction and, to the extent possible, internships.

Unfortunately, many Americans are reluctant to support economic aid to the U.S.S.R. because they view the Soviet Union as a former enemy which continues to be an adversary and which represses its own people. But that view is based on a narrow vision and an ignorance of history. Following World War II, the United States helped its former enemies rebuild their economies—a bold policy decision which has proven to be a very wise expenditure of funds. The United States did not help the Soviet Union at that time, even though the U.S.S.R. had fought on its side, because the former allies were locked in an ideological battle. That battle is now over—with the United States a clear winner—and the case for aid to the Soviet Union is at least as good as it was for aid to the Germans and Japanese in the period following World War II.

In fact, if historical relationships are at all a factor, the case for aid for the Soviet Union today is far better than it was for Germany and Japan in 1945. In World War I the United States and Russia were on the same side. In fact, the United States has been involved in wars against Great Britain, Germany, Italy, Japan, China, and Spain—but never against Russia. And at least one distinguished historian has noted that Russian support for the North during the Civil War probably prevented Britain and France from forcing a negotiated settlement giving independence to the Southern states.[3]

My personal interest in U.S.-Soviet cooperation—which clearly is very strong—did not have its roots in either a knowledge of the Soviet Union or a feeling of affection for the country. Its genesis in the early 1980s stemmed from my belief that economic cooperation was a way to decrease the chances of a nuclear war and to end an arms race that was damaging the economy of the United States as well as that of the Soviet Union. Today the threat of nuclear war between the two superpowers has become very small, but both continue to spend enormous sums for military preparedness. I view a multibillion dollar U.S. aid package to the Soviet Union not as an additional government expense but as part of a program to save tens of billions of dollars a year by being able to make massive cuts in the $300 billion annual military budget.

Not surprisingly, my involvement with the Soviet Union has caused me to reflect on my personal feelings about the country. Like every other Westerner who has dealt with the U.S.S.R., I have experienced inconveniences and frustrations. But, perhaps because I find that it helps me to be patient and persistent in dealing with the Soviets, I have come to realize that I am more in their debt than they are in mine. I was 18 years old on December 21, 1944. Had it not been for the heroism of the Soviet people— and the loss of more than 20 million Soviet lives—World War II would certainly have gone on much longer, many more Americans would have died, and I might have been one of them. My son and my daughter, in whom I take so much pride and from whom I receive so much joy, might never have been born.

Foreign business firms must recognize that there are two types of action they can take with respect to the U.S.S.R. One is to participate directly as sellers, buyers, and investors. The other is to influence their governments to give appropriate economic assistance to the Soviet Union. The second will greatly influence the first—and the future of the entire world.

Notes

Chapter 1

1. Because prices in the Soviet Union have not been related to costs, there is considerable debate among experts about the size of the Soviet GNP. However, most specialists would support a figure of 11 to 14 percent of world GNP. The 1988 edition of the *World Factbook* published by the U.S. Central Intelligence Agency gives 14 percent.
2. John Holusha, "Business Taps the East Bloc's Intellectual Reserves," *New York Times,* February 20, 1990, A-1.
3. Clyde V. Prestowitz, Jr., *Trading Places: How We Allowed Japan to Take the Lead* (New York: Basic Books, 1988).
4. For example, see George S. Day and David B. Montgomery, "Diagnosing the Experience Curve," *Journal of Marketing* 47 (Spring 1983): 44–58.
5. Morton Deutsch, "Fifty Years of Conflict," in *Retrospections on Social Psychology,* ed. Leon Festinger (New York: Oxford University Press, 1980), 46–77.
6. Muzafer Sherif, *In Common Predicament* (Boston: Houghton Mifflin, 1966).
7. Joseph S. Nye, Jr., *Peace in Parts: Integration and Conflict in Regional Organizations* (Boston: Little, Brown, 1971), 116.
8. Tom W. Smith, "The Polls: American Attitudes towards the Soviet Union and Communism," *Public Opinion Quarterly* (Summer 1983): 277–92.
9. This unpublished study was conducted by two Harvard graduate students, Eric Stubbs and William H. Searles, and was completed at the Center for Foreign Policy Development at Brown University.

Chapter 4

1. William Moskoff, *Labor and Leisure in the Soviet Union* (New York: St. Martin's Press, 1984), 29.
2. Details of the pension system are available in Bernice Madison, "The Soviet Pension System and Social Security for the Aged," in *State and Welfare, USA/USSR,* ed. Gail W. Lapidus and Guy E. Swanson (Berkeley: Institute of International Studies, University of California, 1988), 163–212.
3. Ibid., 188, and Moskoff, *Labor and Leisure,* 34–35.
4. *Trud v SSSR* (Labor in the U.S.S.R.) (Moscow: Finansy i Statistika, 1988), 83, 85.
5. See V. Novoselov, "Schools for a Totalitarian-Technocratic Utopia," *Radio Liberty Research,* March 13, 1984.

6. See L. Denisova, "Ne pogreshim protiv istiny: Pravda protiv statistiki" (Let us not sin against truth: Truth versus statistics), *Narodnoe obrazovanie* (no. 7, 1989): 26–32.

7. Ibid.

8. See Richard B. Dobson, "Higher Education in the Soviet Union: Problems of Access, Equity, and Public Policy," in *State and Welfare,* ed. Lapidus and Swanson, 24–25.

9. Denisova, "Ne pogreshim protiv istiny."

10. I. S. Poltorak and Iu. E. Shul'ga, "Adaptatsiia vypusknikov proftekhuchilishch na proizvodstve" (Adaptation of vocational school graduates in production), *Sotsiologicheskie issledovaniia* (no. 2, 1984): 79–80.

11. The introduction of the Gospriemka (state acceptance commission) system in much of industry in 1987, which brought new inspectors into the plants but kept them under the State Committee on Standards, was an attempt to put teeth into quality control, to force bad products into the reject bin. It came, of course, at the wrong end of the production process, and in the end mattered little.

12. Bob Arnot, "Soviet Labour Productivity and the Failure of the Shchekino Experiment," *Critique* (no. 15, 1982): 46.

13. See the summary in Murray Yanowitch, *Work in the Soviet Union* (Armonk, N.Y.: M. E. Sharpe, 1985), 20–47.

14. *Izvestiia,* February 27, 1988, 1.

15. On the fate of such experiments, see Bob Arnot, *Controlling Soviet Labour* (Armonk, N.Y.: M. E. Sharpe, 1988).

16. See Richard Pipes, *Survival Is Not Enough: Soviet Realities and America's Future* (New York: Simon and Schuster, 1984), 127.

17. See William Moskoff, "Popular Attitudes to Food Shortages," *Radio Liberty Report on the USSR,* May 25, 1990, 9–12.

18. As a percentage of "workers and employees" in 1987; excluding collective farmers (of whom 43 percent were women in 1987). See *Trud v SSSR,* 107–8.

19. One can only guess here. The lack of intrinsic interest in routine work is one thing, the crowded living conditions and lack of what might be called a leisure culture for economically favored women, another. It will take substantial alterations in the Soviet economy before the number of women who might leave employment can be estimated realistically.

20. G. V. Morozov and V. N. Pushina, "Otsenka rabotnitsami deiatel'nosti neposredstvennogo rukovoditelia" (Women workers' estimates of the work of the immediate superior), *Sotsiologicheskie issledovaniia* (no. 1, 1983): 136–39.

21. See Gail W. Lapidus, *Women in Soviet Society* (Berkeley: University of California Press, 1978), for a still informative overview of women's problems and opportunities.

22. See Vladimir Treml, "Alcohol Abuse and Quality of Life in the USSR," in *Soviet Politics in the 1980s,* ed. Helmut Sonnenfeldt, (Boulder, Colo.: Westview Press, 1985), 55–65.

23. Ibid., 57, 64.

24. Ibid., 56.

25. Elizabeth Teague, "Soviet Workers Find a Voice," *Radio Liberty Report on the USSR,* 13 July 1990.

26. *Financial Times,* 19 July 1990.

27. Radio Liberty, *Daily Report,* 23 July 1990, 30 July 1990.

Chapter 5

1. See *Behind the Factory Walls: Decision Making in US and Soviet Enterprises,* ed. Paul R. Lawrence and Charalambos A. Vlachoutsicos (Boston: Harvard Business School Press, 1990).

2. See para. 2 of Article 19 and Article 20 of the June 4, 1990, decree no. 1524 of the Supreme Soviet of the U.S.S.R. on the Law on the Soviet State Enterprise.

3. The new (June 4, 1990) Law of the Soviet State Enterprise in the U.S.S.R. provides in sect. 4, "Management of an Enterprise and Self Management," several points relevant to the selection of managers:

    Article 14

    "1. The management of an enterprise shall be carried out in accordance with its charter on the basis of a combination of the principles of self-management of the workers collective and the rights of the owner to the economic use of his property. . . .

    "2. The hiring (appointment, election) of the head of an enterprise shall be the right of the owner of the property of the enterprise and shall be exercised by him directly as well as through the councils of the enterprise. . . ."

    Article 18

    "1. The council (board) of an enterprise shall consist of an equal number of representatives nominated by the owner of the property of the enterprise and elected by its workers collective. . . ."

    Article 20

    "2. Brigade leaders shall be elected at meetings of the collectives of brigades (by secret or open vote) and approved by the head of the subdivision of which the brigade is a part."

4. Hiroaki Kuromiya, "Edinonachalie and the Soviet Industrial Manager, 1918–4.1937," *Soviet Studies* 36 (no. 2, 1984): 186.

5. Michael Waller, *Democratic Centralism: An Historical Commentary* (New York: St. Martin's Press, 1981), 62.

6. Abel Aganbegyan, *The Economic Challenge of Perestroika* (Bloomington: Indiana University Press, 1988), 193, and D. Gvishiani, *Organization and Management* (Moscow, 1972), 31–33.

7. Mikhail Gorbachev, *Perestroika* (New York: Harper & Row, 1987), 34. After three days of tempestuous debate, the Soviet Communist party reached the historic decision on February 7, 1990, "to abandon its 70-year-old hold on absolute power,

paving the way for a multi-party democracy. Key elements in the platform include a radical shift to grass-roots democracy, ending the Leninist tradition of democratic centralism to enforce party discipline" (*Financial Times,* February 8, 1990, 1).

8. These examples are drawn from Chapters 6, 7, 8, and 9 of *Behind the Factory Walls* and were written primarily by Sheila Puffer, Elise Walton, Alexander Naumov, and Vitale Ozira.

Chapter 6

1. Philip Hanson, *Trade and Technology in Soviet–Western Relations* (New York: Columbia University Press, 1981).

2. James L. Hecht and James K. Oliver, "The Experience of U.S. Firms with the Soviet Union: What Does the Past Tell Us to Do in the Future?" *Columbia Journal of World Business* (Summer 1988): 91–98.

3. James L. Hecht, "Soviet Union Use of Technology," *les Nouvelles,* September 1990, 101–5.

4. Robert D. Hisrich and Michael P. Peters, "East-West Trade: An Assessment by Manufacturers," *Columbia Journal of World Business* (Winter 1983): 44–50.

5. Robert Axelrod, *The Evolution of Cooperation* (New York: Basic Books, 1984).

6. Nineteen companies participated in the study; eleven other companies known to have licensed technology for plants in the Soviet Union either were unable or unwilling to supply the necessary information. Also, I estimate that there probably were of the order of six additional companies who licensed technology, but were not included in the study.

7. Ed A. Hewett, *Energy, Economics and Foreign Policy in the Soviet Union* (Washington, D.C.: Brookings Institution, 1984), 75.

Chapter 7

1. Previously the Soviet government had appealed for Western help at times of great peril and vulnerability of the regime: in the 1920s after the end of the civil war and in 1941 following the disastrous consequences of the German attack.

2. Although not required by law, joint ventures should ordinarily be approved by the Ministry of Defense and the KGB.

3. Of those, West Germany had the highest number, with Finland and the United States in close second and third positions, respectively. The United States was nevertheless leading in the amount of overall investment. See "JV Archipelago," *Business in the USSR,* October 1990. It is also worth noting that out of the total, fewer than 500 were fully operational.

4. Joint ventures are not an entirely novel type of business combination in Soviet foreign trade practice. Since the 1960s, Soviet foreign trade organizations have entered into marketing joint venture agreements to distribute Soviet products abroad—such as Belarus tractors in the United States and cars and diamonds in Europe. These ventures were formed outside the Soviet Union, had little impact on Soviet enterprises, and were not publicized in the country.

5. According to a Soviet business publication, foreign investors' average contribution to the authorized capital of joint ventures has declined from an equivalent of 2.4 million rubles to less than 1 million. See "Unfulfilled Hopes," *Business World,* October 1990.

6. Even when convertible currency sales are possible, they may not be an ideal solution for Soviet enterprises, because little of the proceeds remain at their disposal.

7. See N. Belov, "Parfumernyi Conflict," *Rabochaja Tribuna,* July 28, 1990.

8. See N. Anisimov, "Na Razhyh Yazykah," *Nedelja,* November 12, 1989.

9. This concern was also expressed by Keith A. Rosten, "Soviet Joint Ventures Riding on Troubled Waters," *Wall Street Journal,* May 7, 1990.

Chapter 9

1. Information on these products can be obtained from Indian Valley Meats, Indian, Alaska 99540.

Chapter 11

1. Lenin, in his ideas for the long-term use of "external resources" to aid in the development of the country's economy, foresaw concessions to foreign capital for the development of various projects for a period of 60 to 70 years.

2. Today the U.S.S.R. has 1.3 hectares of pasturable land and 0.8 hectares of plowed field per capita, as opposed to the corresponding 0.18 and 0.25 hectares in Western Europe and 1 and 0.8 in the United States.

3. The principal ones are listed, for instance, in *The Post-Containment Handbook: Key Issues in U.S.-Soviet Economic Relations* (Boulder, Colo.: Westview Press, 1990), 190–213.

4. In 1980–84 alone American firms missed 31 large contracts with various countries because of the conditions they placed on countertrade. See "Assessment of Effects of Barter and Countertrade Transaction on U.S. Industry," U.S. International Trade Commission Publication 1766 (Washington, D.C.: The American Countertrade Association, 1985). The American Countertrade Association consists of 138 U.S. manufacturing companies. Information about the association can be obtained by contacting Dan West at (314) 694–5703.

5. For further information on countertrade, see L. Fargo Wells and Karin B. Dulat, *Exporting: From Start to Finance* (Blue Ridge Summit, Pa.: Liberty House, 1989), 318–22.

6. The property law that took effect July 1, 1990, in the U.S.S.R. establishes the property rights of joint ventures, foreign citizens, and other persons legally on the territory of the U.S.S.R. and provides for the protection of those rights. Article 29 of the law, in part, states, "Foreign persons legally in the U.S.S.R. have the right to ownership on the territory of the U.S.S.R. of industrial and other enterprises, buildings, structures and other properties for the purpose of economic and other activity in cases and order established by the legislative acts of the Union of Soviet Socialist Republics."

7. The U.S.S.R. Trade Representation in the United States is located in Washington, D.C., and can be reached by telephone at (202) 232–5988; Amtorg is in New York City and can be reached by telephone at (212) 956–3010.

Chapter 12

1. One way around this problem is to negotiate a countertrade agreement, in which the ruble earnings would be converted into given quantities of Soviet goods. A variation on the Pepsi for vodka compensation deal provides the outline of a structure that could be adapted to joint ventures.

2. A leading Soviet economist, Valery Makarov, director of the Central Economics and Mathematics Institute, expressed the view that power over resource allocation was being lost by the central government: "There are now three centers of power—the center itself, the republics and the cities." Quoted in "Soviet Economists Pessimistic at Gorbachev Reforms," *Financial Times,* July 27, 1990, 3. An example of changes affecting enterprise control over foreign exchange was provided by the introduction in November 1990 of new regulations compelling enterprises to sell 40 percent of all hard-currency earnings to a newly created All-Union Currency Fund. At the same time the commercial exchange rate of the ruble was devalued 66 percent. Quentin Peel, "Debt Needs Prompt Hefty New Soviet Tax," *Financial Times,* November 6, 1990, 3.

3. A concise survey of Soviet banking reforms may be found in "In Search of Greater Financial Discipline," *Financial Times,* March 12, 1990, xii.

4. For example, shareholders in the Moscow Share Innovation Bank include a state bank (Promstroibank), the Ministry of Electronics, the Electronics Central Scientific Research Institute, and a Moscow watch factory.

5. "In Search of Greater Financial Discipline," xii.

6. "Investing in the USSR" (available from the law offices of Cole Corette & Abrutyn, 21 Upper Brook Street, London and 1110 Vermont Ave., N.W., Washington, D.C.), 21. This booklet provides an excellent survey of the banking reforms and issues associated with foreign investment in the Soviet Union.

7. Quentin Peel, "Soviet Bank Law Clears First Hurdle," *Financial Times,* October 10, 1990, 2.

8. "China Stings Banks on State Concerns' Loan Guarantees," *Wall Street Journal,* July 19, 1990, A6.

9. Keith A. Rosten, "Soviet Joint Ventures Riding on Troubled Waters," *Wall Street Journal,* May 7, 1990.

10. Although the BFEA exercises controls on foreign borrowings on behalf of the government, it does not enjoy a Soviet government guarantee. Legally, it is organized as a joint stock company with shares distributed among several ministries and the Gosbank. Its statutes state that the Soviet government is not liable for the obligations of the bank. The BFEA borrows in its own name, not directly on behalf of the Soviet government. In practice, most Western creditors consider the BFEA and the Soviet government as one and the same. "Soviet Bank Brings a Whiff of Glasnost to London," *Financial Times,* November 13, 1989.

11. *Financial Market Trends,* February 1990, 23.

12. "Moscow Faces Import Payments Crisis," *Financial Times,* May 18, 1990.

13. "Soviets Deposit Gold in Western Banks as Collateral for Easing Cash Squeeze," *Wall Street Journal,* June 4, 1990, A3; "Soviets to Sell Diamonds to De Beers's Swiss Arm," *Wall Street Journal,* July 26, 1990, A12.

14. Reuters Newswire, "West German Companies Paid by Soviet Union," July 25, 1990.

15. In September, an official of a Japanese trading company confirmed that his company's subsidiaries in Germany were receiving prompt payment on export shipments, but the head office in Tokyo was still experiencing arrears of over $100 million. Interview material, September 27, 1990.

16. "Bonn Offers Moscow Huge Credit, Seeking to Ease Unification Jitters," *Wall Street Journal,* June 22, 1990.

17. "Soviet Union credit rating to be downgraded by Deutsche Bank," *Financial Times,* January 15, 1991, 1.

18. In Germany and several other countries some facilities have been set up as bank-to-bank lines, with all negotiations handled between the BFEA and banks in the respective country.

19. The following discussion has benefited from Robert Starr's excellent analysis in "Investing in the USSR," 27–30.

Chapter 13

1. For a comprehensive discussion of the development of Russian law from the founding of Russia through the Russian Revolution, see W. E. Butler, *Soviet Law,* 2d ed. (London: Butterworth, 1988), 10–26.

2. The Marxist-Leninist principle that law was merely politics led not only to a belief that law was irrelevant, but that it had no binding effect, with the result that early Bolshevik legal decisions were often based on whim and arbitrariness. See John Hazard and Isaac Shapiro, *The Soviet Legal System* (Dobbs Ferry, N.Y.: Oceana, 1962), 3–5. See also Butler, *Soviet Law,* 27–40. See also Edgar Boden Leimer's review of P. I. Stuchka's legal philosophy in *American Journal of Comparative Law* 38 (1990): 196. Stuchka was among the most eminent of early Bolshevik legal scholars.

3. Stalin, while agreeing with the basic Marxist-Leninist premise that law was politics, transformed the role of law to "safeguard" the strong state that he was building. The "withering away of the state" was replaced by efforts to protect the state. Such protection was necessary because the U.S.S.R. was undergoing forced industralization from above, i.e., dictated and enforced by the central authorities. This protection also provided the justification for Stalin's amassing of great personal power. As Hazard and Shapiro *(The Soviet Legal System)* have noted:

> Stalin called for strict observance of law, but this did not mean to him that he was to be held personally to any humanistic standard. He drew a line between his own freedom to determine policy without regard to rules, other than those created by economics and natural science, and the freedom he denied to subordinates to depart from the rules he established for them to administer. (P. 5)

For a perspective on the historical development of Soviet contract law, see E. Farnsworth and V. Mozolin, *Contract Law in the USSR and the United States* (Washington, D.C.: International Law Institute, 1987), 57–86.

4. Even today, it is widely believed that more than 70 percent of Soviet laws that affect the rights and freedoms of Soviet citizens remain unpublished and are classified as state secrets. *Izvestia,* November 30, 1990.

5. See, for example, Evsey S. Rashba, "Settlement of Disputes in Commercial Dealings with the U.S.S.R.," *Columbia Law Review* 45 (1945): 530, 538.

6. For example, Article 5 of the RSFSR Civil Code, entitled "Enforcement of Civil Rights and Liabilities," states:

> Civil rights are protected by law except in cases where they are exercised in a manner which would be inconsistent with the purposes of such rights in a socialist society during the period of the establishment of communism.
>
> In exercising rights and performing duties, citizens and organizations must comply with the laws and observe the rules of socialist community life and the moral principles of a society building communism.

For an interesting discussion of the "problems of legislative technique" in the U.S.S.R. (described as overregulation [of the trivial]; underregulation [of the important]; and vagueness, particularly regarding the legal consequences of actions), see Brunner, "The Legal Framework of Economic Reform" (Paper presented at NATO Colloquim, Brussels, March 1989).

7. In his article, "Plan and Contract in the Domestic and Foreign Trade of the U.S.S.R.," *Syracuse Journal of International Law and Commerce* 8 (1980): 29, Isaak Dore discusses Soviet *arbitrazh* decisions that demonstrate the primacy of the economic plan goals in the resolution of disputes.

8. Harold Berman and George Berstin focus on the impartiality of the Foreign Trade Arbitration Court in "The Soviet System of Foreign Trade," *Law & Policy in International Business* 7 (1975): 987, 1019–26.

9. Olympiad Ioffe, one of the leading experts in Soviet civil law, argues persuasively that the fundamental purpose of the Soviet legal and economic system is political, i.e., to guarantee the dominance of the state. Ioffe, "Law and Economy in the USSR," *Harvard Law Review* 95 (1982):1591, 1624.

10. Mikhail Gorbachev, *Perestroika: New Thinking for Our Country and the World* (London: Collins, 1987), 105.

11. Ibid., 106.

12. Alexander Yakovlev, "Transforming the Soviet Union into a Rule of Law Democracy: A Report from the Front Lines" (Speech to the Association of the Bar of the City of New York, December 1990).

13. For an analysis of the impact of reform on the Soviet legal system, see "Soviet Economic Law: The Paradox of Perestroika" by Paul Stephan of the University of Virginia, which will be published in 1991 by the University of Pittsburgh as part of the Carl Beck papers; also, see Frances Foster-Simons, "Toward a More Perfect Union? The 'Restructuring of Soviet Legislation,' " *Stanford Journal of International Law* 25 (1989): 331.

14. The views expressed here are those of the author and not necessarily those of his employer.

15. American Intellectual Property Law Association Mid-Winter Institute, the Art of Negotiation and Conciliation, Palm Desert, Calif., February 1990.

16. John Minan and Grant Morris, "Unravelling an Enigma: An Introduction to Soviet Law and the Soviet Legal System," *George Washington Journal of International Law and Economics* 19 (1985): 1.

17. Alex Keviczky, "US-USSR International Arbitration," *les Nouvelles,* March 1990, 21.

18. In the U.S.S.R., as in most other countries, a patent is not a license to practice the invention, but a right to exclude others from practicing the invention, since an earlier patentee may have a dominating patent. The solution is normally a cross-license between the two patentees.

19. If one files a patent application in the United States and then files it in the U.S.S.R. within a year of the U.S. filing date, an international treaty considers the Soviet filing date to be effectively the same as the U.S. filing date.

Chapter 15

1. Starr describes a Soviet public far more sophisticated, better educated, and more demanding than that of 30 years ago. See "Soviet Union: A Civil Society," *Foreign Policy* 70 (Spring 1988): 26–41. Gail W. Lapidus makes a similar point, noting that while Khrushchev ruled over a society still predominantly rural, by the time Gorbachev became Soviet leader two-thirds of the population lived in cities. During the same period, the number of citizens with a higher education grew from 5.5 million to 24 million and the number of "scientific workers" increased tenfold, to 15 million. See "State and Society: Toward the Emergence of Civil Society in the Soviet Union," in *Politics, Society, and Nationality inside Gorbachev's Russia,* ed. S. Bialer (Boulder, Colo.: Westview Press, 1989), 126.

2. Andrei Amalrik, *Will the Soviet Union Survive until 1984?* (New York: Harper & Row, 1970), 64–65.

3. Gertrude Schroeder, "Social and Economic Aspects of the Nationality Problem," in *The Last Empire: Nationality and the Soviet Future,* ed. R. Conquest (Stanford, Calif.: Hoover Institution, 1986), 308–9.

4. See Gorbachev's speech to participants in a military exercise in Odessa, August 17, 1990, in Foreign Broadcast Information Service, *Daily Report: Soviet Union* (hereafter *FBIS*), August 20, 1990, 46; and "Communique of the Joint Meeting of the USSR Federation Council and the Presidential Council," *FBIS,* September 4, 1990, 56.

5. U.S.S.R., *Natsional'niy sostav naseleniya* (National composition of the population) (Moscow: Finansy i statistika, 1989).

6. Orest Subtelny, *Ukraine: A History* (Toronto: University of Toronto Press, 1988), xi.

7. This attempted suppression and the Ukrainian reaction are discussed in Roman Solchanyk, "Ukraine, Belorussia, and Moldavia: Imperial Integration, Russification, and the Struggle for National Survival," in *The Nationalities Factor in Soviet*

Politics and Society, ed. L. Hajda and M. Beissinger (Boulder, Colo.: Westview Press, 1990), 175–203, and Roman Szporluk, "The Ukraine and Russia," in *The Last Empire,* ed. Conquest, 151–82.

8. See also the interview given in London on August 21, 1990, by Bohdan Horyn, a deputy to the Ukrainian Supreme Council and member of the Ukrainian Republican party and Rukh, reported in the RFE/RL *Daily Report,* August 30, 1990.

9. Laurie P. Salitan, "Politics and Nationality: The Soviet Jews," in *Politics, Society, and Nationality,* ed. Bialer, 187.

10. See Leonard Schapiro, "Nationalism in the Soviet Empire: The Anti-Semitic Component," in *The Last Empire,* ed. Conquest, 78–86, and Hugh Seton-Watson, "Russian Nationalism in Historical Perspective," in ibid., 23, 28.

11. On a smaller scale, disputes have arisen between the newly reestablished Ukrainian Autocephalous Orthodox Church and the Orthodox Church of the Ukraine, which is subordinate to the Patriarch of Moscow.

12. Geoffrey Hosking, *The Awakening of the Soviet Union* (Cambridge, Mass.: Harvard University Press, 1990), 132.

13. Gorbachev, speech of August 17, 1990, *FBIS,* August 20, 1990.

14. Ronald Suny, "Transcaucasia: Cultural Cohesion and Ethnic Revival in a Multinational Society," in *The Nationalities Factor,* ed. Hajda and Beissinger, 231.

15. Alexandre Bennigsen, "Soviet Minority Nationalism in Historical Perspective," in *The Last Empire,* ed. Conquest, 137.

16. Suny, "Transcaucasia," 238.

17. Gertrude Schroeder, "Nationalities and the Soviet Economy," in *The Nationalities Factor,* ed. Hajda and Beissinger, Table 1, Table 6.

18. See Hélène Carrère d'Encausse, *Decline of an Empire: The Soviet Socialist Republics in Revolt,* trans. M. Sokolinsky and H. LaFarge (New York: Newsweek Books, 1979), 237–47; Martha Brill Olcott, "Central Asia: The Reformers Challenge a Traditional Society," in *The Nationalities Factor,* ed. Hajda and Beissinger, 269–72; and S. Enders Wimbush, "The Soviet Muslim Borderlands," in *The Last Empire,* ed. Conquest, 226–28.

19. On the other hand, the higher birth rates of Central Asian peoples and the growing outmigration of Russian and other non-Asian minorities are increasing the proportion of native ethnic groups in the population of this region, a trend that may well accelerate.

20. See Olcott, "Central Asia," 254.

21. See ibid., 267, and Wimbush, "The Soviet Muslim Borderlands," 220–22.

22. Gregory Embree, "The Political Emergence of the Soviet Intelligentsia" (Unpublished manuscript, Arlington, Virginia, 1989).

23. Charles E. Ziegler, "Environmental Policy and Politics under Gorbachev" (Paper presented at the Fourth World Congress for Soviet and East European Studies, Harrogate, England, July 1990), 3.

24. Marshall Goldman, "Environmentalism and Nationalism: An Unlikely Twist in an Unlikely Direction" (Paper presented at the Fourth World Congress for Soviet and East European Studies, Harrogate, England, July 1990), 14–15.

25. Ziegler, "Environmental Policy," 5–6, 11–12.

26. Olcott, "Central Asia," 275.

27. See Norton T. Dodge, "Women in the Professions," in *Women in Russia,* ed. D. Atkinson, A. Dallin, and G. Lapidus (Stanford, Calif.: Stanford University Press, 1977), 206–14. Dodge notes that the 1970 census showed women representing 82 percent of Soviet economists and planners, 74 percent of physicians, 77 percent of dentists, 43 percent of teachers in higher education, and 40 percent of engineers and scientific research personnel. (By contrast, women represented 7 percent of physicians in the United States.) However, the proportion of women diminished sharply as the level of rank in each profession increased, with very few women occupying managerial or administrative positions, even in fields where they dominated the lower levels.

28. Janet G. Chapman, "Equal Pay for Equal Work?" in *Women in Russia,* ed. Atkinson, Dallin, and Lapidus, 236–39. Chapman notes that the lower pay scales in sectors dominated by women reflect in part demand–supply dynamics, since the steady increase in women entering the work force over several decades created a more plentiful labor supply in those sectors than in others. Chapman suggests the wage differential may decrease as greater priority is accorded consumer goods and services, where female workers dominate.

29. Gail Warshofsky Lapidus, *Women in Soviet Society: Equality, Development, and Social Change* (Berkeley: University of California Press, 1978), 270–72.

30. For firsthand accounts of these and other challenges facing Soviet women, see the interviews with women occupying a range of social, economic, and professional situations in Francine du Plessix Gray, *Soviet Women: Walking the Tightrope* (New York: Doubleday, 1990), and the collection of articles from the dissident publication "Woman and Russia: An Almanac to Women about Women," in *Women and Russia: Feminist Writings from the Soviet Union,* ed. Tatyana Mamonova and trans. Rebecca Park and Catherine A. Fitzpatrick (Boston: Beacon Press, 1984).

31. Dorothy Atkinson, "Society and the Sexes in the Russian Past," in *Women in Russia,* ed. Atkinson, Dallin, and Lapidus, 14–16.

32. Ibid., 3–5, 36–37.

33. Mary Buckley, *Women and Ideology in the Soviet Union* (Ann Arbor: University of Michigan Press, 1989), 210.

34. Ibid., 200–203.

35. See Rosamund Shreeves, "Mothers against the Draft: Women's Activism in the USSR," in Radio Liberty, *Report on the USSR,* September 21, 1990, 3–8.

36. The yearning for more time in traditional roles is a recurring theme in the interviews recounted by Gray, and Shreeves suggests this strain in Soviet feminism could result in a women's movement that placed far greater emphasis on "female values" than its counterparts in the West.

   Soviet women receive 112 days of maternity leave at full pay and partially paid leave for an additional year (Mamonova, *Women and Russia,* 91).

Chapter 16

1. This assumes that there would be enough corporate applicants. However, even with a government subsidy of 50 percent of the hard-currency investment there may not be enough proposed joint ventures; as a matter of principle, subsidies greater than

50 percent should not be given. On the other hand, an aid program of this type might encourage the Soviets to be more realistic in their negotiations. The willingness of an American company to forgo a large government subsidy would certainly make the point to the Soviets that the terms that they were offering were not good.

2. Robert D. Schmidt, "Business Negotiations with the Soviet Union," in *Private Diplomacy with the Soviet Union,* ed. David D. Newsom (Lanham, Md.: University Press of America, 1987), 85.

3. John Lewis Gaddis, *Russia, the Soviet Union, and the United States: An Interpretive History* (New York: Wiley, 1978), 21.

Recommended Books

One book cannot meet all of the needs of people seriously interested in doing business with the Soviet Union—or even just interested in learning about the country.

Some people would prefer a list of recommended reading to be a short list. However, the selection of such a list would depend on answers to several questions: what are the reader's interests in the Soviet Union; what are the reader's general interests; and how much detail does the reader want? Since the answers for each reader will differ, our list of recommended readings is long but is grouped by subject and includes a brief comment on most of the books.* This should enable readers to develop their own short list quickly.

Some subjects listed, such as literature, may seem out of place. However, particularly for people interested in the literature of their own country, reading Russian literature will be both a pleasure and a way to establish closer relationships with some of their Soviet business counterparts. The same holds for art, music, and foreign affairs.

Agriculture

Medvedev, Zhores A. *Soviet Agriculture.* New York: Norton, 1988. A broad review of agriculture from 1965 to 1986.

Yanov, Alexander. *The Drama of the Soviet 1960s: A Lost Reform.* Berkeley: Institute of International Studies, University of California, 1984. Illustrating his theory of the pendulum swing of reform and counterreform, Yanov describes the struggle for reform in agriculture in the early 1960s—in which he was directly involved.

Arms Control

Arbatov, Alexei G. *Lethal Frontiers: A Soviet View of Nuclear Strategy, Weapons, and Negotiations.* New York: Praeger, 1988. The author addresses the U.S. response to the onset of strategic parity.

Dyson, Freeman. *Weapons and Hope.* New York: Harper & Row, 1984. Contains a great chapter on the Soviet Union. The rest of the book is must reading for anyone with a strong interest in arms control.

---

*Some of the comments are abstracted from book reviews in *Foreign Affairs* and from a reading list supplied by the Citizen Exchange Council of New York.

Flynn, Gregory, ed. *Soviet Military Doctrine and Western Policy.* New York: Routledge, 1989. Explores why Western policy (especially American nuclear policy) has seemed so disconnected from understandings of Soviet doctrine.

Gray, Colin S. *Nuclear Strategy and National Style.* Lanham, Md.: Hamilton Press, 1986. Gray argues that there are distinctive national styles in nuclear politics, based on history and culture, and that the United States consistently misreads the U.S.S.R.

Mandelbaum, Michael, ed. *The Other Side of the Table: The Soviet Approach to Arms Control.* New York: Council on Foreign Relations Press, 1990. A compilation of American assessments of Soviet arms control practices.

Morris, Charles R. *Iron Destinies, Lost Opportunities.* New York: Harper & Row, 1988. A detailed study of the arms race that not only provides an excellent survey on the topic but also points out what went wrong in U.S.-Soviet relations and why.

Newhouse, John. *War and Peace in the Nuclear Age.* New York: Alfred A. Knopf, 1989. The book, the basis of a television documentary series, is good reading for the general reader.

Sherr, Alan B. *The Other Side of Arms Control: Soviet Objectives in the Gorbachev Era.* Boston: Unwin Hyman, 1988. The author is a lawyer who was president of Lawyers for Nuclear Arms Control.

Sloss, Leon, and M. Scott Davis. *A Game for High Stakes: Lessons Learned in Negotiating with the Soviet Union.* Cambridge, Mass.: Ballinger, 1986. Veteran U.S. negotiators discuss Soviet negotiating style and tactics. Soviet negotiations are best described as tenacious, but are often dependent on an initial American proposal.

Arts and Culture

Billington, James. *The Icon and the Axe: An Interpretive History of Russian Culture.* New York: Alfred A. Knopf, 1966. Classic work which started the author on the road to recognition.

Brown, Matthew Cullerne. *Contemporary Russian Art.* New York: Philosophical Library, 1990. Discusses the work of 58 artists.

Brumfield, William. *Gold in Azure: One Thousand Years of Russian Architecture.* Boston: D. R. Godine, 1983. Well written, with many fine photos.

Crankshaw, Edward. *Putting up with the Russians.* New York: Viking, 1984. A collection of essays on Russian and Soviet culture from 1947 to 1984 put together by a leading British expert.

Fedotov, George. *The Russian Religious Mind.* Belmont, Mass.: Nordland, 1975. A reprint of the classic study of Russian spirituality.

Gerhart, Genevra. *The Russian's World: Life and Language.* Fort Worth, Tex.: Holt, Rinehart and Winston, 1974. Detailed explanation of culture, tradition, common habits, and objects.

Kerblay, Basile. *Gorbachev's Russia.* New York: Pantheon, 1989. Contemporary work dealing with the Soviet people and culture.

Maclean, Fitzroy. *Holy Russia.* New York: Atheneum, 1979. An illustrated guide to Russia, with emphasis on traditional culture.

Massie, Suzanne. *Land of the Firebird.* New York: Touchstone/Simon & Schuster, 1980. Popular book. The author later became an adviser to President Ronald Reagan on Russian culture and is credited with changing some of the President's views.

Rice, Tamara. *A Concise History of Russian Art.* London: Thames & Hudson, 1963. A well-illustrated survey.

Schwarz, Boris. *Music and Musical Life in Soviet Russia, 1917–1981.* Bloomington: Indiana University Press, 1983. Music and its political dimensions.

Starr, S. Frederick. *Red and Hot: The Fate of Jazz in the Soviet Union.* New York: Oxford University Press, 1983. A look at the Jazz Age in the U.S.S.R. by a well-known Sovietologist who is president of Oberlin College.

Valkenier, Elizabeth. *Russian Realist Art: The State and Society.* New York: Columbia University Press, 1989. Traces the precursors of Soviet socialist realism in reform-minded nineteenth-century painters.

Ware, Timothy. *The Orthodox Church.* New York: Penguin Books, 1981.

Zenkovsky, Sergei. *Medieval Russia's Epics, Chronicles, and Tales.* New York: Dutton, 1974. Good background reading for those visiting cathedrals, monasteries, museums, and so on.

Economics and Business

Aslund, Anders. *Gorbachev's Struggle for Economic Reform.* Ithaca, N.Y.: Cornell University Press, 1989. Explains many cultural aspects of economic performance. Some people consider this to be the best book so far on economic reform.

Christians, F. Wilhelm. *Paths to Russia.* New York: Macmillan, 1990. The author, the chairman of Deutsche Bank, tells about his 20 years of extensive experience with Moscow.

Fisher, Roger. *Getting to Yes.* Boston: Houghton Mifflin, 1981. This classic work on negotiation gives lots of ideas which can be used when dealing with Soviet negotiators.

Goldman, Marshall I. *Gorbachev's Challenge: Economic Reform in the Age of High Technology.* New York: Norton, 1987. The associate director of the Harvard Russian Research Center offers Gorbachev some quite specific advice, 1987 vintage.

Gregory, Paul R., and Robert C. Stuart. *Soviet Economic Structure and Performance.* New York: Harper & Row, 1986.

Hewett, Ed A. *Energy, Economics, and Foreign Policy in the Soviet Union.* Washington: Brookings Institution, 1984. A well-researched book which looks at the Soviet energy problem.

———. *Reforming the Soviet Economy.* Washington: Brookings Institution, 1988. This highly acclaimed work on the Soviet economy discusses both the formal economy and the system as it actually operates.

Hough, Jerry F. *Opening up the Soviet Economy.* Washington: Brookings Institution, 1988. Hough argues for U.S. policies which do not restrict trade with the U.S.S.R.

Marples, David. *Chernobyl and Nuclear Power in the USSR.* New York: Macmillan, 1987. A thorough study on the Chernobyl nuclear accident, its origins and its repercussions.

———. *The Social Impact of the Chernobyl Disaster.* New York: St. Martin's Press, 1988. A continuation of his earlier study, this book looks into the long-term environmental, political, and social impact of Chernobyl.

Millar, James R. *The ABC's of Soviet Socialism.* Urbana: University of Illinois Press, 1981. Award-winning account by knowledgeable Sovietologist.

———. *The Soviet Economic Experiment.* Urbana: University of Illinois Press, 1990. A collection of essays edited by Susan J. Linz.

Newsome, David D., ed. *Private Diplomacy with the Soviet Union.* Washington: University Press of America, 1987. This small book is filled with sound, practical advice on the pitfalls and opportunities of nongovernmental contacts with the Soviet Union.

Nove, Alec. *An Economic History of the USSR.* New York: Penguin, 1989. Emphasizes the social costs of the rapid transformation from an underdeveloped country to an industrial superpower.

Pisar, Samuel. *Coexistence and Commerce.* New York: McGraw-Hill, 1970. This was the best book to read for those doing business with the U.S.S.R. for over 15 years following its publication. It is detailed, thorough, and scholarly, but now outdated.

Rumer, Boris Z. *Soviet Steel: The Challenge of Industrial Modernization in the USSR.* Ithaca: Cornell University Press, 1989. Valuable study written by a former economist for the Soviet construction industry.

Education

Bronfenbrenner, Urie. *Two Worlds of Childhood: US-USSR.* New York: Russell Sage Foundation, 1970. Comparative study of educational systems and their psychological impact on children.

Grant, Nigel. *Soviet Education.* 4th ed. Baltimore: Penguin, 1970. Brief description of the Soviet higher and secondary education system.

Jacoby, Susan. *Inside Soviet Schools.* New York: Hill and Wang, 1974. Critical of rote learning and lockstep discipline.

Foreign Policy

Bialer, Seweryn. *The Soviet Paradox: External Expansion, Internal Decline.* New York: Alfred A. Knopf, 1986. Discusses the roots of Soviet foreign policy.

Carrère d'Encausse, Hélène, trans. George Holoch. *Big Brother: The Soviet Union and Soviet Europe.* New York: Holmes & Meier, 1987. First published in France in 1983, this book focuses on how successive leaders in the Kremlin saw their vital interests.

Cockburn, Alexander. *The Threat: Inside the Soviet Military Machine.* New York: Random House, 1983. Argues that the bear's growl is worse than his bite.

Collins, Joseph J. *The Soviet Invasion of Afghanistan: A Study in the Use of Force in Soviet Foreign Relations.* Lexington, Mass.: Lexington Books, 1986. A study in the use of force in Soviet foreign policy.

Kennan, George. *Russia and the West Under Lenin and Stalin.* Boston: Little, Brown, 1961. Authoritative interpretation by one of the most respected Sovietologists of our time.

Lynch, Allen. *Soviet Study of International Relations.* New York: Cambridge University Press, 1987. Summarizes and analyzes the Soviet literature.

MccGwire, Michael. *Military Objectives in Soviet Foreign Policy.* Washington, D.C.: Brookings Institution, 1987. Written by a respected expert on Soviet military strategy, this is an analysis of the motivations behind Moscow's policy.

Menon, Rajan. *Soviet Power and the Third World.* New Haven: Yale University Press, 1986. Menon concentrates on Soviet theories on East-West competition in the Third World, Soviet capabilities for projecting power into those regions, and the role of arms transfers in Soviet policy.

Shevchenko, Arkady N. *Breaking with Moscow.* New York: Alfred A. Knopf, 1985. A former Soviet diplomat who defected to the West describes his career in Moscow's foreign service with many details on decision-making processes and Soviet understanding of the West, America in particular.

Suvorov, Victor. *Inside the Soviet Army.* New York: Macmillan, 1982. An intimate view of how the Soviet military works by a high-ranking defector.

General and Miscellaneous

Arbatov, Georgi A., and Willem Oltmans. *The Soviet Viewpoint.* New York: Dodd, Mead, 1983. Skillful presentation of the Soviet side of the Cold War by the director of the Institute of United States and Canadian Studies of the Soviet Academy of Sciences.

Brezezinski, Zbigniew. *The Grand Failure: The Birth and Death of Communism in the Twentieth Century.* New York: Scribner, 1989. Brezezinski sees the ideology and the system in rapid decline and that communism is approaching its end as a significant world phenomenon.

Clemens, Walter C., Jr. *Can Russia Change? The USSR Confronts Global Interdependence.* Boston: Unwin Hyman, 1990. This book argues that Russia *can* change.

Custine, Astolphe, Marquis de. *Empire of the Czar: A Journey through Eternal Russia.* New York: Doubleday, 1989. This classic by a French traveler, first published in 1843, can be likened to Tocqueville's *Democracy in America.* Contains insights on the Russian character that are unchanged to this day.

Fainsod, Merle, and Jerry Hough. *How the Soviet Union Is Governed.* Cambridge, Mass.: Harvard University Press, 1979. "Revisionist" updating of a classic, originally based on Communist party archives seized in Smolensk by the Nazis.

Ford, Robert A. D. *Our Man in Moscow: A Diplomat's Reflections on the Soviet Union.* Toronto: University of Toronto Press, 1989. The author was Canadian ambassador to the U.S.S.R. from 1964 to 1980 and has been concerned with Soviet affairs since then. The book includes conversations with Soviet literary and artistic figures as well as officials.

Gorbachev, Mikhail. *Perestroika: New Thinking for Our Country and The World.* New York: Harper & Row, 1987. The Soviet leader describes his program of restructuring.

Graham, Loren R. *Science, Philosophy, and Human Behavior in the Soviet Union.* New York: Columbia University Press, 1987. The author is widely recognized as one of the foremost authorities on Soviet science.

Hazard, John. *The Soviet System of Government.* 5th ed. Chicago: University of Chicago Press, 1980. A description of the Soviet political system by one of the first Americans to study it.

Hosking, Geoffrey. *The Awakening of The Soviet Union.* Cambridge: Harvard University Press, 1990. An assessment of Gorbachev's domestic policies.

Hough, Jerry. *Russia and the West.* New York: Simon & Schuster, 1988. The book is about Russia and the pressures which are driving Gorbachev in the direction of radical reform more than about Russia and the West.

Jamgotch, Nish, Jr., ed. *Sectors of Mutual Benefit in US-Soviet Relations.* Durham, N.C.: Duke University Press, 1985. Includes agriculture, science, space, and environmental protection.

Jones, Ellen. *Red Army and Society: A Sociology of the Soviet Military.* London: Allen & Unwin, 1985. Includes political indoctrination and control, treatment of ethnic minorities, and the interdependence of the military and civilian sectors of Soviet society.

Judy, Richard W., and Virginia L. Clough. *The Information Age and Soviet Society.* Indianapolis: Hudson Institute, 1989. How the "information revolution" is doing in the Soviet Union.

Kaiser, Robert. *Russia, the People and the Power.* New York: Atheneum, 1976. Overview by the former Moscow Bureau Chief of the *Washington Post.*

Kerblay, Basile. *Gorbachev's Russia.* New York: Pantheon, 1989. Looks into the social aspects of change under Gorbachev.

Nagorski, Andrew. *Reluctant Farewell.* New York: Holt, Rhinehart and Winston, 1985. *Newsweek*'s former Moscow correspondent reports on his tour of duty, cut short when he was expelled. The book also paints a picture of the system and how it works.

Roxburgh, Angus. *Pravda: Inside the Soviet News Machine.* New York: Braziller, 1987. A brief history of the official Communist party newspaper and description of its role.

Sakharov, Andrei. *My Country and the World.* New York: Alfred A. Knopf, 1975. Sakharov was more than a courageous and good man. He was one of the most brilliant men of the twentieth century.

Salisbury, Harrison. *Russia.* New York: Macmillan, 1965. Very good short primer.

Shipler, David. *Russia: Broken Idols, Solemn Dreams.* New York: Times Books, 1983. Well-written overview.

Smith, Hedrick. *The New Russians.* New York: Random House, 1990. Smith describes his return to the land of *perestroika* in vivid detail.

———. *The Russians.* New York: Times Books, 1976. Somewhat outdated, but a classic in its day, by the *New York Times* man in Moscow.

Symons, Leslie, ed. *The Soviet Union: A Systematic Geography.* Totowa, N.J.: Barnes & Noble, 1983. Covers demography, natural resources, physical features, and climate.

Tucker, Robert C. *Political Culture and Leadership in Soviet Russia: From Lenin to Gorbachev.* New York: Norton, 1987. A leading Sovietologist explains the evolution of the Soviet system.

Voinovich, Vladimir. *The Anti-Soviet Union.* San Diego: Harcourt Brace Jovanovich, 1986. A distinguished Russian novelist, an émigré, writes about a broad range of Soviet society. Full of anecdotes.

Walker, Martin. *The Waking Giant.* New York: Pantheon, 1986. Deals with the people, culture, politics, and economics.

Yanov, Alexander. *The Russian Challenge and the Year 2000.* New York: Basil Blackwell, 1987. The author's thesis is that if Gorbachev's reforms fail the result will be an oppressive and aggressive nation based on the ideology of anti-Western Russian nationalism.

History and Biography

Biola, Lynne. *The Best Sons of the Fatherland: Workers in the Vanguard of Soviet Collectivization.* New York: Oxford University Press, 1987. The vanguard was the group of some 25,000 urban workers sent out into the countryside as pioneers in 1930–31 to help put through the drive to collectivize the farms.

Bonner, Elena. *Alone Together.* New York: Alfred A. Knopf, 1986. Andrei Sakharov's wife tells of their years of enforced exile in Gorky.

Conquest, Robert. *The Great Terror: A Reassessment.* New York: Oxford University Press, 1990. The author uses new material in this update of his classical study of the purges in the 1930s, but few of his original insights and judgments need to be changed.

————. *The Harvest of Sorrow: Soviet Collectivization and the Terror-Famine.* New York: Oxford University Press, 1986. Stalin's campaign against the kulaks and the drive for farm collectivization accompanied by force, terror, and famine, especially in the Ukraine.

Doder, Dusko. *Shadows and Whispers: Power Politics Inside the Kremlin from Brezhnev to Gorbachev.* New York: Random House, 1986. Doder, of the *Washington Post,* writes of the U.S.S.R. in the early 1980s, focusing on the struggles that marked the shifts in leadership.

Frankland, Mark. *The Sixth Continent: Mikhail Gorbachev and the Soviet Union.* London: Hamish Hamilton, 1987. A former Moscow correspondent of the London *Observer* concentrates on the crisis of leadership and the politics of successions following Brezhnev.

Gilbert, Martin. *Shcharansky: A Hero of Our Time.* New York: Viking, 1986. Describes the struggle of Shcharansky and other Jews to emigrate from the U.S.S.R. to Israel.

Hazard, John N. *Recollections of a Pioneering Sovietologist.* New York: Oceana, 1987. An autobiography of one of the foremost Western experts in Soviet law.

Hosking, Geoffrey. *The First Socialist Society: A History of the Soviet Union from Within.* Cambridge, Mass.: Harvard University Press, 1985. A British historian's readable account of the changes in society, as well as the politics and decisions at the top.

Kelly, Laurence, ed. *Moscow: A Travellers' Companion.* New York: Atheneum, 1984. Moscow's history. Includes details about the city's landmarks.

Laqueur, Walter. *Stalin: The Glasnost Revelations.* New York: Scribner, 1990. The most up-to-date portrait of the dictator by an eminent Soviet expert using the most recently available evidence and documentation.

Lincoln, W. Bruce. *Red Victory: A History of the Russian Civil War.* New York: Simon & Schuster, 1989. A fine history of a trauma that still affects events in the Soviet Union.

———. *In War's Dark Shadow.* New York: Dial Press, 1983. Russia before World War I.

Massie, Robert. *Nicholas and Alexandra.* New York: Atheneum, 1967. Well-written account of the end of the Romanoff dynasty.

———. *Peter the Great: His Life and Times.* New York: Knopf, 1980. Magnificent biography. Massie's description of Peter's Russia enhances the reader's understanding of today's Soviet Union.

Medvedev, Roy. *Let History Judge.* New York: Columbia University Press, 1989. A Soviet Marxist dissident's updated version of his 1971 exposé of the Stalin era.

Medvedev, Zhore A. *Gorbachev.* Oxford: Basil Blackwell, 1986. Medvedev, a Soviet scientist living in London, discusses the Soviet system and the rivalries and maneuvers of those contending for power.

Pipes, Richard. *The Russian Revolution.* New York: Alfred A. Knopf, 1990. The ultimate work in scholarship, intellect, and detail on what happened by one of the Soviet Union's strongest critics.

Riazanovsky, Nicholas. *A History of Russia.* 2d ed. New York: Oxford University Press, 1969. Readable textbook with an excellent bibliography.

Salisbury, Harrison. *The 900 Days: The Siege of Leningrad.* New York: Harper & Row, 1969. Unforgettable story of the Nazi siege. The events described still influence Soviet life.

Sanders, Jonathan. *1917: The Unpublished Revolution.* New York: Abbeville Press, 1990. An elegant collection of photographs from the revolutionary year of 1917.

Scammel, Michael. *Solzhenitsyn: A Biography.* New York: Norton, 1984. A portrait of Solzhenitsyn in the context of the Soviet system and of Russian culture.

Schmidt-Hauer, Christian. *Gorbachev: The Path to Power.* Topsfield, Mass.: Salem House, 1986. The author is a West German correspondent stationed in Moscow for many years.

Troyat, Henri. *Catherine the Great.* New York: Dutton, 1980. Readable biography about a great leader and the Russia of her time.

———. *Ivan the Terrible.* New York: Dutton, 1984. There are parallels between Ivan and Stalin. Ivan's life is an important part of the Russian past.

Tucker, Robert. *Stalin as Revolutionary.* New York: Norton, 1973. Psychological study of the dictator's career up to 1930.

Ulam, Adam. *The Bolsheviks.* New York: Macmillan, 1968. Exciting story of Lenin's revolutionary party and the November 1917 coup.

———. *Expansion and Co-existence: Soviet Foreign Policy, 1917–1973.* New York: Praeger, 1974. A comprehensive interpretation of Soviet international behavior.

Von Laue, Theodore. *Why Lenin, Why Stalin?* Philadelphia: Lippincott, 1964. A thoughtful essay on historical causes.

Yeltsin, Boris. *Against the Grain: An Autobiography.* New York: Summit, 1990. Published before his election as President of the Russian Republic.

Literature

Anything written by one of the giants of Russian literature, such as Anton Chekhov, Fëdor Dostoevski, Nikolai Gogol, Maxim Gorky, and Leo Tolstoi is worth reading. Among their best-known works are Tolstoi's *War and Peace* and *Anna Karenina;* Chekhov's *The Cherry Orchard* and *The Three Sisters;* Dostoevski's *Crime and Punishment* and *The Brothers Karamazov;* Gogol's *The Government Inspector* and *Dead Souls;* and Gorky's *Lower Depths* and *Mother.* The many excellent books by lesser known writers include the following.

Bulgakov, Mikhail. *Master and Margarita.* New York: Grove Press, 1967. A surreal account of the adventures of the devil in the Moscow of Stalin.

Chernyshevsky, Nikolai. *What Is to Be Done?* Ithaca, N.Y.: Cornell University Press, 1989. This extraordinary novel, published in Russia in 1863, allegedly was to the Russian Revolution what *Uncle Tom's Cabin* was to the American Civil War. Its dominant preoccupation is the emancipation of women.

Voinovich, Vladimir. *The Ivankiad.* New York: Farrar, Straus and Giroux, 1977. The tribulations of a writer trying to claim a vacant apartment.

Nationalities

Alexeyeva, Ludmilla. *Soviet Dissent: Contemporary Movements for National, Religious and Human Rights.* Middletown, Conn.: Wesleyan University Press, 1985. Written by a well-known human rights activist who emigrated in 1977, this book is a massive compendium of opposition in the Soviet Union since Stalin.

Carrere d'Encausse, Helene. *Decline of an Empire.* New York: Harper & Row, 1981. Argues there is an erosion of Moscow's authority in the non-Russian republics. A good introduction to the "nationalities problem" which has proven accurate.

Conquest, Robert, ed. *The Last Empire: Nationality and the Soviet Future.* Stanford, Calif.: Hoover Institution Press, 1986. A number of scholars deal with the subject from many angles, but agree that the nationalities problem has been misunderstood and underestimated in the West.

Gitelman, Zvi. *A Century of Ambivalence: The Jews of Russia and the Soviet Union, 1881 to the Present.* New York: Schocken, 1988. A vivid description of Jewish life over the decades, with rare photographs.

Katz, Zev, et al., ed. *A Handbook of Major Soviet Nationalities.* New York: Free Press, 1975. Useful preparation for visiting specific national regions.

Sociology

Atkinson, Dorothy; Alexander Dallin; and Gail W. Lapidus, eds. *Women in Russia.* Stanford, Calif.: Stanford University Press, 1977. Based on a conference held at Stanford University.

Binyon, Michael. *Life in Russia.* New York: Pantheon, 1983. Anecdotal account of experiences in the U.S.S.R. by a London *Times* correspondent.

Ebon, Martin. *The Soviet Propaganda Machine.* New York: McGraw-Hill, 1987. Contains a mixture of history, policy explanations, and descriptions of propaganda instruments and the people involved.

Gerhardt, Genevra. *The Russian World: Life and Language.* New York: Harcourt Brace Jovanovich, 1974. Good introduction to Soviet culture and everyday life.

Gray, Francine du Plessix. *Soviet Women: Walking the Tightrope.* New York: Doubleday, 1990. Highly praised book about the role of women and their problems in dealing with Soviet life.

Hansson, Carola, and Karin Liden. *Moscow Women.* New York: Pantheon, 1983. Interviews with 13 women offer a candid glimpse into the lives of Soviet women.

Hayward, Max, and William Fletcher, eds. *Religion and the Soviet State: A Dilemma of Power.* New York: Praeger, 1969.

Herlemann, Horst, ed. *Quality of Life in the Soviet Union.* Boulder, Colo.: Westview Press, 1987. Discusses living standards, trends in consumption, housing, services, medical care, education, working conditions, and alcoholism.

Hollander, Paul. *Soviet and American Society: A Comparison.* New York: Oxford University Press, 1973. Excellent comparative analysis of American and Soviet values and behavior.

Kerblay, Basile. *Modern Soviet Society.* New York: Pantheon, 1983. French sociologist's overview, with attempts to identify directions for the future.

Lapidus, Gail W. *Women in Soviet Society: Equality, Development and Social Change.* Berkeley: University of California Press, 1978.

Matthews, Mervyn. *Poverty in the Soviet Union: The Life-Styles of the Underprivileged in Recent Years.* New York: Cambridge University Press, 1986.

————. *Privilege in the Soviet Union.* London: Allen & Unwin, 1978.

Mickiewicz, Ellen. *Media and the Russian Public.* New York: Praeger, 1981. A book about the Soviet media and propaganda.

Millar, James R., ed. *Politics, Work, and Daily Life in the USSR.* New York: Cambridge University Press, 1987. Describes contemporary Soviet life. Based on interviews with 2800 émigrés.

Shlapentokh, Vladimir. *Public and Private Life of the Soviet People: Changing Values in Post-Stalin Russia.* New York: Oxford University Press, 1989. This Soviet sociologist's study of Soviet society from the end of Stalin's era to the beginning of Gorbachev's helps one understand the shift in attitudes toward privatization and consumerism.

Index

Abalkin, Leonid, economic reform plan of, 221–22
Accreditation of foreign companies, 116–17, 187–88
Agroprombank, 170
Alaska Airlines, 125, 130
Alaska Commercial Company, 133–34
Alcohol abuse, 60–61, 121
Alibegov, Thomas, 10
Amalrik, Andrei, 228
American Countertrade Association, 158
Amtorg Trading Corporation, 166
Anti-Semitism, 235
Apartment ownership, 32
Archer Daniels Midland, 98
Argus Trading, Ltd., joint venture and, 144
Asea Brown Boveri, joint venture and, 140, 146, 149
Asetco, 181
Axelrod, Robert, 87

Baltic Republics, 25, 231–33
Barter, 36, 102, See also Countertrade
BFEA, 170, 171, 173, 174, 175, 178, 179, 180
Blat ("pull"), 22, 30, 43, 44
Brainard, Lawrence
    on joint ventures financing, 169–83, 251
Brelsford, Virginia, 127
Brezhnev, 38
Burke, Edmund, 81
Bush, George, 179, 204

Cash-flow financing. See Project financing

Caterpillar, 2
Caucasas Republics, 25, 230–31, 236–37, 242
Central Asian Republics, 25, 90, 157, 230–31, 237–38, 241–42
Chernyshevsky, Nikolai, 243
Churchill, Winston, 13
Cohon, George A., 141, 248
Combustion Engineering, joint venture and, 140, 143, 144, 145, 146, 147, 148, 150
Communications infrastructure, Soviet, 115
Connor, Walter D.
    on Soviet work force, 47–62
Contract research, 4–5
Cooperatives, 33–34
Corporate experience, See U.S.-Soviet trade experience
Counterpurchase, 159
Countertrade, 4–5, 157–58, 175
Country risk, 172–73
Cowper, Steve, 127
Credit risk, 172, 173
Currency. See Hard currency

Dean, Richard N.
    on Soviet legal system, 185–97
Dederichs, Mario R.
    on understanding Russian culture, 13–27, 249
Deficit commodities, 35–36, 37, 39, 43, 44
Deutsch, Morton, 11
Dialogue, 164
Du Pont, 5, 203

Economic aid, to Soviet Union
    advantages of, for U.S., 252–53
    advantages of, for U.S.S.R., 252
    case for, 254
    consumer goods, 253
    management training, 253
    tax rebates, 252–53, 267n1
    undesirable aspects of, 252
Energy-Buran space project, 156
Environmental movement, 238–42
    foreign business opportunities and,
      242
    in RSFSR, 241
European Bank for Reconstruction and
    Development (EBRD), 179–80
Evolution of Cooperation, The
    (Axelrod), 87
Experience curve, 6, 9–10
Export Credit Agencies (ECAs), 173,
    174, 175, 178, 179
Export credit agencies. *See* ECAs
Export-Import Bank, 178, 179

Family, Soviet, 29, 44–45
Financial assets, ownership of, 32–33
Financing guarantees, Soviet, 173,
    174–78
    See also Joint venture financing
Financing guarantees, Western,
    178–80
    See also Joint venture financing
Finkelstein, William A., 198
Ford, 8
Foreign trade, Soviet
    compensational transactions/barter,
      158–59
    constraints on, 152
    counterpurchase, 159
    countertrade, 157–58, 159
    imbalance, 153–54
    import needs, 157
    joint ventures in Soviet Far East,
      160–62
    need for organization/management
      specialists, 165
    perestroika and, 154
    Soviet-American cooperation, U.S.
      policies and, 166–67
    structure of, 152–53
    U.S. misconceptions about, 155–57
    U.S.S.R. trade representatives
      contacts with, 165–66
    See also Joint Ventures

Foreign Trade Arbitration Court
    (FTAC), 191
Forstner, James A.
    on licensing/protecting intellectual
      property, 197–204
Friedman, Gail
    on joint venture pioneers, 139–50

Glasnost (openness), 13, 63, 93, 186,
    219
    anti-Semitism and, 235
    environmental movement and,
      240
    women's issues and, 242
Gorbachev, Mikhail, 21, 22, 29, 29, 37,
    97, 101, 151, 160, 186, 187, 193,
    194, 196, 215, 216, 219, 225–27,
    243
Gosbank, 170, 171
Gosplan, 21, 32, 38, 113, 194
Grass-roots democracy, Soviet
    decision-making and, 64, 69–71
    collective leadership and, 69
    democratic centralism and, 69–70
    one-person leadership and, 69
Gross National Product (GNP), Soviet,
    1, 257n1

Hamilton, Alexander, 10
Hanson, Philip, 81, 89
Hard currency, 3–4, 105, 157, 162–63,
    164, 250
    repatriation of, 6–8
Hecht, James L.
    on corporate experience in Soviet
      Union, 81–92
    on doing business in Soviet Union,
      1–12, 247–55
Henry, Patrick, 81
Hewett, Edward A., 90
Hisrich, Robert D., 87
Hosking, Geoffrey, 235

Indian Valley Meats, 128, 129, 133,
    134, 135
Intellectual property, in Soviet Union
    arbitration issues, 202–3
    guidelines for protecting/licensing,
      198
    language of agreements, English vs.
      Russian, 202

late payment penalty provisions, 200

memorandum of understanding and, 199

patent law, Soviet, 203–4, 265*n*18, 265*n*19

patent warranties and, 201

plant performance guarantees and, 201

Intelligent Resources International, 156–57

International Monetary Fund (IMF), 179, 183

Jackson-Vanik Amendment, 178–79

Job security, 44

Joint venture financing, 169–83
  alternate financing structures and, 173–83
  country risk and, 172–73
  credit risk and, 172, 173
  resource allocation and, 170, 262*n*2
  risk/reward balance and, 169–70
  Soviet banking system and, 170–72

Joint ventures
  advantages, 5–6, 100, 101–2
  asset acquisition and, 103–4
  attitudes toward, of U.S. firms, 85
  authority issues, 149
  background of, 97–100, 260*n*4
  employee incentives, 147–48
  financing, 169–83
  impact on people involved, 106–7
  increase in, 96, 260*n*3
  legal aspects of, 107–8
  living conditions, expatriate, 148
  low cost work force and, 8–9
  negotiating strategies for, 108–11
  new product development and, 9–10
  and non-joint venture agreements, 104–5
  patience and, 143–44
  pioneers of, 139–50
  property rights of, 261*n*6
  quality issues, 144–45
  real estate and, 103
  repatriation of profits and, 6–8
  and Soviet culture, adapting to, 146–47
  in Soviet Far East, 159–65
  Soviet Joint Venture Law and, 94–96, 98, 101, 105

Soviet supply infrastructure and, 6, 8, 82, 92, 248

technology utilization study and, 82, 87–92

Joint venture financing structures
  guarantees, Soviet, 173, 174–78, 262*n*10
  guarantees, Western, 178–80
  project financing, 180–83
  stand-alone financing, 173, 174

Kendall, Donald, 4, 9

KGB, 149, 187, 189, 190, 223, 226

Khabarovsk, 130, 132

Kiev, 30, 123, 149

Kobe Steel, 200

Komatsu, 2

Laurita, Tom
  on operating in Moscow, 113–23

Lawrence, Paul R.
  on managerial decision making, 63–80

Legal system, Soviet
  basic goals of, 192
  business tax law, 194–95
  conducting business under, 185–204
  confusion/uncertainty regarding, 195–97
  historical background, 186–93, 263*n*2, 263*n*3, 264*n*6
  intellectual property and, 197–204
  irrelevance of, for foreign business transactions, 189–91
  laws, unavailability of, 188–89, 196–97
  perestroika and, 193–97
  personal tax law, 195
  property law, 195
  rule of law and, 193–94
  Soviets' approach to, 192

Lenin, Nicolai, 22, 69

Leningrad, 30, 107, 123

Levine, Herbert
  on future of Soviet economy, 205–24, 249

Licensing Executives Society, 82

Living conditions, Soviet
  consumer cooperatives, 40
  improvements in, 40–41
  labor market, 42–43

labor participation rates, 41–42
material incentive system and,
43–44
perestroika and, 45–46
private enterprise, 33–34
private property, 31–33
sellers' market and, 41, 45–46
state retail outlets, 34–37
urban vs. rural, 29–30, 32
Local level business operations, 125–37
assessment of potential partners in,
131–33
examples of, 125–27, 128–30
and resources, adequacy of, 133–34
role of Moscow in, 135–36
rules/regulatory policies and,
136–37
state enterprises and, 131
subjective values and, 135
training programs and, 133–34
value of, 128
Logovaz, 163
Louis Harris and Associates, 11

Madara, Eugene, 140, 143, 144–45,
146, 148
Main Service Bureau for the Diplomatic
Corps (UPDK), 119, 120, 188
Magadan, 127–30
Management Partnering International,
164
Market Knowledge, 165
McDonald's, 8, 12, 35
joint venture and, 140, 141, 143,
146, 147, 150, 248
Millar, James R.
on daily economic life in U.S.S.R.,
29–46
Miller, Elisa B.
on doing business outside of
Moscow, 125–37
Minimum simultaneity, 218, 220, 249
Ministry of Foreign Trade. *See*
Ministry of Foreign Economic
Relations
Ministry of Foreign Economic
Relations, 97–99, 101, 137, 189,
194, 196
Minsk, 123
Modisett, Lawrence E.
on future of Soviet Union, 225–45,
247, 250
Monsanto, 4

Moscow, 30, 31, 35, 39, 113–23, 127
accredited agents in, 116–17
alcohol consumption in, 121
City Council, 110, 119
costs of operating in, 120
doing business outside of, 125–37
family life of business
representative in, 121–22
hotel accommodations, 115, 116,
149
management/control issues in,
120–21
need for business expertise in, 114
need for business presence in, 114,
115–16
schools for foreigners, 121–22
selecting executives to work in,
122–23
setting up office in, 118–19
women executives in, 122–23
Moscow World Market Reserve
Institute, 165
Most-favored-nation (MFN) status, 166,
179

Nakhodka, 162, 164
Nalevo ("under the counter"), 37, 38,
39, 43, 44
National Opinion Research Center, 11
Nationalism, 227–38
in Baltic republics, 232–33
in Caucasus, 236–37
in Central Asia, 237–38
forms of, 227
and secession vs. federation, 228–32
in Slavic republics, 233–35
New Economic Policy (NEP), 22,
209–11, 215
Nomenklatura, 23

Ohaniian, Constantin, 139, 140, 143,
147, 148, 149, 150
Oliver, James K., 82

Palace Hotel, 181
Pamyat, 235
Patent law, Soviet, 203–4, 265*n*18,
265*n*19
Pepsico, 4, 98, 158, 198
Perestroika (restructuring), 13, 22, 41,
42, 70, 85, 105, 123, 154, 224

Soviet legal system and, 186, 192, 193
Perestroika (Gorbachev), 70
Personal wealth, inheritance of, 33
Peter the Great, 15, 187, 206–7, 212, 227
Peters, Michael P., 87
Pipko, Roman
  on joint ventures, 93–111
Pompa, Yevgeniy Y.
  on Soviet foreign trade, 151–67
Prestowitz, Clyde, 7
Private enterprise
  pervasiveness of, 43
  restrictions on, 33
Private property, legal status of, 31
Private land ownership, 31–32
  opposition to, 33
Project financing, 180–83
  major financings, 181
  See also Joint venture financing
Promstroibank, 170
Protocols of the Elders of Zion, 235
Provideniya, 125–127
Public Agenda Foundation, 11

Queuing, 20, 41, 45

Rae, Michael, 143, 144, 145, 148
Rasputin, Valentin, 227
Repatriation of profits, 6–8, 162
Retail outlets
  illegal, 37
  prices in, 38–39
  space/service in, 39
  state, 34–37
  subsidies to, 34–35
Risk-taking
  economic aid and, 251–54
  labor utilization and, 248
  personnel problems and, 248–49
  political turmoil and, 249
  in RSFSR, 247
  supply infrastructure and, 248
  uncertainty of economic future and, 249–50
Rubles
  convertibility, 95, 169
  exchange rate, 55, 195
  investment of, 140, 142, 164
  joint venture sales and, 95
  purchasing power of, 102

risk-reward structure of, 169
  See also Hard currency
RSFSR, 226
  environmental movement in, 241
  investment in, 247
  nationalism in, 227, 228, 229, 233, 234
  private enterprise and, 235
Russian character
  economic system and, 18, 21–23
  endurance, 21
  envy, 23
  inconsistency, 24
  mistrust, 17
  patience, 20
  pride, 16
  Russian vs. non-Russian views on, 19
  secretiveness, 14–16
  sex differences and, 24–25
Russian culture, 13–27
  agents of power, 15
  bureaucracy, 23–24
  and business culture, 22
  cultural heritage, 16
  guidelines for dealing with, 25–27
  language, 17
  male chauvinism and, 122–23
  multiethnicity and, 25
  risk-aversion, 198, 201
  Russian character and, 14–16, 17, 18, 19, 21–23, 24–25
  self-denial, 17–18
  and Soviet culture, 18–20
  travel restrictions, 16–17
  uniformity, 18
  women and, 24–25
  work incentives, 21
Russian Revolution, 186, 209
Russian Soviet Federated Socialist
  Republic (RSFSR). *See* RSFSR
Rynok (private market), 30, 36, 40, 44
Ryshkov, 221
  economic reform plan of, 222

Sberbank, 170
Schmidt, Robert D., 253
Shatalin, Stanislav, economic reform plan of, 222–23
Sherotel Novotel, 181
Shevardnadze, Eduard, 226
Siberia, 41, 90, 157
Smith, Tom, 11

Solzhenitsyn, Alexander, 227
Sovbutital, 181
Soviet American Travel and Trade
Association, 149
Soviet decision making, managerial,
63–80, 259n3
grass-roots democracy in, 69–71,
259–60n7
phases of, 70–71
structural task unit (STU) in,
64–68
US misconceptions about, 63–64
Soviet economy, future of, 205–24,
249
Abalkin plan, 221–22
competition and, 218
economic reform and, 215–24
historical background, 205–15
macroeconomics and, 220–21
managerial issues and, 216–17
market system and, 215–16
monetary control and, 217–18
political aspects, 218–19,
223–24
property rights and, 221
reform/destabilization and, 218
Ryzhkov plan, 221–22
Shatalin plan, 222–23
Soviet Far East, 125–27, 129–30,
160–62
Soviet Joint Venture Law, 94–96, 98,
101, 105
Soviet Union
business culture, 2–3
coproduction with, 5
countertrade with, 4–5
daily economic life in, 29–46
desirability of trade with,
10–12
future of, 225–45
hard currency, 3–4
hierarchy of living conditions in,
30
legal system, 185–204
market share increase and, 1–2
U.S. corporate experience in, 81–92
work force, 8–9, 41–43, 47–62, 92
See also selected topics
Soviet Union, future of
consumer's movement and, 244
environmental movement and,
238–42
Gorbachev and, 225–27
labor organizations and, 238–40

nationalism and, 227–38, 266n19
women and, 242–44, 267n27,
267n28, 267n30, 267n36
Soviet work force, 8–9, 41–43, 47–62
alcohol abuse and, 60–61
company stores and, 57
discontent of, 54–55
education and, 48–53
hours worked, 47–48
living standards of, 55–57
motivation of, 54, 55
quality control and 54, 258n11
regional/cultural variations in,
53–54
retirement from, 47
strikes/stoppages and, 61–62
utilization of, 53–54
women in, 57–60, 258n19
work ethic and, 53
Stalin, Josef, 13, 37, 43, 186, 211–12
Stand-alone financing, 173, 174
See also Joint venture financing
Stevenson Amendment, 179
Stimpfle, Jim, 127
Structural task unit (STU), 64–68,
70–71
examples, 72–79
operating rules, 66, 68
Supply infrastructure, Soviet, 6, 8, 82,
92, 248

Tambrands, joint venture and, 139, 140,
144, 146, 147, 148, 149, 150
Trade and Technology in Soviet-Western
Relations (Hanson), 81–82
Trading Places (Prestowitz), 7
Tyurchev, Fedor, 14

Ukraine, 25, 230, 233–35, 241
U.S. Commercial Office (USCO),
116
U.S.-U.S.S.R. Trade and Economic
Council (USTEC), 116
United States-Soviet trade experience,
81–92
by industry type, 85–86
joint ventures, attitudes toward, 85
marketing issues, 84–85
technology utilization study of, 82,
87–92
Soviet reliability, 82–83
United Workers Front (UWF), 239

Vlachoutsicos, Charalombos
    on managerial decision making,
        63–80
Vnesheconombank, Bank for Foreign
        Economic Affairs (BFEA). *See*
        BFEA

War Communism, 209, 210, 211
West, Dan, 158
What Is to Be Done (Chernyshevsky),
        243
Women, in Soviet Union
    future of, 242–44

glasnost and, 242
    women executives in, 122–23
    work force, 57–60
World Bank, 179, 183

Yakolev, Alexander, 193
Yeltsin, Boris, 222, 223, 226,
        238

Zeiger, Shelley, joint ventures and,
        141–42, 146–47, 150
Zhilsotsbank, 170

About the Authors

James L. Hecht is an adjunct professor in the Department of Political Science at the University of Delaware, where he is director of the Project for the Study of the American Future. His work at Delaware has included two pioneering studies on the experience of U.S. Corporations in the Soviet Union. He came to the University of Delaware in 1986, following his retirement from E. I. du Pont de Nemours & Company after a 31-year career in a variety of research and development positions. Dr. Hecht is the author of *Because It Is Right: Integration in Housing* (Little, Brown, 1970) and received a Public Service Award from the Department of the Interior for achievements in safety. A graduate of Cornell University, he received his Ph.D. degree is chemical engineering from Yale University.

Lawrence J. Brainard is director of research for the Emerging Markets Group at Goldman Sachs. Prior to his present position, he was responsible for economic and political analyses at the Bankers Trust Company, where he was a senior vice president. He is considered an authority on financing nonmarket economies and has published extensively in this field. Dr. Brainard received a B.A. from Northwestern University in Russian studies and has a Ph.D. degree in economics from the University of Chicago.

Walter D. Connor is a professor of political science, sociology, and international relations at Boston University and a fellow of the Russian Research Center at Harvard. The most recent of his five books is *The Accidental Proletariat: Workers, Politics and Crisis in Gorbachev's Russia* (Princeton University Press). He worked eight years for the Department of State, and received the department's Meritorious Honor Award. A graduate of Holy Cross, he received his M.A. and Ph.D. from Princeton University.

Richard N. Dean is a partner in the international law firm of Coudert Brothers. In February 1988, with Mr. Dean in charge, Coudert became the first foreign law firm to open an office in Moscow. He resided in Moscow for the next 30 months before joining Coudert's Washington office, where he continues to supervise the firm's Soviet practice which now involves more than 20 attorneys. A graduate of Vanderbilt University, he also has a master's degree in foreign affairs and a law degree from the University of Virginia.

Mario R. Dederichs is a German journalist who was Moscow bureau chief of *Stern* for over three years, until 1988. He has been with *Stern* since 1976 and currently is Washington bureau chief. In previous assignments he reported on German politics and served as deputy foreign editor. Since coming to the United States he has been a frequent panelist for the Cable News Network.

James A. Forstner is an attorney who is a managing counsel in the legal department of E. I du Pont de Nemours & Company. He also is Chair of the International and Foreign Law Committee of the American Intellectual Property Law Association. In addition to his J.D. in law, which he received from the University of Maryland, he holds a Ph.D. in chemistry from Carnegie-Mellon University.

Gail Friedman currently is a free-lance writer in New York. A 1980 graduate of the Medill School of Journalism at Northwestern University, she has won several awards, including a National Magazine Award. for work appearing in the *Washingtonian* magazine.

Tom Laurita is a vice president of VITAS Corporation, a U.S. firm which specializes in Soviet strategic and financial consulting and in the representation of foreign firms in the U.S.S.R. From 1988 to 1990 he was U.S.S.R. country manager for the Monsanto Company. His initial experience in Moscow was with the US-USSR Trade and Economic Council, and this was followed by four years as head of representation in Moscow for SATRA Corporation. He is a graduate of Brown University and holds a master's degree in management from Yale.

Paul R. Lawrence is the Wallace Brett Donham Professor of Organizational Behavior Emeritus at the Harvard Business School, where he has been on the faculty since 1950. He also is a fellow at the Russian Research Center at Harvard. He is the author or co-author of 24 books, including *Behind the Factory Walls: Decision Making in Soviet and U.S. Enterprises.*

Herbert S. Levine is a professor of economics at the University of Pennsylvania, co-director of the Lauder Institute of Management and International Studies at the University of Pennsylvania, and chairman of the board of PlanEcon, a Washington-based research firm which specializes in Soviet and East European trade and investment. Widely recognized as one of the world's foremost experts on the Soviet economy, his many awards include two University of Pennsylvania prizes for distinguished teaching. He received his Ph.D. in economics and an M.A. in Russian studies from Harvard University.

James R. Millar is the director of the Institute of Sino-Soviet Studies and a professor of international affairs at the George Washington University. His published books include *The ABC's of Soviet Socialism,* which received the 1981 award in nonfiction from the Society of Midland Authors. Dr. Millar was the project director of the multimillion dollar Soviet Interview Project (1979–89), which interviewed more than 5000 former Soviet citizens about their lives in the U.S.S.R. A graduate of the University of Texas, he received his Ph.D. degree in economics at Cornell University.

Elisa B. Miller is a lecturer in Soviet business and trade at the University of Washington and is managing director of Soviet Market Information Services, a company that assists businesses interested in the Soviet market. She has served as a consultant to the states of Oregon and Alaska in organizing trade missions to the U.S.S.R. A graduate of the University of California at Berkeley, she received a Ph.D. degree in Soviet-East Asian economic relations from the University of Washington.

Lawrence E. Modisett is a senior analyst in the Office of Soviet Analysis of the Central Intelligence Agency, and is currently serving as a visiting faculty member at the Naval War College in Newport, Rhode Island. He has worked as a Soviet and Eastern European analyst for the Library of Congress and the State Department. He holds a master's degree in foreign service and a Ph.D. degree in modern diplomatic history from Georgetown University.

Roman Pipko is an attorney in the New York office of Paul, Weiss, Rifkind, Wharton & Garrison. He was born in the Soviet Union and studied law there before emigrating to the United States. On behalf of his firm's clients, he now makes frequent trips to the Soviet Union where he has negotiated commercial agreements in a variety of sectors. He is a graduate of Columbia University and received his law degree from Yale University.

Yevgeniy Y. Pompa is the chief economist of the Trade Representation of the U.S.S.R. in the U.S.A. He received his doctoral degree in economics from the National Market Research Institute of the Ministry for Foreign Economic Relations and, prior to his assignment in the United States, was a senior researcher at the institute.

Charalombos A. Vlachoutsicos is a Greek businessman who has been engaged in trade with the Soviet Union since 1956. With Paul Lawrence, he co-edited *Behind the Factory Walls.* He is a fellow at the Russian Research Center at Harvard University and a senior research fellow at the Harvard Business School. He has an M.B.A. from the Harvard Business School.